WHO'S BETTER, WHO'S BEST in BASKETBALL?

Mr. Stats Sets the Record Straight on the Top 50 NBA Players of All Time

ELLIOTT KALB

Contemporary Books

Chicago New York San Francisco Lisbon London Madrid Mexico City
Milan New Delhi San Juan Seoul Singapore Sydney Toronto

Library of Congress Cataloging-in-Publication Data

Kalb, Elliott.
    Who's better, who's best in basketball? : Mr. Stats sets the record straight on the
top 50 NBA players of all time / Elliott Kalb. — 1st ed.
        p.   cm.
    ISBN 0-07-141788-5
    1. Basketball players—United States—History.   2. Basketball players—Rating
of—United States.   3. Basketball players—United States—Records.   I. Title.

GV883.K35   2003
796.323'02'1—dc21   2003011298

To my wife, Amy, for her love and support

1 2 3 4 5 6 7 8 9 0   AGM/AGM   2 1 0 9 8 7 6 5 4 3

ISBN 0-07-141788-5

Interior design by Nick Panos

McGraw-Hill books are available at special quantity discounts to use as premiums and
sales promotions, or for use in corporate training programs. For more information, please
write to the Director of Special Sales, Professional Publishing, McGraw-Hill, Two Penn
Plaza, New York, NY 10121-2298. Or contact your local bookstore.

This book is printed on acid-free paper.

CONTENTS

FOREWORD
Bob Costas

I have worked with Elliott Kalb for 20 years now—baseball, basketball, and football— play-by-play and studio shows of every description. Without exaggeration, his work is beyond excellent.

He is a tireless worker and unfailingly accurate. But, here is what separates "Mr. Stats" from a mere statistician. He thinks in storylines. He uses numbers and history to make compelling and original points. With Elliott, you get much more than just facts, however useful. You get an informed, often provocative point of view.

He has a broad frame of reference and thinks very quickly on his feet, making him exceptionally valuable in live situations. He writes well and has a sharp sense of humor, separating him from most of those whose primary work is with facts and figures. Whatever the issue or debate in sports, Mr. Stats has more than just the facts. He has a well-researched, carefully reasoned, and cleverly presented "take."

If I had simply saved all of his production notes and background material through the years or had taped his comments at our meetings and dinners, I would probably have a book of my own. But this is a book he should write, and I hope you see it the same way.

FOREWORD
Bill Walton

I have known Elliott Kalb—Mr. Stats—for more than 10 years. He is a basketball historian, with an encyclopedic knowledge of the NBA. We have worked nonstop together during some of the greatest moments in NBA history.

Some narrow-minded, shortsighted hypocrites occasionally complain that I am opinionated. They need to listen to my friend Elliott deliver the truth for a while. We have shared our lives for the last decade debating anything and everything in the universe. A conversation might start with "What's the best Dylan cover song ever?" and end up with a lengthy appreciation of center Dave Cowens. *Who's Better, Who's Best in Basketball?* is what Kalb lived, died, and researched every day to make national televised broadcasts better.

When the New Jersey Nets met the Los Angeles Lakers in the 2002 NBA Finals, Kalb's notes were the backbone, structure, and foundation for the broadcasts—stacked with provoking questions, answers, and debates: Was Jason Kidd the "real" MVP? Was the trade for Kidd one of the best of all time? How good could Nets forwards Kenyon Martin and Richard Jefferson become? Who were the greatest players in history to hail from New Jersey? Kalb was able to recite Nets head coach Byron Scott's NBA Finals history as a player and Kidd's shooting percentage in fourth quarters—to say nothing of some of history's greatest players who flopped in the Finals!

I always tell Elliott that, when judging players of different eras, one can never say who's best—we can only say who's among the best. But I can unequivocally say this: for NBA fans, there is no one better at what he does than Elliott Kalb. He's much like my coach John Wooden—simply the best.

ACKNOWLEDGMENTS

I would like to express my heartfelt love and gratitude to my parents for taking me to my first NBA games at the fabulous Forum in the early 1970s. I need to thank David and Randi for being my brother and sister and putting up with me. I'd like to thank Marv Albert for teaching me what is—and what isn't—important when watching an NBA game. To Boomer Esiason, who in addition to being one of the all-time top quarterbacks, is a great sports fan and friend and who hooked me up with the right laptop. I have to give thanks to John Colombo, Ellen Columbus, and Charessa L. Scott for their help with the microfilm. Many thanks to Dick Ebersol and David Neal for giving me the best seat in the house for 12 years; and to Jamie Reynolds, Brian Sherriffe, Tim Corrigan, and Mike Tirico for letting me continue at ABC/ESPN; to Hannah Storm for her friendship and guidance; and to Carol Mann, the best literary agent in the business.

Many thanks to Bill Walton, for his friendship and hospitality (the kids had a blast!), and for his insights into the NBA that only a true superstar can provide. More thanks to the St. Louis delegation of Bob Costas and Steve Horn. If I had one lifeline to phone a friend, I'd call area code 314. To my friends that I pestered and ran things by during the last few months: Gary Gilbert, Scott Leabman, Ricky Diamond, Phil Harmon, and Ethan Cooperson, thanks. The insights and contributions from these intelligent men have been surpassed only by their combined 90 years of friendship. David Harmon deserves special mention. He has been a best friend whose sharp wit, strong opinions, and recommendations are almost always impeccable.

This book has been heavily influenced by the founding fathers of intelligent statistical analysis. Harvey Pollack has been "Super Stat" in Philadelphia for more than 50 years. He is a historian of the first order. There is no greater authority on the game I love. Seymour Seywoff has not only recorded the information, he has made sense of it. His Elias Sports Bureau has raised the nation's consciousness and sporting intelligence. For someone who makes his living in numbers, he is one of the great storytellers and raconteurs around. I know Bill James only through his writings. His analysis in baseball raised the bar for analysis in all sports and proved that people not directly connected with the leagues had valid—sometimes more valid—opinions than people who were connected. Also, thanks to the various public relations directors who were the best sources of information—people such as Jeff Twiss, John Black, Dennis D'Agostino, Matt Dobek, Tom James, Gary Sussman, and Tim Donovan. My thanks also go to Matthew Carnicelli and Michele Pezzuti for helping to shape and edit the manuscript. Finally, to my wife, Amy, and Wyatt, Heath, Alissa, and Jordan, thank you for always being there for me and my crazy schedule.

INTRODUCTION

More than 28 million people tuned in to watch the 2002 NBA All-Star game. That same season, more than 20 million people paid to see a game in person (which breaks down to more than 17,000 fans per game). In 2003, more than 71 million people viewed games on ESPN, ESPN2, and TNT. The list of foreign-born players in the NBA has grown exponentially, from a handful just a few years ago to 66 in the 2003 regular season. The NBA Finals are shown in 210 countries and broadcast in 41 different languages. According to a recent ESPN Sports poll, 75 percent of American teenagers consider themselves NBA fans and, since 1990, the NBA's popularity with teen girls has increased 17 percent.

There are more people following the league than ever before in history. Those new to the party—including younger fans, more women than ever, and an exploding international following—have little to compare the modern stars to.

Each day players, general managers, owners, and fans ask the question: Who's better, who's best? First for NBC Sports and now for ESPN, I've researched many of the debates concerning NBA players from Magic Johnson to Kobe Bryant.

Is Shaquille O'Neal the most dominant player of all time? Or is Michael Jordan really the greatest player the game has ever seen? Is Dennis Rodman a Hall of Famer? Who's better—Kareem Abdul-Jabbar or Wilt Chamberlain? Who was the greatest head coach in NBA history—Red Auerbach or Phil Jackson?

The idea for this collection of essays and debates started in 2002 during the NBA Finals. Without great championship games to write and talk about, the national and local media focused on Shaquille O'Neal's—and the Lakers'—place in history.

NBA legends such as Jerry West, the Hall of Famer who played with Wilt Chamberlain, weighed in: "I can't believe I'm saying this, but I think Shaquille is the best center to ever play this game. You feel kind of bad saying that because of Abdul-Jabbar and Wilt, but I just haven't seen anyone else with the whole package like him, now or ever."

Everyone, it seemed, had an opinion. My then seven-year-old son, Wyatt, chipped in with a popular response. "Shaq's just a big bully—Michael Jordan is the greatest."

Just a month after the 2002 Finals had ended, I would wind up in a shuttle bus at a celebrity golf tournament in Lake Tahoe next to NFL legend Jerry Rice.

"Are you an NBA fan?" I asked Rice.

"Yes, a big one," he replied.

"Who's the greatest NBA player of all time?" I asked.

"MJ, of course," was his response.

When Rice asked my opinion, I gave him the answer of someone who has watched NBA basketball for more than 30 years.

"Shaquille O'Neal," I said.

Rice's jaw dropped. Another celebrity golfer began yelling at me, "There isn't a player alive or dead who is close to Michael Jordan."

Welcome to *Who's Better, Who's Best in Basketball?* I told the former football players that indeed there is one alive and one who passed on (Chamberlain) who were better players.

Rice wasn't buying it. He asked me if I had actually seen Jordan play.

I didn't get into it too much with the best wide receiver to ever play—but the fact is I was courtside for every Finals game and more than 100 of Jordan's playoff games. It was my job to compare Jordan's work—to instantly critique it—to put it in perspective—to document it—for a national televised audience of millions. As part of NBC Sports' production team, I took notes while Ahmad Rashad or Mike Fratello or Marv Albert or Doug Collins talked with Michael on the day of the game. I saw Jordan—personally—damn near every Christmas, Mother's Day, Father's Day, and Easter Sunday for most of a decade. Yeah, I told Rice, I saw him play.

Jerry told me that saying Shaq was better than Jordan was "like saying that Kurt Warner was better than Joe Montana."

I finally told him that I wasn't "dissing" Jordan by placing him behind O'Neal in the all-time rankings. I also reminded him that O'Neal had performed at a high level for (then) nine years—three times longer than Warner. O'Neal had won three consecutive NBA titles—while Warner had won just one championship. Warner had also lost a Super Bowl to an inferior team—something that Montana never did.

Are the rest of you going to be that hard to convince?

Just a month earlier, the debate raged among the MVP selections. The Nets' Jason Kidd lost to the Spurs' Tim Duncan. Kidd told me that several of his New Jersey teammates told him to go down to the police station and file a robbery report. Again, many players and fans thought that the award belonged to Jason. Again: Who's better, who's best?

During the 2001 Finals, the best big man in the game, O'Neal, bested the team with the best little man, Allen Iverson. Then, the debates were about Iverson's place in history. It's hard to believe, but as recently as 1996, O'Neal was the most controversial choice when the NBA selected its list of the 50 greatest players. In 1991, after his sixth season in the league, the consensus on Michael Jordan: he was an extremely talented player but he didn't make his teammates better—as Magic Johnson and Larry Bird did. That changed, of course, when Jordan won his string of championships. Following the 2003 Finals, a new debate emerged: was Tim Duncan the greatest power forward in history?

For anyone growing up in the 1960s, there were two camps among NBA fans: those who favored Wilt Chamberlain ahead of Bill Russell and those who favored Russell. Once Kareem Abdul-Jabbar entered the league, a whole new set of arguments ensued. Chamberlain put down Kareem in two of his autobiographies. Abdul-Jabbar, in a 1981 *Inside Sports* article penned by his biographer, Peter Knobler, wrote, "The only place that Wilt could out-rebound me is in his sleep."

This book will take a historical and long-range perspective on these and other arguments.

I have spent a lifetime asking questions of various players, coaches, writers, and executives connected with the NBA. For this book, I have canvassed the opinions of some of the most respected experts in NBA history. How good was Julius Erving in the ABA? I asked his then coach, Kevin Loughery. Did Kareem dominate Wilt in their head-to-head matchups? I asked Pat Riley, who played in every one of those contests. Why were there fewer assists awarded in Bob Cousy's era? His former teammate Tom Heinsohn had the answer. How dominant was Hakeem Olajuwon in the mid-1990s? I asked Sam Cassell, who was the point guard on the two championship teams.

Marv Albert had finished a radio interview with Willis Reed just an hour before Reed's heroic appearance on the court before Game 7 of the 1970 Finals. Harvey Pollack wore seven different hats that night in Hershey, Pennsylvania, when Wilt scored 100 points. If Leonard Koppett told me about Andy Phillip and Dolph Schayes and Bill Sharman, I listened.

This book isn't a product of looking at dry statistics. It is a book of informed opinions. It is the informed opinions of three dozen experts who were closely identified with the league. It is the informed opinions of superfans such as Jeff Hamilton and Jimmy Goldstein (a fan who has followed the league for more than 35 years and who has sat in the first row at Clippers, Lakers, and West Coast playoff games on a nightly basis). It is these opinions based on trends, league averages, and firsthand accounts.

Who's Better, Who's Best in Basketball? will serve several purposes. The first is to present an updated—and ranked—list of the NBA's 50 greatest players. The second is to explain why these are the all-time great players.

There really is no place on a televised NBA game to present evidence. This book has evidence. On television, one must be content with saying that Elgin Baylor never won the big game. In this book, I can present the evidence of Baylor's performances in the eight games he could have won and been champion, and I can better make the argument to place him ahead of forwards who did win NBA Championships, including Julius Erv-

ing. Is Reggie Miller the best three-point shooter in history? How many would Pete Maravich have hit, if the rule had been in effect when he played? Is Moses Malone really the
best offensive rebounder? I will present hypothetical arguments about the realistic number that Chamberlain or Russell would have garnered, if the league had kept track of
offensive rebounds in the 1960s. These hypothetical arguments do one of two things:
they either build more of a case for the elite player who excelled pre-1974, or they add
to the modern-day player by clearly showing that no player could have reached their feats
even if the league had a way of going back and counting the statistic.

It's not enough to say the Celtics of the 1980s had one of the best frontcourts in history. In this book, I'll give the other contenders. Was Dennis Rodman the greatest defensive forward in the history of the game? I believe he was. His coaches had him defend
four different positions. He guarded Michael Jordan at the end of the Pistons-Bulls games.
He guarded Shaquille O'Neal for Phil Jackson in the 1996 playoffs. Dave DeBusschere
tried his hand at Wilt in the 1970 Finals, but he never chased guards around. Scottie Pippen chased Kobe and all the guards but never took on the center.

Who's Better, Who's Best in Basketball? will also put the modern stars in context with the
legends that preceded them. I love Robert Horry as much as the next person—more, in
fact. But I can't hear one more person call him the best clutch shooter in NBA playoff history. Does anyone remember Sam Jones? Isiah Thomas? Thomas scored 16 points in 94
seconds against the Knicks in the postseason. He had 16 points in the fourth quarter of
a 1990 Finals game (10 points in the final 2:27) to rally the Pistons to victory. He had a
stunning 25-point quarter in Game 6 of the 1988 Finals against the Lakers. And Thomas
doesn't even equal Reggie Miller when it comes to game-winning three-pointers in the
postseason.

These are the types of arguments that I'll present in this book. This book will utilize
a number of different sources—and present logical arguments—to answer dozens of NBA
questions. Along the way, I'll revise and rank the list of the 50 greatest players in NBA
history. You might recall that in 1996, as part of the 50th anniversary of the league, the
NBA selected the following players (in alphabetical order):

Kareem Abdul-Jabbar, center
Nate "Tiny" Archibald, guard
Paul Arizin, forward-guard
Charles Barkley, forward
Rick Barry, forward
Elgin Baylor, forward
Dave Bing, guard

Larry Bird, forward
Wilt Chamberlain, center
Bob Cousy, guard
Dave Cowens, center
Billy Cunningham, forward
Dave DeBusschere, forward
Clyde Drexler, guard
Julius Erving, forward
Patrick Ewing, center
Walt Frazier, guard
George Gervin, guard
Hal Greer, guard
John Havlicek, forward-guard
Elvin Hayes, forward-center
Earvin "Magic" Johnson, guard
Sam Jones, guard
Michael Jordan, guard
Jerry Lucas, forward-center
Karl Malone, forward
Moses Malone, center
Pete Maravich, guard
Kevin McHale, forward
George Mikan, center
Earl Monroe, guard
Hakeem Olajuwon, center
Shaquille O'Neal, center
Robert Parish, center
Bob Pettit, forward
Scottie Pippen, forward
Willis Reed, center
Oscar Robertson, guard
David Robinson, center
Bill Russell, center
Dolph Schayes, forward
Bill Sharman, guard
John Stockton, guard
Isiah Thomas, guard

Nate Thurmond, center
Wes Unseld, center-forward
Bill Walton, center
Jerry West, guard
Lenny Wilkens, guard
James Worthy, forward

Here is how I'll revise the list.

I'll look at players who dominated seasons. The NBA Most Valuable Player award was selected by a vote of NBA players from 1956 to 1980. After that, it was selected by writers and broadcasters. The All-NBA teams were selected by writers and broadcasters beginning in 1947. Until 1988, there was only an All-NBA First and Second Team. To restore integrity and maintain a balanced playing field, I'm only considering the years a player was named to the All-NBA First or Second Team. Being named one of the 5 or 10 best players of a particular season is a greater honor than being named to a Third Team (best 15 players) or All-Star game (best 24 players). I'm also considering NBA Championships. You'll notice the first five players on my list have won a collective 28 NBA titles.

Also, I should point out that I've made a style change that hopefully will make this book easier to read. Instead of the bulky, cumbersome convention of writing, for example, "the 1971–72 season," I will write about seasons in the year the championship series was held. So, in the above example, I will refer to that year as "the 1972 season."

I'd like to think that no one is more qualified, more of an NBA historian, more *opinionated* than I am.

I grew up for several years with Chick Hearn in my ear nightly, teaching me about the Lakers. After my family moved back to the East Coast, I became a Knicks fan following the great title teams. In 1979, I went to college at UMass, where Dr. J had played. This exposed a whole set of Boston Celtics fans to me. I may as well have been from another planet, for these Celtics fans had never met anyone who hadn't accepted as gospel that Russell was better than Chamberlain. If the college years are meant to prepare people for their life's work, UMass prepared me well.

My first job out of college was with NBA Films. I was a logger, paid to watch two- to three-day-old NBA games as they were shipped to New York and look for (log) great and unusual plays. It was here that I first met Commissioner David Stern.

I would be at NBC Sports when the network acquired the rights to broadcast the NBA beginning in the 1991 season. Working alongside Marv Albert, I became witness to NBA history. I was center court for 66 consecutive Finals games and 11 consecutive All-Star games. Working next to Albert, Bob Costas, and brilliant basketball analysts, I learned about the league. Mike Fratello broke down the Bulls' triangle offense for me. Collins told me what to look for—he would get excited about watching David Robinson stand for the national anthem! Guokas regaled me with stories about playing with Chamberlain.

I chronicled the careers of Michael Jordan and Shaquille O'Neal. I was in Barcelona for the Dream Team games. I worked alongside of, and became friends with, many of the heroes of my youth.

I noticed something that we all had as a common denominator. When I began working with Isiah Thomas—who didn't know me at all at the time—he would soon begin engaging me in debates. Who did I think was better—Wilt or Russell? He would put together a team of players who grew up in Chicago and want me to put together a team from New York. Which team would win? How could I put Olajuwon ahead of Kareem Abdul-Jabbar?

I would read a long-form interview with Michael Jordan and learn that he played the same "Who's Better, Who's Best" game that I always had with friends and co-workers. He picked his all-time team in the early 1990s once, with his then general manager Jerry Krause picking his. Krause had ties to the old Baltimore Bullets and picked old-timers such as Gus Johnson and Earl Monroe. He had Jerry West and Oscar Robertson as his starting guards. Michael had himself and Magic, along with more modern frontcourt stars.

When I began with ESPN for the 2003 season, I worked with former Spurs star Sean Elliott, who told me that he would debate players on their all-time teams constantly. But he and Chuck Person had to stop because the answer to every question was the same: Michael Jordan. (Who would you rather have take the last shot in a one-point game? Who was the best defensive guard? Who was the best at . . . ?)

I spent the better part of one of my semesters at college debating many of the same issues with my friends Scott Leabman and Gary Gilbert. Twenty years later, the arguments had moved from a dorm at Amherst, Massachusetts, to Edie's Diner in Marina Del Rey—but I was arguing the same debates, this time with Doug Collins.

My notes to the broadcasters included many of the opinions that are sprinkled throughout *Who's Better, Who's Best in Basketball?* This book will provide research and ammunition for those fans who engage in these debates and arguments themselves.

I may not move Russell fans over to Chamberlain, and I am prepared for an E-mail avalanche for not proclaiming Michael Jordan the greatest ever—but hopefully, you'll enjoy the give-and-take opinions on this great game.

In the course of making decisions on the ranking of the 50 greatest players in NBA history, I interviewed and enlisted the help of the following people:

Marv Albert: The Hall of Fame NBA announcer has covered the Knicks for more than four decades. He has been the lead voice of NBA basketball on network television for more than 10 years.

Nate Archibald: He played in the NBA from 1971 to 1984 and was elected to the Hall of Fame in 1991. A five-time All-Star, he won a championship and a scoring title and led the league in assists.

Quinn Buckner: He played in the NBA from 1977 to 1986 with the Celtics, Bucks, and Pacers. He won a National Championship in college with Indiana University in 1976, when they went 30–0. He won an NBA title in 1984 with the Celtics.

P. J. Carlesimo: He was head coach of the Trail Blazers for three seasons and of the Warriors for three more. He's also served as a television analyst, and most recently has returned to the bench as an assistant with the Spurs. He was also an assistant to Chuck Daly on the 1992 Dream Team that went to Barcelona.

Sam Cassell: He has played in the NBA for 10 years, winning NBA Championships in his first two seasons with the Houston Rockets. He's played against the great point guards of the last decade, including Jason Kidd, John Stockton, and Gary Payton.

Doug Collins: He was the star of the 1972 U.S. Olympic team and hit the arguably two most pressure-packed free throws of all time against the Soviet Union. He was the first pick overall of the 1973 draft and played eight seasons with the 76ers before injuries curtailed his career. He made the All-Star team four times and played with Billy Cunningham and Julius Erving. He coached Michael Jordan early and late in his career. He also coached the 1997 Pistons to 54 victories.

Mark Cuban: He owns the Dallas Mavericks. He grew up in Pittsburgh, an ABA fan of Connie Hawkins and Julius Erving.

Mike Dunleavy: He was head coach for two years with the Lakers in the early 1990s, replacing Pat Riley and leading the Magic Johnson Lakers to the Finals against the Bulls. He spent four seasons in charge of the Milwaukee Bucks and then four more as head coach of the Portland Trail Blazers. He played on the 1977 Philadelphia team with Julius Erving that went to the NBA Finals. He also played on the 1981 Houston Rockets team with Moses Malone that went to the Finals.

Sean Elliott: He played 12 seasons, 11 with the San Antonio Spurs. He played with David Robinson, Tim Duncan, Dennis Rodman, and Isiah Thomas in his career. His moment came on Memorial Day, 1999, in Game 2 of the Western Conference finals when he hit a game-winning three-pointer to beat the Portland Trail Blazers. That was the Spurs' first championship season.

Mike Fratello: He was a head coach for 14 years in the NBA, with the Atlanta Hawks and Cleveland Cavaliers. Since 1981, he has been a head coach or courtside for television networks, working NBA games.

Walt Frazier: He played for the Knicks from 1968 to 1977 and finished up with the Cleveland Cavs. He was inducted into the Hall of Fame in 1987. He has also served for more than a decade as the Knicks' broadcast color analyst.

Matt Guokas: He played with Wilt Chamberlain and coached Charles Barkley, Julius Erving, and Shaquille O'Neal. He has been connected to the NBA in some fashion since 1967, when he was a rookie with the champion 76ers. He, too, was the lead analyst for NBC for four seasons.

Derek Harper: He played 16 seasons and 1,199 games in the NBA with the Dallas Mavericks, New York Knicks, Orlando Magic, and Los Angeles Lakers. He hit 17 three-pointers in the 1994 NBA Finals for the Knicks.

Del Harris: He spent 14 years as a head coach in the NBA with the Houston Rockets, Milwaukee Bucks, and Los Angeles Lakers. He has spent several more seasons as the defensive coordinator for Don Nelson's Dallas Mavericks. He has coached Moses Malone, Rick Barry, Shaquille O'Neal, and Kobe Bryant.

Tom Heinsohn: In 1957, he (not Bill Russell) was voted Rookie of the Year. He went on to be named to the All-NBA Second Team four times. He won eight championships as a player with the Celtics. He succeeded Bill Russell as head coach of Boston and won two more titles with John Havlicek and Dave Cowens as the stars.

Phil Jasner: He has covered the NBA—mostly for the *Philadelphia Inquirer*—for more than three decades.

Steve Jones: He was an ABA original with the 1968 Oakland Oaks. He was a three-time ABA All-Star. He was one of 12 players to score 10,000 points in the ABA. He was known for his three-point shooting (34 percent career average) and never had a technical foul called against him in his ABA career (680 games). He played one year in the NBA with the Trail Blazers.

Leonard Koppett: A former NBA writer for the *New York Times*, Koppett wrote the definitive book on the early years of the NBA, *Twenty-Four Seconds to Shoot*, in 1970. Mr. Koppett passed away in the summer of 2003.

Kevin Loughery: He was a head coach for 20 years. In his three-year stint with the Nets, he won a pair of ABA Championships. He played from 1963 to 1973 with the Pistons, Bullets, and 76ers. He played with Earl Monroe and Wes Unseld and was the coach of such greats as Julius Erving, Bernard King, Moses Malone, Dominique Wilkins, and Michael Jordan.

Joe Maloof: He and his brother Gavin own the Sacramento Kings. In the early 1980s, their late father owned the Houston Rockets, which starred Moses Malone and went to the Finals against the Boston Celtics.

Cedric Maxwell: He played with Boston from 1978 to 1985 and with the Clippers for two years after that. He finished his career with the Rockets. He averaged 12.5 points and 6.3 rebounds in his 11 years. He was the MVP of the 1981 NBA Finals.

Harvey Pollack: A member of the Basketball Hall of Fame, Pollack is the only individual who worked in the NBA in its inaugural 1947 season who is still working for an NBA team. He was the longtime public relations director of the Philadelphia Warriors (and later, the 76ers).

Dr. Jack Ramsay: The 76ers general manager in 1967 and 1968, he coached 21 years in the NBA in Philadelphia, Buffalo, Portland, and Indiana. He coached Chamberlain, Cunningham, McAdoo, Drexler, and Miller, among the list of my top 50.

Pat Riley: He is the second-winningest head coach in NBA history (by wins) and has coached more playoff games than anyone in history. He has won four NBA Championship rings as a coach, one more as a player with the 1972 Lakers, and another as an assistant coach. He has played with Wilt Chamberlain, Jerry West, and Elvin Hayes, among others. He has coached Magic Johnson, Kareem Abdul-Jabbar, and Patrick Ewing. He served as the head coach in nine different All-Star games.

Bob Ryan: He has covered the NBA—mostly for the *Boston Globe*—for more than three decades.

John Saunders: One of the voices of the NBA on ESPN, the well-respected Saunders was the Toronto Raptors' announcer when Tracy McGrady entered the league.

Paul Silas: He played 16 years in the NBA with the Hawks, Suns, Celtics, Nuggets, and Sonics. He's one of the leading rebounders in history and has won three titles as a player. He's been a head coach of three teams, and has coached Bill Walton and LeBron James.

Jerry Sloan: From 1989 to 2003, Sloan has been the head coach of Karl Malone and John Stockton with the Utah Jazz. Sloan played with the Chicago Bulls, where he was selected by the league's coaches for the All-Defensive teams in six of the first seven seasons that they were awarded.

Isiah Thomas: The second overall pick of the 1981 NBA draft, Thomas enjoyed spectacular success for the next 13 years with the Detroit Pistons. Following his Hall of Fame career, he was part-owner of the Toronto Raptors, majority owner of the Continental Basketball Association, and head coach of the Indiana Pacers.

Rod Thorn: He is the president and general manager of the New Jersey Nets. He is also a former player and head coach and was the NBA's vice president of operations. In 1964, he was drafted by the Baltimore Bullets and spent eight years playing for Detroit, St. Louis, and Seattle, averaging 10.8 points per game. As the general manager of the Chicago Bulls, he drafted Michael Jordan.

Dr. Ernie Vandeweghe: Dr. Vandeweghe played for the Knicks from 1950 to 1955, playing for the NBA title against the Minneapolis Lakers in 1952 and 1953. He worked for the Lakers from 1960 to 1974. His son, Kiki, played from 1981 to 1993 and is currently the general manager of the Denver Nuggets.

Pete Vecsey: He has covered the NBA—mostly for the *New York Post*—for more than three decades. There is no better source than Vecsey, whose *Hoop Du Jour* is required reading for any real NBA fan.

Bill Walton: One of the greatest centers to ever play the game, Walton had an injury-plagued career that took him to stops in Portland, San Diego, and Boston. He was elected to the Basketball Hall of Fame in 1993.

SHAQUILLE O'NEAL
The Case for Number One

MVP: 1	
MVP VOTING: 6 years in top 4	
NBA TITLES: 3	
ALL-NBA FIRST TEAM: 5	
ALL-NBA SECOND TEAM: 2	

Shaquille O'Neal is the best of the almost four thousand NBA players who have ever suited up in a uniform, and in this chapter, you'll find out why. Statistics will help separate O'Neal from most of the competition, and I will also share the informed judgments of NBA experts. Finally, I will explain why never before in history has the best player in the game been that much better than the second best.

By the close of the 2003 NBA season, O'Neal had played 11 seasons and close to 800 games. By his thirty-first birthday, he had scored more points than all but two dozen or so players in the history of the league. O'Neal is one of the most prolific scorers not only of his time but of all time. While he may not have scored as much or as quickly as Wilt Chamberlain, he won more. And although O'Neal may not have won more than Bill Russell or Kareem Abdul-Jabbar, he won almost as much in a league that had 28 competing teams, as opposed to 8 or 16 squads.

No one ever entered the NBA with the hype that O'Neal did. All first-round draft picks enter the league amidst high expectations, but players picked first overall have even higher standards that they need to meet. Of all those players selected first overall, none entered the league under higher expectations than Shaq. Despite the pressure, he has dominated from Day One. He has won two scoring titles and narrowly missed four others. He has won an MVP award and has been in the top four in voting in six other seasons. He was the NBA Finals MVP for three consecutive seasons. There are no other big centers like him, and no centers in the league can challenge him. He can seemingly do anything he wants to. You would have to say that he has produced.

As a rookie, O'Neal was instantly among the top six or seven players in the league. At that time, there were three dominant centers who were at the peak of their careers—Hakeem Olajuwon, Patrick Ewing, and David Robinson. It didn't take long for O'Neal to surpass the accomplishments of all three. O'Neal—in repeated interviews through the years—has said that Olajuwon took the longest to slay. These weren't just three good players, by the way. They represented three of the league's all-time best centers.

All-NBA First Team Selections

Hakeem Olajuwon	6
Shaquille O'Neal	5
David Robinson	4
Patrick Ewing	1

Those 16 selections represent a 17-year history in the NBA. Only in the 1999 condensed lockout season was there a center chosen other than those four—Alonzo Mourning. Mourning was the All-NBA First Team selection in that season. Centers are judged like NFL quarterbacks, with an emphasis on playoff success. Ewing didn't play in an NBA Finals until his ninth season. O'Neal led his Orlando Magic to the Finals in just his third season. By 1998, O'Neal had surpassed Ewing in All-NBA First Team selections and MVP votes. He had clearly outplayed Ewing in their head-to-head meetings. A year later, O'Neal was devastating in the playoff series against Olajuwon's Houston Rockets. Following the 1998 season, O'Neal's teams were 13–6 against the Rockets and Spurs in the postseason. The Lakers swept David Robinson's team out of the playoffs in 2001 and defeated them 4–1 in 2002. In the first half of O'Neal's career, he has surpassed the three best centers he had to overcome.

O'Neal's Stats

Shaquille dominates the most important statistics in the game of basketball. His teams win more than any other. He has led expansion teams into the Finals at a record rate. He has led the Lakers with an assortment of help at the other positions. He has scored more points than almost everyone. He has pulled down more rebounds. He is one of the best passing centers. Annually, he leads the league in field goal percentage. In addition, he can write and sing rap songs, act in movies, sell products, and move comfortably in his celebrity lifestyle.

Shaq's Rankings Based on Points/Game

Year	Rank in League	Points/Game
1993	8th (tie)	23.4
1994	2nd	29.3
1995	1st	29.3
1996	3rd	26.6
1997	didn't play enough games to qualify	
1998	2nd	28.3
1999	2nd	26.3
2000	1st	29.7
2001	3rd	28.7
2002	2nd	27.2
2003	4th	27.5

As these stats show, O'Neal has ranked near the top in scoring each year after his rookie season. And O'Neal's four second-place finishes were by four of the narrowest margins in the scoring title races. Just a handful of points (or free throws, to be more accurate) have kept him from winning five or six scoring titles in his first 11 seasons. Only Chamberlain and Michael Jordan have accomplished that, and they rate right behind O'Neal in this book. Chamberlain didn't win as much as O'Neal. Jordan won three titles in his first 10 seasons (to match O'Neal) but Shaquille's size enabled him to grab twice as many rebounds.

The 1994 Scoring Title Race

Going into the final day of the 1994 season, O'Neal had scored 2,345 points in 80 games (29.31 average) to lead the league. The Magic were playing the New Jersey Nets. Later that night, Robinson's Spurs were going to play the Clippers in Los Angeles. Robinson had scored 2,312 points in 79 games (29.26 average).

1994 Scoring Leaders by Average

1. David Robinson   29.8
2. Shaquille O'Neal   29.3

Shaquille knew that he was signing his score card and going into the clubhouse first. (By the way, it was a meaningless game for the Magic, who were locked into their playoff seed.) This was the situation for Shaq as he headed out to play New Jersey:

If Shaq scored 20 points . . . Robinson would need 24 points to win the scoring title.

If Shaq scored 25 points . . . Robinson would need 29 points.

If Shaq scored 30 points . . . Robinson would need 35 points.

If Shaq scored 40 points . . . Robinson would need 44 points.

The Magic coaching staff allowed O'Neal to play enough in the 29-point victory over New Jersey to score 32 points. This is well within the confines of what a star player would play and score in an average game. Although the scoring title was important to O'Neal, the Magic never let the scoring race between O'Neal and Robinson become a sideshow to their game.

Robinson, however, with the generous help of Spurs head coach John Lucas and Clippers head coach Bob Weiss, scored 71 points on April 24, 1994. Robinson was the good guy, the player who meant so much to the league. O'Neal was a brash 22-year-old kid who would have many more chances to lead the league. Robinson must have been defensive about his 71-point outburst; there were a rash of quotes following the game that implied it was his teammates who wanted him to win the scoring title and that he personally didn't "rub it in."

Put an asterisk next to Robinson's 1994 scoring title. People always talk about how Chamberlain or O'Neal played for "numbers and stats." In this case, David Robinson was totally out of character.

Was Robinson "helped out" in a plot to gain him the scoring title? You be the judge.

Robinson's Season-High Point Totals/Game

Year	Points
1990	41
1991	43
1992	39
1993	52
1994	71
1995	43
1996	45
1997	27
1998	39
1999	39
2000	38
2001	34
2002	27
2003	20

Robinson has played in about 1,000 regular-season games in his NBA career. In exactly two of them (once in 1993 and once in 1994) did he score as many as 52 points in a single game. He won a scoring title because on the final night of the 1994 season, he scored 71 points. Is it unusual for a player to better his career best by almost 30 percent? Here is a sampling of some of the greatest scorers in history.

Great Scorers	Career Best	2nd Best
Wilt Chamberlain	100	78
Elgin Baylor	71	64
Michael Jordan	69	64
Rick Barry	64	57
Karl Malone	61	56
Kobe Bryant	56	52
Dominique Wilkins	57	57
Shaquille O'Neal	61	53

O'Neal's Narrow Misses in 1998 and 1999
In 1998, O'Neal lost a second close scoring race under different circumstances.

1998 Scoring Leaders
1. Michael Jordan   28.7
2. Shaquille O'Neal   28.3

This race was different because the playoff positioning was still on the line in the season's final days. The Chicago Bulls finished with 62 wins. The Lakers finished with 61 victories. The last game of the season meant a lot to both Jordan's Bulls and O'Neal's Lakers. You could forgive either one of them if they went off and scored a bundle.

Going into the final games for each player, the scoring race looked like this:

O'Neal	1,656 points in 59 games	28.06 points/game
Jordan	2,313 points in 81 games	28.55 points/game

Shaq again led off, this time on Saturday night, April 17, against the Dallas Mavericks. Jordan would finish on Sunday against the New York Knicks.

Shaquille hit 18 of 22 field goals and made 7 of 13 free throws. He finished with 43 points and went into the clubhouse with 28.32 points per game. Jordan needed the equivalent of a tap-in putt to win his 10th scoring crown. He would wind up with 44 points and a 28.7 average. Jordan could have lollygagged around the court for three hours and he would have won with just 10 points.

1999 Scoring Leaders
1. Allen Iverson   26.8
2. Shaquille O'Neal   26.3

History repeated itself in 1999. Those three narrow second-place finishes kept O'Neal from his third, fourth, and fifth scoring titles. Only the two men ranked directly below him (Chamberlain and Jordan) have won more than four. Shaquille would finish second a fourth time (in 2002, again to Iverson) but this time by a larger margin.

It's hypothetical, but one could state that O'Neal would have won those three additional scoring titles simply by hitting an average amount of free throws. If Shaquille had shot just 60 percent from the free throw line in those three seasons (1994, 1998, and 1999), he would have edged out Robinson, Jordan, and Iverson. Or, at least he would have forced Robinson to threaten Chamberlain's single-game record of 100 points in that season-ending mockery of 1994.

That brings me to a very important point about my ranking players. I do not take away from Shaquille's greatness because of his weakness in shooting free throws. Similarly, I do not take away from Babe Ruth because he lacked the range and speed to play center field and he struck out a lot. (I will explain more about this in Chapter 2 on Chamberlain.)

O'Neal's Scoring Machine
One thing Shaq has always done well is put the ball in the hoop.

Shaq's Place Among Field Goal Percentage Leaders
1994	1st
1995	2nd
1996	3rd
1997	4th
1998	1st
1999	1st
2000	1st
2001	1st
2002	1st
2003	1st

Shaquille is one of the *most* accurate shooters in history. He almost never takes a low percentage shot. According to Harvey Pollack's 15-year study of slam dunks (published in
his annual *Statistical Yearbook*, in conjunction with the Philadelphia 76ers), no one is close
to O'Neal in the number of dunks.

Most Slam Dunks, 1987–2002

1. 2,447   Shaquille O'Neal
2. 1,595   David Robinson
3. 1,491   Shawn Kemp

Of 7,421 field goals, 2,447 have been dunks for Shaq (33 percent). Is that a lot? Let's
compare him to the other big men from that same 15-year period.

Percentage of Field Goals That Were Slam Dunks

Dikembe Mutombo	39 percent
Shaquille O'Neal	33 percent
Shawn Kemp	28 percent
Alonzo Mourning	26 percent
David Robinson	22 percent
Tim Duncan	15 percent
Hakeem Olajuwon	12 percent
Patrick Ewing	11 percent
Karl Malone	9 percent

While I am sure Shaquille has missed his share of dunks, his field goal percentage on slam
dunks is pretty close to 99 percent. In a 1994 interview with *Sport Magazine*, Shaquille
said, "People want to see power. My role is to be a power player and dominate and dunk.
That's what made Shaq Shaq."

Rebounding Prowess

One of my main criteria for ranking the great players of all time (at least, the frontcourt
players) is rebounding. Since rebounding totals fluctuate by era (because of a change in
field goal percentage and shots attempted), the best measure is to judge players against
their competition within their eras. To qualify for the rebounding crown, the league states
that a player must either play in 70 games or have 800 total rebounds. This is how Shaq
has finished yearly:

Rank Based on Rebounds/Game

1993	2nd
1994	2nd
1995	3rd
1996	didn't play enough games to qualify
1997	didn't play enough games to qualify
1998	didn't play enough games to qualify
1999	7th (tie)
2000	2nd
2001	3rd
2002	didn't play enough games to qualify
2003	didn't play enough games to qualify

Won-Loss Record

Of course, most great players—and all the great centers—are judged on their wins and losses. This is where little is known about O'Neal's dominance. Remember, the year before he arrived in Orlando, the third-year expansion Magic were 21–61.

First Year Won-Loss Record

1993	41–41 (one game out of playoffs)

Matt Guokas: "Shaquille was still raw then, his body still forming. Shaquille was a different player in his rookie season. He didn't throw those elbows around like he did in later years—and if he did, he wouldn't have gotten away with it. If he had his toe in the three-second lane, they would call it. I had one of my assistants chart it—I remember he was called for something like 27 traveling violations halfway through the season. And he had 17 or 18 calls of three seconds in the lane. We missed the playoffs that season by a five-point differential against Indiana. It must have gone down to the fourth or fifth tiebreaker. We would have drawn New York in the first round."

Won-Loss Record, 1994–2003

1994	50–32
1995	57–25
1996	60–22
1997	56–22

1998	61–21
1999	31–19
2000	67–15
2001	56–26
2002	58–24
2003	50–32

His teams have won 587 of 870 games in his first 11 years for a winning percentage of .674. When O'Neal is able to play, his team's winning percentage is even higher. In 2003 the Lakers were 45–22 with Shaq, only 5–10 in the 15 games he missed.

The greatest winner in NBA and team sports history is Bill Russell, so it's important to compare Russell's winning percentage with O'Neal's. There is a sizable contingent of people who would argue that Russell is the greatest player of all time, on the basis of his team's success.

Bill Russell's Celtics: Won-Loss Record, 1957–1969

1957	44–28
1958	49–23
1959	52–20
1960	59–16
1961	57–22
1962	60–20
1963	58–22
1964	59–21
1965	62–18
1966	54–26
1967	60–21
1968	54–28
1969	48–34

Bill Russell's teams won 716 out of 1,015 regular-season games—a winning percentage of .705.

To put it in context, during an 82-game season, Shaquille's teams won an average of 56 games. Russell's teams won an average of close to 58.

Take away Shaquille's rookie season when he was drafted by a 21–61 Orlando team and O'Neal's teams played at a winning percentage of .703—essentially the same as Russell's Celtics.

Remember, Russell went to a Celtics team that was 39–33 and featured the best backcourt in the game—Bob Cousy and Bill Sharman.

Well, you say, what about the playoffs? After all, playoff success is even more important than regular-season dominance in my view. Let's look at the postseason:

Russell's 13 Seasons, Celtics	108–59	.647	won 27 playoff series
O'Neal's First 11 Seasons, Magic/Lakers	83–53	.610	won 22 playoff series

O'Neal in the Postseason . . .
Or Why He's Listed First in This Book

O'Neal had a reputation early in his career for losing. He never won a National Championship in college. He didn't win an NBA title in his first seven years.

Here is how O'Neal has done in the playoffs since:

2000 Postseason

Lakers 15–8	Shaq 30.7 points	15.4 rebounds

2001 Postseason

Lakers 15–2	Shaq 30.4 points	15.4 rebounds

2002 Postseason

Lakers 15–4	Shaq 28.5 points	12.6 rebounds

2003 Postseason

Lakers 6–6	Shaq 27.0 points	14.8 rebounds

Even before the 2000 postseason, Shaquille had his memorable playoff games. Jordan's teams were 24–1 in his last 25 playoff series. The only series loss was to O'Neal and the Orlando Magic in 1995.

In that series, Chicago and Orlando were tied 2–2 after four games. In the fifth game, O'Neal grabbed 14 offensive rebounds—still an NBA playoff record for a regulation game (Moses Malone once had 15 in an overtime game). Shaquille had 23 points, 22 rebounds, five blocks, four assists, and two steals to lead Orlando to victory. In the sixth game, he eliminated Jordan and the Bulls with 27 points, 13 rebounds, four assists, and four steals.

Later in the 1995 playoffs, the Magic played the Indiana Pacers in the Conference finals. Everyone remembers Game 4 of that series—a wonderful Memorial Day game where the Pacers tied the series up 94–93 in a game that featured four lead changes in the final 13 seconds. The fifth game had less fanfare because it lacked the "fantastic finish" but the game was equally vital. Shaquille had 35 points and 13 rebounds in a 108–106 Orlando victory. Indiana then blew Orlando out in Game 6, but Orlando blew Indiana out in Game 7. O'Neal went to the Finals.

In Game 1 of the 1995 NBA Finals, O'Neal came up with a beauty. In his first NBA Finals game, he came within a whisker of a triple double. He had 26 points, 16 rebounds, and nine assists. It would have been enough for a victory, too, if teammate Nick Anderson hadn't missed four free throws in the final 12 seconds of regulation play.

Shaquille's first playoff game with the Lakers was against Portland in 1997's first round. All he did was score 46 points.

In the first round of the 1999 playoffs against Houston, Shaquille put an end to playing second fiddle to Olajuwon. In the fourth and final game of the series, Shaq scored 37 points and had his way with The Dream.

In the 2000 playoffs, O'Neal came to the rescue (with Kobe Bryant) in Game 7 against Portland.

In the 2000 Finals, O'Neal was brilliant. He had 43 points and 19 rebounds in the first game. In the second, he had 40 points and 24 rebounds. He hit 18 free throws in that game. (That was the game he went to the line 39 times—a postseason record. No one ever attempted 39 in a regular-season game, either.)

In the 2001 playoffs, O'Neal had his way with the Spurs and Robinson. In the Lakers' four-game sweep, O'Neal outscored The Admiral 108–57. That's one series after the Lakers swept Sacramento, and Shaq outscored Vlade Divac 133–42.

In the 2001 Finals, O'Neal dominated Dikembe Mutombo, the best defensive center of the generation. Shaquille averaged 33 points per game in leading the Lakers to their second consecutive title.

Then, he was unstoppable in the 2002 Conference finals versus Sacramento. After getting to the line just one time in Game 5 (played in Sacramento), Shaquille hit 13 of 17 free throws in Game 6 to tie up the series 3–3. In the seventh game, O'Neal hit 11 of 15 free throws. In the two biggest games of the season, O'Neal scored 76 points, had 30 rebounds, and stayed on the court for 95 minutes.

In 19 NBA Finals games, Shaquille O'Neal has averaged 34.2 points per game. Only Rick Barry (in 10 Finals games) had a higher scoring average: 36.3.

Money is not a criterion for me but incentive is. Unlike the great centers and players of the past, Shaquille has been richly rewarded from Day One. He has always been one of the highest-paid players in the league. In the summer of 1996, when he was a free agent, he signed what was then the richest contract in NBA history, seven years for $120 million, luring him away from the Orlando Magic to the Lakers. It was also the biggest bargain in sports. Prior to the 2001 season, the Lakers extended O'Neal's contract for three additional years for $88 million. The $200+ million over 10 years doesn't even take into consideration the millions of dollars that O'Neal was able to parlay his basketball abilities and personality into with other endorsement deals.

It is worth asking about O'Neal's future motivation. He has little competition for being the most dominant player in the game. Chamberlain always had Russell. Russell always had Chamberlain. Abdul-Jabbar always had Chamberlain or Walton or Moses Malone. All of those mentioned had money as a motivating factor, as well.

It remains to be seen whether O'Neal will use the Lakers' loss to the Spurs in the 2003 postseason as a motivating force to push him to greater feats, but it certainly appears that will be the case. O'Neal hired an ex-marine personal trainer and vowed to dedicate himself to being even more dominant (as Jordan did after losing in the 1995 postseason).

Of course, the Lakers' defeat in 2003 can hardly be pinned on Shaq. Critics will point out that Shaq was heavier than in previous seasons and had begun both the 2002 and 2003 seasons out of shape. In the first round of the 2003 playoffs, the Lakers lost starting forward (and defensive specialist) Rick Fox to injury. Fox's replacement, Devean George, then suffered a severely sprained ankle. In the four Lakers losses to the Spurs, George made just five baskets in 21 attempts, averaging just 4.3 points per game in the three losses that he played in (George missed one game). During the season, Fox and George had combined to average 50 minutes and 16 points per game. Against the Spurs in the second round of the 2003 playoffs, the Lakers were down 10 points per game just from the small forward spot.

And then there was the Robert Horry problem. Horry was one of the great playoff performers of all time, consistently hitting big shots throughout his five championship seasons in Houston and Los Angeles. But against the Spurs, Horry was 0 for 18 from three-point range, including a crushing miss at the end of Game 5. Horry averaged only 4.3 points per game in the series (after averaging 6.5 during the season). Even worse, Horry had the responsibility of Tim Duncan, who averaged 28 points, 12 rebounds, and five assists against the Lakers.

Kobe Bryant had injured his right shoulder during the first round. He played the Lakers' final 10 postseason games (including all six of the Spurs series) with a shoulder that would require surgery immediately after the season. And, of course, Phil Jackson needed a heart procedure that would leave him at home for Game 4 of the San Antonio series.

Despite all that, Shaquille was the one who took the brunt of the criticism for the Lakers' defeat. Never mind that he tied the series at 2–2 when he sank a pair of free throws with 67 seconds remaining to tie Game 4, and then stole a pass by Tim Duncan. Twelve seconds later the Lakers had the lead for good. Never mind that Shaq scored 152 points on just 102 field goal attempts in the series. Never mind that Shaq averaged over 25 points, 14 rebounds, and nearly four assists and three blocks per game.

If that was Shaq bottoming out, then he is clearly the best of all time.

Who's Better, Who's Best
Shaquille O'Neal or Kareem Abdul-Jabbar

Pat Riley: "There's no comparison as far as their size and skill, they're different kinds of players. Kareem was more of a finesse player; Shaq is more of a power player."

Bill Walton: "Kareem versus Shaq: two of the five greatest players in history. . . . For Shaq to be the greatest, he has to play better the rest of his career."

Who's Better, Who's Best
Shaquille O'Neal or Wilt Chamberlain

Rod Thorn: "I used to compare Shaq to Wilt, but O'Neal is quicker and bigger than Wilt. . . . Wilt had incredible athletic ability and probably more basketball skills than O'Neal."

Joe Maloof: "To me, the three best players in history are Shaq, number one. Wilt Chamberlain, number two. And Jordan, number three. I like the big men. Look at this league. The dominant teams have always had the big man—except for the Bulls."

Kevin Loughery: "I put Shaquille ahead of Wilt. Chamberlain didn't have enough titles. But he had enormous numbers. And that's part of greatness."

Matt Guokas: "Shaquille isn't even close to Wilt defensively. Chamberlain would block about eight shots a game. And Wilt was much better at controlling the lane."

I'm not saying that O'Neal has won as many championships as Russell. I'm not saying he's won as many championships as Abdul-Jabbar (although Kareem only won two in his first 11 years). Shaq also hasn't scored as many points or pulled down as many rebounds as Chamberlain. But, listen to this: Chamberlain averaged more points early in his career—*but* Wilt entered a very different NBA. One with a lot more offense, a lot more shots, and very little emphasis on defense.

In Chamberlain's rookie season, the average team in the NBA scored 118.1 points per night. In 1962, the average team scored almost 119. The average team took 108 shots per game!

O'Neal is scoring points in an era when no one else is. The average team took just 78 shots per game in 1999 and scored just 91 points per game. In 2002, the average was up to only 81 shots per game and 95 points per team. If Chamberlain's numbers for his first four seasons were adjusted to fit the NBA average in the late 1990s, then Chamberlain's first four years (where he averaged 42.9 points per game) would drop to 34.3 points per game in Shaq's era. Not that there's anything wrong with that. If you adjust for Shaq/Wilt against the league average, I suspect their scoring average would be about the same.

Shaquille has proved he is head and shoulders above most of the current centers in the NBA. He proved himself against the best of the last 10 years. He has scored like Chamberlain, won like Russell and Abdul-Jabbar, and been as dominant as any of them. On March 26, 2003, O'Neal outplayed Rockets rookie sensation Yao Ming in their second meeting. After the game, O'Neal said, "Everybody knows the type of player I am. I've been doing this for 10 years, and just because he had one good game against me doesn't mean he has the MDE (most dominant ever) title. I took that from Hakeem when he left Houston a couple of years ago."

O'Neal is well aware of his place in history.

As for not placing Jordan ahead of O'Neal, I just feel that O'Neal was so much better than the second-best player in the game during the early 2000s than Jordan was against the next best player in the 1990s. Jordan wasn't that much better than Magic Johnson, Charles Barkley, Clyde Drexler, and Karl Malone in respective seasons. That's what made Jordan so compelling to watch. The outcome was frequently in doubt.

There were only a few close to Shaq from the moment he entered the league. Beginning in 1998, his dominance was so superior that it was often overlooked. It will not be overlooked, or discounted, here.

A Better Analogy

Shaquille O'Neal and Frank Sinatra When Shaquille O'Neal came up, he competed against some of the greatest centers in NBA history. Most of them were much older and had little success left. O'Neal then became the only true center in the league, competing against an influx of younger, athletic 7-footers who played a different position (Kevin Garnett, Tim Duncan, Dirk Nowitzki). Many of these later opponents were foreigners, who made a big splash in the NBA.

Frank Sinatra came up with trumpeter Harry James's band as the boy singer. Sinatra's success with the James band led to his recruitment by the king of swing bands, trombonist Tommy Dorsey. Sinatra stepped behind the microphone fronting for Dorsey's band, the most popular of its time. You might compare this band to the Los Angeles Lakers. Sinatra freely admitted learning his trademark phrasing and intonation from listening to Dorsey play. You might say it is similar to Shaquille learning how to play the pick and roll from playing for Coach Phil Jackson.

Sinatra competed against other crooners, mainly older guys such as Bing Crosby who were still at the top after dominating popular music for many years. Then, Sinatra became the only pop music star left, it seemed, as the rock n' roll era came in, led by an influx of younger, more athletic stars. Many of these later opponents were foreigners. Remember the British Invasion in the early 1960s?

Yet, with the rock era rolling along, Frank Sinatra had a number-one hit, "Strangers in the Night."

As Bono said in presenting Sinatra with a special Grammy tribute one year, Sinatra had plenty of swagger and attitude. He was cocksure. He didn't like talking to the press much, preferring to reveal himself in his music.

Shaquille O'Neal will have a place in NBA history . . . oh, let's just say, From Here to Eternity.

WILT CHAMBERLAIN
The Babe

MVP: 4	
MVP VOTING: 10 years in the top 5	
NBA TITLES: 2	
ALL-NBA FIRST TEAM: 7	
ALL-NBA SECOND TEAM: 3	

Wilt Chamberlain was the Babe Ruth of his sport. He changed it. He brought it into the modern era. He set standards that would either be unapproachable, or not altered for decades. He dominated the statistics and was the most compelling force in the game's history.

The knock on Chamberlain was that he didn't win. He won a lot, actually. All it would have taken for him to have retired with five NBA Championships is three Game 7s going his way toward the end of his career.

I want to examine his statistical accomplishments and which of his records are the most impressive as well as look back at his history in Game 7s. I want to find out why 30 years after his last game, people are so polarized in their impressions of him.

I should state my feelings in any argument concerning Chamberlain. He was my favorite player growing up and you'll see why in the coming paragraphs. I saw him play—only with the Lakers in the last three or four years of his career. I read his books not once, but a hundred times. I memorized his statistics.

The Stats According to Chamberlain

Even I don't know how to begin a list of his Ruthian feats. He started as a rookie in the 1960 season. Prior to that season, no one had ever averaged as many as 30 points per game in an NBA season. In Wilt's *first* game, he scored 43 points.

In that rookie season, Chamberlain averaged 37.6 points per game—shattering the old record of Bob Pettit's 29.2. That means he broke the record by about 30 percent in only his first year. It's as if a rookie came up in baseball in the 1960 season and beat Babe Ruth's home run record—not by hitting 61, but by hitting 79.

In his second season, Wilt averaged 38.4 points per game. By 1963, the Big Dipper averaged the nice, neat number of 50 points per game. That season, he scored more than 4,000 points. Only five other players that year scored 2,000 points.

Chamberlain doesn't merely have the most points per game in a season. He has the three top seasons and five of the top seven seasons.

Most Points/Game, Single Season

Rank	Points	Player	Year
1.	50.4	Wilt Chamberlain	1962
2.	44.8	Wilt Chamberlain	1963
3.	38.4	Wilt Chamberlain	1961
4.	38.3	Elgin Baylor	1962
5.	37.6	Wilt Chamberlain	1960
6.	37.1	Michael Jordan	1987
7.	36.9	Wilt Chamberlain	1964

Chamberlain led the league in scoring his first seven years in the league and then concentrated on other aspects of the game. But he didn't just lead the league in scoring. He was so far ahead of everyone else it wasn't even a scoring race. In 1960, Jack Twyman was second to Wilt—and he finished 6.4 points per game behind Chamberlain. In 1963, Elgin Baylor averaged a magnificent 34 points per game—and was 10.8 points per game behind Wilt. In the same number of games (80), Wilt scored 867 more points than the second-place Baylor and 1,322 more points (in the same number of games) than the third-leading scorer, Oscar Robertson.

The year Chamberlain averaged 50 points per game, Walt Bellamy averaged 31.6 points per game. Baylor averaged 38.3 points per game—but played only 48 games due to military service. The fact is Baylor and Bellamy barely beat Chamberlain in alphabetical order. In scoring, they weren't within 20 percent of Chamberlain.

Only Michael Jordan won more scoring titles than Chamberlain. But Jordan never dominated a season's scoring as Chamberlain did. Jordan won his 10 scoring titles by an average of 3.3 points more per game than the second-place finisher. Wilt won his seven scoring titles by an average of more than seven points per game over the second-place finisher.

Most 50-Point Games

Rank	Games	Player
1.	122	Wilt Chamberlain
2.	37	Michael Jordan
3.	18	Elgin Baylor
4.	15	Rick Barry
5.	10	Kareem Abdul-Jabbar

Chamberlain scored 50+ points in 45 different games in 1962—more than any other player did in a career!

An argument against Wilt: 118 of his 122 games of 50+ points came in the regular season. Chamberlain played in 160 postseason games, with only four of them reaching 50+ points.

Most 60-Point Games

Rank	Games	Player
1.	32	Wilt Chamberlain
2.	4	Michael Jordan
3.	3	Elgin Baylor

There have been 52 games in which a player has scored 60 or more points in a single game. Chamberlain did it more than everyone else in the history of the league combined. He also did it 27 of the first 33 times it was done.

Most 70-Point Games

Rank	Games	Player
1.	6	Wilt Chamberlain
2.	1	David Thompson, Elgin Baylor, David Robinson

Some more unbelievable scoring machine records: Chamberlain once had 65 consecutive games of 30+ points.

He was also the league's great ironman. Wilt Chamberlain once played 47 consecutive games without missing a second of playing time. For his career, he averaged almost 46 minutes per game. In 1962, Chamberlain "pitched 79 complete games." That represents the number of games he didn't rest for a second of playing time: not for fouls, not for injuries, not for fatigue.

In Chamberlain's final season, he averaged 43.1 minutes per game. As I recall, Lakers coach Bill Sharman always sat Chamberlain down at precisely the same time in every game—with two minutes remaining in the first quarter. Wilt came back after two minutes were played in the second quarter. In his final year, he played the entire second half of every game.

He was also the most accurate shooter in NBA history. Chamberlain led the league in field goal shooting in nine different seasons. He holds the record for hitting over 72 percent of his shots in the 1973 season.

Chamberlain once hit 15 of 15 field goal shots in a game. He hit all 16 shots he attempted in another. In yet another, he hit all 18 shots he took. According to Philadelphia's former public relations director (and statistical wizard and Wilt historian) Harvey Pollack, Chamberlain once hit 35 consecutive shots.

Above all, Chamberlain was (by far) the greatest rebounder in the history of the game. Chamberlain led the league in rebounds 11 different seasons. The only two seasons that Wilt played where he didn't win the rebounding title were 1964 and 1965—losing both rebounding titles to Bill Russell. In 1964, Chamberlain was second with 22.3 rebounds per game, and, in 1965, he was second with 22.9 rebounds per game.

Most Rebounds, Career
1. 23,924   Wilt Chamberlain
2. 21,620   Bill Russell
3. 17,440   Kareem Abdul-Jabbar

Most Rebounds/Game, Career
1. 22.9   Wilt Chamberlain
2. 22.5   Bill Russell
3. 16.2   Bob Pettit

It is not enough to say that Chamberlain has the highest number of rebounds in a season. He has six of the seven highest rebound totals.

Most Rebounds/Game in a Season

1. 27.2   Wilt Chamberlain, 1961
2. 27.0   Wilt Chamberlain, 1960
3. 25.7   Wilt Chamberlain, 1962
4. 24.7   Bill Russell, 1964
5. 24.6   Wilt Chamberlain, 1966
6. 24.3   Wilt Chamberlain, 1963
7. 24.2   Wilt Chamberlain, 1967

Most 40-Rebound Games

1. 14   Wilt Chamberlain
2. 8   Bill Russell

Only two other players ever had as many as 40 rebounds in a game (Nate Thurmond and Jerry Lucas). Chamberlain had 55 rebounds in one game.

Some people will attempt to downplay Chamberlain's rebounding feats because there were so many shots taken in those games. But if that were the case, everyone's rebounding numbers would look ridiculous. Only one other player, Bill Russell, even approached Wilt.

Most Rebounds in the 1960s

1. 19,112   Wilt Chamberlain
2. 17,501   Bill Russell
3. 9,786   Elgin Baylor
4. 9,716   Walt Bellamy
5. 8,831   Jerry Lucas

The Complete Player

Wilt Chamberlain wasn't just a scorer. He was the complete package.

Wilt the Passer

Chamberlain had 21 assists in a single game, which remains the record for a center. In 1968, Chamberlain led the league in assists with 702 assists. Oscar Robertson had a higher per-game average.

Wilt the Shot Blocker

They have only kept track of blocked shots since the 1974 season, a year after Chamberlain retired. Matt Guokas played with Wilt and swears he averaged about eight per game. Even accounting for the fact that there were more shots taken in those days, that number is incredible. Newspaper accounts from many of the games talk about Chamberlain blocking 10 or 12 shots, so perhaps eight isn't a high enough amount. Even if it wasn't eight per night, he most certainly would have blocked more than any other player (except for possibly Bill Russell).

Matt Guokas: "Wilt, for much of his years in the league, was into numbers. He would count his points, rebounds—he wasn't concerned about points after a certain year, but he was always big on rebounds—and he would test himself. He kept mental notes to himself—and would check the stat sheets at halftime. He would have questions to Harvey (Pollack, the Philadelphia public relations director) if the official numbers were different than his."

Wilt the Wage Earner

When Chamberlain entered the NBA, there was a ceiling on salaries of $25,000 a year. Wilt broke that mark with ease as soon as he agreed to a contract. He left college a year early and signed with the Harlem Globetrotters for a reported $75,000. No one will really know what his early salaries were, but by the most conservative estimates, Wilt always signed the largest contracts in league history. He was the first to play for $100,000 per year. He was the first to play for $250,000 a year. When he was traded to the Lakers, Jack Kent Cooke signed him to a five-year, $3 million contract.

When Chamberlain entered the league, Bob Cousy was earning a reported $22,000 a year. He and Bob Pettit were the highest-paid players. Chamberlain raised the bar for everyone. (If you're wondering, Bill Russell wrote in his 1965 autobiography *Go Up for Glory* that his first contract was for $22,000—less $3,000 for showing up late for playing in the Olympics.)

In the 2002 NBA season, there were 28 different players who earned at least $11 million per season. Kevin Garnett earned the most, $22,400,000. In 2003 and 2004, Garnett was paid over $28 million per year.

Wilt the Foul Shooter

It is harder to defend him at this. I could say that even though he was one of the worst free throw shooters in history, he made more than most because he took so many. In fact, he led the league in free throws made in one year. Only one player in history—Karl Malone—has attempted more free throws than Chamberlain. And Karl has played in about 400 more games. Besides, it's not as if Chamberlain was out there on "Great Player Island" as the only participant who couldn't shoot a high percentage of free throws.

Career Free Throw Percentages

Wilt Chamberlain	.511
Shaquille O'Neal	.542
Bill Russell	.561

Chamberlain pointed out that after five years in the league, he was actually a better foul shooter than Russell. Indeed, Wilt came into the league a much better foul shooter than when he left:

First five seasons	55 percent (3,043 of 5,537 free throws)
Rest of career	48 percent (3,014 of 6,325 free throws)

Wilt played for eight different head coaches, with eight different systems and personalities. Some were former great players. Some were former college coaches. It's no wonder his seasonal stats look so different. If you look at his list of head coaches, he actually played for two of the greatest foul shooters in history.

Chamberlain's Head Coaches
Neil Johnston
Frank McGuire
Bob Feerick
Alex Hannum
Dolph Schayes
Butch van Breda Kolff
Joe Mullaney
Bill Sharman

How did he do playing for two of the greatest foul shooters?

- In 1965 Chamberlain shot .464 FT playing for Dolph Schayes (career .843 FT, led the league three times).
- In 1972 Chamberlain shot .422 FT playing for Bill Sharman (career .883 FT, led the league seven times).

Those were his two worst foul-shooting seasons. He explained what happened in 1965 in his first autobiography. Chamberlain wrote that the first thing Dolph did when Wilt joined the 76ers was have him shoot free throws. "I must have made 400 a day. And I usually converted about 80 percent of them in practice. Then, during the games, I reverted to my old habits and hit about 50 percent, and Dolph finally realized that my problem wasn't laziness."

My take on Chamberlain's free throws is that athletes—even great athletes—have weaknesses. Pitching sensation Sandy Koufax was one of the worst hitters in baseball history. Slugger Babe Ruth didn't have the range to play center field. For Chamberlain to have been as great as he was without being able to make more than half his free throws is actually a testament to his greatness.

Wilt's Record Clarified

The other great criticism of Chamberlain was that he wasn't a winner. Chamberlain wrote three books defending his record. He pointed out that with two titles, he won more than Bob Pettit or Dolph Schayes or Oscar Robertson or Elgin Baylor—to say nothing of sports stars like Hank Aaron and Willie Mays and Joe Namath and Jim Brown and Ted Williams.

Chamberlain also wrote that most knowledgeable observers readily agree that Boston almost invariably had better players, better coaching, and better luck. (Of course, it's all in whom you talk to. In *Go Up for Glory*, Russell wrote, "Wilt came into the league playing with Tom Gola and Guy Rodgers and Woody Sauldsberry and Paul Arizin. You couldn't find greater teammates. But the Celtics were champions.")

If just three or four games spanning the more than 1,200 regular and postseason games that Chamberlain played had gone the other way, he would never have been labeled a loser. In fact, his career came close to looking like this: the first seven years would have been spent winning scoring titles and leading lesser-talented teams to the verge of the NBA elite. The last seven would have been spent playing defense and winning four or five championships. He came close. Oh, so close.

Losing Game 7s in 1968, 1969, and 1970

Here's how close Chamberlain came to winning NBA Championships in three seasons.

Eastern Conference Finals, 1968

For the first time in his career, Chamberlain played a season as the defending champion. The Sixers again had the best record in basketball, winning 62 games. Despite playing

82 games (and the Celtics eight times), they had to defeat Boston to make a return trip to the NBA Finals.

Chamberlain made a big deal in his book that the series was played with heavy hearts on both sides. Dr. Martin Luther King Jr. had been assassinated the day before the series was to have started. Matt Guokas told me that he remembers Chamberlain walking down to the Boston locker room before Game 1 to discuss if there should be a game or not. Guokas remembers the body language—he said you could tell the players were overwhelmed and didn't want to play. Boston won that first game 127–118 in Philadelphia.

Then, after five days between games (rescheduled because of Dr. King's funeral), the Sixers took command, winning three straight games.

Game 5 was in Philadelphia.

Matt Guokas: "We relaxed a little in the fifth game, up 3–1. A lot of people don't remember that Billy Cunningham was hurt in the earlier playoff series versus the Knicks—which meant I had to play a lot more. That didn't help. But anyway, in Game 5, Russell blocked a couple of Chamberlain shots, pushing him farther and farther away from the basket. Bill smacked one of Wilt's finger rolls all the way to halfcourt one time. Oh, Chamberlain had a bad knee then, too."

The Celtics blew out the Sixers by 18 points in Philadelphia in Game 5. Back in Boston, the Celtics won 114–106, setting up a seventh game in Philly.

The Celtics won 100–96. This is the game that is remembered for one thing: Chamberlain took only one shot in the second half. Chamberlain wrote about the game in his autobiography, saying that he was playing the way he had played and won all year. He was passing and rebounding, even outrebounding Russell 34–26. He wrote that Boston had half their team guarding him. Russell was behind him, and K. C. Jones and Sam Jones were collapsing on him. That left his teammates open for easy shots, but they kept missing. Hal Greer hit 8 of 25 field goals and Guokas hit 2 of 10 field goals.

There is no bigger Wilt fan on this planet, but I would have gone crazy watching that game. Chamberlain couldn't afford to play the way he had all year. Billy Cunningham (a 19-point scorer during the season) was out with an injury. This was the seventh game—against Boston. The guards couldn't hit their shots. And Chamberlain—who averaged 24 points (and 17 shots) per game during the season—took just one shot in the second half!

Harvey Pollack: "I remember right after the seventh game, everyone asked Coach Hannum why he didn't tell Wilt to shoot more. Hannum said, 'I never had to tell him to shoot before.'"

Chamberlain was criticized for shooting too much and scoring too much early in his career. Now, with a championship under his belt, perhaps he felt he not only wanted to win—he wanted (needed) to win like Bill Russell—without scoring.

He played the game correctly—if you're doubled, pass it out to the open teammate for an easier shot. At what point does a great player have to become selfish and take control?

1969 NBA Finals: Game 7

After the 1968 season, Chamberlain was traded to the Lakers. Wilt wanted a piece of the 76ers team, which had been promised to him by the late owner. That wasn't going to happen. Instead, he was traded to the Lakers and played alongside Jerry West and Elgin Baylor. It's almost as if Shaquille O'Neal had been traded to the Utah Jazz following the 1996 season and played alongside Stockton and Malone—before any of the three of them had won a championship.

Despite Chamberlain and Baylor getting in each other's way at times (both played best on the low blocks), the Lakers finished 1969 with 55 wins. They made the Finals against the Boston Celtics, who had won only 48 games in Russell's final season.

The Lakers took the first two games (with West scoring 94 points), and Boston won the third game. Chamberlain was quick to point out in his autobiography (correctly) that Baylor made 4 of 18 field goals in that game and West missed 13 of 14 fourth-quarter shots. The series went to seven games.

In the seventh game, Lakers owner Jack Kent Cooke had thousands of balloons hanging from the ceiling in huge nets, ready to be cut loose the instant the Lakers won. In the third quarter, the Lakers missed 15 straight shots at one point and trailed by 17 points. Los Angeles then rallied. With five minutes left in the game, the Lakers trailed by nine points. To that point, Chamberlain had 18 points and 27 rebounds. On his 27th rebound, Chamberlain banged his knee and was forced to come out of the game. A minute of game time later, Chamberlain said that he signaled Coach van Breda Kolff that he was ready to come back into the game. The coach figured he could win without Wilt—determined to prove he was boss. The Lakers were continuing to come back with Mel Counts at center. Van Breda Kolff humiliated Chamberlain and cost his team a chance at an NBA Championship.

Russell's remarks cut deep when he said after the game, "Any injury, short of a broken leg or a broken back, isn't good enough. When he took himself out of the game when he hurt his knee, well, I wouldn't have put him back in the game, either, even though I think he's great."

Now, remember the context in which this was said: that was Russell's final game ever and he wanted to go out with a victory. He not only wanted a victory, he wanted one against Chamberlain. In more recent years, Russell softened his statements concerning that game.

Leonard Koppett wrote the game story for the *New York Times*, and Chamberlain's absence in the final 5 minutes 19 seconds was a real sidebar. Koppett didn't mention Chamberlain sitting out until the 12th paragraph. In the sidebar story these were the only quotes offered from van Breda Kolff. He felt his team "missed the open man too often." About Wilt asking to go back in for the final minutes after injuring his right knee, the Lakers head coach said, "I thought we were playing fairly well without him."

The sensibilities of 1969 and those now in the early 2000s are much different. There was no intense media circus. There was no ESPN. There was no Internet. Today, the superstar player being unable to get back into the closing minutes of a championship game would have overshadowed Jerry West's brilliant performance in a losing cause. It would have shared headlines with the Celtics winning their 11th title in 13 seasons.

The coach and the center had had an adversarial relationship all season, and van Breda Kolff knew that Chamberlain wasn't going anywhere after just his first season in Los Angeles. If we put ourselves in van Breda Kolff's mind, why let Chamberlain be a hero? He probably knew he was coaching his final game with the Lakers. If he could win a title without Wilt, it would have been better than winning it with him.

From Chamberlain's point of view, he again did the honorable thing. He played his heart out in the seventh game. This time, unlike the previous year, he shot early and often. He played great defense. He got hurt, but then heroically tried to re-enter the game.

More than 30 years later, it has been debated whether Chamberlain could or should have insisted he go back in. Some people think Chamberlain should have forced himself into the game—made a scene with the coach, if he had to. That wasn't Wilt's way. That wasn't anyone's way in sports in 1969. How honorable was Chamberlain that after the game, he didn't publicly blast the coach for his decision?

1970 NBA Finals, Game 7

Chamberlain tore a tendon in his right knee just nine games into the season and was expected to miss the remainder of the season. But he returned to play the final three games and then the entire playoffs. In the Finals against the Knicks, with the series tied 2–2, it was New York center Willis Reed who left the game with a hip injury in the second quarter. But the Lakers couldn't take advantage and lost that fifth game 107–100 as Wilt was played by the much smaller forwards Dave DeBusschere and Dave Stallworth.

In the sixth game, sans Reed, Chamberlain scored 45 points and pulled down 27 rebounds. In the famous seventh game, Reed brought the house down when he came out for warm-ups. But Reed's playing in the game meant little. He scored only those two early field goals. Chamberlain took only 16 shots (making 10) and scored 21 points. But he missed 10 of 11 free throws! Chamberlain wrote later in his autobiography that Walt Frazier whipped West's ass that night. Not only did Frazier score 36 points and dish for 19 assists, Wilt says he must have stolen the ball right out of West's hands five or six times in the first half alone.

Marv Albert: "Wilt *couldn't* do more than he did. He wasn't the same player he was in the past. He wasn't the same physically, for sure. The Knicks played great defense."

In 1968, Chamberlain's team held a 3–1 lead on Russell's Celtics. In 1969, Chamberlain's team held a 3–2 lead on Russell's Celtics in the Finals. In 1970, Wilt's team was tied 2–2 with the Knicks—and suddenly had to essentially play the rest of the series without their MVP center. Chamberlain needed one or two of those critical games to go his way.

Chamberlain's teams won in 1967 and 1972. His teams weren't good enough to win prior to 1965. They were good enough to compete for the title every year after that.

Leonard Koppett: "No one has ever come close to the degree of dominance Wilt had over anyone. Shaq today isn't playing against other Shaqs. But Wilt was playing against three or four others in his class. No one could stay with him one on one."

Matt Guokas: "Wilt had the sphere of peers. He played Russell, Thurmond, Bellamy, even Zelmo Beatty. Shaquille, on the other hand, doesn't have the concentrated talent to play against."

There are those (including veteran Boston sportswriter Dan Shaughnessy and Philadelphia historians Harvey and Ron Pollack) who feel that Chamberlain was the best player in NBA history. Most experts, such as Rod Thorn, feel that Chamberlain was behind only Jordan and Russell.

Chamberlain was so dominant that people tended to downgrade his accomplishments. Pete Vecsey told me that Wilt always wanted to prove people wrong. If they said he couldn't shoot from outside, he'd shoot from outside to prove them wrong. That's why he took so many turnaround bank shots.

Bill Bradley wrote in his 1976 *Life on the Run* that Wilt pointed to his statistical achievements as specific measurements of his ability, and they were. But to someone who knows basketball they are, if not irrelevant, certainly nonessential. When I asked Kevin

Loughery to name the three best players in NBA history, he left out Chamberlain for not winning enough . . . then paused, and said, "But he had enormous numbers. You can't ignore that. That's part of greatness."

Bradley also captured that by saying that Chamberlain's career was a paradox. The more Wilt's teams lost (perhaps because of his teammates) and he tried to absolve himself by referring to his individual accomplishments, the more he became, in the eyes of fans, a giant who should never lose. Bradley also wrote that Chamberlain was almost too passive in a game where aggressiveness is rewarded. He never developed the killer instinct necessary for team victory. According to Bradley, "Chamberlain would pat Russell on the behind when Russell made a good play, showing what Wilt thought was magnanimity. It was as if he were paralyzed within his enormous body, unwilling to strike out for fear of injuring an opponent or demeaning himself."

Matt Guokas: "Wilt was not a mean guy. He played hard. He didn't barrel into people. He didn't commit hard fouls."

Connie Hawkins stated in his 1970 *Foul*, written with David Wolf, that Chamberlain was held in higher esteem by the black players. Hawkins saw Chamberlain as someone who didn't play along with the system. He was an individual no one could make conform—on or off the court.

One player who didn't see it that way was Kareem Abdul-Jabbar. Abdul-Jabbar and Chamberlain played against each other for the last four years of Wilt's career. He became Chamberlain's greatest rival, replacing Russell. But, in his later years against a young, militant, outspoken Abdul-Jabbar, Wilt became the good guy in a lot of fans' eyes. Abdul-Jabbar saw it like this: "I always rooted for Wilt. I always appreciated his position in the game. But Wilt always saw everything as a personal attack on his place in history." Abdul-Jabbar said many times that basketball gave Chamberlain his only identity.

Looking Back on Chamberlain's Career

I have to use some baseball references to summarize Chamberlain's career. He set marks as huge and enduring as Babe Ruth's. But Ruth was on winning teams—championship teams. Chamberlain, then, is a cross between Babe Ruth and Barry Bonds, the surly star of the San Francisco Giants. Bonds would often be criticized for walking and taking too many pitches. In the regular season, it is one thing to walk twice a game. It is another in the playoffs and World Series. Chamberlain "took too many pitches" in the 1968 series against the Celtics. Good strategy can always topple a team with Wilt Chamberlain or Barry Bonds. You can't walk them (or put them on the line or triple-team them) every single time. You have to take your shots. But you can't let them beat you. Hal Greer and Jerry West and Jeff Kent had to come up big, because teams would not let Chamberlain/Bonds win a championship against them. That meant that Chamberlain/Bonds sometimes had to be a little more selfish, a little more aggressive—a little more yes, Jordan-like—to overcome that strategy.

In my mind, O'Neal is just as dominant as Chamberlain was. In an era with far fewer points and far more emphasis on team defense, O'Neal has averaged almost as many points in his 11 years as Chamberlain averaged in his 14. O'Neal has won a little more than Chamberlain, as well. Chamberlain won his individual duels with Russell and Abdul-Jabbar. I'm not sure he would have won them with a young Shaquille O'Neal.

They say that Jordan, in his prime, was the best offensive and best defensive player in the game. Chamberlain, for sure, was the best offensive player for many years. In his last few years, he may have been the best defensive player. Chamberlain's career was like a buffet table. Everything was there, in abundance, you just had to look for what's important and limit yourself in portions.

Here's an interesting factoid about Wilt Chamberlain I learned in researching this book.

Dr. Ernie Vandeweghe: "I'll tell you a stat about Wilt you probably never knew. He never was knocked down and never sat on the court. In that seventh game against the Celtics, when he hurt his knee—he hopped off the court. He was like a boxer that took great pride in never being knocked down."

One More Interesting Factoid About Wilt Chamberlain

He was once called "Big Musty" when he avoided showers because he thought it would age his skin. What, you thought Shaquille was the first to come up with these clever nicknames ("The Big Aristotle")?

A Better Analogy

Wilt Chamberlain and Babe Ruth Babe Ruth played for two teams in Boston (the Red Sox and the Braves) but was known mostly for his time with the Yankees. Wilt Chamberlain played for two teams in Philadelphia (the Warriors and 76ers) but was mostly known for his time with the Lakers. Babe Ruth played in one ultimate Game 7 in his career. That was Game 7 of the 1926 World Series. Ruth was thrown out attempting to steal second for the series' final out. Chamberlain's Game 7 history has already been documented.

In 1920, Ruth's most dominant season, his total of 54 homers surpassed every other team in the league except Philadelphia. That same season, Ruth slugged an astonishing .847, a record that stood for more than 80 years until broken by Barry Bonds. Ruth kept his incredible pace up, and by 1921 he had already hit more homers than anyone in baseball history. And he was only 26 years old. Chamberlain needed only a few years until he became the NBA's all-time leading scorer in 1966—when he was 29 years old.

The Yankees, after reaching the World Series and losing in 1921 and 1922 to the Giants, finally won their first world championship in 1923. Chamberlain, after losing playoff series to the Celtics in 1960, 1962, 1964, 1965, and 1966, finally won the NBA Finals in 1967.

Both men had huge appetites and huge vices and huge salaries. Ruth, of course, responded, "I had a better year than him," when asked about making more money than President Herbert Hoover. Chamberlain built a mansion in Los Angeles that columnist Jim Murray called "a monument to the dunk shot, and other social advances."

But the most poignant comparison comes from the end of their careers. Ruth was offered the Tigers managerial job before Mickey Cochrane but refused to give a firm answer before traveling to Hawaii on a publicity tour. When he returned, the Tigers offered Cochrane the job. Ruth was on the sidelines as a coach for the Brooklyn Dodgers in the late 1930s. It was a publicity stunt, and Babe was never given a real shot at managing the team, though he thought he would be given a chance.

Chamberlain never got a chance to coach in the NBA. His coaching tree could be traced back to Charles Darwin. (That's a joke: it could literally be traced back to the game's inventor, Dr. James Naismith.) Wilt retired prematurely, to coach the ABA's San Diego Conquistadors (he wanted to be a player-coach). All the other great stars of his era (West, Russell, and Reed) held head coaching jobs in the NBA. Not Chamberlain. Similar to Ruth, he wasn't taken seriously. All Ruth/Chamberlain did was bring their games into the modern era and dominate like no other athlete this side of Wayne Gretzky.

MICHAEL JORDAN

MJ Isn't the Automatic Choice Anymore

MVP: 5	
MVP VOTING: 2nd in 1987, 2nd in 1989, 2nd in 1997	
NBA TITLES: 6	
ALL-NBA FIRST TEAM: 10	
ALL-NBA SECOND TEAM: 1	

If one had asked someone on the street in the 1950s who the greatest NBA player was, the answer most likely would have been George Mikan. If someone had asked the same question in the 1960s, the answer would have been either Wilt Chamberlain or Bill Russell, depending on what part of the country one was in. In the 1970s, the answer would have been Kareem Abdul-Jabbar. In the 1980s, the answer would most likely have been either Magic Johnson or Larry Bird, depending on what part of the country one was in. Around 1990, Michael Jordan became "the answer," and it has stayed that way until recently. That question has about a 10-year cycle. It is time for Shaquille O'Neal to be the answer to that most basic of all NBA questions. But that shifting of the guard does not detract from Jordan as a player.

Jordan was not only the MVP in five different seasons, he came darn close to winning it a sixth time. In 1997, Karl Malone had 63 first-place votes and 986 total. Jordan had 52 first-place votes and 957 total.

NBA Stardom

Jordan has been universally acclaimed as the greatest NBA player of all time. The nation has been following his career since his freshman season at the University of North Carolina. He has earned the respect of other top athletes and celebrities. He has been called a player with absolutely no weaknesses and has been thought of as the best offensive player while being the best defensive player. That combination has never really existed at the same time.

Wilt Chamberlain may have been the best defensive player in the early 1970s, but that was long after he was the dominant offensive player. Most of the great defensive players in the history of the game (Bill Russell, Dikembe Mutombo, Scottie Pippen, Dave DeBusschere, Dennis Rodman, Gary Payton, and Dennis Johnson) didn't have nearly Jordan's offense. Most of the great offensive players (George Gervin, Lenny Wilkens, and Allen Iverson) didn't have the defense. Jordan had everything, the whole package. He wowed them early in his career, and he wowed them late. He was a different player in his 20s, though, than the one we saw in his 30s.

Jordan in his 20s

638 games	32.3 points	4.9 rebounds	5.9 assists	2.7 steals	7.7 free throws/game

Jordan in his 30s

404 games	27.3 points	6.0 rebounds	4.3 assists	1.9 steals	5.7 free throws/game

Even though only a handful of NBA players ever played into their forties, Jordan set the record for most points by a 40-year-old in his very first week on the job. He turned the Big 40 on February 17, 2003. God stopped him from breaking the record for 40-year-olds on his actual birthday: a major snowstorm dumped almost three feet of snow in Washington, canceling a game against Lenny Wilkens's Toronto Raptors. So, four nights later, against the Nets, Michael Jordan scored 43 points. Kareem Abdul-Jabbar once scored as many as 27 points in his forties. That had been the record.

Jordan's MVPs

One way of measuring greatness is, of course, the test of time. A player in another sport—Willie Mays—won his first MVP in 1954 and his last in 1965. That is an incredible span in a ballplayer's life.

Jordan won his first MVP award in 1988—and his last in 1998. That is the longest span between first and last MVP in NBA history.

Chamberlain came close. He won his first in 1960, was third in 1972, and was fourth in 1973. His last MVP season was 1968—with eight years between his batch of MVP seasons.

Kareem Abdul-Jabbar came even closer. He won his first in 1971 and his sixth in 1980. But he was third in 1970 and third in 1981. He got a ton of votes into the mid-1980s.

Bill Russell won five MVPs. They came within an eight-year span, from 1958 to 1965.

Larry Bird won his three MVPs consecutively while Moses Malone won his three in a five-year period. Magic Johnson won thrice in four seasons.

Say Hey! No one in the NBA had MVP seasons 10 years apart except for Michael Jordan.

His Coaches

During his basketball career, Jordan played for a number of coaches.

Michael Jordan's Teachers

Dean Smith
Kevin Loughery
Stan Albeck
Doug Collins
Phil Jackson

Jordan has been extremely loyal and respectful to all his coaches. Albeck was only the Bulls coach in 1986, when Michael was injured and limited to just 18 regular-season games. Essentially, he's played for legendary college coach Smith (about whom it was said was the only individual who could hold Jordan under 20 points), Loughery, Collins (who tutored young pups Jordan, Pippen, and Horace Grant and brought them to the brink of a dynasty), and Jackson, who reaped the rewards. A 1991 candid conversation with Jordan in *Playboy* magazine included this question and answer: "You've had four pro coaches. Whom did you like to play for the most?" Jordan's answer was Kevin Loughery. When asked why, he responded, "He gave me the confidence to play on this level. My first year, he threw me the ball and said, 'Hey, kid, I know you can play. Go play.' I don't think that would have been the case going through another coach's system."

In later years, Jordan was very respectful to Jackson as Jackson teetered on whether to continue on as Bulls head coach. And of course, Jordan turned to his other old coach, Collins, to help guide another group of youngsters on the art of basketball, when Jordan needed a basketball wizard to coach his Washington Wizards. Only Jackson, however, coached MJ in the NBA Finals.

Michael Jordan's 35 Finals Games

I chronicled each of Jordan's 35 Finals games (and each of his 32 Conference finals games beginning in 1991) from a courtside seat working for NBC Sports. It was my job to study the statistics, spot, and then report immediately—without the filter of a deadline or editor—any trends, records, or notable accomplishments. It was also my job to take notes as the national broadcasters sat and talked to Jordan on the day of each Finals game.

There wasn't a producer or director or executive who worked every single Finals game that Jordan played. Ahmad Rashad was the only announcer with perfect attendance. It is a body of work that I have studied and lived through, and I am the authority on.

Jordan has had so many memorable moments in the Finals. Everyone remembers the last image—making the steal against Karl Malone and hitting the final shot with five seconds to play that would clinch the 1998 Finals.

But I remember a Jordan in the Finals even better than that.

1991 NBA Finals: Michael Jordan and Magic Johnson

Johnson entered those Finals as a rite of summer. His Lakers were in the Finals for the ninth time in 12 seasons. Johnson had already won five NBA titles. No Bulls player had ever been in a Finals game, much less won one. The Lakers went into that Finals with as much collective Finals experience as any team has ever had. They had five players—Magic Johnson, Byron Scott, James Worthy, A. C. Green, and Mychal Thompson—with 123 games of Finals experience. Even the great Celtics teams from the 1960s would be hard-pressed to top that for experience.

Game 1 of the series was the first time Jordan had ever played in a Finals game. To that point, he had played 509 regular-season and 65 postseason games.

The first game of that series was a tightly contested affair that came down to three North Carolina products. The Lakers had a pair of Tar Heels alums (James Worthy and Sam Perkins) who combined for 44 points. The Bulls had Jordan and Scott Williams. They combined for 36 points (Jordan 36, Williams 0). Perkins hit a shot to put the Lakers up 92–91 with 14 seconds remaining. Jordan had a chance to win it at the end, but the ball went in and out. In that game, the Bulls had 38 field goals—Jordan made 14 of them and assisted on 12 others.

The Lakers used Byron Scott to guard Jordan; he "held" Jordan to 36 points. Earvin Johnson had a brilliant game. He controlled the game, despite taking just five shots. He was content to pass out of the constant double teams and had a triple double: 19 points, 10 rebounds, and 11 assists. (It was the 137th triple double of his career. His triple double in Game 5 would be his last, though no one knew it at the time.) The Bulls trailed 1–0 in the Finals.

In the second game, Jordan played point guard and was better than Magic. In this game, Jordan shot 15 of 18 field goals and had 33 points, 13 assists, and seven rebounds. Jordan also made his famous move, switching hands in midair to score. The Bulls shot a Finals record 62 percent with John Paxson a perfect eight of eight in field goal shooting. The Bulls had tied the series.

In Game 3, you didn't have to be a statistician to notice Lakers shooting guard Byron Scott had missed all eight of his shots. I don't believe I've ever seen a shooting guard play 43 minutes in a game of that magnitude and go 0 for 8 in field goal shooting. Scott was injured and didn't play in the fifth game of the series. In the first four games, in 140 minutes, he made just five field goals. He had averaged 14.5 points per game during the season. In the Finals—against the suffocating defense of Pippen and Jordan—he averaged 4.5 points per game. The Bulls won.

In the fourth game, Jordan had 13 assists to go along with his 28 points. Surprisingly, that victory came easy for the Bulls. Chicago's defense was again the story, holding the Lakers to just 14 points in the third quarter.

Jordan won his first NBA title in Los Angeles in the fifth game. That was a routine game for Jordan (30 points, 10 assists, 48 minutes), but two of his teammates played the game of their lives. Pippen had 32 points, 13 rebounds, and seven assists, and Paxson hit 9 of 12 field goals, including all five he took down the stretch, as the Bulls won their fourth in a row, and concluded the playoffs 15–2. Following that game, Jordan broke down holding the trophy, with his father by his side.

The memory of Jordan's performance in that series gets blurred with each passing year. People tend to remember Jordan in his thirties, going against Karl Malone and John Stockton. In his first Finals, though, with everything to prove, Jordan came through as only he could. He averaged 31.2 points and 11.4 assists in the series. He shot 56 percent from the floor and 85 percent from the line. He had 14 steals in the five games. And he was a big reason why the Lakers scored only 92 points per game in the series—14 points per game less than their season average.

1992 NBA Finals: Michael Jordan and Clyde Drexler

A lot had changed in 12 months. Jordan was back in the Finals, prepared to defend his title. But Johnson had gone from a spot on the floor to a seat next to me (and broadcasters Marv Albert and Mike Fratello). Jordan needed a number-one challenger, and Drexler was the man. This time, it would be more mano-a-mano action, unlike with Johnson. Drexler and Jordan played the same position (the year before, Michael had guarded Magic, but the Lakers had used—er, *sacrificed*—Byron Scott on MJ). If Drexler hadn't been taken by Portland the year before he came out, Jordan most likely would have spent his entire career in Portland (near Nike headquarters in Beaverton, Oregon).

Overcoming the drafting of Sam Bowie eight years earlier, the Blazers had made the Finals for the second time in three seasons, thanks to Drexler. The media quickly built this series up as Michael versus Clyde.

Steve Jones: "That should have been a defining moment in the greatness of Clyde Drexler. He should have taken it as a personal challenge. Clyde didn't take that mental approach. Jordan has always gone insane trying to prove that no one else could beat him."

Mike Fratello: "People tend to make it closer than I believe it was . . . Michael had a better understanding of what it took to win."

Portland's strategy in Game 1 was not a bad one. They wanted Jordan to take a steady diet of long-range shots. After all, he had shot only 27 percent from behind the three-point line during the season. Remember, though, all Jordan needed was a little challenge. Jordan hit six three-pointers in the first half! After the sixth, Jordan was captured on tape shrugging his shoulders when glancing at our broadcast table and Magic Johnson. It is a memorable shot of Jordan, for in that one second, we saw the great athlete as stunned by his prowess as the rest of us. Jordan opened the first game of the 1992 Finals by going for the first-round knockout. He had 35 points in the first half of Game 1.

1993 NBA Finals: Michael Jordan and Charles Barkley

These longtime friends had met each other in the playoffs once before, in 1991 when Barkley was a Philadelphia 76er. Jordan's Bulls had struggled during the 1993 season and in the playoffs against the Knicks. The Suns were actually favorites, with the home court advantage. When Chicago took the first two games in Phoenix, it appeared a Bulls third straight title was in the bag. But Phoenix took two of the next three games in Chicago. They might have swept the Bulls in the middle three games, but Jordan scored 55 points in Game 4, the second-highest total ever in a Finals game (trailing Elgin Baylor's 61).

The Bulls avoided a seventh game in Phoenix because Jordan scored every point for Chicago in the fourth quarter of Game 6 except for the final three: those came from Paxson's game-winning three-pointer.

Jordan did everything in that 1993 series. He set a Finals record by averaging 41 points per game in the series. During the three NBA Championship Finals, the Bulls had won eight out of nine road games. The Celtics never had a three-year run that equaled that. They almost always needed the luxury of having a seventh game at the Boston Garden.

Then Michael retired. In a mid-career crisis, he decided he really wanted to play professional baseball. And spend more time with his family. And make movies like *Space Jam* with Bugs Bunny, and go to spring training with Frank Thomas. So he walked away from the game at the age of 30.

He returned for the final 17 games of the 1995 season. Although he was not quite in Michael Jordan shape for the NBA, he and the Bulls were still able to get past the Charlotte Hornets in the first round of the playoffs.

In the second round of the 1995 playoffs, the Bulls faced the Orlando Magic. In Game 1, in Orlando, the Bulls had a chance to win in the final seconds until Chicago native Nick Anderson stole the ball from Jordan. You don't tug on Superman's cape and get away with it! Exactly one month later, in the first game of the 1995 Finals, it was Anderson (a 70 percent foul shooter during the season) who missed all four free throws in the final 12 seconds to blow a game—and probably the championship. Anderson was never again the same player he had been.

The Bulls had their chances in that 1995 series—even holding an eight-point lead in the final minutes of Game 6. But the Magic—led by former Bulls forward Horace Grant—scored the last 14 points of the game and won the series on the Bulls' home court. That would serve as the motivation for Jordan to rededicate himself to basketball and provide all those memorable moments in the 1997 and 1998 Finals.

1996 NBA Finals: Michael Jordan and Gary Payton

The Bulls added Dennis Rodman to the mix for the 1996 season, and the result was a 72–10 regular season that set the NBA record for most wins. Strangely, it was Jordan's worst Finals performance—by a lot. Most of that was due to 1996 Defensive Player of the Year Gary Payton.

The Bulls won the first game, and Seattle coach George Karl scrapped his idea of conserving Payton's energy and put him on Jordan. Payton and Jordan were the supreme trash talkers of their day, and Payton gave an earful to Jordan in Game 2.

"I didn't say nothing to him [in Game 1] and he was still fired up. So what difference does it make?" Payton said in June 1996, after a reporter questioned the wisdom of Payton trash-talking Michael Jordan in Game 2 of the NBA Finals. Once again, you don't tug on Superman's cape. Or spit into the wind. Or pull the mask of the Lone Ranger. In Game 3 of the series, Michael Jordan had his series high in points and, more important, led the Bulls to a commanding 3–0 lead.

Payton would outplay Jordan the next two games, delaying the inevitable, but Jordan won the Finals MVP. I don't think Jordan deserved it. Rodman won two games with his offensive rebounding. Shawn Kemp and Payton were extremely good in a losing cause. It was a tough call.

1997 NBA Finals: Michael Jordan and Karl Malone

During the season, the Mailman narrowly won the MVP over Jordan. Again, you don't tug on Superman's cape. Malone (a 76 percent foul shooter during the season) missed two shots at the end of the first game that would have given Utah the victory. Instead, Michael Jordan came down and calmly sank the game-winning jumper.

Prior to the fifth game, a bad pizza made Jordan sick. Somehow, though, he found the strength to deliver 38 points, including the backbreaking three-pointer to give Chicago a 3–2 lead going back to Chicago.

And in the sixth game, Jordan scored 39 points with 11 rebounds, but his biggest play was an assist: he found Steve Kerr to drill the game-winner that won the series.

For every other player who ever played the game, any of those three moments in the series would be a crowning achievement.

1998 NBA Finals: Rematch Between Jazz and Bulls

The end of Game 6 cemented MJ's reputation for all time. The Bulls won 87–86 on Jordan's steal and jumper in the final seconds. Everyone remembers Jordan's last shot. How about his last game? The Bulls had 87 points. Jordan had 45 of them.

That meant all of the following became true:

- Jordan's teams were 25–1 in their last 26 playoff series. (It was only MJ that you could say that about. Pippen and Coach Phil Jackson had lost to the Knicks in 1994, remember.)
- Jordan had scored at least 20 points in all 35 NBA Finals games. In 22 of those games, he scored at least 30 points.
- Jordan—in his six championship seasons—needed to win only two seventh games (a 1992 second-round series with the Knicks and the 1998 Eastern Conference finals against the Pacers).
- Jordan had all of these playoff heroics and victories after starting his NBA career 1–9 in his first 10 playoff games.
- Jordan's teams were 53–27 in the last two rounds of the playoffs. (That included a 5–8 start, losing the Eastern Conference finals to Detroit in both 1989 and 1990. After that, his teams were 48–19 in the last two rounds.)

The thing about Jordan's moments in the NBA Finals: they don't begin to showcase the entire postseason history of Michael Jordan. From his series-winning shot against the Cleveland Cavs in 1988 against Craig Ehlo to his NBA-record 63 points against the 1986 Celtics in Boston Garden to the 54 points he put on the Knicks to tie the Eastern Conference finals at 2–2 on Memorial Day 1993, it seemed as if he *always* came through.

Derek Harper: "The more success he had, the more he craved. Here's the thing that made Michael Jordan so great. We all knew that in the last couple of minutes the ball was going to him. Everyone in the building knew it. And yet, he still came through every single time. That's what made him so special."

Jordan's Numbers

Jordan went to the line about 10 times per game in his twenties. He went to the free throw line about seven times per game in his thirties. He became less of a slasher and driver to the basket, and more of a jump shooter.

Jordan is second all time in career steals, trailing only John Stockton. But Stockton has played about 430 more games than Jordan. Stockton has averaged 2.18 steals per game in his career. For his career, Jordan has averaged 2.37 steals. Only a talented flame-out such as Michael Ray Richardson (2.63 steals per game in his 556 games) and Gary Payton (more than 2.7 per game in a 13-year career) have surpassed Jordan's steals per game. Only a few others (notably Fat Lever and Mookie Blaylock) have approached the steals numbers.

Jordan made the All-Defensive First Team nine different seasons. In his prime, he was probably the best defender in the league, bar none. He played the passing lanes extremely well, which is why his steals totals were so high. In my opinion, Jordan and Chamberlain are the only players who would have been among the 50 greatest in history *if they had scored 10,000 fewer points each.*

Jordan's offensive game expanded over the years. In his first four seasons, he didn't even have a three-point shot to speak of.

Michael Jordan's Three-Point Shooting

1985	9 of 52	17 percent
1986	3 of 18	17 percent
1987	12 of 66	18 percent
1988	7 of 53	13 percent

In 189 attempts in his first four seasons, Jordan made just 31 treys. But he would finish his career with close to 600. In 1992, he shocked the world (and himself) with six three-pointers in the first half against Portland in Game 1 of the Finals. In 1996, he made 111 for the season, hitting 43 percent for the season.

Who's Better, Who's Best
Michael Jordan or Wilt Chamberlain

Games Needed to Reach 30,000 Points
1. 941   Wilt Chamberlain
2. 960   Michael Jordan

After 1,045 Games
Chamberlain   30.1 points/game
Jordan   30.3 points/game

Chamberlain averaged almost four times as many rebounds per game as Jordan. Wilt averaged 22.9 rebounds per game, while Jordan averaged just more than 6 boards. Jordan averaged a little more than one assist per game more than Wilt. Wilt shot a higher percentage from the field. Michael shot a much better percentage from the line. Wilt was a great shot blocker. Michael was great at stealing the ball.

Chamberlain dominated any statistical category he wanted. He was held well under his seasonal averages in the biggest games he played in. Jordan was one of the greatest big-game performers ever.

A Better Analogy
Michael Jordan and Willie Mays Considered by many the greatest baseball player of all time, Mays was the prototype of the complete player. He hit for average and power, ran the bases with intelligence and speed, played a spectacular center field, and possessed a great arm. He was also remarkably durable, playing in at least 150 games for 13 consecutive years. Jordan was similarly the prototype of the complete basketball player, with seemingly no weaknesses. He was also remarkably durable, playing all 82 games eight times.

A Better Analogy
Michael Jordan and David Stern Michael Jordan was similar to the most popular kid in school who just happened to be the best athlete and the smartest kid, as well. Sometimes,

those kids feel like they can get away with anything. And when it's their money that paid for the schools and the teachers, they pretty much can. That was the case with Jordan. He pretty much was able to get away with anything. After all, he did more for the league than anyone. The Bulls weren't worth more than $20 million when Jordan joined the team. He practically built that United Center and filled it—even years after he left Chicago. The television ratings soared with Jordan, and the league needed him every time a renewal of multimillion-dollar negotiations came up.

Jordan had a history of doing things his way, with NBA Commissioner David Stern only putting his foot down on the real important stuff. Jordan didn't accompany the Bulls to the White House after winning his first championship. He initially didn't plan on playing for the U.S. Olympic team in Barcelona, saying that he had already experienced being an Olympian. He didn't march in the Olympics Opening Ceremonies. He played golf the day before the NBA Finals in Phoenix. He made a habit of skipping All-Star weekend duties, preferring to pay the fine. There were times he chose not to talk to the press. There was the famous incident in which he changed his number (from #45 back to #23) without informing the league. There was the book by a former golfing buddy that detailed big-stakes gambling losses. There was the move with super agent David Falk planning to decertify the union.

There was also social criticism of Jordan, most notably by football great Jim Brown. Brown long contended that Jordan didn't do enough for the black community.

Of course, the league, under Stern, did a lot for Jordan. It gave him a platform on which he could compile a portfolio of many lucrative endorsements. It gave him worldwide fame and publicity. It gave a great competitor constant competition. As a youngster, Jordan competed against Julius Erving and Larry Bird and Magic Johnson. As a 40-year-old, he competed against Kobe Bryant and Tracy McGrady. It was Stern who allowed Jordan to bounce between basketball and baseball, ownership and player, legend and partner.

When Jordan retired for the first time, Stern angrily dismissed suggestions that there was a link between Jordan's gambling and his retirement, calling the idea "scurrilous and disgusting." Yet it came at a time when Stern had made an effort to talk to Jordan about his gambling before the 1994 season opener, just weeks away. In baseball and football, commissioners past and present have kicked out and kept out superstars of the highest order. In 1979, Major League Baseball Commissioner Bowie Kuhn forced Willie Mays to choose between a job as a casino greeter and his association with baseball. In 1963, the NFL suspended the leading scorer on the championship team (Paul Hornung) for a year because he bet on his own team to win. The NBA's investigation into Jordan's high-stakes gambling was over before it had begun. Both parties benefited. Remember, you don't tug on Superman's cape.

Michael Jordan probably preferred not to play in his final All-Star game, in February 2003. At least, that's what Jordan hinted at in public statements. The NBA needed him there, and they turned the weekend into a long, celebratory graduation party for him. Stern needed Jordan, and Jordan needed Stern. They made beautiful money together.

Why MJ Isn't the Automatic Choice Anymore

Among the experts that I spoke to, several were adamant about Jordan being the best player of all time. Rod Thorn, Pete Vecsey, Del Harris, Mike Fratello, Derek Harper, Marv Albert, Mike Dunleavy, P. J. Carlesimo, Tom Tolbert, Bill Walton, Sean Elliott, Isiah Thomas, and Doug Collins all agreed on Jordan. It took each of them all of a second to make that decision.

It wasn't nearly a unanimous landslide, however. Bob Ryan and Kevin Loughery gave their votes to Bill Russell. Ryan even put Magic ahead of Michael. The *Boston Globe*'s Dan Shaughnessy, the *Philadelphia Inquirer*'s Stephen A. Smith, former player Dr. Ernie Vandeweghe, and Matt Guokas went with Wilt Chamberlain. Sacramento Kings owner Joe Maloof picked Shaquille O'Neal. Leonard Koppett of the *New York Times* told me that one has to do it by eras, but came close to picking Oscar Robertson ahead of Jordan when he told me, "No one has ever been a better all-around player—including Michael Jordan—than Oscar. Anything Jordan could do, Robertson could do better. He could shoot better, defend, pass better, and he was two inches shorter." Steve "Snapper" Jones didn't hesitate or put qualifiers on his choice. Oscar Robertson was the best of all time, he told me. Snapper had Wilt second, also ahead of Jordan.

To me, it should not be a popularity contest. Too often elections are won by the candidates with the most money. Commissioner Stern cared deeply about creating, cultivating, and maintaining Jordan's popularity and image.

Did anyone in charge of the league back in Chamberlain's day broker a deal that would have allowed Wilt to play for the Lakers in the 1974 playoffs, after his ABA Conquistadors' season was over?

Did Converse do as much for Magic Johnson as Nike did for Jordan? Did CBS do as much for Magic Johnson and Larry Bird as NBC did for Jordan?

No, no, and no.

Jordan, for his part, held up his end of the bargain quite nicely. For all the small infractions, he was every bit the positive role model the league sold. Unlike other superstar players in this book, he never was caught with drugs and never had to do time in rehab. He transcended the game, as only a few athletes (Muhammad Ali, Tiger Woods) ever have. He was always great theater.

He was the political candidate with the money and media knowledge. He also was the rarest of birds: he was always better than the hype.

But I can't quite cross the line and join the people who think Jordan was the greatest basketball player of all time. He took too much time off during his prime. Bill Walton would have killed to have back even one of the nine years he lost due to injury. It took a potentially life-threatening illness to get Magic Johnson off the court—and even then, the disease couldn't stop him from returning. Jordan had many reasons to retire in both 1993 and 1998. In 1993, that included a desire to play professional baseball. You don't think Chamberlain wanted to field offers to play other sports? The man had a contract to fight Muhammad Ali! Chamberlain also mourned the loss of his father late in his career. In 1998, Jordan walked away after a storybook championship season. But Oscar Robertson didn't walk away after his long-awaited 1971 title. Jerry West didn't leave after his long-awaited first NBA Championship in 1972. It took John Elway a lifetime to win his first Super Bowl. He returned anyway, to defend his title (and win a second consecutive Super Bowl).

People talk about maximizing their abilities to the fullest. Jordan gave everything he had—except he cheated himself (and his fans) out of five years. These weren't five years of wartime service, which is what Ted Williams lost. These weren't five years of rehabilitation to gain back his physical prowess. They weren't even five years of playing against somewhat inferior competition in a competing league.

Jordan had every right to live his life the way he chose. He retired in 1993, after just nine full seasons. Shaquille O'Neal has made just as much money in the same spotlight. He has had just as many offers for movies and still had time for the NBA and raising a family. He didn't stop after nine seasons. Kareem Abdul-Jabbar didn't stop after 15. It doesn't mean that Jordan was right or wrong. It just means—in my opinion—that it tilts the balance to Who's Better, Who's Best.

BILL RUSSELL
The Lion in Winner

MVP: 5	
MVP VOTING: 10 consecutive years in top 5	
NBA TITLES: 11	
ALL-NBA FIRST TEAM: 3	
ALL-NBA SECOND TEAM: 8	

Bill Russell was the most celebrated victor in the sport. He was the most celebrated victor in American team sports. He won five Most Valuable Player awards—and would have won a bucketful of Finals MVPs, had someone thought of awarding them in the 1960s.

Most historians would agree that Russell was the greatest defensive force in the history of the NBA. Despite not averaging as many as 15 points per game, he was regarded as the greatest player ever by many experts and fans. No one concentrated on his weaknesses—and he had some offensively. He couldn't shoot foul shots much better than Wilt Chamberlain or Shaquille O'Neal. He made costly turnovers in some big spots in the seventh game of the NBA Finals. But the bottom line was that his teams always won.

It was at the University of San Francisco that Russell began to display the abilities to lead his team to victory that NBA fans would later see in the 1960s. He so dominated the college game that the NCAA widened the foul lane from 6 to 12 feet. He tasted life as a champion first in college and then in Rome at the 1956 Olympics.

He became a student of blocking shots. Of course, no one kept track of that statistic until much later. When he arrived in Boston to play for the Celtics, they had never won a championship. As soon as he arrived, a dynasty—the greatest in team sports history—began. Boston won its first title in Russell's first season.

Who's Better, Who's Best
Bill Russell or Wilt Chamberlain (or Anyone Else, for That Matter)

Doug Collins: "You know what's funny, Elliott. If those guys played today, Russell would be a power forward. . . . There was more competition for the great centers in those days: Thurmond, Bellamy, Reed. That's part of what made Russell and Chamberlain so great. They were pushed by those guys, and pushed by each other."

Bob Ryan's All-Time Top Three Players
1. Bill Russell
2. Magic Johnson
3. Michael Jordan

Tom Heinsohn's All-Time Top Three Centers
"I have to give it to you in terms of geography," said Heinsohn. "In geography terms starting in Boston, Massachusetts:
1. Bill Russell—from Boston
2. Wilt Chamberlain—in Newton, Massachusetts [a neighboring suburb]
3. Kareem Abdul-Jabbar—in Mississippi somewhere, and
4. No one else in the continental United States."

Del Harris: "Michael Jordan is the best. Now, in regard to Russell or Chamberlain, I was in Chamberlain's corner for many years, but I have to defer and listen to Nellie (Don Nelson). Nelson played with Russell and has convinced me to place Russell ahead of him."

Matt Guokas: "I played with Chamberlain. There was no one better than him."

Rod Thorn: "My all-time top three would have Jordan first, Russell second, and Chamberlain third."

Kevin Loughery's All-Time Top Three
1. Bill Russell
2. Michael Jordan
3. Shaquille O'Neal

Pete Vecsey's All-Time Top Three
1. Michael Jordan
2. Bill Russell
3. Kareem Abdul-Jabbar

Russell's Rebound Numbers

There are only 24 NBA games in history in which a player had 40-plus rebounds. Only four players accomplished this feat.

40 or More Rebounds in a Game

1.	14	Wilt Chamberlain
2.	8	Bill Russell
3.	1	Nate Thurmond
4.	1	Jerry Lucas

Russell's Rebound Rankings

1957	4th	943 rebounds (Missed 24 of 72 games. 19.2 average would lead NBA.)
1958	1st	22.7 per game
1959	1st	23.0 per game (6.6 more per game than second-place Bob Pettit)
1960	2nd	24.0 per game (behind Chamberlain)
1961	2nd	23.9 per game (behind Chamberlain)
1962	2nd	23.6 per game (behind Chamberlain)
1963	2nd	23.6 per game (behind Chamberlain)
1964	1st	24.7 per game
1965	1st	22.9 per game
1966	2nd	22.8 per game (behind Chamberlain)
1967	2nd	21.0 per game (behind Chamberlain)
1968	3rd	18.6 per game (behind Chamberlain and Jerry Lucas)
1969	3rd	19.3 per game (behind Chamberlain and Wes Unseld)

Note: If we awarded rebounding crowns by average per game (as they've done since Russell's retirement), Russell would have led the league in 1957. He would have finished fourth in 1968. He would have finished second only to Chamberlain in his final season of 1969.

Russell averaged 22.5 rebounds per game in his career. In 165 postseason games, he averaged 24.9 rebounds per game.

Was He the Greatest Rebounder of All Time?

First, a quick sidebar to why Chamberlain and Russell are superior to today's rebounders.

Tim Duncan pulled down a career-high 25 rebounds in a pathetic 67–65 game against the Miami Heat on February 1, 2003. It was the 417th game in Duncan's career. In his first five seasons, Duncan was ranked number 3, 5, 3, 4, and 2 in rebounds.

In that career-high rebounding effort, Duncan pulled down 25 rebounds in a game with 101 missed shots. That "career high" would be very comparable to hundreds of routine games for Chamberlain or Russell.

1970 Finals

Game 1	The game had 106 missed shots. Chamberlain had 24 rebounds.
Game 2	The game had 105 missed shots. Chamberlain had 24 rebounds.
Game 6	The game had 90 missed shots. Chamberlain had 27 rebounds.
Game 7	The game had 91 missed shots. Chamberlain had 24 rebounds.

I could do that comparison for any Chamberlain game I had a box score for (in the 1960s, for Russell's career, box scores only had field goals made, not attempted).

1972 Finals

Game 5	The game had 108 missed shots. Chamberlain had 29 rebounds.

Duncan has been one of the NBA's best rebounders for a five-year period. In his first 416 games, he never had as many as 25 rebounds in a game. Chamberlain averaged 25 rebounds per game over the course of the 1962 season (25.7 per game).

Chamberlain	1,045 games	22.9 rebounds/regular season	24.5 rebounds/postseason
Russell	963 games	22.5 rebounds/regular season	24.9 rebounds/postseason

Take away Chamberlain's last season:

Chamberlain	963 games	22,398 rebounds	23.3 rebounds/game
Russell	963 games	21,620 rebounds	22.5 rebounds/game

Chamberlain Against Russell

They played 142 games against each other in their careers. That in itself is an amazing stat.

Bill Russell played 963 regular-season and 165 postseason games. That's 1,128 career games with the Celtics. He played 142 of those 1,128 games (almost 13 percent) against Chamberlain.

Russell entered the NBA three years before Chamberlain. In those three years, he played 217 games, including the 30 postseason games. Once Chamberlain entered the league, Russell had to play him 142 times out of 911 games (15.6 percent of the time).

In the 142 games they played against each other, their stats were:

Chamberlain	28.7 points/game	28.7 rebounds/game
Russell	14.5 points/game	23.7 rebounds/game

Chamberlain's teams	58 wins
Russell's teams	84 wins

Russell's teams won 59 percent of the time against Chamberlain's teams. By the late 1960s, Chamberlain's teams won more regularly. Once Chamberlain went to the 76ers and Lakers, his teams were 34–35 against Russell. But Russell won the last meeting: Game 7 of the 1969 NBA Finals—the last game of Bill Russell's career.

How fitting.

Bill Russell in Game 7s

Russell's teams won every Game 7 they played.

Most Amazing Stat in Russell's Career

His teams were 10–0 in Game 7s. How come no one ever called him "Mr. April"?

Bill Russell in Game 7s

1.	April 13, 1957	Boston 125, St. Louis 123	2 OT
2.	April 1, 1959	Boston 130, Syracuse 125	
3.	April 9, 1960	Boston 122, St. Louis 103	
4.	April 5, 1962	Boston 109, Philadelphia 107	
5.	April 18, 1962	Boston 110, Los Angeles 107	1 OT
6.	April 10, 1963	Boston 142, Cincinnati 131	
7.	April 15, 1965	Boston 110, Philadelphia 109	
8.	April 28, 1966	Boston 95, Los Angeles 93	
9.	April 19, 1968	Boston 100, Philadelphia 96	
10.	May 5, 1969	Boston 108, Los Angeles 106	

Okay, let's examine these games.

1. First off, the first eight of these Game 7s were played in Boston. The last two the Celtics were forced to play on the road.
2. Five of these games decided the NBA Finals.
3. Russell was 4–0 against Chamberlain in a Game 7 situation. Those four games were decided by two points, one point, four points, and two points.

April 13, 1957; NBA Finals: St. Louis at Boston

Russell scored 19 points and pulled down 32 rebounds in one of the most thrilling games of all time. Russell kept the Celtics alive late in the fourth quarter. After he hit a shot from the pivot with 20 seconds remaining to put Boston up by two points, he blocked an almost certain field goal by the Hawks' Jack Coleman. But Russell wound up fouling the great Bob Pettit, who made a pair of foul shots to tie the game and send it to the first of two overtimes.

April 1, 1959; Eastern Finals: Syracuse at Boston

The Nationals had a 16-point lead in the second quarter, but the Celtics pulled even by the third quarter. The game swung back and forth in the final four minutes. Each game of this series was won by the home team. Russell played the first 46 minutes before fouling out. He scored 18 points and had 32 rebounds before departing.

April 9, 1960; NBA Finals: St. Louis at Boston

This was the easy one. The lone Game 7 blowout. Russell was a man among men. He scored 22 points. He pulled down 35 rebounds. The game was decided by rebounds.

Boston had the advantage on the boards, 83–47. The Hawks were so physical with Russell that he once had to ask for a timeout after being cuffed on the head once too often.

April 5, 1962; Eastern Finals: Philadelphia at Boston
Russell scored 19 points, while holding Chamberlain to a mere 22. That, my friends, was a major blow to the Warriors. Boston led 107–102, but Wilt hit on two free throws and then had a three-point play to tie the game. Sam Jones hit a jumper with two seconds left to win the game, and the Celts advanced to the Finals.

April 18, 1962; NBA Finals: Los Angeles at Boston
The Celtics won their fourth consecutive NBA title—this time, in overtime—and Russell was brilliant. This had to be the best game of his NBA career. It came, naturally, in the seventh and deciding game of the NBA Finals.

Russell scored 30 points and tied an NBA playoff record by grabbing 44 rebounds (a mark that has stood for 40 years). Boston needed every last point and rebound.

The Lakers had a legitimate shot at this title, especially when foul trouble sent Tom Sanders, Jim Loscutoff, and Tom Heinsohn to the bench late in the game. In the overtime, Russell scored 5 of Boston's 10 points.

Another measure of the greatness of Bill Russell. In this climactic game, he converted 14 of 17 free throws.

April 10, 1963; Eastern Finals: Cincinnati at Boston
Bob Cousy had announced his retirement upon season's end months earlier. Russell made sure his friend didn't end his career with a loss. Russell had 20 points. The game was actually decided by the Celtic guards: Sam Jones scored 47 points (still a record for a seventh game), and Cousy added 21 points and 16 assists.

April 15, 1965; Eastern Finals: Philadelphia at Boston
The last five seconds of this game are as memorable as any five seconds in the history of the league. Does "Havlicek steals the ball" ring a bell? It was a wild finish. The Celtics led 110–107 and Boston seemed certain to advance, since only five ticks of the clock remained. Wilt Chamberlain scored on a layup—no Celtic would dare risk a foul—and that cut the lead to one. Then Russell tossed the ball inbound over Chamberlain's long arms. The ball hit the wire supporting the backboard and the 76ers were awarded possession. Now, it was Philly that had one last chance for a winning shot. Hal Greer stepped out of bounds and tossed it in toward Chet Walker, 30 feet away.

John Havlicek stole the ball, and Russell was saved from being the goat. This was Chamberlain's sixth season in the league, and he had a great game with 30 points and 32 rebounds. But it was one point short of what his team needed. Russell had the following line: 15 points, 29 rebounds, nine assists.

April 28, 1966; NBA Finals: Los Angeles at Boston

This is getting silly. Russell scored 25 points and had 32 rebounds in Game 7 of the NBA Finals, which was decided by a mere two points. This was the Celtics' ninth title in 10 seasons, and the one that sent Red Auerbach out with one last victory cigar. The game was decided by two points, but it wasn't that close. Boston scored the first 10 points of the game and never looked back. Red lit the cigar with 35 seconds remaining, after Sam Jones hit a 35-foot bank shot.

April 19, 1968; Eastern Finals: Boston at Philadelphia

You can't help but think Russell—in fact, all the players—had to be affected by the assassination two weeks earlier of Dr. Martin Luther King Jr. This was the first Game 7 that Russell had played in away from the Boston Garden. Boston won 100–96 because player-coach Russell made three plays in the game's final minute. First there was the free throw he made to put his team up by a deuce with 34 seconds remaining. Then, Bill blocked a Chet Walker shot. After Hal Greer missed, Russell snared the rebound. Following the game, Russell called it the most satisfying of his career. He only scored 12 points, but held Chamberlain to 14. Strangely, Wilt took only two shots in the second half and scored only two points after halftime.

May 5, 1969; NBA Finals: Boston at Los Angeles

This was the game that Boston was supposed to lose. The Lakers thought so. This was Russell's 13th season and 11th championship. This was the first time his team had defeated a squad comprising old rivals Chamberlain, Baylor, and West. Chamberlain picked up his fourth foul in the opening minutes of the second half. He picked up number five late in the third quarter. Chamberlain had never fouled out of a game before and wasn't going to start in this one. But he hurt his right knee coming down for a rebound with 5:45 to play in the fourth quarter. At the time, the Lakers trailed by seven points. Wilt said he wanted to go in for the final four minutes. But van Breda Kolff said that he thought his team was playing fairly well without him.

Russell scored 6 points, and Chamberlain 18.

Boston won 108–106.

A Better Analogy

Bill Russell and Joe DiMaggio Bill Russell went to high school in Oakland, California. Joe DiMaggio was born across the bay two decades earlier. Russell was the greatest winner his sport has ever known. DiMaggio was the greatest winner his sport has ever known. Both men played exactly 13 years. Russell won 11 championships in 13 seasons. His teams went 11–1 in the NBA Finals. DiMaggio's Yankees won 10 pennants and went 9–1 in the World Series. Neither man lost an ultimate game.

In a 2003 book by Morris Engelberg titled *DiMaggio: Setting the Record Straight*, the longtime business manager/attorney for DiMaggio revealed that the Yankee Clipper privately gloated over the fact he had nine World Series rings and Ted Williams had none, ignoring that he got more support from his team than Williams did from his Red Sox teammates.

Does that sound familiar? Neither revolutionized his sport. Neither of the players had the gaudy statistics of others. DiMaggio hit just 361 homers, with an average of 118 RBI per year and a .325 lifetime batting average.

In 1941, DiMaggio won the Most Valuable Player award despite Ted Williams hitting .406 for the season. No player has averaged .400 in a season since.

In 1962, Russell won the Most Valuable Player award despite Chamberlain averaging 50 points for the season. No player has come close since then.

Williams was considered by many the greatest hitter (offensive player, in his sport) in the history of the game. Chamberlain was considered by many the greatest scorer (offensive player, in his sport) in the history of his game. Russell's defense was harder to quantify, but deeply appreciated. DiMaggio's defense was equally hard to quantify, but deeply appreciated by all who saw him play.

The Eagle with the Beard, as Russell was known, was a winner. He didn't have the statistics that the three players ahead of him have. He does have the hardware. Just as DiMaggio spent the last two decades being introduced as the "Greatest Living Baseball Player," Russell deserves a huge amount of respect and love for what he meant to the game. He was the best player on the best team for his entire career. And the best part: we all know where Russell has gone. He hasn't left us. A nation doesn't turn its lonely eyes to him.

KAREEM ABDUL-JABBAR
K-Tel Presents "The Best of the 1970s!"

MVP: 6	
MVP VOTING: 14 years in top 5	
NBA TITLES: 6	
ALL-NBA FIRST TEAM: 10	
ALL-NBA SECOND TEAM: 5	

I have never bought any "Greatest Hits" albums. I would never purchase the compilations of the greatest hits of a certain year or era. If I wanted to evoke a certain memory of a time and place, I would buy an album of one of the best representatives of the era. Following that line of thinking, there is no need to read or watch anything from the NBA in the 1970s or 1980s unless it involves Kareem Abdul-Jabbar. Pick a game, a year, a score from Kareem's career. It is the league's history from that period.

Kareem Abdul-Jabbar had a peak value like few others. He had a career value that no one else came close to. He was great on bad teams. He was great on great teams. He won at every level.

Abdul-Jabbar Before the Pros

When he was a high school player at Power Memorial in New York City, his team won more than 70 consecutive games before being beaten. Here's how dramatically times have changed. In Lew Alcindor's four years of high school, no sportswriter or college scout ever talked to him! It was a Coach Jack Donahue rule: no interviews. He believed his players had enough to worry about in high school without worrying about giving interviews. Coach Donahue also didn't believe in running up scores. He'd sit down his star center and the other starters when the lead got out of hand. Kareem's coach wouldn't let him pad his stats in high school.

At UCLA, Alcindor was a freshman on the Brubabes, the Bruins freshman team (at the time, freshmen weren't allowed to play on the varsity). As a first-year student, he had the same protective fence around him. UCLA had a rule forbidding freshmen to grant interviews. Beginning with his sophomore year, the Bruins won three National Championships and had a record of 88–2. After the first National Championship, they changed the rules and outlawed dunking. This rule's purpose wasn't to make Abdul-Jabbar a better professional, but it surely did. One of the two losses was to the University of Houston, with Elvin Hayes. The UCLA Bruins had eliminated Houston from the NCAA tournament the year before, and both teams entered the game with winning streaks. UCLA had won 47 in a row; Houston had won 16 straight. But Alcindor had a badly scratched cornea and was suffering with it. He shot only 4 of 18 field goals and couldn't contain Hayes, who scored 39 points and had 15 rebounds. In the NCAA tournament, UCLA won the rematch, with Hayes being held to just 10 points. The Bruins won the rematch 101–69 and advanced to the finals, where they defeated North Carolina for their second consecutive National Championship. The following year had one blemish: a two-point upset to USC, which used stall tactics.

Abdul-Jabbar was voted Outstanding Player of the NCAA Tournament three consecutive times.

Abdul-Jabbar's NBA Career

Upon entering the NBA, Kareem felt that the no-dunk rule in college actually helped other aspects of his game. He had to work on other shots, unlike later 7-footers such as Shaquille O'Neal, who entered the league with just the basic power game.

Kareem led the expansion Milwaukee Bucks to an NBA title in his second year (and the franchise's third). He led the Lakers to a bunch of titles in the 1980s. His sky hook remains the game's most singular unstoppable move.

Nobody ever approached his six MVP seasons. He was second in 1973 to Dave Cowens as well. If you include a third-place finish in his rookie season of 1970 and another in 1981, Abdul-Jabbar spent nine years as one of the three most valuable players in the NBA. As late as 1986, Abdul-Jabbar was fifth in the MVP voting.

He won his MVPs in his 2nd, 3rd, 5th, 7th, 8th, and 11th seasons.

His first season was the 1970 season, and he dominated the 1970s. Not only was Abdul-Jabbar the leading scorer in that decade, he was the fifth-leading scorer in the decade of the 1980s!

Kareem Abdul-Jabbar entered the NBA as Lew Alcindor. In his first of 1,560 regular-season NBA games, he scored 29 points in a 119–110 Bucks victory over the Pistons. He played all 48 minutes and hit 12 of 27 field goals from the field. He added 12 rebounds, six assists, and three blocked shots. (It wasn't quite Wilt Chamberlain's debut of 43 points, but it was close enough to warrant all the hype.)

Who's Better, Who's Best
Kareem Abdul-Jabbar or Wilt Chamberlain

Pat Riley: "It was an absolute spectacle every time they played against one another. At that particular time Wilt was not much of a scorer when I was there because we had Jerry West, Gail Goodrich, and Jim McMillian taking most of the shots. He was a defender and dominant rebounder, and every now and then he would be criticized about not being able to score anymore and he would get 60 points on somebody. Wilt and Kareem would always be somewhat of a standoff. They would equal one another."

Kareem played against Wilt only 27 times in their careers. In Abdul-Jabbar's rookie season of 1970, Chamberlain missed 70 games and played against the Bucks only once.

They played against each other 15 times in regular-season play in the following three seasons before Chamberlain's retirement. They also met in the 1971 and the 1972 playoffs.

In his 1983 autobiography with Peter Knobler, *Giant Steps*, Kareem wrote:

You can't ever say that Wilt didn't give his best, or that his best wasn't superlative. Wilt was one of the great centers to play the game, and the next three years we had a very fierce competition. In the years since, he has said that I played extra hard against him, as if I had something to prove. He is right, I did play extra hard. If I hadn't, he would have dominated me, embarrassed me in front of the league, and undermined my whole game and career. Wilt demanded my best, and I gave it to him with a vengeance. I was definitely aware that I was posting up with the man against whom all comparisons would be made. . . . Toward the end of his career, when he was 36 and I was 25, I had it any way I wanted. The Bucks would play the Lakers at the Forum, and I'd be getting 50 points against him; he'd try the fade-away, but I'd be there to block it, and he'd storm out to halfcourt. With his career being closed in his face, he must have taken the defeat to heart.

Hold on there, Big Fella. "Any way" you wanted? You could count the number of 50-point games that Kareem had in his lifetime on two hands. He had exactly one of those against Chamberlain.

50+-Point Games

Chamberlain	122
Abdul-Jabbar	10

One of the 10 games in which Kareem scored 50+ *was* against Wilt. It came late in the 1972 season, and the Lakers won the game 123–107. When the Bucks made a drive within two points midway through the fourth quarter, Wilt held Abdul-Jabbar scoreless in six straight shots while the Lakers went on a run to finish off the Bucks.

Wilt Chamberlain Against Kareem Abdul-Jabbar

They met 27 times. Chamberlain's teams won 14. Abdul-Jabbar's teams won 13.

They met in the 1971 postseason, with the Bucks taking the Western Conference finals 4–1, on their way to the 1971 NBA title.

They met in the 1972 postseason, with the Lakers taking the Western Conference finals 4–2, on their way to the 1972 NBA title.

In the first 11 meetings, Chamberlain was still able to (read that *inclined to*) score with Abdul-Jabbar. In their first 11 meetings, Chamberlain scored 251 points (22.8 points per game) along with 194 rebounds (17.6 per game). Abdul-Jabbar averaged 26.0 points and 15.6 rebounds in those games.

Then, as Wilt and Kareem wrote about, Abdul-Jabbar turned on the afterburners, and probably (as he stated) gave it to him with a vengeance.

In the 1972 season, Kareem outscored Wilt 201–70 in their five regular-season games (40.2 versus 14.0). Kareem averaged 34 against the rest of the league, but 40 in the games against Chamberlain. In that year's playoffs, Kareem outscored Wilt 202–67 in the six games. But Chamberlain outrebounded Abdul-Jabbar and played better defense. In the sixth game in Milwaukee with the Bucks down three games to two, Milwaukee led by 10 points late in the third quarter. Chamberlain then went on a tear and led the Lakers to a four-point win, ensuring there would be no Game 7.

But while Abdul-Jabbar played Chamberlain all the time with a tenacity reserved especially for his greatest rival, Wilt often . . . well, here's how he put it in his 1973 autobiography, *Wilt*:

One time in Boston, this last February, three girls called me in my hotel room within 20 minutes after I got back from the game. I invited one of them over at midnight, and the other two at 2 A.M. All four of us wound up frolicking in the sack by breakfast. Then, the very next afternoon—in Milwaukee—a girl called me within five minutes after I checked in to the Pfister Hotel. . . . It was a very nice visit . . . even if I was a bit weary that night when the Bucks blew us off the court by 21 points.

I actually checked. The Lakers did fly from Boston to Milwaukee for the second game of a back-to-back in February 1973. Chamberlain had it right, Milwaukee won by a score of 109–88. Although I'm not sure if it was the Bucks who blew out Chamberlain that night. There might have been a more pressing head-to-head matchup for Wilt that morning at the Pfister.

When Abdul-Jabbar played Chamberlain, Wilt's history was repeating itself. This time, however, it was Chamberlain who played the good guy and Kareem was the villain. This time, it was Chamberlain losing the scoring battles, but winning more often.

Who's Better, Who's Best
Kareem Abdul-Jabbar or Shaquille O'Neal

After their 11th seasons in the NBA, this is how Shaq stacked up against Kareem.

Abdul-Jabbar	855 games played
O'Neal	742 games played

(O'Neal has missed parts of several seasons. Abdul-Jabbar missed one-quarter of a season due to injury when he punched center Kent Benson in retaliation for a thrown elbow.)

Abdul-Jabbar	28.3 points	14.4 rebounds
O'Neal	27.6 points	12.1 rebounds

(Adjust for the league average in points per game and number of rebounds, and it's a virtual wash.)

Abdul-Jabbar	.555 average FG
O'Neal	.577 average FG

Kareem made more; Shaq shot a higher percentage.

Abdul-Jabbar	4,217 free throws made (.711)
O'Neal	4,242 free throws made (.542)

Shaq made more, Kareem shot a higher percentage.

In his first 11 seasons, Abdul-Jabbar had won six MVP awards. O'Neal had only won one. Abdul-Jabbar had won two NBA titles. O'Neal had won three.

By the end of Abdul-Jabbar's ninth season, he was already ninth in the NBA's list of career scorers, with 20,238 points. He was the career field goal percentage leader, with .549. He was second all time in career scoring average (29.2 points per game) and had become just the 14th player in history to get 10,000 rebounds.

It's a pretty close call between O'Neal and Abdul-Jabbar—at least by comparing those first 11 years.

But look at the back nine holes that Kareem played.

Abdul-Jabbar				
First 11 years	855 games	28.3 points	14.4 rebounds	4.1 assists
After that	705 games	20.2 points	7.2 rebounds	2.6 assists

A Look at the Awards Kareem Won . . . and Didn't Win

Kareem was one of the greatest-ever collectors of trophies and awards. He won six championships. He was season MVP six times. He was Finals MVP twice. He was Rookie of the Year.

But he didn't win several times when he should have.

1970 MVP

In 1969, the league gave the MVP to a center who led his team from 36 wins to 57. Wes Unseld was both Rookie of the Year and MVP in 1969. Now, Kareem came along the next year and vaulted an expansion Bucks team from 27 wins to 56. Kareem was second in scoring and third in rebounds. He put up better numbers than Unseld the previous year, and the team improved even more dramatically. But there was a tough choice for voters. Los Angeles fans felt Jerry West deserved it in a season that saw Wilt Chamberlain go down for 70 games and Elgin Baylor a shell of himself because of his knee problems. I would have gone with the Milwaukee center. But superstars in New York (Reed) and Los Angeles (West) beat him out.

1971 All-Star Game MVP

It was one of two games ever in which Wilt and Kareem were on the same team. Kareem started for the West. Kareem wanted to show the world that Willis Reed did not own Kareem. Willis only made 5 of 14 shots. Kareem—with the game on the line—scored the last six points, blocked a shot, and put the game to bed with a three-point play with less than 10 seconds to go in the game. The West won 108–107, yet the MVP award went to Lenny Wilkens. Even then, the All-Star game wasn't about winning. It was about which player would be elected MVP. It's similar to the election of a student body president. The popular kids always win. Kareem played in more All-Star games than anyone but never won the award.

1974 NBA Finals

I remember reading Abdul-Jabbar's *Giant Steps* when it was published in 1983. He felt that the officiating was very poor. Abdul-Jabbar wrote that Richie Powers allowed the Celtics' center Dave Cowens to dive on Kareem's back for rebounds and defense. Well, I checked out the box scores. Powers didn't officiate just one or two games. Richie Powers was the referee in Games 1, 3, 5, and 7 of those Finals. Boston was 4–0 in those games, but 0–3 in the ones when Powers *wasn't* in charge of the whistles.

1980 NBA Finals MVP

Kareem was the Finals MVP in 1971 and 1985. He would have been Finals MVP in both 1974 and 1984 if the seventh game had a different outcome. The best Finals performance Abdul-Jabbar ever had was obscured by his own teammate, however. That was in 1980.

It's not just the numbers that Abdul-Jabbar put up in those 1980 Finals. He scored more than 33 points per game in the series, with more than 13 rebounds and 4.5 blocks per game. In the first game of the Finals, Michael Cooper and Jamaal Wilkes stopped Julius Erving and the Lakers cruised to a victory. Two days prior to the first game, the Lakers' top frontcourt reserve, Spencer Haywood, passed out while on the floor during stretching exercises. The day after Game 1, Haywood arrived 10 minutes late for team practice. Following Game 2, Lakers coach Paul Westhead met with Haywood and suspended him for "activities disruptive toward the team." The Lakers—after splitting the first two in Los Angeles—won the third game in Philadelphia, led by a terrific performance from Abdul-Jabbar. In Game 4, Kareem was held below 33 points for the first time in the series. He scored only 23, and the Sixers tied the series 2–2.

In the fifth game, Kareem injured his left ankle in the third quarter. He missed only four minutes of action (and the Lakers outscored the Sixers 12–6 in that span). Kareem said later the doctors thought his ankle was fractured and asked him if he wanted to go to the hospital right away. He told them to tape it up, as long as he wouldn't be able to injure it further. They taped it tightly, and the pain was intense. He wrote that the first few times back on the court the pain intruded like an electrical storm. Kareem scored 40 points in that fifth game, and the Lakers took a 3–2 lead back to Philadelphia. But Kareem headed straight to the hospital. His ankle had swollen, making it impossible to travel. You know the rest. Magic Johnson played center and scored 42 points. Jamaal Wilkes scored 37.

Kareem averaged 33.4 points per game, had 23 blocks in five games, and had performed on a badly injured ankle. Magic Johnson had averaged 17.4 points per game in the first five games of the Finals—with 25 turnovers in the first five contests. Magic turned it over 30 times in the six games—still a record for most turnovers in a Finals. Abdul-Jabbar was never going to get the respect in some people's eyes. Magic was the MVP of Game 6. Kareem was the real MVP of that series.

Kareem in the Finals

He had so many dramatic moments. In 1971, he helped Oscar Robertson win his first and only NBA Championship. It was a four-game rout of the Bullets. In 1974, Kareem's game-winning hook shot to win Game 6 remains one of the all-time greatest moments in the history of the Finals. His 1980 Finals performance was described previously. In 1984, Kareem averaged 26.6 points per game on 60 percent shooting. Kareem overcame a migraine headache to score 32 points in the first game—a victory for the Lakers. He had 32 points to lead the Lakers in the sixth game, setting up a seventh and deciding game. Amazingly, however, Kareem's best performance in the Finals came in 1985, at the age of 38.

Abdul-Jabbar in the 1985 Finals

6 games	25.7 points	9 rebounds	5.2 assists	67 of 111 field goals	.604 FG average

Abdul-Jabbar held Robert Parish to 17.2 points per game on 48 percent shooting. Following the "Memorial Day massacre," the Lakers defeated the Celtics four out of five games to finally defeat Boston. In Game 2, Kareem scored 30 points and pulled down 17 rebounds to tie the series at 1–1. He had 26 points in Game 3. And in the deciding sixth game, Kareem scored 29 points. He was voted MVP of the Finals, 14 years after winning the same award in 1971. It was an amazing series for Kareem.

After that, his seasonal performances and his play in the Finals dropped. In 1987, the Lakers won a championship—but Kareem was the Lakers' third-leading scorer (and scoring just barely more than Byron Scott). In that Finals, however, Kareem still averaged 21.7 points per game and seven rebounds—despite being 40 years old. In the 1988 Finals, the Lakers repeated, with Kareem averaging 13 points per game in the seven-game series. Even in that series, he hit 21 of 26 free throws, including two of the biggest of his career.

He played in nine Finals and won six of them. In the three Finals that he lost, he lost in seven games in 1974, seven games in 1984, and four games in 1989, when his two starting guards pulled up lame.

Abdul-Jabbar played his best against the best, and when the games were the biggest. If he wanted to crush an old Chamberlain or dominate Willis Reed in his hometown of New York, he could. If his team needed a big basket in the postseason, Abdul-Jabbar took it. It is very slight criticism to hint that Abdul-Jabbar didn't always play his best. He played more than 1,500 regular-season games and had "only" 70 games of 40+ points, and "only" 10 games of 50+ points. Did Abdul-Jabbar conserve strength and energy, preferring to save it for when he felt he or the team needed it? In the 1980 movie *Airplane!*, 10-year-old Joey says to the airline pilot, "You're Kareem Abdul-Jabbar. I think you're the greatest. But my dad says you don't work hard enough on defense. And that lots of times you don't even run downcourt. And that you don't really try, except during the playoffs."

The pilot denies it, showing his tag. "The hell I don't," Abdul-Jabbar says in character. "Listen, kid, I've been hearing that crap ever since UCLA. I'm out there busting my buns every night! Tell your old man to drag Walton and Lanier up and down the court for 48 minutes."

Abdul-Jabbar answered his critics with humor, but there was truth in it. He *was* busting his buns every night, but the average fan saw someone who conserved energy and didn't play to his capabilities every single time downcourt.

Kareem was the best player in the league at least six different seasons. But he didn't live up to the potential that we all knew he could unlock at a moment's notice.

Against Chamberlain, it was a standoff in their 27 meetings, but those were Chamberlain's least productive seasons and Abdul-Jabbar's most productive. In a November 1980 *Inside Sports* article, Chamberlain, 44 years old at the time, said that if he was still playing, he would be averaging more than 20 rebounds per game. Wilt saw fit to put down Kareem's rebounding. Kareem answered back by saying, "The only place Wilt out-rebounds me is in his sleep, when he's dreaming."

Chamberlain has since passed. Hopefully he can rest in peace, knowing that in his dreams (and in my dreams and my memory) as well as pressed in the microfilm machines at public libraries, Chamberlain is still out-rebounding Abdul-Jabbar.

LARRY BIRD

The Best Forward Ever

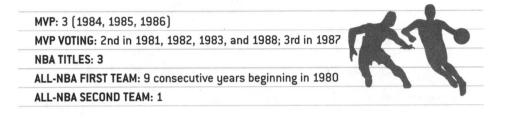

MVP: 3 (1984, 1985, 1986)	
MVP VOTING: 2nd in 1981, 1982, 1983, and 1988; 3rd in 1987	
NBA TITLES: 3	
ALL-NBA FIRST TEAM: 9 consecutive years beginning in 1980	
ALL-NBA SECOND TEAM: 1	

Is Larry Bird the greatest forward of all time? I believe so. I don't believe there is too much doubt. In an era of great players (Kareem Abdul-Jabbar, Moses Malone, Julius Erving, and Magic Johnson), Bird was either first or second in the MVP voting for *six straight seasons*. He was in the top three in voting for *eight consecutive seasons*.

Bird's Legacy

He was an automatic choice for All-NBA First Team in the 1980s. The other forwards had to battle for the second spot on the team. Erving was the other forward for the first four years of the 1980s but gave way to Bernard King in 1984. King kept his slot for two seasons, before giving way to Dominique Wilkins in 1986 and Kevin McHale in 1987. Charles Barkley made his first appearance on the First Team as a forward in 1988.

Bird would win three MVPs, but in 1981, he just missed. Erving had 28 first-place votes and 454 total points compared to Bird's 20 first-place votes and 423 total votes.

Bird was such a fan favorite. He brought the NBA to heights in public popularity that it had never reached before. When he entered the NBA, the Finals were broadcast on tape-delay following the 11 P.M. local news on the East Coast. Bird represented the "Great White Hope" to a great franchise in a great media market. He brought passing back into vogue. He was also a great rebounder.

Bill Walton: "I used to think Larry Bird was a good basketball player. Then I played with him. Larry is much better than I ever dreamed. I think that today Larry Bird is the greatest forward in the history of the game of basketball."

Bob Ryan: "Larry Bird is unarguably the greatest forward of all time."

More Walton: "Bird was an unbelievable rebounder. He knew where the ball was going before the ball knew. I wish he were a stock so I could buy some. He should start his own religion."

Magic Johnson: "I admire Larry Bird for many reasons. He's got to be the most dedicated athlete imaginable. A lot of guys I've played with and against are not really that dedicated. To them, it's just a job. With Larry, basketball is his life. He has great heart and guts. He always seemed to make the big shot or make the big play."

More Walton: "Of course, he did all of this without being able to jump over two pieces of paper."

Who's Better, Who's Best
Larry Bird or Julius Erving

Rod Thorn: "You know, I love Dr. J. Everything about him. But the team he was on in Philadelphia—well, I just think he never approached the level he was at in the ABA. I'd have to say Bird. Larry was a better shooter, better passer. Doc was a better defender."

Cedric Maxwell: "They were both great—and both great for the game. Larry could do more in all areas of the game."

Pete Vecsey: "I love Julius. He was the best man at my wedding. But—that being said—Larry Bird is one of the top five or six players of all time. There was nothing he couldn't do. Julius, in many ways, was a lot of hype."

Leonard Koppett: "Julius Erving is in the very top group of basketball players ever. . . . He was superior to Bird . . . it is the all-around play that lifts him above the rest of the pack—especially in his early years when he played in the ABA."

Steve Jones: "I would put Erving over Bird. When Julius was in the ABA, that was when the full-blown Doctor was playing. When he went to Philly, he toned his game down. But nobody had the stuff Dr. J had. Nobody. He and Bird were totally different players.

I'll say this for Bird: he was a better 'big game moments' player in the NBA than Erving was."

Bob Ryan: "Bird, Bird, Bird. When Larry entered the league, he was the young Turk. It took him all of one year to figure [Erving] out. It culminated on the night of the fight—November 1984—when Doc had 6 points and Bird had 42."

It's very hard to compare Bird and Erving without considering that Bird was born in December 1956 and Erving was born in February 1950. Bird had almost seven years on Erving.

Erving was past his prime almost as soon as Larry Bird entered the room. After Larry's first three to four years, it was (as Ryan observed) not even a contest anymore. There was a moment in time, however, where a 31-year-old Erving battled a 24-year-old Bird in a seven-game playoff series for the right to go to the NBA Finals.

The 1981 Eastern Conference finals is one of the greatest playoff series of all time.

Why do I consider this Eastern Conference finals series so special? The Celtics and 76ers had both won 60 games that season, the best record in the NBA. The teams had split their six regular-season matchups. The home court advantage for this playoff series wasn't decided until the final day of the regular season, when the Sixers played in Boston Garden. The winner would have home court advantage throughout the playoffs. The Celtics won the regular-season finale for the right to host Game 7 if they met in the postseason.

The year prior, in 1980, Boston had won 61 games and Philadelphia 59. They met in the Eastern Conference finals. Philadelphia handled the Celtics in five games—but that was Larry Bird's rookie season and first taste of the NBA playoffs.

In 1981, it was official. The long-standing rivalry of the 1960s that featured historic matchups such as Wilt Chamberlain/Bill Russell, Hal Greer/Sam Jones, and Billy Cunningham/John Havlicek was resurrected.

In 1981, Erving was still close to the top of his game. He would narrowly defeat Bird for the MVP that season; no one else was even close.

| Erving | 24.6 points/game | 8.0 rebounds | 4.4 assists |
| Bird | 21.2 points/game | 10.9 rebounds | 5.5 assists |

There were other great matchups when those teams squared off. The Celtics had Robert Parish at center. His nickname "Chief" came from the silent character in the film

One Flew over the Cuckoo's Nest. The 76ers had Darryl Dawkins, who nicknamed each of his dunks and said he was from "Planet Lovetron."

Tiny Archibald was closer to the end of his career at point guard for Boston—and Maurice Cheeks was closer to the beginning of his—but because of that, it was an even match for both in 1981.

The most valuable players for each team may have been the most unheralded—defensive specialist Bobby Jones for Philly and Kevin McHale for Boston.

1981 Eastern Conference Finals
Game 1: Philadelphia 105–104 at Boston, Series 1–0 Sixers
Bird had 33 points, 10 rebounds, and three assists on 14 of 29 field goals, but those numbers still fell short as the Sixers broke through for a win in Boston Garden. Archibald had a brilliant game in defeat: 20 points, seven rebounds, and nine assists. Erving made only eight of 20 field goals and scored 25 points. But it was Celtic-killer rookie Andrew Toney who provided the heroics with 26 points off the bench. (The Celtics in later years would acquire defensive specialist Dennis Johnson for just such moments. Chris Ford, M. L. Carr, and Gerald Henderson were not able to stop Toney.) With eight seconds remaining and the Sixers down by a point, Toney drove the right side as Erving set a pick on Henderson. Toney headed to the hoop, and, on the switch, Maxwell fouled Toney. The Sixers guard hit both foul shots, giving Philly the first game.

Game 2: Boston 118–99 at Boston, Series 1–1
This game was played the very next night, and it was too much to expect Philadelphia to win back-to-back on the road in the Garden. Boston jumped to a 66–47 halftime lead, and the game was over. Bird put on a vintage shooting display: 34 points (14 of 21 field goals), with 16 rebounds and five assists. Erving did not score in the game's first 17 minutes.

Game 3: Philadelphia 110–100 at Philadelphia, Series 2–1 Sixers
Would fans who recently started watching the NBA even recognize the game if they put in this tape from 1981? The teams combined for 46 fast-break opportunities. They also combined to take just two three-pointers (without making one). Billy Cunningham made a switch before this game, putting Erving on Bird. Erving's tight defense gave the Sixers an early lead. It also allowed Caldwell Jones to play good defense on Robert Parish, who had an uncharacteristic 1-of-14 field goal shooting night with four fouls and three

turnovers. It seems impossible—but the official box lists the time of game at just two hours and 13 minutes.

| Bird | 8 of 16 field goals | 6 of 7 free throws | 22 points | 13 rebounds | 4 assists |
| Erving | 9 of 21 field goals | 4 of 4 free throws | 22 points | 7 rebounds | 7 assists |

Game 4: Philadelphia 107–105 at Philadelphia, Series 3–1 Sixers

Jake O'Donnell and Bill Saar were the referees. That's important, as the game was in Philadelphia and the Sixers shot 20 more free throws than Boston. The Sixers jumped out to a 17-point lead at the half and built that up to 19 early in the third quarter. But the Celts went on a furious rally. Philadelphia scored 26 fast-break points and another 29 points from the charity stripe. Dr. J outscored Bird by the two-point margin the game was decided by—but Philly won this game because Bobby Jones (18 points) and Andrew Toney (17) came off the bench to spark Philadelphia to the commanding 3–1 series lead.

There was another thrilling ending. Philly had a two-point lead when Jones missed a shot with six seconds remaining. The Celtics' Maxwell grabbed the rebound and gave the ball to quarterback Archibald, who didn't call a timeout. Tiny tried to get the ball to Bird, but it was intercepted by Jones as time ran out.

| Bird | 7 of 19 field goals | 4 of 5 free throws | 18 points | 17 rebounds | 6 assists (48 min.) |
| Erving | 8 of 16 field goals | 4 of 6 free throws | 20 points | 7 rebounds | 5 assists (5 blocks) |

Game 5: Boston 111–109 at Boston, Series 3–2 Sixers

With all the pressure in the world on both teams, Boston hit 35 of 39 from the foul line (90 percent as a team). They needed every one. Philadelphia hit 33 of 39 from the line (85 percent). The guards provided some much-needed spark. Lionel Hollins hit 11 of 15 field goals on the way to scoring 23 points, to go along with a floor game of five rebounds and five assists. Nate Archibald matched Hollins with 23 points and seven assists of his own. The Celtics were down by six points with a minute and a half left to play, but Archibald came up with a huge three-point play on the break to get the Celtics back into it.

| Bird | 11 of 24 field goals | 8 of 8 free throws | 32 points | 11 rebounds | 5 assists |
| Erving | 9 of 18 field goals | 3 of 4 free throws | 21 points | 2 rebounds | 5 assists |

Game 6: Boston 100–98 at Philadelphia, Series 3–3

Philadelphia jumped to a 31–18 first-quarter advantage, hoping to close out the series and advance to the Finals. The Celtics pecked away, led by another strong game from Tiny Archibald (19 points, six assists). Robert Parish added 21 points to help set up a seventh game. Once again there was a dramatic finish. With less than 20 seconds left, Toney moved into the lane to take a shot that could give the game and series to the Sixers. But Kevin McHale made a huge block, and Maxwell hit two free throws for the series-saving game.

| Bird | 10 of 22 field goals | 5 of 6 free throws | 25 points | 16 rebounds | 4 assists |
| Erving | 5 of 17 field goals | 6 of 7 free throws | 16 points | 6 rebounds | 4 assists |

Game 7: Boston 91–90 at Boston, Series 4–3 Boston

In any context, this was a great game. The 76ers had the lead for most of the game, by as many as 11 in the first half and 11 in the second half. But the Boston defense tightened, and Philadelphia could score only 15 points in the final quarter. When Dr. J hit a layup with 4:34 remaining to put the Sixers up 89–83, it was the last field goal of the season for his team.

The officiating crew (Darrell Garretson, Jake O'Donnell, and alternate Jack Madden) knew they were in Beantown: they called 27 personals on the Sixers, only 18 on the Celts. The Celtics had 35 free throw attempts to only 15 for Philadelphia. Larry Bird was quoted as saying that with about five minutes to go, the refs just put their whistles away. Bird said Darrell and Jake were letting everything go. Players were knocking each other down on both ends of the court. Dawkins was clearing out and Boston was hammering Dawkins. Bird recalled the last five minutes of Game 7 like this: "It was all-out war. I've never been through anything so brutal."

It ended like this: with one second remaining, Bobby Jones inbounded the ball—an alley-oop to Erving that hit the top of the backboard. Fans streamed onto the court as time expired. It was the first time Boston fans could celebrate a playoff series victory over Philadelphia since 1969.

It seems fairly certain that Bird had several steals off Erving and that Bird went to the line courtesy of Erving fouls. Their individual battle was as close as the game.

Bird

9 of 12 field goals	6 of 7 free throws	23 points	11 rebounds	5 assists	1 turnover	1 foul	5 steals

Erving

11 of 21 field goals	1 of 2 free throws	23 points	8 rebounds	5 assists	6 turnovers	5 fouls

For the series:

Bird	26.7 points/game	13.4 rebounds	7.8 assists
Erving	19.9 points/game	5.9 rebounds	4.1 assists

Now, this was not Julius in his mid-thirties. This was Erving at 31 years old in his MVP season. During the season, Erving outscored Bird by 3.4 points per game. In the seven-game series—matched against each other—Bird outscored Erving by 6.8 points per game. Meanwhile, look at the game scores of this fabulous series between two great rivals. Games 1, 4, 5, 6, and 7 were all decided by one or two points!

The fact that the Celtics went on after that series to capture the NBA title was anticlimactic. More than two decades after the games were played, that Eastern Conference finals remains one of the greatest playoff series of all time.

My Choices for the Greatest Playoff Series of All Time

1.	1981	Eastern Conference finals	Boston 4	Philly 3
2.	2002	Western Conference finals	Lakers 4	Sacramento 3
3.	1998	Eastern Conference finals	Chicago 4	Indiana 3
4.	1957	NBA Finals	Boston 4	St. Louis 3

The bottom line on Larry Bird: Bird's ranking as the greatest forward to ever play the game was one of the easier choices in this book. No one can seriously put Tim Duncan ahead of Bird. Pettit and Baylor didn't win as much as Bird. That leaves Erving. Erving did things that Bird couldn't do in his dreams—but most of what Dr. J did was unseen by the nation. No one ever saw Erving play in college. Only a lucky few saw Erving play with Virginia in the first two years of his professional career. We see more—and know more—about high school players today. Bird we saw coming. Television created such a hit with Bird on the NCAA tournament that they spun a whole series out of it. Bird was featured a lot in his first year. In his second year, he won an NBA Championship.

Bird versus Erving was in many ways the ultimate NBA matchup. Boston versus Philadelphia. The white hick against the black New Yorker. I could say that Bird had a better NBA career and Erving a better professional career. Why do I feel so guilty putting Bird ahead of Erving? Bird was a better player than Erving. There, I said it.

EARVIN "MAGIC" JOHNSON
Showtime!

MVP: 3	
MVP VOTING: 9 finishes in the top 3	
NBA TITLES: 4	
ALL-NBA FIRST TEAM: 9	
ALL-NBA SECOND TEAM: 1	

E arvin Johnson Jr. got his nickname while he was playing at Everett High School in Lansing, Michigan. When his mother, a devout Seventh-Day Adventist, first heard her son referred to as "Magic," she considered it blasphemy. Growing up, everyone called him "June Bug." While he may have been a June Bug as a young man, he grew into a life of magic and the name of "Magic."

Johnson's Achievements

His winning percentage rivals Bill Russell. His rebounding and assist numbers dwarf Oscar Robertson. He was more instrumental to the four Lakers titles in the 1980s than Kareem Abdul-Jabbar. For the first half of Michael Jordan's career, it was Jordan who played in Johnson's shadow. If Johnson hadn't left the stage prematurely—or if Jordan hadn't resumed his career after his short-lived baseball career—then a case could be made for Magic over Michael.

Only one player in history ever had more top three finishes in the MVP voting: Jordan placed 10 times in the top three.

Only two players in history ever played in more NBA Finals series. They are Bill Russell, with 12, and Sam Jones, with 11.

Magic's teams made the NBA Finals nine times in 12 seasons. They won five rings in the 1980s, defeating teams led by Julius Erving, Larry Bird, and Isiah Thomas. Magic had rivalries with them all, also losing NBA Finals series to each of the same teams.

By the end of Johnson's first eight seasons, he had three NBA Championships (and an NCAA title) under his belt and four consecutive assist titles. He had yet to win the MVP of the league. That would change, as he won three in four years beginning in 1987.

In 1987, this is how good Johnson was. Jordan averaged 37.1 points per game (the highest in the league since Chamberlain two decades earlier). Jordan that year also averaged 5.2 rebounds and 4.6 assists and had more than 200 steals and 100 blocked shots. He also improved the Bulls from 30 wins (when he was injured for most of the season) to 40 wins. Yet Johnson received 65 of 78 first-place votes that year in the MVP voting. In some seasons, the MVP voting can be taken as a popularity contest. In 1987, Johnson deserved the award—despite Jordan's explosion of basketball genius.

That's how good Magic Johnson was in the 1987 season—it may have been his best. The Lakers won 65 games that year—the most a Magic Johnson team ever won in a season.

What Made Magic Johnson So Great?

Pat Riley: "Magic Johnson is one of the great winners, great team players, and he understands exactly what it takes to win and he went out and proved it year in and year out. I think he ranks right there near the top; right at the top of the all-time greats."

Bob Ryan: "To me, Bill Russell is the greatest NBA player ever. But Magic is second, and Michael third."

Bill Walton: "Stats meant nothing to Magic . . . and also, it should be pointed out that Kareem willingly allowed Magic to be the spirit and face and voice of the team."

Nate Archibald: "When I first had to play against him, I was like, 'Do I have to play this guy?' His size reminded me of Gervin—but Magic was an all-around player. A much better player. He was a great post-up player, great passer, great rebounder. He was always out to win."

Derek Harper: "E.J. was the toughest player I ever played against. The way he would post me up, he had just so much ability. Take Jason Kidd. He's a great player, one of the best pure point guards of all time. But Magic could do more offensively—he was craftier around the basket. He made a living posting guys like me."

Sean Elliott: "He would take advantage of your mistakes like no other player. That's what I remember about playing him."

Who's Better, Who's Best
Magic Johnson or Larry Bird

Despite the fact that Magic Johnson played guard and Larry Bird played forward, their careers will always be linked. They played against each other in 1979 for the NCAA Championship in the highest-rated basketball game of all time. Magic's team won the game, and he was picked first in the NBA draft.

Magic's Lakers also won a championship before Bird's Celtics—in Magic's rookie year. Bird's Celtics took the title the next year (maybe because Magic missed 45 games due to torn cartilage after the Hawks' Tom Burleson landed on his left knee). In 1982, the Lakers not only won a second championship with Magic, Johnson received his second Finals MVP.

Allowing one season for the 76ers and Julius Erving to claim their championship, the next four years were all about Lakers/Celtics, Magic/Bird.

They met for the first time in the NBA Finals in 1984.

1984 NBA Finals The first game was as eagerly anticipated as any matchup in NBA history. The Celtics versus Lakers was always enough to hype. The Celtics had never lost to the Lakers in the NBA Finals. Of course, it wasn't as if Bird guarded Johnson. In fact, Magic spent much of the series being guarded by 6-foot-2 Gerald Henderson. Bird had a defender worthy of guarding him—Michael Cooper. But still, the Finals had a matchup similar to the Russell/Chamberlain Finals confrontations.

Once again, the Celtics mystique prevailed in (yet again) seven games. Johnson was tormented after that series. He had a good Game 1 (18 points, six rebounds, 10 assists) as the Lakers won in Boston. After the Celtics won an overtime game to even the series, Magic had a Finals-record 21 assists in Game 3 to give the Lakers a 2–1 advantage. The Celtics then won another overtime game to even the series at 2–2. In that game, Magic Johnson threw away a crucial pass with the game tied and only four seconds remaining. He also missed a pair of free throws in the overtime. In Game 7 at Boston Garden, Johnson shot just 5 of 14 field goals and turned the ball over seven times. The story following the final game of that series was that Magic disappeared into the showers for so long that people became concerned and went in after him.

Following 1984 NBA Finals: First Five Years

	Regular-Season Games	FG Att.–FG Made	FG %	FT %	Pts	Reb	Asst
Bird	399	7,403–3,628	.490	.858	22.8	10.7	5.6
Johnson	338	4,285–2,323	.542	.790	18.2	8.4	9.8

Bird had won NBA Championships in 1981 and 1984. Johnson had won NBA Championships in 1980 and 1982.

It was as close to an even matchup as one could have. It is hard to believe, but both players improved. Bird or Magic won the MVP six times in a seven-year period (Bird in 1984, 1985, 1986 and Magic in 1987, 1989, 1990). Only an upset by the Houston Rockets in 1986 prevented four consecutive Lakers-Celtics matchups in the Finals.

Johnson became a much better NBA player with each season, constantly working on improving his game.

First five seasons	18.2 points	9.8 assists
Last seven seasons	20.7 points	12.3 assists

Those stats show how Magic took on more of the scoring load as Kareem Abdul-Jabbar got older and older. He also made himself a better scorer.

Magic was outscored by Abdul-Jabbar in each of their first seven seasons together. Kareem outscored Magic by almost seven points per game in 1980. No one ran the fast break better than Magic Johnson, and no one helped Abdul-Jabbar achieve his 20-point average better than Magic throughout the 1986 season. In 1987, Kareem's average went from 23.4 points per game to 17.5. The same season, Magic improved his scoring from 18.8 points to 23.9.

Who's Better, Who's Best
Magic Johnson or Kareem Abdul-Jabbar
In the 1980s, it was Earvin. Of course, Kareem had an entire decade of the 1970s where no one was close to him. That being said, Kareem earns a higher ranking in this book.

Johnson and the Lakers' History of Three-Point Shots
Magic Johnson, Larry Bird, and the three-point shot came into the NBA in the same year: 1980. Johnson and Bird made the game more aesthetically pleasing to watch. The three-point shot did not. I will show why, using Johnson's and Kobe Bryant's Lakers as prime examples.

Early in the 2003 NBA season, Lakers guard Bryant hit a dozen three-pointers in one game, including nine in a row at one point. The Lakers hit only 20 treys in their 1980 championship season! The NBA adapted the three-point shot in 1980, Magic Johnson's first season. Here is what Magic and the Lakers did with the shot in the early days.

Evolution of the Three-Point Shot

Year	Lakers Team	Magic Johnson
1980	20–100	7–31
1981	17–94	3–17
1982	13–94	6–29
1983	10–96	0–21
1984	58–226	6–29

Johnson made just 22 three-pointers in his first five seasons (just 17 percent of his three-point attempts). Earvin went on to make 117 three-pointers in his first 10 seasons and then made 106 in 1990, his 11th season. He would finish his career with 325 made on 30 percent shooting.

The Lakers, by the way, won those three consecutive championships in the early 2000s by making 344 three-pointers in 2000, 439 in 2001, and 510 in 2002. Sure, the Lakers made close to 1,300 successful three-pointers in their last three championship seasons, but is it a better brand of basketball? It sure was more fun to watch Magic and Worthy and Cooper get up and down the court, rather than watching Shaq kick it out and re-post.

Showtime

The Lakers ran a lot during their Magic Johnson days, leading to easy layups. The NBA record for team field goal percentage is held by the 1985 Lakers, who shot 55 percent for the season. The next two teams on the list were also Johnson-led Lakers teams, who shot 53 percent in 1984 and 53 percent in 1980. During that 1985 season, the NBA league average was 49 percent.

November 7, 1991

It was an announcement that shook the world. People who were born just a few years before me (1961) have recollections of where they were when President John F. Kennedy was assassinated. Similar to JFK's death, Magic's abrupt retirement announcement in 1991 was mourned worldwide. He was perhaps the most popular athlete of his time.

Of course, since then, Magic has remained healthy and my generation (and others after mine) had more tragic dates that the world shared. The events of September 11,

2001, overshadowed any announcement from 1991. But at the time of Johnson's announcement, it was big. No one knew much about HIV. All anyone knew was that it was incurable. It was almost unthinkable for a major sports star to put a face on what had been until that time considered a gay disease. It represented a creeping, grudging awareness that AIDS was not just a disease that afflicted gay people.

That wasn't the last NBA fans would see of Magic Johnson. Very few men or women have a second act in life as Magic has had. He would return triumphantly to play in (and be the MVP of) the 1992 All-Star Game in Orlando. He played in Barcelona, Spain, on the Olympic Dream Team. He took a spin as coach of the Lakers. He returned to play the final 32 games of the 1996 season.

Johnson built a chain of state-of-the-art multiplex movie theaters in inner cities called Magic Johnson Theatres. (I remember suggesting to Magic that an on-premises babysitting service for infants and toddlers would encourage more attendance at movies. Magic gave me the one-word answer to my suggestion: "Insurance.")

I might not know the movie business, but Magic didn't quite master the television talk show biz. "The Magic Hour" was a late-night talk show that didn't make it. In almost every other venture, this guy hit home run after home run.

The Lakers have been blessed with more than their share of all-time great guards. Bryant may reach—may have already reached—Jerry West status. But he has a long way to go to catch the Magic Man.

So, really:

Who's Better, Who's Best
Magic Johnson or Larry Bird

My friend Gary Gilbert will not separate Magic from Larry. They are joined as one, taking up two consecutive spots. More than one expert felt the same way. Mike Fratello and Jerry Sloan both had Magic and Larry tied among the top three players in the game. Heck, Bird and Magic don't separate each other. Sloan had only Michael Jordan ahead of them; Fratello had Jordan and Abdul-Jabbar. Magic won four NBA titles; Bird won three. Both won three MVP awards. Magic retired first, but would wind up playing 906 games because of the 1996 season. Bird limped his way to a final total of 897, winding up with a bad back that made it painful to even sit on the bench.

Together Magic and Bird ushered in a new era of the NBA, one that saw the advent of great teams and great passing.

I can't take a pass and declare a tie. Magic backers point to the fact that point guard is a more demanding position. Bird fans will unite in the theme that Johnson was playing against much smaller opponents. Both came up big on the NBA Finals stage, but Johnson had some costly failures in the biggest of shows. In my estimation, it comes down to this: There was a better guard than Magic Johnson. There was not a better forward than Larry Bird.

OSCAR ROBERTSON
The Original Triple Double

MVP: 1	
MVP VOTING: 1st in 1964; 8 other years in top 5	
NBA TITLES: 1	
ALL-NBA FIRST TEAM: 9	
ALL-NBA SECOND TEAM: 2	

Oscar Robertson belongs on the short list of everyone putting together the game's all-timers. He was instrumental in the early 1960s as one of the first African-American superstars. He was among the first great backcourt players. He was influential in the 1970s for his role in the development of Kareem Abdul-Jabbar. He was later influential for his work as the head of the players union. He was even the standard-bearer for Magic Johnson and Jason Kidd in later years as they took on Oscar's line of statistics, which came to be known as the triple double (at least 10 points, 10 rebounds, and 10 assists in the same game).

Robertson may have been better than Michael Jordan, except Cincinnati was not Chicago and the 1960s were not the 1990s. Finally, Oscar did not have the benefit of Scottie Pippen (who made Jordan a better player) or Nike, Gatorade, and Spike Lee (all of whom marketed Jordan superbly). Robertson was—no matter what later historians would write—on the first, real "Dream Team." I'm sure that Oscar Robertson, Jerry West, Walt Bellamy, Jerry Lucas, and company would have given the 1992 U.S.A. team a run for their money. They might have even won. Robertson averaged a triple double for an entire NBA season. Even though Johnson popularized the term, it was Robertson who was better at compiling points, rebounds, and assists in the same game.

Who's Better, Who's Best
Oscar Robertson or Magic Johnson

There was not a stronger guard in the game than Robertson. At 6-foot-5, 220 pounds, he was big for a guard in his day. He was also the forceful leader of the Players Association and has an important role in that history, as well.

Robertson after 1972 season	897 games	27.5 points	8.0 rebounds	9.9 assists
Johnson's entire career	906 games	19.5 points	7.2 rebounds	11.2 assists

Leonard Koppett: "No one has ever been a better all-around player—including Michael Jordan—than Oscar. Anything Jordan could do, Robertson could do better. He could shoot better, defend, pass better, and he was two inches shorter."

Nate Archibald: "I got a chance to play against him as a point guard. He was the best all-around player ever. He was a great rebounder, defensive player . . . best at running a team. Triple doubles, you name it, he could do it."

Stephen A. Smith: "I would take Magic over Oscar Robertson. Oscar could probably do more, but Magic Johnson transcended the game. He made passing an art—something more than just numbers on a stat sheet. He made an assist something you strived for. If there was no Magic Johnson, there would be no John Stockton or Jason Kidd. I suppose you could say that if there was no Oscar Robertson, there would be no Magic Johnson . . . so it's extremely close. I'm only 35 years old, and I only remember seeing Magic."

Everyone has said for years that Magic Johnson made his teammates better. I recall a passage in Bill Bradley's *Life on the Run*, where he wrote about Oscar Robertson making his teammates better:

Perhaps he doesn't give lesser players a large enough margin of error, but when they listen to him he makes All-Stars of meager talents. He controls events on the court with aplomb and the authoritarian hand of a symphony conductor. The NBA Finals in 1971 showed Oscar's mood as he sensed the possibility of his first championship. He drove his young teammates, placing blame on those who made mistakes, urging them not to let up, telling them when and where to move, and insisting on perfect execution.

Who's Better, Who's Best
Oscar Robertson or Jerry West

West played his final season in 1974 but only played in 31 games that final season. It is very rare to have two superstars playing the same position who came into the league and left the same seasons. Robertson and West both played the same 14 seasons. Oscar was more durable (playing 108 more games—although it was only 69 more games in the first 13 seasons). Oscar was a more accurate shooter. He was a better rebounder. He had many more assists.

West played on teams that won more games. He played in the Finals nine times. Robertson played in the Finals twice. Both won one NBA Championship at the tail end of their careers. West was All-NBA First Team 10 times to Robertson's nine.

It is one of the truest "Who's Better, Who's Best" comparisons. It is virtually a dead heat statistically.

West	932 games	27.0 points	5.8 rebounds	6.7 assists	.474 field goal %
Robertson	1,040 games	25.7 points	6.7 rebounds	8.9 assists	.485 field goal %

Nate Archibald: "Jerry West. You have to understand, when I was growing up, there were only six channels on television. You only saw three teams play—Boston, Philly, Los Angeles. Jerry was the ultimate ambassador of the game, before Julius Erving. He never said a word on the court. I had the ultimate respect for him. Oscar was a better rebounder—what do they say, the best pound-for-pound player ever. I only played Oscar one season. I played Jerry a few years—although it seemed like he never got old."

There is no other noncenter who ever kick-started his NBA career as Robertson did. Only a handful of noncenters have ever scored 2000+ points in their rookie seasons. They include Robertson, Jordan, Billy Knight, Rick Barry, Geoff Petrie, and Sidney Wicks. Players who did it in the ABA include Connie Hawkins, Julius Erving, Spencer Haywood, and Dan Issel.

Here are the first five seasons for comparable players to Oscar. All are noncenters who entered the NBA with a bang.

First Five Seasons in NBA

Player	Min/Game	Pts/Game	Reb/Game	Asst/Game
Oscar Robertson	44.4	30.3	10.4	10.6
Larry Bird	37.9	22.6	10.7	5.6
Magic Johnson	37.4	18.2	8.4	9.8
Michael Jordan	39.0	32.6	6.2	5.9
Allen Iverson	42.0	26.2	4.0	5.6

Only Iverson comes close to Robertson in minutes played. Only Jordan (who scored more) is in Oscar's ballpark in points per game. Only Larry Bird could rebound as well as Robertson. Only Johnson came close to matching Robertson in assists per game.

If you took the best category from each player, this is what it would look like:

Bird/Magic/ Michael/A.I.				
best marks	42.0 minutes	32.6 points/game	10.7 rebounds	9.8 assists/game
Robertson	44.4 minutes	30.3 points/game	10.4 rebounds	10.6 assists/game

Robertson's First Five Years

1961	30.5 points	10.1 rebounds	9.7 assists	42.7 minutes
1962	30.8 points	12.5 rebounds	11.4 assists	44.3 minutes
1963	28.3 points	10.4 rebounds	9.5 assists	44.0 minutes
1964	31.4 points	9.9 rebounds	11.0 assists	45.1 minutes
1965	30.4 points	9.0 rebounds	11.5 assists	45.6 minutes

In 1962, Oscar Robertson had 985 rebounds and 899 assists. No other player before or since has had as many as 800 rebounds and 800 assists in the same season. Oscar came within an assist of getting 900/900. In that 1962 season, Oscar had 45 games that would now be labeled triple doubles. That's as many as Jason Kidd had in his first nine seasons.

In fact, no other players except Wilt Chamberlain (in 1968) and Magic Johnson (in 1982) had as many as 700 rebounds and 700 assists in the same season. Oscar, of course, did it in 1962, 1963, and 1964.

Even before he hit the NBA, Robinson had an impact on the game. Pete Newell was the coach of the 1960 U.S.A. Olympic basketball team. This was the best collection of amateur talent ever assembled. The team swept through the eight games by at least 24 points per game. The team was top-heavy in centers (Walt Bellamy, Darrall Imhoff, Bob Boozer, Burdette Holdorson, and Jerry Lucas), but why not, if you have Jerry West and Oscar Robertson in the backcourt?

U.S.A.	101.9 points/game
Opponents	59.5 points/game

Robertson was the star of this team, the leading scorer and playmaker. He scored 16, 19, 22, 16, 13, 16, 22, and 12 points. Oscar would later win an NBA title to join the Olympic gold medal, but it took a long time.

Robertson's 1971 Bucks

It is hard to say that the NBA has ever produced a more devastating combination of dominating center and guard than Shaquille O'Neal and Kobe Bryant. Shaq and Kobe combined to win three consecutive NBA Championships in the early 2000s. There are really only a handful of other combos worthy of mention. Kareem Abdul-Jabbar and Magic Johnson teamed up to win five NBA titles in the 1980s, but Kareem was 33 years old when Magic joined the team. Kareem averaged only 17 points and then 10 points for the back-to-back Lakers title teams in 1987 and 1988.

For one season, it is hard to top the 1971 season that Kareem Abdul-Jabbar and Oscar Robertson had for the Milwaukee Bucks. Those Bucks are almost forgotten in the talk about great teams. They were sandwiched between the overhyped 1970 Knicks championship team and the 1972 Los Angeles Lakers team that won a then-record 69 games. Of course, New York and Los Angeles teams would get the attention, but look what the Milwaukee club accomplished.

1971 Bucks

10–0	preseason
66–16	regular season
12–2	playoffs

It wasn't a great team. It was a great one-two combination. The rest of the Bucks that saw significant time were starting forwards Bob Dandridge and Greg Smith and guards

Lucious Allen and Jon McGlockton. Bob Boozer was the third forward, and Dick Cunningham backed up Abdul-Jabbar.

The championship happened because Cincinnati Royals coach Bob Cousy couldn't get along with the Big O and shipped Robertson to the Bucks.

The result was a championship for Robertson in his 11th season, and yet another trip to the Finals (in 1974) before he packed it in and called it a career.

Robertson Finally Wins a Title

There was little suspense about which team would win Game 4 of the 1971 NBA Finals; the Bucks were up 3–0. It was assumed that Abdul-Jabbar would win others. The Bullets were just happy to be there—having defeated their nemesis New York in the seventh game of the Eastern finals. The first three games of the series weren't even close: Milwaukee had won them by 10, 19, and 8 points. There was one storyline going into Game 4 on April 30, 1971. Finally, Oscar Robertson was going to be rewarded for a lifetime of NBA excellence. Robertson made 11 of 15 field goals on his way to 30 points and made nine assists. The Bucks swept the Bullets with a 118–106 victory.

It would not prove to be a dynasty, however. In 1972, the Lakers finally won their first championship in Los Angeles, and the Lakers defeated the Bucks in the Western finals 4–2, as Chamberlain outplayed Abdul-Jabbar and Robertson was slowed by a groin injury. In 1973, the Golden State Warriors would upset the Bucks in the Western semis 4–2 behind Rick Barry. By 1974, the Bucks were able to squeeze 59 wins out of their team and earn a trip to the Finals, despite a 35-year-old Robertson playing out his final games.

Robertson's Career				
10 years with Cincinnati	29.3 points/game	8.5 rebounds	10.3 assists	44 min.
4 years with Milwaukee	16.3 points/game	4.9 rebounds	7.5 assists	37 min.

But Oscar played more playoff games in his final four seasons (47) than he did in his first 10 years with the Royals (39). By 1974, his last season, he was down to 35 minutes per game and averaged only 12.7 points and 6.4 rebounds. They were career-low numbers.

Robertson was trying to end his career—which began with the Original Dream Team of the 1960 Olympics—with a second NBA Championship.

The 1974 NBA Finals
Game 1
Oscar Robertson had a very forgettable 2-of-13 field goal shooting performance. In 46 minutes, he scored just six points (to go with six rebounds and eight assists). Boston blew out the Bucks in Milwaukee.

Game 2
The Bucks evened the series, but Robertson again shot poorly—this time a measly 4 of 10 field goals. Robertson played an incredible 52 minutes in the double-overtime game (more than anyone else in the game and at that time, a Finals record). Robertson—at the time one of the three leading scorers in NBA history—put up only 10 shots in those 52 minutes.

Game 3
Robertson scored only 12 points, giving him a total of just 28 so far in the three-game Finals. The Celts led 2–1.

Game 4
Milwaukee won in Boston Garden, and Robertson played better, getting 10 points and nine assists.

Game 5
The Big O turned the clock back and delivered 23 points while pitching a complete game (48 minutes). Still, the Celts held on to win 96–87 in Milwaukee.

Game 6
In a double-overtime Milwaukee victory that has been reduced to a single shot (Abdul-Jabbar's sky hook), the Bucks extended the series with a 102–101 victory. John Havlicek, Kareem, and Oscar played a then-Finals-record 58 minutes each. Oscar had 18 points and 10 assists. Robertson would play at home in Milwaukee in a Game 7 that would end his career one way or another.

Game 7
Robertson hit just 2 of 13 field goals in the last game of his career. The Celtics were up by 13 at halftime and cruised to a 102–87 victory.

Kareem Abdul-Jabbar, in a 1981 *Inside Sports* article: "I may achieve a lot in terms of statistics, but I still think Oscar Robertson is the best ever." At the time, Oscar was the second all-time leading scorer and first in career assists. Thirty years after his retirement, a strong case could be made for him to be called the best player in NBA history. No one who follows him in this book can make a similar claim. He is on the short list with Mr. O'Neal, Mr. Chamberlain, Mr. Jordan, Mr. Russell, Mr. Abdul-Jabbar, Mr. Johnson, and Mr. Bird.

Although he grew up in a ghetto of Indianapolis, Indiana, Oscar Robertson was born on November 24, 1938, on his grandfather's farm near Charlotte, Tennessee. His grandfather, who had been a slave and was at one point the oldest living person in the United States, was 116 years old when he died.

Oscar served as president of the NBA Players Association from 1963 to 1974 and had been president of the Retired NBA Players Association as well. The famed Oscar Robertson lawsuit, so named because he was the president of the players union at the time (1970), led to free agency in the NBA.

His real legacy, however, came in 1997, when he donated his kidney to his daughter, Kia. It was the most important assist in a lifetime full of assists.

TIM DUNCAN
The Big Fundamental

MVP: 2 (2002, 2003)	
MVP VOTING: 5th in 1998, 3rd in 1999, 5th in 2000, 2nd in 2001	
NBA TITLES: 2	
ALL-NBA FIRST TEAM: 6	
ALL-NBA SECOND TEAM: 0	

Prior to Game 6 of the 2003 NBA Finals, I was approached on the court by longtime friend (and NBA superfan) Jeff Hamilton. Hamilton asked me if Duncan had a place in the top five players of all time. Not one to react (or overreact) to the last image or game, I replied, "Not yet, although he is ranked high."

"Well, he's at least the greatest power forward, right?" Jeff asked.

To be honest, he wasn't at the time. Not in this book, anyway. A handful of forwards following Bird (Duncan, Karl Malone, Pettit, Baylor, and Erving) are so close that one could put them in almost any order and justify it. In Duncan's case, I don't have the back end of his career to judge. In Erving's case, I don't have the beginning (he didn't join the NBA until he was almost 27).

In Game 6 of the NBA Finals, Duncan almost had a quadruple double (at least 10 points, rebounds, assists, and blocks). It was a spectacular performance, and it pushed him ahead of Karl Malone in this book.

After the game, Hamilton wasn't the only one positively gushing about Tim Duncan. I went back and asked everyone I could.

Should Tim Duncan (two MVP seasons, two NBA titles, two NBA Finals MVPs) be ranked ahead of Karl Malone (two MVP seasons, zero NBA titles, but 18 consistently brilliant seasons compared to six for Duncan)?

Pete Vecsey: "Duncan won two titles, dominating throughout. Of course he's ahead of Karl Malone, a guy who couldn't win a title with John Stockton and only cares about himself and his stats. [Note: Pete said this in June 2003, prior to Malone signing with the Lakers for much less money than he could have received with another club.] Those factors must be gauged. Duncan is incredibly humble, hardworking, loves the game. Never a bad word for his teammate. No pressure from him to produce. Even if you suck, he's laughing and joking with you at practice, keeping everyone upbeat. Amazing defender—smart, long arms, great hands, uses his body well without fouling. Gets every rebound. He's the best. And as I said, amazingly unaffected. Of all the superstars in the history of the game, he's the number one teammate in terms of ability, personality, quality of person, work ethic, likability . . . he's number one. Not even close."

As a nod to fans (represented by Hamilton), longtime media scribes (represented by Vecsey), and players (Jason Kidd was effusive in his praise of Duncan at the conclusion of the 2003 Finals), I'm putting Duncan ahead of Malone and all other forwards save for Larry Bird.

Tim Duncan was the first player picked in the NBA draft in 1997, and that choice has kept the San Antonio Spurs near the top of the Western Conference ever since. He has had back-to-back MVP seasons (joining only Russell, Wilt, Kareem, Moses Malone, Bird, Magic, and Michael). He probably deserved the MVP in 1999, but the voters were in love with old warhorses Karl Malone and Michael Jordan. He probably didn't deserve it in 2002, when Jason Kidd elevated the Nets to elite status and Shaquille O'Neal did whatever he wanted. But I'm being picky. In Duncan's first six years in the league, he's been voted in the top five of the MVP each year.

Duncan—as Vecsey pointed out—is simply stunning as a defender. Duncan was First Team All-Defense in each of the seasons following his rookie year (when he was Second Team All-Defense).

Here is but one way to look at Duncan's defensive contributions. Other teams just do not shoot well against the Spurs. Casual fans may have noticed how dominating the Spurs can be on defense in the 2003 Finals versus the Nets. It is something that careful observers have known ever since Duncan entered the league.

1998	NBA average field goal percentage: .450	vs. Duncan's Spurs: .411 (#1 in NBA)
1999	NBA average field goal percentage: .437	vs. Duncan's Spurs: .402 (#1 in NBA)
2000	NBA average field goal percentage: .449	vs. Duncan's Spurs: .425 (#5 in NBA)
2001	NBA average field goal percentage: .443	vs. Duncan's Spurs: .419 (#2 in NBA)
2002	NBA average field goal percentage: .445	vs. Duncan's Spurs: .426 (#4 in NBA)
2003	NBA average field goal percentage: .442	vs. Duncan's Spurs: .427 (#3 in NBA)

In every season that Duncan plays, his team rates among the top in defensive rankings for fewest points allowed and opponent field goal percentage. And because of that, the Spurs are always near the top in the most important statistic, point differential.

1998:   Spurs +4.0
1999:   Spurs +8.1
2000:   Spurs +5.9
2001:   Spurs +7.8
2002:   Spurs +6.2
2003:   Spurs +5.2

Tim Duncan's team has mirrored his own play. He is fundamentally sound, a true sportsman, and remarkably consistent.

1997 NBA Draft

This draft moved the power from the East to the West. During the 1997 NBA season, the Boston Celtics bottomed out at 15 wins (15–67). M. L. Carr was fired, and a giddy Rick Pitino took over. Pitino knew that Boston had the best chance of winding up with the first overall selection, the one that everyone coveted: Tim Duncan from Wake Forest.

San Antonio had finished 20–62 that same season (Robinson was injured and limited to just six games the entire season). Vancouver won even fewer games and had more of a chance at gaining the rights to draft Duncan.

The NBA had changed their rules every few years about the draft selection. At first, teams just picked in the reverse order of their standings. The team with the worst winning percentage selected first, and so on. This was equitable until teams figured out they would be better off losing (to increase the prospects of adding a Tim Duncan–like player).

In 1985, the NBA instituted a lottery, and it was simple. The league had 23 teams. Sixteen made the playoffs. The other seven teams essentially picked out of a hat. In 1985, the two worst teams were Indiana in the East and Golden State in the West. Each had 22 wins. Instead of a coin toss to determine which franchise would pick first, all seven non-playoff teams entered the first "lottery." That is how the Knicks wound up with Patrick Ewing. In a prior year, he would have been either a Warrior or a Pacer.

The NBA noticed that it was unfair that the Clippers were a league-worst 12–70 in 1987 but received only the fourth pick in the draft. That meant Reggie Williams instead of David Robinson.

And hey, it didn't stop teams from tanking. The 1987 Spurs were 28–54. They finished their season 2–11 in their final 13 games and won the David Robinson lottery. The Spurs "knew when to hold them . . . and knew when to fold them." In the 1997 season, the Spurs lost 15 of their last 19 (and eight of their last nine) as they geared up for their lottery run at Duncan. It paid off many times over when they won the rights to draft him.

So, the NBA began tinkering. The team that "just" missed the playoffs would have fewer chances for getting the top pick or the top three selections.

In some years, superstars emerge from draft selections in the top six picks. That wasn't going to be the case in 1997, when Rick Pitino was hoping to start his Celtics era with the big man from Wake Forest.

1997 NBA Draft
1. Tim Duncan
2. Keith Van Horn
3. Chauncey Billups

When Shaquille O'Neal left Orlando as a free agent following the 1996 season and signed with Los Angeles, it was the beginning of the shift in the balance of power from East to West. A year later, Duncan was the pick of a Western team, San Antonio. A year after that, Washington traded Chris Webber out west to Sacramento for an aging Mitch Richmond, and the shift was complete.

The Numbers on Duncan

In 1998, Duncan's rookie season, he was Rookie of the Year. If I had an award to give, I would have awarded him Rookie of the Decade. Players like him only come around once every ten years or so. In that 1998 season, he averaged 21.1 points (remember, the league average was only 95 points per game that season), 11.9 rebounds, and 2.5 blocks, while shooting 55 percent from the field (league average: 45 percent). Plus, he started all 82 games for a 56-win team that had won only 20 games the year before. It was one of the greatest rookie seasons of all time.

Only eight other players had ever been All-NBA First Team in their rookie seasons. Duncan was the second youngest player (behind Max Zaslofsky in 1947) to be First Team All-NBA.

Duncan got better with each season. In his second season, he went from Second Team All-Defense to First Team. He went from fifth in the MVP vote to third. He was tied for sixth in the NBA in points per game. His team became a runaway train that was impossible to derail in the playoffs. He was the unquestioned leader of the 1999 championship team.

That 1999 season was known for several things. Michael Jordan had retired again following the 1998 Finals, and the Bulls dynasty was dismantled. Phil Jackson spent the year on the sidelines. The lockout shortened the season to 50 games. Jackson would later denigrate the 1999 champions because they hadn't proved themselves as others had, over an 82-game schedule.

That, of course, is nonsense. Joe Gibbs heard the same cracks, since his Redskins twice won Super Bowls in strike seasons. If Jackson had competed in that 1999 season, he would have given that campaign equal importance with the others.

In the 1999 postseason, defense was the operative word.

1999 NBA Finals: New York Versus San Antonio

In the first game, played in San Antonio, the Knicks were held to 10 points in the second quarter. The Knicks were playing the series without Patrick Ewing. Against other clubs, they might have started their 6-foot-11, 235-pound youngster Marcus Camby (who had been the spark for the Knicks in their Conference finals victory over the Pacers) or the undersized Kurt Thomas. Against David Robinson and Tim Duncan, however, Knicks coach Jeff Van Gundy elected to start Chris Dudley at center.

Chris Dudley may be the worst player ever to start an NBA Finals game. He'll be mentioned again in this book if I ever put together the list of the worst free-throw shooters in history, or perhaps a list of Ivy League players in the NBA.

The Knicks scored 37 points in the first half of the first game. They scored 34 points in the first half of the second game.

Chris Dudley started the first two games and missed all five of his shots. He scored two points. He would score just two field goals in the five-game series.

The Knicks shot 38 percent in the first game and lost 89–77. They shot just 33 percent in the second game and lost 80–67.

Without Patrick Ewing (injured) and Charles Oakley (traded the year before for Camby), the Knicks didn't have the size. Tim Duncan was guarded by Larry Johnson.

Tim Duncan in Game 1
33 points　　　16 rebounds　　　13 of 21 field goals

Tim Duncan in Game 2
25 points　　　15 rebounds　　　9 of 17 field goals

The Knicks knew they were in trouble in the first half of Game 1, when Duncan had 19 points at halftime. On the last play of the first half, Duncan had a vicious block of Dudley to hold the Spurs' lead at eight.

In the second game, Duncan and Robinson combined to block nine shots by the Knicks—four by Duncan.

If people remember anything about the 1999 Finals, they remember the personal duel between Tim Duncan and Latrell Sprewell in the fifth and (what turned out to be) final game. At one point, Sprewell had 14 consecutive Knicks points and Duncan had 14 of 15 for San Antonio.

Duncan had 31 points in the deciding game and was the Finals MVP. For the series, he averaged 27.4 points per game (in a series where the Spurs averaged 84 points and the Knicks 79.8). Duncan scored 32 percent of the Spurs' points in the Finals.

2000 Playoffs

In the 2000 season, Duncan finished fifth in the MVP voting. His Spurs won only 53 games, as Duncan missed eight games with injuries. It was the timing of the injuries that cost San Antonio their chance to repeat. Duncan missed four games in late February with a lower abdominal strain. He missed the final four games of the season—and all of the playoffs—after suffering a torn left lateral meniscus on April 11 in Sacramento.

How valuable was Duncan? With him, they won the NBA title in 1999. Without him, the Spurs lost in the first round to the Phoenix Suns, 4–1.

Tim Duncan's Record in Playoff Games

1998	4–5
1999	15–2
2001	7–6
2002	4–5
2003	16–8
Total	46–26

The Spurs have played five postseason games in the Tim Duncan era without Duncan (four versus Phoenix in 2000, and Game 4 of the first round in 2002, when Duncan missed a game for personal reasons). The Spurs are 1–4 in playoff games without Duncan.

After winning the first two rounds of the 2001 playoffs (against Minnesota and Dallas), Tim Duncan was 26–9 in his first 35 playoff games. He then ran into a Lakers dynasty, and despite Duncan, the Lakers beat the Spurs eight of nine times in the 2001 and 2002 playoffs.

2001 Western Conference Finals: Lakers 4, Spurs 0

Going into the series, the Spurs were on equal footing with the Lakers. San Antonio had won in 1999, sweeping the Lakers on their way to the title. The Lakers had won in 2000—but remember, Tim Duncan missed the playoffs with an injury.

The Spurs even had the homecourt advantage in the series. In the first game, in San Antonio, the Lakers won by 14 points despite 28 from Duncan. In the second game, Duncan scored 40 points. It still wasn't enough—the Lakers won by seven. When the series moved to Los Angeles, the Lakers won by scores of 111–72 and 111–82.

Which is why Tim Duncan is a great player—one of the greatest of all time—but he's no Shaquille O'Neal.

In the 2002 playoff series against Los Angeles, Duncan led his team in scoring and rebounding all five games. He scored more with each game.

Game 1	26 points
Game 2	27 points
Game 3	28 points
Game 4	30 points
Game 5	34 points

The 2003 Postseason

Tim Duncan and the Spurs didn't steamroll through the postseason as the 1999 Spurs did. San Antonio needed six games to polish off the Suns, Lakers, Mavericks, and Nets. In some ways, they were the lucky benefactors of fate befriending them. In some ways, they were their own worst enemy.

- In Game 1 of the first round against the Suns, Duncan missed a pair of free throws with five seconds remaining, allowing Phoenix's Stephon Marbury the chance to bury a three-pointer that defeated the Spurs.
- In Game 4 of the first round, the Spurs blew a 12-point lead in the fourth quarter as a player named Jake Voskuhl hit a hook shot over Duncan with two seconds left in the game. Duncan then missed a fallaway jumper as time expired.

- In Game 5 of the second round versus the Lakers, the Spurs blew a 25-point lead. Duncan dropped into the paint and left Robert Horry on the perimeter for a good look at a potentially game-winning three-pointer. Horry missed, and the Spurs held on for a 3–2 series lead.
- In Game 1 of the Western Conference finals, the Spurs blew an 18-point lead as Tim Duncan (40 points, 15 rebounds, 7 assists) shot an air ball with six seconds remaining and then missed a pair of free throws with four seconds remaining.
- In Game 2 of the NBA Finals, Duncan missed 7 of 10 free throws as the Nets evened the series with a two-point victory.

Mike Tirico: "It's hard to reconcile that Tim Duncan—known as Mr. Fundamentals and the most fundamentally sound player in the NBA—struggles with his free throws, the single most basic fundamental skill in basketball."

As luck would have it . . . the Spurs faced the Lakers in the conference semis. The Lakers had three key players injured in their prior first-round series with Minnesota: Rick Fox, Devean George, and Kobe Bryant. Bryant played, George did so less effectively, and Fox not at all.

In the conference finals, the Spurs faced the Dallas Mavericks. Dirk Nowitzki, the Mavs superstar, went down with a sprained left knee late in Game 3 and missed the rest of the series.

In the NBA Finals, the Nets' lone offensive threat, Kenyon Martin, played the final two games with a flu-like condition that caused him to miss practice. Martin made only two of eight field goals in the fifth game. Martin missed 20 of 23 shots in the sixth and final game.

San Antonio avoided the Sacramento Kings because the Kings bowed out to the Mavericks—when Kings star Chris Webber was forced to the sideline with injury.

So, in many ways, San Antonio were the last men standing.

What the Spurs and Duncan Did So Well

The Spurs never needed a seventh game, closing out all four series in six contests. They did this mostly with Duncan setting up his teammates.

- In the sixth game of the first round, Duncan had 15 points, 20 rebounds, 10 assists, and four blocks. He did not score a point in the fourth quarter.
- In the sixth game of the NBA Finals, Duncan had 21 points, 20 rebounds, 10 assists, and eight blocks.

- In the sixth game of the Conference finals, the Spurs outscored the Mavs 34–9 in the fourth quarter. The Spurs had a 23–0 run that knocked out the outmanned Dallas team.
- In the sixth game of the NBA Finals, the Spurs outscored the Nets 31–14 in the fourth quarter, with a 19–0 run that put the game and series out of reach.

Where does Duncan's Finals performance rank?

Tim Duncan in 2003 NBA Finals

24.2 points	17 rebounds	5.3 assists	5.3 blocks

But it was more than just the numbers. In Game 1, with the score tied at halftime, Duncan scored 13 points in the third quarter and took over the game. In Game 3, Duncan boxed out Kenyon Martin and beat him to the boards on a missed Tony Parker free throw that was the single biggest play of the game. In Game 6, Duncan kept his team in the game for the first three quarters, until the other Spurs started hitting shots.

Still, he was not as dominating as Shaq had been the previous three years. And Jordan averaged 41 points, 8.5 rebounds, and 6.3 assists per game in the 1993 Finals. Larry Bird averaged close to a triple double (24 points, 9.7 rebounds, 9.5 assists) in the 1986 Finals. Magic Johnson in the 1980 Finals averaged 21.5 points, 11.1 rebounds, 8.7 assists, and 2.9 steals.

Bill Walton's 1977 Finals matches up quite nicely with Duncan's 2003 performance.

Walton, 1977 Finals:	18.5 points	19.0 rebounds	5.1 assists	3.6 blocks
Duncan, 2003 Finals:	24.2 points	17.0 rebounds	5.3 assists	5.3 blocks

Again, I'm super-critical, but I want my superman to put up more than 18 shots per game in the biggest games of his life. I want him to hit a higher percentage of foul shots—particularly with the game on the line. In the two Nets victories, Dikembe Mutombo played over 20 minutes per game and played Tim Duncan straight up, causing Duncan and the Spurs problems. Mutombo's skills and playing time had eroded markedly since the 2001 Finals, when Dikembe was a defensive force in the league. Mutombo couldn't stop O'Neal for a minute in those 2001 Finals—and yet, he contained Duncan for stretches in the 2003 Finals.

Who's Better, Who's Best?
Tim Duncan or Shaquille O'Neal

Steve Kerr: "Shaq will always be the most dominating big man ever. He's like a man among boys out there. But Tim is fundamentally the best big man in the game and the fact is, he outplayed Shaq in our series. And we beat them. So for right now, anyway, Tim has the edge over him."

Kevin Willis: "Shaq's number one because of what he's done. He's got three championships and the only way you can stop him is to double-team or triple-team him and hope he doesn't want to play that night."

Willis has it right, and Kerr could be excused for his loyalty to his teammate. Shaq's better. Shaq's the best. But Duncan is very, very, very good.

Who's Better, Who's Best
Tim Duncan or Charles Barkley

Joe Maloof: "Don't ask me why, but I take Barkley. He was a great player who was great for a long time."

There is no player that really compares to Duncan. As P. J. Carlesimo said to me, "Name me another seven-footer who uses the glass as well as Timmy." There isn't one, of course. NBA.com used a comparison to Bob Pettit, who was 6-foot-9 and 215 pounds, far from Duncan's 7-foot-0. Pettit, though, was an inside force who beat the Celtics in 1958, putting off by a year the Celts' run of consecutive championships. Duncan was an inside force whose Spurs defeated the Lakers in the 1999 postseason, putting off by a year the Lakers' run of consecutive titles.

Duncan could have played in almost any era (like John Stockton). Shaquille calls Duncan "The Big Fundamental." Pettit was named to the All-NBA Team 11 times (10 times on the First Team). That is very much within the grasp of "The Big Fundamental."

A Better Analogy

Tim Duncan or Pete Sampras During the 2003 NBA Finals, Bill Walton made this point. He compared Tim Duncan to tennis great Pete Sampras. Walton noted that both were classically trained, with facial expressions that never change. Plus, both win all the time.

Actually, Bill, I agree with you about Sampras and Duncan. But more than that, they are compared because of their boring or pleasant personalities. Both have had to defend their personality. Neither of them owes us flamboyance or charisma. Duncan followed handsome multitalented superstars like Jordan and Shaq. They were "movie-star" big and appealed to a wide cross-section of people. Sampras followed the likes of Connors and McEnroe. Duncan and Sampras didn't hang in those circles. They didn't join rock bands and make movies and host game shows and sell a million different products. They appealed to serious fans of their sport.

And neither has to apologize for who he is.

BOB COUSY
Houdini of the Hardwood

MVP: 1	
MVP VOTING: 3rd in 1956, 6th in 1958, 4th in 1959, 4th in 1960	
NBA TITLES: 6	
ALL-NBA FIRST TEAM: 10	
ALL-NBA SECOND TEAM: 2	

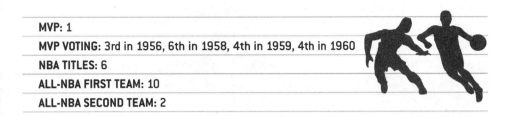

Bob Cousy was a general on the court and one of the most dominant players in the history of the game. He was known as the "greatest little man" among the pros. He won only one MVP, but the NBA didn't award an MVP until 1956. Based upon voting by writers and broadcasters of the time, Cousy finished fourth in the All-NBA First Team voting in 1952. He placed second to George Mikan in 1953. He would have won the MVP in 1954 had one been awarded. And he would have been second again in 1955.

That would add up to two MVPs, and five years in the top three.

Do you need more credentials? He was selected for the 25th, 35th, and 50th NBA Anniversary teams. He played in 13 consecutive All-Star Games and was MVP of the game in both 1954 and 1957.

It's not the numbers; it was his style. He revolutionized the game with his ball handling and razzle-dazzle. His story was one of legend. His parents were poor French immigrants. He was cut twice from the Andrew Jackson High School junior varsity team. At the age of 13, he fell out of a tree and broke his right arm. He learned to dribble and shoot with his left arm. When his former coach saw him play in neighborhood leagues, he invited him back on the team as a playmaking guard.

Cousy's Pro Career

Cousy was drafted by the Tri-Cities Blackhawks, who soon traded him to the Chicago Stags. The Stags folded before the 1951 season even started, so the names of Cousy and two other much-sought-after Stags players were placed in a hat. The owners of the Knicks, Warriors, and Celtics gathered in a hotel room and each drew out of a hat. The story goes that the Celtics wanted Max Zaslofsky first, Andy Phillip second, and then Cousy. After the Knicks drew Zaslofsky, Boston was "stuck" with Bob Cousy.

Cousy's 1951 Rookie Season

15.6 points/game (ninth in NBA)

6.9 rebounds

4.9 assists (fourth in NBA)

Remember, at the time, the league was only shooting about 37 percent and teams would average only 84 points per game. There were tons of rebounds to go around—and comparatively few hoops. Prior to Cousy, Boston was 22–46. In 1951 with him, they were 39–30.

In his second season, he jumped to third in the league in scoring and second in assists. That 1952 season saw him average 21.7 points, 6.4 rebounds, and 6.7 assists per game in a year when the average team scored only 83 points per game.

Leonard Koppett: "Cousy: You're asking me about his style of play . . . three people come to mind . . . Andy Phillip, Dick McGuire, and Cousy. They were masters of true passing . . . but where to pass . . . how to deliver the ball in just the right spot . . . Cousy was a great scorer, which is what separated him from Phillip. In a later era, Oscar Robertson and Jerry West had that passing ability as well."

The Defining Game of Cousy's Career

Prior to the arrival of Bill Russell, the Celtics weren't exactly a dynasty-in-training. Going into the first-round playoff series against the Syracuse Nationals at the end of the 1953 season, the Celts had never even survived so much as a single playoff round.

During the 1953 campaign, Boston had finished third in the Eastern Division but only a game behind the division champion New York Knicks. Cousy had proved that season that he could play the big man's game despite his 6-foot height. In his third NBA season, Cousy was the third-leading scorer in the game and was the assist king by 150 assists.

1953 Assist Leaders

1. Bob Cousy   547 (7.7 per game)
2. Andy Phillip   397 (5.7 per game)

That year, Cousy led the NBA in shot attempts as well as assists. Only Philadelphia's Neil Johnston and Minneapolis's George Mikan averaged more points than Cooz. He was as big a star as the NBA had east of Minnesota then. Remember, this was in a year where the shooting percentages were around 37 percent.

When the Celtics won the first game of the best-of-three playoff series against the Nats, they took the upper hand. But with less than a minute left in the second game, it all began to slip away. The Nats were leading by a point and Boston had the ball. Cousy had 25 points to this point and had played brilliantly, but he tried to bullet a pass to a teammate beneath the basket. Ironically, it flew wildly out of bounds. All Syracuse had to do was hold on to the ball and the series would be tied on Cousy's turnover.

But the Celtics stole the ball and quickly got it back to Cooz, who dribbled in fast. Syracuse fouled him for a one-shot foul. Cousy tied the game up with a free throw, sending the game into overtime.

In the first overtime, Cousy needed another free throw to extend the game into a second overtime. Again, he converted the one-shot opportunity. Bob had scored six of the Celtics' nine points in overtime.

In the second overtime, neither team wanted to shoot, the pressure was so great. Syracuse scored four points, and it might have held up except Cousy (who else?) drove in and scored to tie the game at 90–90, forcing overtime number three.

By now, Syracuse was in real trouble. Only five players were left who hadn't fouled out, and one of them, Paul Seymour, had sprained his ankle. Seymour stayed under the basket, so Boston basically had a power play opportunity for the entire period. But despite the power play, Syracuse led by five with 13 seconds remaining. Cousy drove and shot. If a pre-adolescent Marv Albert was somehow calling the game, it would have sounded like this: "Yes, and it counts." Cousy hit the shot and the free throw to cut the lead to two. There were only five seconds left.

Boston stole the ball in the backcourt and passed it to Cousy. He dribbled across the midcourt line and hit from 25 feet away. The buzzer went off as the ball was released. The shot forced overtime number four. Boston had scored nine points in the third overtime—and Cooz had scored eight of them.

Someone should have realized right there that shots from that far away should be worth three points, but that would come years later, of course. In 1953, Cousy had to settle for a deuce.

In the fourth overtime, Syracuse's four healthy players scored the first five points of the extra session. Boston eventually wore the Nats down, winning 111–105 in four overtimes. Cousy scored another nine points in the fourth overtime. In the four overtimes, he scored an amazing 25 points. He had 50 for the game; unheard-of for that time and inconceivable since he had only 7 points at halftime. Cousy had hit 30 of 32 free throws in that pressure-packed game. He would never score 50 in a game again.

Who's Better, Who's Best
Bob Cousy or John Stockton

The most comparable modern-day player to Cousy has to be John Stockton. Cousy was ahead of his time, and Stockton was a throwback. They could have both probably played in any era. Cousy led the NBA in assists for eight straight seasons. Stockton led the NBA in assists for nine straight seasons.

Tommy Heinsohn: "He was the ultimate creator. Let me put it in perspective—if you think Magic Johnson could pass, if you think John Stockton could pass, multiply by 10 and you have Bob Cousy."

Cousy's Rankings When He Retired

After the 1963 season, Cousy was the fourth-highest scorer in NBA history (16,955 points). He also had the all-time record for assists (6,949).

The Era Cousy Played In		
Year	NBA Average Points	Field Goal Percentage
1951	84.1	.358
1952	83.7	.367
1953	82.5	.370
1954	79.5	.372
1955	93.1	.385
1956	99.0	.386
1957	99.6	.380
1958	106.6	.383
1959	108.2	.394
1960	115.3	.403
1961	118.1	.415
1962	118.8	.412
1963	115.3	.439

Somehow, this guy played in equal amounts of both the dead ball era and the highest-scoring time in history. Of course, the dividing line was the advent of the 24-second clock. But if you average out all 13 seasons, the NBA average for those 13 years is a little more than 100 points per game.

Now, if Cousy played in a 13-year era where the average team scored just over 100 points per game (not much different than the modern-day game), then why are his (and everyone's from his era) assists totals so much lower than the modern-day game?

The fact is . . . one has to adjust for assist totals. For the last two decades, assists have been credited on about 60 percent of all field goals scored in the NBA.

That wasn't the case in Bob Cousy's time. Even spotty or poor statisticians can identify baskets and fouls. There is little left to subjectivity. But the awarding of an assist (a pass leading directly to a basket) is subjective.

The advent of the computer—and a standardized one in which each team's local statisticians are trained—help account for regional differences. With no disrespect to Jerry West and Magic Johnson, the Los Angeles assist totals have always been very liberal. Not only are there regional differences, but the league over time has given out more and more assists. For instance, in 1962, the average team scored more than 118 points per game, yet only one player averaged more than eight assists per game. Wilt Chamberlain scored 20 baskets per game that year, yet his point guard Guy Rodgers averaged "only" eight assists per game.

Percentage of Assisted Field Goals in Cousy's Era

1957	assists awarded on 52 percent of all field goals
1958	assists awarded on 50 percent of all field goals
1959	assists awarded on 49 percent of all field goals
1960	assists awarded on 51 percent of all field goals
1961	assists awarded on 53 percent of all field goals
1962	assists awarded on 52 percent of all field goals
1963	assists awarded on 50 percent of all field goals

Percentage of Assisted Field Goals in Stockton's Era

1986	assists awarded on 60 percent of all field goals
1987	assists awarded on 61 percent of all field goals
1988	assists awarded on 61 percent of all field goals

1989	assists awarded on 60 percent of all field goals
1990	assists awarded on 60 percent of all field goals
1991	assists awarded on 60 percent of all field goals
1997	assists awarded on 61 percent of all field goals
1999	assists awarded on 61 percent of all field goals
2000	assists awarded on 61 percent of all field goals
2001	assists awarded on 61 percent of all field goals

Okay, what can we take from this list? After an interview with Cousy's longtime teammate Tommy Heinsohn, I had an explanation.

Tommy Heinsohn: "Elliott, you know why Cooz didn't have many more assists? IF YOU DRIBBLED THE BALL, YOU WEREN'T GIVEN AN ASSIST." *What?* "It had to be a catch-and-shoot situation. Guys weren't given assists on fast breaks. If you dribbled the basketball and dished it to someone who scored, no assist."

All-Time Career Assist Leaders

Bob Cousy was number one following the 1963 season when he retired. In the next 20 years, despite being the greatest offensive years in NBA history, only two men would pass his assist total (Oscar Robertson and Lenny Wilkens).

Career Assist Leaders Through 1982

Rank	Player	Assist Total
1.	Oscar Robertson	9,887
2.	Lenny Wilkens	7,211
3.	Bob Cousy	6,955
4.	Guy Rodgers	6,917
5.	Jerry West	6,238

In the following 21 years, when teams "moved the fences in" (awarded assists on 10 percent more field goals) the numbers skyrocketed.

Career Assist Leaders Through 2003

Rank	Player	Assist Total
1.	John Stockton	15,806
2.	Mark Jackson	10,215
3.	Magic Johnson	10,141
4.	Oscar Robertson	9,887
5.	Isiah Thomas	9,061

Cousy didn't show up on the Top 10 list, trailing guards like Rod Strickland, Terry Porter, and Tim Hardaway. Cousy was 12th all-time in assists following the 2003 season.

In Defense of Cousy and the Old-Timers

Cousy played the first four years of his career in the "dead ball era" before the 24-second clock encouraged teams to run and shoot quickly. Players didn't know assists totals were so coveted. They didn't have incentives in their contracts. Cable television networks weren't putting up lists of all-time assists leaders.

More than one player on a team could distribute the ball. There wasn't such a thing as a "point" guard. Both guards shared responsibility for bringing the ball upcourt and dishing out assists. Cousy regularly received credit for less than 40 percent of the Celtics' assists totals in any given season. Stockton routinely would receive credit for more than 50 percent of the Jazz totals in any given season. Give Cousy an extra 10 percent assists for crossing time lines and playing in the modern day when more assists are awarded. Give Cousy an extra 10 percent for being "the" point guard who concentrates on accumulating and stockpiling statistics.

Give Cousy four to five more years of playing by throwing millions of dollars at him.

Cousy's Eight Consecutive Years of Leading the League in Assists

1953	7.7 per game	Only two other players had more than 4.9 per game
1954	7.2 per game	Only three other players had more than 4.5 per game
1955	7.9 per game	Teammates Sharman, Macauley also in top 10
1956	8.9 per game	No one else in the league even had 6.5 assists per game
1957	7.5 per game	50 percent more assists than runner-up Jack McMahon (5.1)
1958	7.1 per game	Only four other players with more than 4.6 per game
1959	8.6 per game	Ninth in scoring (20 points/game), 2.4 more per game than runner-up
1960	9.5 per game	Only Guy Rodgers had more than 6.3 per game

Stockton's Nine Consecutive Years of Leading the League in Assists

1988	13.8 per game	No one else had more than 12 per game
1989	13.6 per game	Magic and Kevin Johnson had more than 12 per game
1990	14.5 per game	Scored or assisted on close to 1,600 field goals
1991	14.2 per game	1,164 assists; a season record that still stands
1992	13.7 per game	Only Johnson and T. Hardaway had 10 per game
1993	12.0 per game	250 more assists than anyone else in game
1994	12.6 per game	Same story: more than 1,000 total assists, no one else had 800
1995	12.3 per game	Kenny Anderson second with 9.4 per game
1996	11.2 per game	Jason Kidd second with 9.7 per game

Who's Better, Who's Best
Bob Cousy or John Stockton

Come on. Cousy was a player who changed the game. He dominated with his playmaking—but also with his scoring and rebounding. He won six NBA Championships. If Stockton had played in Cousy's era, he would have averaged slightly fewer assists than Cooz—based on the aforementioned aspects (fewer assists awarded, more players sharing playmaking, et cetera).

Who's Better, Who's Best
Bob Cousy or Jerry West

That's one of the toughest calls I have to make in this book. West was known as "Mr. Clutch" and his playoff career is filled with legendary shotmaking. There was no three-point shot for either of them, although you have to figure West would have benefited more. West had Baylor and little else for most of his career. Cousy had a bushelful of Hall of Fame teammates. I'll leave this one to Cousy's teammate Bill Russell—and his 1966 opinion as expressed in this list from his *Go Up for Glory*.

Bill Russell's All-Time All-Star Team—1966

Jerry West—guard
Oscar Robertson—guard
Wilt Chamberlain—center
Elgin Baylor—forward
Bob Pettit—forward

Russell added: "I might make a change at center, if you'll pardon a personal prejudice. As an alternate, I'd also have to pick Dolph Schayes. And of course the great Bob Cousy."

Wow. If I read that correctly, Russell most definitively put West ahead of Cousy—despite writing while having vivid, recent memories of the Cooz.

But at the back of that same book, as an All-Time NBA team (as decided by a poll of the sports editors of the nation's 100 largest newspapers), the Academy of Sports selected the following as the all-time NBA team:

69 percent named Bob Cousy
67 percent named Bill Russell
65 percent named George Mikan
57 percent named Elgin Baylor
53 percent named Wilt Chamberlain

Those numbers tell us plenty. Almost 70 percent of the educated media saw fit to put Bob Cousy as the best player on the All-Time NBA team. Not even 15 percent of those who voted put West at the top of the list.

Tommy Heinsohn: "Jerry West or Bob Cousy. That's a tough one. I'll give you my all-time top five team. Russell is the center. Bob Pettit and Elgin Baylor are the forwards. Bob Cousy and Jerry West are the guards." I came back at Heinsohn, because of what I perceived as a glaring omission of Oscar Robertson and/or Michael Jordan. "We Celtics had the best offense . . . and by far the best defense. You heard me right. Jerry West was a great, great player. West and Cousy are my guards."

In summary, Cousy was the best guard of his era. For a short period (between Mikan's end and Russell's beginning), he was the best player period. He was the gold standard for point guards. My favorite Cousy story involves the late Al McGuire. The Knicks and the Celtics were always rivals, even back in the 1950s when the Knicks weren't very good. Al was a Knicks guard, not nearly as highly regarded as his brother Dick. In fact, if he scored two points it was a good game for him. But after one game in which the precocious Al did a good job defensively, Al stood on a Knicks dressing room table, confronted the mass of Boston's media, and, with clenched fist raised, humbly announced to the world, "I own Cousy."

It was a funny story because no one owned Cousy. It's been 40 years since he retired, and he still merits a place among the top 10 players of all time.

BOB PETTIT

First to Score 20,000 Points

MVP: 2	
MVP VOTING: 5 top 3 finishes; 8 years in the top 5	
NBA TITLES: 1	
ALL-NBA FIRST TEAM: 10	
ALL-NBA SECOND TEAM: 1	

Bob Pettit played between 1954 and 1965. He entered the league just at the end of the "dead ball era" and played in an era when offenses exploded. In his first year, teams averaged 79.5 points per game. The next year, the 24-second clock came in and teams averaged 93.1 points. By Pettit's eighth season, the league average was up to 118 points. Pettit took advantage of the new rules and was the all-time leading scorer in the time after George Mikan and before Wilt Chamberlain. Pettit was known for his clean living and for his second efforts. He did things that were noticed and counted: he scored a ton of points and pulled down a ton of rebounds. He was part of the St. Louis Hawks when they dominated the West and seemingly played the Boston Celtics each year in the Finals.

He retired as the all-time leading scorer in the NBA in 1965. You can't do much better than that.

MVP Voting

In the first year of the MVP vote, Bob Pettit easily outdistanced Paul Arizin to win the first MVP. It was in the year 1 B.B.R. (Before Bill Russell). In 1957, Pettit's Hawks would lose to the Celtics in the Finals and Pettit would lose to Boston guard Bob Cousy in the MVP voting, finishing second. The following year, 1958, Pettit fell to fourth in the MVP voting, but he won his only NBA Championship.

In 1959, Bob Pettit rewrote the NBA record books. He not only led the league, he set single-season marks for most field goals (719), most free throws made (667), most points scored (2,105), most points per game (29.2), and most games of 50+ points (three). If the league record keepers had kept more stats, Pettit would have broken additional records.

The 1959 MVP vote went like this: Pettit had 59 first-place votes. The other 23 first-place votes were split up by eight other players. Pettit finished with 317 points. Bill Russell was second with 144 points.

The following year, Pettit stepped back one notch. He finished third in the MVP vote, trailing rookie Chamberlain and Russell. In 1961, Pettit was again second in the voting, trailing only Russell.

That's one outstanding five-year period. His team went to the Finals four times, winning once. And Pettit was always one of the three or four best players in the entire league.

In 1962, Pettit's team dropped back and he finished sixth in the MVP voting, trailing the usual suspects (Russell, Chamberlain, Oscar Robertson, Elgin Baylor, and Jerry West). It only took a year to rebuild, and by 1963 the Hawks were back in the playoffs and Pettit was back to fourth in the MVP vote. He was fourth again in the MVP vote in 1964, this time trailing Robertson, Chamberlain, and Russell.

The MVP voting and being named to the All-NBA teams were testament to Pettit's abilities and what people thought of him. But it is his playoff career that puts him in the class of the top dozen players of all time.

The Greatest Finals Ever Played

In late March 1957, the St. Louis Hawks defeated the Minneapolis Lakers to advance to their first NBA Finals. The Boston Celtics defeated the Syracuse Nats to advance to their first.

The Celtics, with their rookie center Bill Russell, were heavily favored. But in the first game, St. Louis staged a rare road victory, taking the Celtics in double overtime, 125–123.

Here are a few nuggets from that game. In this, the first NBA Finals game ever played in Boston, the attendance was 5,976. Boston forced the first overtime when Tom Heinsohn tapped in a ball with five seconds remaining. The Celtics forced a second overtime when Bob Cousy threw in a long set shot with 15 seconds remaining in the first extra session.

As the first overtime began, Bill Russell fouled out, attempting to block a Pettit drive. Pettit was brilliant, scoring 37 points. His layup with a minute left in the second overtime tied the game 123–123. After that, Cousy missed a free throw and a player named Jack Coleman hit a 15-footer to give the Hawks the win.

As you might expect, the Celtics came back the next day and crushed the Hawks by 20 points to even the series.

The teams split the next four games to set up a Game 7 on April 13, 1957, in Boston. That seventh game was perhaps the greatest game in the history of the league. It was the second game of the Finals to go into double overtime. (To show how close the series was, two other games in the series were decided by two points.)

1957 Finals Game 7 Trivia

Some nuggets from the *New York Times* story written after the seventh game: Red Auerbach shook hands with Ben Kerner, the Hawks owner, before the game. Days earlier, Auerbach had punched Kerner in St. Louis after a heated oral discussion. Among the onlookers at the game were members of the Red Sox.

In the seventh game, there were 38 lead changes and 28 additional ties. Pettit was a stud, contributing 39 points and 19 rebounds (on 14 of 34 field goals). Tom Heinsohn hit 17 of 33 shots and scored 37 points.

Before a capacity crowd of 13,909 in Boston, the "action was so feverish that the fans were left limp when the last buzzer sounded," according to William Briordy's account in the *New York Times*.

It was Pettit who forced the first overtime in Game 7, hitting a pair of free throws with the season on the line and six seconds remaining. In the first overtime, Heinsohn hit a layup with 15 seconds left to put the Celts up. The Hawks' Jack Coleman tied it. Sharman then missed at the buzzer, sending the game into double overtime.

In the final extra session, Frank Ramsey's shooting led the Celts to their first championship.

My question is this: How come this game didn't push the NBA to greater heights in popularity? On December 28, 1958, at Yankee Stadium, the NFL had a similarly great NFL Championship game between the Baltimore Colts and the New York Giants.

The Colts had an offense featuring quarterback John Unitas, Alan Ameche, Lenny Moore, and Raymond Berry. The Giants had players such as Frank Gifford, Roosevelt Brown, and Sam Huff. Steve Myrha's 20-yard field goal tied the game with seven seconds remaining, forcing the first sudden-death overtime in NFL Championship history.

Johnny Unitas marched the Colts down the field and the game ended with Alan Ameche going into the end zone. A very large television audience saw that game, which many maintain was the greatest game ever played in the NFL. That game is credited with putting the league on the radar screen of America. It helped gain lucrative television contracts and more.

Wasn't the nationally televised NBA Finals Game 7 of 1957 even close?

Apparently not.

The problem with the NBA's history is that a fan in his early forties, such as me, has never seen Pettit play. I've seen film of the great baseball stars from the 1950s. There isn't a baseball star from the era that I can't pick out of a police lineup. I know the batting stance of most of those stars. Once we get into the 1960s, there are NBA games—usually Finals games—between the Celtics and Lakers. It seems that most of the footage that people have seen—certainly most of the games from the 1960s shown on Classic Sports—involves the Celtics, Sixers, and Lakers. Fans my age have seen Russell, Baylor, and West. If we don't remember seeing them in our youth, we've seen them on ESPN Classic. But not Pettit, who retired by 1965—and whose last Finals appearance was in 1961.

The 1958 Finals: Redemption

The St. Louis Hawks were losers in the NBA Finals in 1957, 1960, and 1961. They would have been considered losers—and Pettit would have joined Chamberlain and Baylor among the losingest losers—if not for the 1958 Finals against Boston.

After splitting the first two games, the series shifted to St. Louis for the third game. Bill Russell was injured in the third quarter, when he fell heavily on his right leg after being charged with goal-tending.

St. Louis led by as many as 15 points in the third quarter, and by as many as 12 in the fourth, but had to hold on to win 111–108 to take a 2–1 lead in the series. Pettit scored 34 points to lead the Hawks.

In the fourth game, Russell sat out with his injury. With Russell in St. Louis with his teammates, a sidebar story in the next day's paper reported that Russell's home in Reading, Massachusetts, was ransacked and more than $1,500 in property stolen. Police reported that thieves broke in during the day, while Mrs. Russell and her young son were at an Easter parade.

In St. Louis, the Celtics staged one of the most memorable playoff wins of all time in Game 4. They evened the series 2–2, despite the loss of Russell. They used great defense and slowdown tactics. Auerbach used guard Bob Cousy in the pivot, and the Cooz had

24 points, 16 in the second quarter. This should be as known and memorable as Magic Johnson playing center, replacing an injured Kareem Abdul-Jabbar in 1980.

Imagine, the great Bob Pettit—at home—being held to just 12 points. Even without Russell, the Celtics out-rebounded the Hawks 73–71. St. Louis missed 20 free throws in this game.

The series went back to Boston, and the Celtics had to feel great about stealing Game 4 minus Russell. Russell was able to rest the fifth game and have two additional days to prepare for the sixth game in St. Louis. In the fifth game, Pettit scored 33 points and the Hawks won 102–100. That set up Game 6—the greatest game of Bob Pettit's career.

Game 6

Russell played on a heavily taped ankle. Unlike Willis Reed's presence 12 years later in a Finals, Russell's appearance (he played 20 minutes, scoring eight points) didn't lead his teammates to victory.

Pettit scored 19 points in the fourth quarter, scoring with 6:16 remaining to put the Hawks up 95–93. Every time the Celts got close, Pettit was there to score another field goal. Pettit's 50 points set a playoff record for a regulation game. The old mark was 47 by Mikan. Cousy had scored 50 in a playoff game, with four overtimes. Pettit's 50 points also represented a Finals record.

Pettit averaged 29.3 points per game in the Finals and scored 83 points in the final two games, after the Celtics had tied the series 2–2. The way Pettit played, it might not have mattered if Russell had been healthy throughout the series.

Then again, it might have.

Matt Guokas: "Bob Pettit: He was a tough, physical player. He had a mid-post game. Not a deep low post. Kind of like how Yao Ming now plays. One hand over his head—a little push shot. Similar to Oscar Robertson's shot. He was a great foul shooter. He became a successful businessman. He was a banker in his playing days."

Harvey Pollack: "He was clutch. What a player. He was thin and not that big—but he gave off the impression that he was taller and bigger than he was."

At least one great player from the modern game remembers Bob Pettit. Shaquille O'Neal tried to quiz me the day before a game in the 2002 season. He asked me what university produced the most of the 50 greatest players in NBA history. Figuring out that it had to be Shaquille's school, I answered Louisiana State. He told me I was correct, and identified Pete Maravich, Bob Pettit, and himself. (Pettit was actually from Baton Rouge, went to Baton Rouge High School, and lived only a mile away from LSU.)

Something else that Shaq shares with Pettit is the ability to get to the free throw line. Pettit averaged over 10.3 free throw attempts per game in his career, a testament to his relentless play under the basket.

Most Free Throw Attempts/Game, Career
1. 11.4   Wilt Chamberlain
2. 10.5   Shaquille O'Neal
3. 10.3   Bob Pettit
4. 9.4   Jerry West

Pettit would have been one of the all-time leading offensive rebounders, if such matters were charted back in his day.

Here's one more interesting tidbit about Pettit. His first NBA coach was Red Holzman, who coached the Hawks from the middle of the 1954 season to the beginning of the 1957 season. Holzman kick-started the Hawks' string of Western championships and the 1958 NBA title by moving young Bob Pettit from center to forward. Pettit was eternally grateful not to have to bang against the bigger centers night after night. More than a decade later, Holzman would shift power forward Willis Reed to center and have equally successful results.

In summary, Pettit didn't excite many people outside St. Louis. He didn't revolutionize the game. He wasn't acrobatic. He wasn't flamboyant. He wasn't a wizard with the basketball as Cousy was. He was—and I heard this word over and over when asking about Pettit—*relentless.* He got the job done enough to rank ahead of all but 10 players in the history of the game. That's what happens when you retire as the leading scorer in the history of the league.

In Pettit's time, he was compared favorably to the two other great forwards (Schayes and Baylor). Schayes preceded Pettit and Baylor succeeded him, although their careers overlapped. Today, Tim Duncan is the player who would be most compared to Pettit. Both Duncan and Pettit were not flamboyant or flashy. Both were yearly picks for the All-NBA First Team. Both won a title early in their careers. Pettit did it first. He did it longer.

Who's Better, Who's Best
Bob Pettit or Tim Duncan
Bob Pettit was the original Tim Duncan. They both do everything really well. Pettit was the best player in the league until Russell came along in 1957. I don't think Pettit was as

good as Baylor turned out to be, but he's in a class with him and the other great forwards of all time. Duncan has size over Pettit, but Pettit was as big as he needed to be for that time. Pettit played straight up, and he could score from the outside. He didn't have too many weaknesses.

The answer to this question depends on the age of the person you ask. In another couple of seasons, Duncan may pull convincingly ahead.

A Better Analogy

Bob Pettit and Stan Musial Baseball was the first sport then as it is now for St. Louis sports fans. The biggest St. Louis sports star in the 1950s was Stan Musial. Musial, like Pettit, played his entire career in St. Louis. Musial was a three-time MVP and, upon retirement, held 17 major league records. He was elected to the Hall of Fame in 1969. Pettit was a two-time MVP who was elected to his Hall of Fame in 1970. The big difference between the two is that St. Louis put up a statue of Musial in front of the baseball stadium in 1968. The Hawks moved to Atlanta shortly after Pettit's retirement. There is no statue of Pettit in St. Louis, in Atlanta, or anywhere. When a franchise moves away, the memories sometimes get lost in the moving boxes.

JERRY WEST
"Zeke" from Cabin Creek

MVP: 0

MVP VOTING: 2nd in 1966, 1970, 1971, and 1972

NBA TITLES: 1

ALL-NBA FIRST TEAM: 10

ALL-NBA SECOND TEAM: 2

If you were lucky enough to see him play, it would be hard to imagine four better guards in the history of the game. Jerry West was a superior offensive and defensive talent. It is easier to compare big men from different eras than the backcourt stars. The guards of the modern age almost play a different game. West wasn't a high-flying, spectacular dunker. He did have all the criteria for being one of the 12 best players in the history of the game. He dominated his position. He was one of the two best players in the league no less than four different seasons (as judged by the MVP votes). He played in the NBA Finals nine times. Unlike his longtime teammate Elgin Baylor, West stayed healthy enough to win an NBA Championship as a player. West also was able to stay with the Lakers organization for more than four decades, building championships as a general manager.

Because of West's success in upper management—and the subsequent arrival in the league of Magic Johnson, Michael Jordan, and Kobe Bryant—it is difficult to convey to younger fans the greatness of West's playing career.

The first way is to examine the results of the four second-place finishes in the MVP voting. I'll also post the contributions West made to the Lakers' record 33-game win streak in 1972, when West was 34 years old. The real measure of Jerry West was his performance in the postseason, particularly in the Finals. Finally, I'll compare him to the modern stars who are the most similar (Bryant, Allen Iverson, Reggie Miller, and Allan Houston).

MVP Voting

As great as Jerry was, he didn't deserve the MVP in any of those seasons. It's hard for a guard to be as, er, *valuable* as a dominant big man.

1966 MVP Voting	1st	2nd	3rd	Total
1. Wilt Chamberlain	48	15	7	181
2. Jerry West	16	20	13	101

1970 MVP Voting	1st	2nd	3rd	Total
1. Willis Reed	61	55	28	498
2. Jerry West	51	59	25	457

1971 MVP Voting	1st	2nd	3rd	Total
1. Kareem Abdul-Jabbar	133	10	3	698
2. Jerry West	4	34	44	166

1972 MVP Voting	1st	2nd	3rd	Total
1. Kareem Abdul-Jabbar	81	52	20	581
2. Jerry West	44	42	47	393

Here's what happened. West was soundly beaten by Chamberlain in 1966. In 1971, Kareem received 133 of 153 first-place votes. It's mind-boggling how the Big Fella didn't get the remaining 20 first-place votes. In 1970, West had a legitimate shot—especially since Walt Frazier (fourth in voting) took some votes from teammate Willis Reed. But Frazier only received 4 of 150 first-place votes—and finished a distant fourth.

1972 MVP Voting

In 1972, West was on the 69–13 Lakers team that won 33 games in a row and went on to finally win the NBA Championship. West received 44 first-place votes and teammate Chamberlain received 36. They finished second and third, respectively, behind Kareem Abdul-Jabbar.

In that 1972 campaign, West and Chamberlain combined for 687 MVP votes, and 582 would have defeated Kareem. It would have been an impossible task for an 11-year-old Lakers fan who followed every game that season to choose between Chamberlain and West. (I'm fairly certain that if anyone had asked, I would have gone with Wilt first.) I'm sure it wasn't easier for the 1972 MVP voters. The number of blocks (for Chamberlain) and steals (for West) weren't kept in that season. West didn't help Chamberlain block shots, but Chamberlain did help West steal the ball. West could take chances at swiping the ball with his long arms, knowing that Chamberlain was behind him as the last line of defense. Chamberlain played defense and rebounded and was on the court more than 45 minutes per game. That's not to take anything away from Jerry's 1972 season.

Kareem Abdul-Jabbar deserved the MVP that year.

The Case for Abdul-Jabbar in 1972 That season, Kareem Abdul-Jabbar averaged 34.8 points per game. That not only led the league, it led the league by 6.6 points per game. He pulled down 16.6 rebounds per game—third in the league behind Chamberlain and Wes Unseld. The Bucks were 63–19. That was a drop of only three games from the previous NBA Championship season—despite the fact that Oscar Robertson missed 18 games with an injury. Kareem was successful on more than 57 percent of his shots—second to Chamberlain although Abdul-Jabbar took almost three times as many shots. Let's just put it like this: it wasn't a bad choice to vote this guy MVP that season.

The Case for Chamberlain in 1972 Prior to the season, Lakers coach Bill Sharman asked night owl Chamberlain to attend day-of-game practices, a previously unheard-of practice. Chamberlain bought into Sharman's practices and his running offense; he did everything asked of him. Chamberlain made 65 percent of his field goals, while averaging close to 15 points and 20 rebounds per game. If blocks were kept, Chamberlain might have averaged eight per game. The Lakers were 69–13, including defeating Abdul-Jabbar's Bucks 4–1 in the regular season. Then in the playoffs, the Lakers defeated them 4–2. The only way the Lakers could defeat the Bucks 8 of 11 games was if Chamberlain did the job on Abdul-Jabbar.

The Case for West in 1972 Kareem led the league in scoring, Chamberlain was first in rebounding, and West led the league in assists. West also averaged 25.8 points per game (seventh in the league) and 4.2 rebounds per game. He made the defensive first team. He performed brilliantly in the Lakers' 33-game winning streak. That streak started when Elgin Baylor retired. Baylor had played with West for 12 seasons—at that time, that was as long as any teammates had ever played alongside each other.

West's Contributions During Lakers' All-Time Winning Streak

No team—not even Jordan's great Bulls teams—ever approached 33 consecutive victories. West was 34 years old (ancient by 1972 standards). Here is what he did in 33 straight early-season games.

	Points	Rebounds	Assists
1.	19	5	6
2.	28	7	8
3.	29	1	8
4.	24	2	13
5.	20	8	10
6.	28	6	8
7.	19	4	11
8.	26	6	9
9.	25	5	4
10.	17	8	6
11.	22	5	13
12.	26	7	13
13.	25	2	18
14.	Did not play. Pat Riley started in his place.		
15.	45	6	5
16.	32	9	9
17.	20	7	10
18.	33	1	6
19.	38	6	11
20.	28	5	11
21.	26	1	14
22.	23	5	15
23.	22	5	9
24.	18	3	7
25.	24	3	10
26.	33	5	10
27.	37	6	9
28.	34	1	17
29.	24	2	8
30.	28	6	11
31.	27	5	12

	Points	Rebounds	Assists
32.	25	4	14
33.	12	1	13

The totals for those 32 games were 837 points (26.1 points/game), 147 rebounds (4.5 rebounds/game), and 328 assists (10.1 assists/game).

This guy didn't just lay it on the line every night during the regular season. He picked it up in the postseason. Oh, how he picked it up!

West's Career

Regular season	27.0 points/game
Postseason	29.1 points/game
NBA Finals	30.5 points/game

Highest Scoring Average in NBA Finals (min. 10 games)

1. Rick Barry	10 games	36.3 points/game
2. Shaquille O'Neal	19 games	34.2 points/game
3. Michael Jordan	35 games	33.6 points/game
4. Jerry West	55 games	30.5 points/game

Obviously, there aren't a lot of players who have been in more than 15 to 20 Finals games.

Most Finals Games Played

1. 70   Bill Russell
2. 64   Sam Jones
3. 56   Kareem Abdul-Jabbar
4. 55   Jerry West

West averaged 43.1 minutes per game in his 55 Finals games. Only Russell played more minutes. West averaged almost 31 points per game in the Finals—without benefit of a three-point shot. Jordan made 42 treys in his 35 NBA games. West had at least Jordan's range. It's fair to say West would have approached Jordan's 33 points per game in the Finals.

Of the 11 highest-scoring performances in NBA Finals history, West has three of them. He scored 53 points in Game 1 of the 1969 Finals (still the highest-scoring Game 1 of all time), and had a 45-point game in both the 1965 Finals and the 1966 Finals.

Chick Hearn called Jerry "Mr. Clutch," and the name was appropriate.

The Irony in Jerry's Finals Records

Until Michael Jordan surpassed it years later, West held an NBA Finals record by scoring 20 or more points in 25 consecutive Finals games. West finally scored less than 20 points in his team's greatest season. The irony: West scored fewer points (and shot worse) in the 1972 Finals—the only one the Lakers won in which Jerry played.

West's Lakers were 1–8 in NBA Finals. No one in history has suffered more losses in the championship round. The whole league was relieved and happy for him when the Lakers finally won in West's 12th season.

West in 1972 NBA Finals

Game 1	3 of 15 field goals	12 points	Lost 114–92
Game 2	6 of 21 field goals	15 points	Won 106–92
Game 3	10 of 28 field goals	21 points	Won 107–96
Game 4	9 of 25 field goals	28 points	Won 116–111
Game 5	10 of 28 field goals	23 points	Won 114–100

West averaged 19.8 points per game in the 1972 Finals on 38-of-81 field goal shooting. Let's just say that while everyone was happy that West finally drank champagne and won a title, it wasn't a hard choice in selecting Chamberlain (24 points, 29 rebounds in the final game) as Finals MVP.

Jerry West's Career Record in NBA Finals

Eight years the Lakers lost	50 games	31.6 points/game
One year the Lakers won	5 games	19.8 points/game

That's not meant to downgrade West. Prior to 1970, West had only Elgin Baylor to rely on to score points. Hey, Michael Jordan, *you* try to defeat a team full of Hall of Famers with Frank Selvy or Rudy LaRusso as your third-best player. West had Baylor and needed to shoot as much as he did in those 1960s NBA Championship series.

For example, in Red Auerbach's final NBA Championship, the Celtics defeated the Lakers 95–93 in Game 7. With the Celtics defense concentrating on Baylor (or Elgin just suffering from a poor shooting night, hitting 1 of 9 field goals in the first half and finishing with 18), the Lakers needed every one of Jerry's 36 points. Leroy Ellis was not going to do much against Bill Russell.

Typical Celebrities at the Lakers Games During the Early 1970s:

Buddy Hackett, Karl Malden, Walter Matthau, Andy Williams, Mike Connors, and Lorne Greene. Dr. Ernie Vandeweghe told me that it was actually his idea in the early 1960s—when the Lakers played in the Sports Arena—to give out four tickets courtside to celebrities. He said the first one was Dean Martin.

Who's Better, Who's Best
Jerry West or Michael Jordan
It's hard to imagine any player having similar statistics to Michael Jordan, but West can place his body of work next to anyone—including Jordan.

West	27.0 points	5.8 rebounds	6.7 assists
Jordan	30.1 points	6.2 rebounds	5.4 assists

I'm not crazy. One can't ignore Jordan's six titles to Jerry's one. For similar reasons, Magic Johnson and Bob Cousy won way too often to be ranked behind West. Oscar Robertson didn't win more than Jerry, but he nudges ahead of West as well.

Who's Better, Who's Best
Jerry West or Allan Houston
P. J. Carlesimo: "It's hard to find a comparable modern player to Jerry West. I'd say Allan Houston, because he's such a good shooter, but Jerry was in a different stratosphere than Allan."

West had 11 consecutive years averaging at least 25 points/game. Houston never averaged as many as 23 points/game.

Who's Better, Who's Best
Jerry West or Reggie Miller

No one in history hit more game-winning three-pointers than Miller. Of course, Jerry played in an era without benefit of the three-point shot *or* four rounds of playoffs that created many more opportunities for memorable postseason moments.

Jerry was the West Virginia boy who played his entire career in Los Angeles. Reggie was the L.A. city kid who played his entire career in the Midwest. *Everybody knows that "Beverly Hillbillies" was a better show than "Green Acres."* And everybody knows that West was a much better player than Miller.

Reggie Miller never averaged as many as 25 points in a game for a season. He has career averages of just three rebounds and three assists per game. He never made the All-Defense teams as West did. Reggie was selected for only five All-Star games.

Who's Better, Who's Best
Jerry West or Allen Iverson

Now, we're getting somewhere. We're getting closer.

| West | 27.0 points | 5.8 rebounds | 6.7 assists |
| Iverson | 27.0 points | 4.1 rebounds | 5.6 assists |

Iverson, similar to West, led the league in scoring. Iverson, like West, was spectacular in the NBA Finals. Iverson, similar to West, was MVP of an All-Star game. Allen knows the burden of carrying the offensive load—just as West did. Allen knows the pain Jerry suffered from breaking his nose nine times. No one takes a bigger pounding than Iverson when he drives to the hoop. West was the face of the league when he played. Iverson is as good a representative of the league as you'll find in the early 2000s. West played longer and won a title. But Iverson is gaining on the all-time greats, including Jerry West.

Who's Better, Who's Best
Jerry West or Kobe Bryant

Dr. Ernie Vandeweghe: "I would take Jerry for a couple of reasons. Jerry had two things over Kobe: speed and defense. Kobe plays great defense, but he didn't his first few years. And Kobe has speed, but not like West."

The first NBA games I ever saw in person were Lakers games in which the star was West. My father took me to those games at the Forum in Los Angeles—and deserves at least as much credit in making me a fan as West, Chamberlain, Goodrich, and Chick Hearn. I didn't see Oscar Robertson play much as a kid—maybe a couple of times in the playoffs, certainly. But I saw West. To me—and to my dad—West was the best guard of all time. When people are young, they tend to believe (a) what their dad tells them and (b) what they see firsthand. Then, they get older and form their own unique opinions. I had the opportunity to see Magic Johnson and Michael Jordan and Kobe Bryant play hundreds of times, often from courtside. But they'll never compare to Zeke from Cabin Creek. Not in my mind. Johnson was a better playmaker—and Jordan a better scorer and defensive player—and Bryant a wunderkind who might turn out to be better than the whole lot of players we're talking about. After people grow out of their rebellious youth, they often realize that those things their dad told them years ago make an awful lot of sense. Jerry West is a Cadillac. The world is driving sportier cars now.

They made a statue for Michael Jordan and put it in front of the basketball arena. They named a conference after Jerry. All the teams in the Lakers' geographic region play in the West. He's the symbol of the league and the symbol of my youth.

When I take my sons, Wyatt and Heath, to their first NBA games, it is to see Jason Kidd's teams. Kidd is not a flavor of the month, any more than West was. The Nets star has basketball genius running through his veins. Wyatt would fight before conceding that anyone is better than Kidd. I only hope my kids remain fans and take their children to a game in 30 years or so. They'll tell them how Kidd was awesome, but even he couldn't overcome the mighty Lakers.

Sometimes, east is east and West is west . . . but in this case, the twain certainly meet. In other chapters, I'll be objective about everything from kids to Kidds. But in this chapter, Jerry West is forever Mr. Clutch.

ELGIN BAYLOR
Everything But the Ring

MVP: 0	
MVP VOTING: 2nd in 1963; 7 years in top 5	
NBA TITLES: 0	
ALL-NBA FIRST TEAM: 10	
ALL-NBA SECOND TEAM: 0	

Elgin Baylor put up incredible numbers for the Lakers throughout the 1960s and was instrumental in bringing NBA basketball to the West Coast. Long before Julius Erving or Michael Jordan, Baylor was the unstoppable force, with a million moves that frustrated opponents and pleased fans. Baylor had many chances to win a championship, but fell just short. In this chapter, I'll examine how much that should weigh in ranking Baylor against the other elite players.

Baylor was All-NBA First Team in 10 different seasons, and only one player has ever achieved that distinction in more seasons. (Karl Malone has been selected 11 times.) Similar to Malone, Baylor was a scoring machine who played virtually his entire career with one of the great playmaking guards of all time, Jerry West. And similar to Malone, Baylor never won a scoring title, because another great player was hogging all the scoring championships during the era.

A Scoring Machine with No Titles

Elgin Baylor never won a scoring title. But just like Karl Malone, he came oh-so-close.

Year	Rank
1959	4th
1960	3rd
1961	2nd

Year	Rank
1962	8th (see below)
1963	2nd
1964	6th
1965	5th
1967	5th
1969	8th

In the 1962 season, Elgin played in only 48 of 80 games. He averaged 38.3 points per game during the season. The scoring title at the time went to the player who scored the most total points. Baylor finished eighth that season, despite missing 32 games. If the scoring title was decided (as it is today) by points per game—Baylor's 38.3 would have been second in the league that season, right behind Wilt Chamberlain. Only Chamberlain has ever averaged more per game in a season than Baylor's 38.3 in 1962.

Here's the interesting scoop on why Baylor only played 48 games that year. Elgin was healthy. If he wasn't the government would have reclassified him. Baylor had to go into the Army in midseason—although, he was able to play occasionally on weekends. If you're wondering why in the world this was necessary, Communist leaders were testing President Kennedy. They erected the Berlin Wall to divide the city. The president met the challenge by activating Army Reserve and National Guard units throughout the nation. The nation's military forces and retaliatory capability were expanded overnight. Private Elgin Baylor was ordered to report. From then on, Baylor was available to the NBA only during infrequent weekend passes. The Lakers and Baylor "saved" most of his leave time for the playoffs.

Dr. Ernie Vandeweghe: "I was the team doctor for the Lakers from 1960 to 1974. When the army called for Elgin, the Lakers sent me up to Seattle with him to see if I could get him better accommodations. Like a bed, instead of a cot. They figured since I had been an air force major, I had a little pull."

Baylor's Rookie Season

Do you think David Robinson or Larry Bird or Tim Duncan wrote the book on improving a team in his rookie season? Check back to 1959, when Elgin Baylor came into the league. He averaged 24.9 points per game (fourth in the NBA), and only Bill Russell and Bob Pettit had more rebounds. More important, he took a 19-win Lakers team and led them to the NBA Finals. In the All-Star game that year, Baylor shared MVP honors with Pettit. Minneapolis upset St. Louis (and Pettit) in the Western Conference finals, and the first Lakers-Celtics Finals would be played.

Also in Baylor's first two seasons, the team still played in Minneapolis. Bob Short had purchased the team but wasn't able to make it financially in Minneapolis. Short capitalized on Baylor's popularity on the West Coast by "farming out" Minneapolis home games to the West Coast. With the Boston Celtics as the opponent, the Lakers drew more than 11,000 fans for a game in Seattle, and then for Bill Russell's homecoming to San Francisco, drew more than 13,000 fans for a game at the Cow Palace. These games generated some much-needed revenue for Short.

Another way for Short to save money on travel costs was by purchasing a rebuilt World War II DC-3 to charter his team. One Sunday night in the middle of January 1961, after a game in St. Louis, the old plane's generator went out. With no electrical power, there was suddenly no interior lighting, no radio, and no heater in the plane. A light snow turned into a blizzard. The pilot finally told the team that he was lost—with fuel running dangerously low. The pilot plowed miraculously through a cornfield, pulling up just short of a fence. They had landed in a cornfield in Iowa. *Build it, and the sporting heroes will come.*

When the players flew west the next fall to Los Angeles, they flew commercial. Short got permission to move the Lakers only after promising to pay for the other teams' additional travel costs to Los Angeles.

Baylor's Scoring Feats

On December 11, 1960, the Lakers traveled to New York to take on the Knicks in the old Madison Square Garden. Back then, the hottest show on Broadway was "Camelot," and the nation had passed its torch to a new generation four weeks earlier by electing John Fitzgerald Kennedy president of the United States. Baylor was hotter that night at the Garden than Marilyn Monroe was in the same building a year later when she sang "Happy Birthday" to Kennedy. Baylor hit 15 of his first 20 shots that night, on his way to 34 first-half points—a Madison Square Garden record. The 10,132 fans were in an uproar in the fourth quarter. Their Knicks were not close, and the fans wanted Baylor to get the scoring record. Elgin picked up his fifth personal foul one minute into the fourth quarter. He all but ignored his defensive responsibilities after that, continuing to score on his twisting drives and outside shots. With less than five minutes remaining, he equaled the all-time mark of 64 points. In the game, Baylor made 28 of 48 shots. He also made

15 of 19 free throws. Not only that, but Elgin pulled down 25 rebounds. He went for 71 points—a record at the time.

There have been thousands of NBA games played since then, and rule changes have made some field goals worth 33 percent more points—but 70 points in a game is still a monumental achievement. Get this: Michael Jordan never did it. The only place Michael has ever shot 71 was on a golf course. By the way, Baylor broke the record of 64 points . . . that he himself had set, breaking Joe Fulk's 11-year-old record.

Michael Jordan Never Did This, Either

Jordan never scored 61 points in the NBA Finals. Baylor did—on April 14, 1962, in the fifth game of the NBA Finals between the Boston Celtics and Los Angeles Lakers. The series was tied 2–2. Baylor was guarded by Tom Sanders, considered a defensive specialist. If Baylor got past Sanders, then he had to deal with Bill Russell, considered the best defensive player of all time. Baylor hit 22 of 46 shots from the floor and scored 61 points to set a new Finals record, which has stood for 40 years. More important, it put Baylor's Lakers up 3–2 with a chance to go back to Los Angeles and win the NBA Championship.

Most 40-Point Games, Career

1. 271   Wilt Chamberlain
2. 173   Michael Jordan
3. 87   Elgin Baylor

Most 50-Point Games, Career

1. 118   Wilt Chamberlain
2. 31   Michael Jordan
3. 18   Elgin Baylor

Most 70-Point Games, Career

1. 6   Wilt Chamberlain
2. 1   Elgin Baylor, David Thompson, David Robinson

More Baylor Feats

Baylor's best MVP showing came in 1963, when he placed second to Bill Russell. Russell beat Baylor 256–196. Baylor was only 6-foot-5 but was a ferocious rebounder. In his rookie season, the Lakers played in Minneapolis, but he became a star in Los Angeles. In the 1960s, the city of Los Angeles had a lot of stars: Sandy Koufax and Don Drysdale.

Merlin Olsen and Deacon Jones. Jerry West and Elgin Baylor. Throw in Maury Wills in the early 1960s. There were college stars from UCLA, including Lew Alcindor in the mid-1960s, and from USC, such as O. J. Simpson in the late 1960s. The greatest testament to Baylor's greatness is that he never got squeezed out by these stars. No. 22 was as big a star in the sporting world as Los Angeles had to offer up.

Who's Better, Who's Best
Elgin Baylor or Bob Pettit

Pete Vecsey: "Pettit: I put him right behind Bird. Ahead of Baylor. . . . Elgin was not even close. Why? The day he retired, Jim McMillian—a steady influence—took his place in the starting lineup and the Lakers won 33 in a row."

Bob Ryan: "Elgin Baylor: he changed the game. He revolutionized the game more than anyone since Hank Luisetti, taking a mostly horizontal game and making it diagonal. He brought in all the reverse layups, the double fakes. He contributed so much after being hurt. He was a power forward—a great rebounder despite his 6-5 size."

Dr. Ernie Vandeweghe: "Pettit wasn't as mobile as Baylor. Elgin had it all. Elg could bring the ball up the court—he was a work of art."

Rod Thorn: "Elgin had a great fake . . . one of the first to hang in the air . . . one-handed shots . . . before he got hurt, he was a great player . . . by the end, he was playing with one-eighth of his kneecap gone—and he was still great."

What Thorn is referring to is that after six years of NBA play during which he had a leaping, driving style, Baylor's knees began to give out. The Lakers sent him to the Mayo Clinic, where they felt surgery wouldn't be worth the risk. But Baylor—following the 1965 season—wound up having surgery anyway. Dr. Robert Kerlan and Dr. Frank Jobe, the surgeons, peeled back the skin of Baylor's damaged knee. They removed the split and shattered upper eighth of the kneecap and then re-attached the tendons of the thigh muscles to the remaining part of the patella through tiny, carefully drilled holes.

This was not at the end of Baylor's career. He played another six seasons.

Although he had to miss the beginning of the 1966 season (because he put too much pressure strain on his "other" leg), he was soon almost as effective.

Vecsey referred to the Lakers winning the 33 consecutive games immediately following Baylor's retirement. The Lakers had added Chamberlain to their team of Baylor and West, beginning in the 1969 season. In that 1969 season, new Lakers coach Butch van Breda Kolff demanded that Chamberlain—for the first time in his career—play the high post, near the free throw line. Wilt was used to playing the low post, under the basket. But that is where Baylor set up and was most comfortable. The Lakers won 55 games and lost a seventh game in the Finals at home. In 1970, Chamberlain was limited to just 12 games due to an injury. In 1971, Baylor missed all but two games. Prior to the 1972 season, the Lakers named Bill Sharman as the new coach. Sharman installed a fast-breaking offense, in which the Lakers needed the forwards to constantly run. It was an ideal system for Chamberlain and a poor one for Baylor.

The addition of rookie Jim McMillian also posed problems for Baylor. Sharman and the Lakers handled the problem well. Sharman began the season with Baylor as a starter. When it became obvious the team needed to find more time for McMillian, Sharman met privately with Baylor. Elgin chose to retire rather than take a reduced role in a system that was foreign to him after 13 years.

Certainly, other superstars have been shown less respect at the end of their careers. It doesn't take anything away from Baylor's greatness, either. He did everything but win the last game of the season.

The Elusive Championship

Why couldn't Baylor win the big one—just once?

His teams lost the NBA Finals no less than eight times. Let me repeat that for speed readers who don't quite pay attention to every last word: Elgin's teams lost in the Finals eight different seasons!

They didn't get overmatched in those Finals, either. In college, Baylor led his Seattle University team to the NCAA Championship game. Naturally, they lost to the University of Kentucky (the Celtics of college ball, you might say). This was the first—but the first of many times—that Elgin was a single game away from winning it all.

If Baylor's teams had won any of these seven games, he would have been a champion:

1. **1958 NCAA Championship** Baylor was the tournament MVP despite the loss to Adolph Rupp's "Fiddling Five" at Freedom Hall in Louisville. Baylor was bothered by a rib injury, saddled with foul trouble, and benched by his coach John Castellani—prematurely, most basketball experts felt at the time—for most of the second half.

2. **1962 NBA Finals—Game 6: Boston 119–105 at L.A. Sports Arena** The Lakers led the series 3–2 and were home. At the half, the Lakers were in front 65–57 as Baylor had scored 21 points by intermission. But he would score only 13 in the second half, and Sam Jones (remember that name) would go nuts, winding up with a game-high 35. Boston forced a deciding Game 7.

3. **1962 NBA Finals—Game 7: Boston 110–107 at Boston** This one went to overtime. Boston led most of the way, but with 74 seconds left, the Lakers cut the lead to four. Frank Selvy made two hoops to tie the game. Selvy actually missed a potential game- and series-winner with three seconds left in regulation that would have prevented the Celtics' fourth championship in a row. Baylor scored 41 points but missed six free throws in the game (15 of 21 free throws)—any one of which might have been the difference. The papers reported he had to return to his army duties at Fort Lewis, Washington.

4. **1966 NBA Finals—Game 7: Boston 95–93 at Boston** This was the Celtics' eighth consecutive NBA Championship, and Red Auerbach's last game on the bench. He was able to light one last victory cigar mainly because Elgin's jumper took a vacation at the absolute worst time. Baylor hit only one of nine field goals for two points in the first half. Boston jumped out on top 10–0, and the Lakers never got as close as two points again until the final four seconds of the game.

5. **1969 NBA Finals—Game 6: Boston 99–90 at Boston** Jerry West had pulled a hamstring early in the series, and he was hobbling in this one. Baylor and West each scored 26 points, but it was not enough. Don Nelson scored 25 points. Game 7 time again . . . but it would be played in Los Angeles.

6. **1969 NBA Finals—Game 7: Boston 108–106 at the Forum** Jack Kent Cooke was the owner of the Lakers then. His to-do list the morning of Game 7 looked something like this: "Make sure West and Baylor get to game on time. Buy enough balloons. Hire a band." West got to the arena and scored 42 points. Nelson hit a shot that bounced in. Don't ask. The Celtics won their 11th title in 13 seasons in Russell's last game. In a bizarre coaching decision, Lakers coach Butch van Breda Kolff kept his star center, Chamberlain, tied to the bench for the final four minutes of the contest. After the game, van Breda Kolff said, "We were playing well without him."

7. **1970 NBA Finals—Game 7: New York 113–99 at Madison Square Garden** This was the game that Willis Reed hit a couple of shots early to inspire his team. Walt Frazier went off for 36 points and 19 assists. Often tagged with the role of loser, Chamberlain contributed 21 points and 24 rebounds. Elgin hit just 9 of 17 field goals and had a total of 19 points and five rebounds. The Lakers were never in this game.

How many players get one game away from a championship? Elgin had seven chances—including one that went into overtime.

I think my good friend Vecsey is a little harsh about Baylor. By all accounts, his knees were shot and he should have retired prior to the 1972 season. He could sense that the Lakers would be special and wanted so badly to be a part of it. When it became apparent that Baylor was slowing the team down, he willingly stepped aside for the good of the team. For that, he should be applauded, even three decades later.

In fact, there is a close comparison in another sport. Baylor, of course, was drafted by the Minneapolis Lakers in 1958 and retired in November 1971. The Lakers had dominated play just a few years prior to Baylor's arrival (winning five early NBA titles) and had a record-setting championship season as soon as he left. Sound familiar, Yankees fans? Don Mattingly missed the Yankees pennants in 1976, 1977, and 1978. He was called up in 1983 and led the Yankees for a dozen seasons. In 1994, with Mattingly slowed by back problems, it appeared the Yankees would finally get to the World Series again. But a work stoppage called the season off. Mattingly finally sniffed the postseason in his last season, 1995—but the Yankees lost in the first round. As soon as Donnie Ballgame left New York, the Yankees proceeded to make the postseason every year, winning the World Series in 1996, 1998, 1999, and 2000. It doesn't take anything away from Mattingly that the Yankees were able to win with a different first baseman (Tino Martinez). By 1996, Mattingly was not the batting champion he once was.

Was Baylor better than Pettit? Jeez, that's awfully close. Pettit retired as the NBA's all-time leading scorer. He was the first to score as many as 20,000 points. He won a championship. He won two MVPs (1956, 1959). He was thrice the MVP of the All-Star Game. Pettit averaged 26.4 points in his career, and Baylor averaged 27.4.

It's not just the extra point per game in the same era—although if we're splitting hairs, that counts—that explains why I have to give the nod to Pettit. He was more durable and he didn't have a superstar on the same level as West to play with. And he won. Still, some experts disagree. Tom Heinsohn was a superstar with the Celtics and actually was matched against Baylor. He puts Baylor on his list of all-time top five players—even ahead of Oscar Robertson. (Heinsohn gave me a starting five of Bill Russell, Larry Bird, Baylor, Bob Cousy, and West.) He didn't say Karl Malone. He didn't say Bob Pettit. He did make it a point to specifically mention Elgin Baylor.

Who's Better, Who's Best
Elgin Baylor or Charles Barkley
- Baylor played 134 playoff games without winning a championship.
- Barkley played 123 playoff games without winning a championship.

- Barkley was not even 6-foot-5 but pulled down 12,546 rebounds in his career.
- Baylor was listed at 6-foot-5 but pulled down 11,463 rebounds in his career.

Jack Ramsay: "Elgin had all kinds of herky-jerky moves. He was much quicker—and more fluid—than Charles. Elgin wasn't much on defense, but Charles was a horrendous defensive player himself."

Who's Better, Who's Best
Elgin Baylor or Rick Barry

Their careers overlapped a few years, as Barry entered the NBA in 1966. They played against each other for two years, although neither was near his best. Barry lasted 1,020 games in the ABA and NBA combined, whereas Baylor's career only lasted 794 games. Barry averaged 24.8 points per game in his career to Baylor's 27.4. Assuming Baylor could have played longer (with a lesser role, as Barry had), the scoring would be about a draw. Baylor was a much better rebounder. Barry was a much better passer. Barry was All-NBA or All-ABA First Team nine times, one less than Elgin. Baylor wasn't as good a shooter, but he was a better scorer.

Dr. Ernie Vandeweghe: "I'd compare them this way. Elg was a more physical athlete. Rick was so focused, so hyperactive as a player that it was almost more mental. Rick had a win-at-all-costs mentality. If you could stand Rick Barry, he made you a winner. Rick's teammates didn't care all that much for him. Baylor's teammates loved him."

In 1970, Leonard Koppett wrote in his *Twenty-Four Seconds to Shoot* that in 1959, the all-league team consisted of Pettit, Baylor, Russell, Cousy, and Sharman. One might put Schayes on it instead of Sharman, and assert that that was the best five-man unit imaginable in the history of the game to that point. A mere seven years later, one could name another all-time, all-star team that any of the above would have trouble making. Robertson and West would certainly usurp the backcourt positions, and Chamberlain would be the center. And who knows what levels Barry and Lucas might reach as forwards, pushing Schayes and Pettit into an honored but outdated category with Mikan. Baylor would be the hardest man to displace on this imaginary team.

He still is.

I have none of the personal recollection with Baylor that I do with West and Chamberlain. I saw Baylor play, but I didn't see what the fuss was all about. I saw Elgin at the end of his career. I wish I could have seen him at the top of his game.

MOSES MALONE
The Offensive Rebounding Master

MVP: 3	
MVP VOTING: Tied for 3rd in 1981, 5th in 1985	
NBA TITLES: 1	
ALL-NBA FIRST TEAM: 4	
ALL-NBA SECOND TEAM: 4	

In Petersburg, Virginia, in the early 1970s, Moses Malone was the best high school player in the country. He led Petersburg High to 50 consecutive wins and two consecutive state championships. At Five Star Basketball camp, led by a New Yorker named Howie Garfinkel, players were rated from one to five stars—Moses earned seven stars. Three to four *hundred* colleges went after Malone, offering all sorts of door prizes. It was reported that Oral Roberts offered to cure Malone's mother's bleeding ulcers by faith healing if he enrolled at Oral Roberts University.

The winner was the University of Maryland, coached then by Lefty Driesell. It was close to home and Malone enrolled. But after two days of classes, he learned that he had been drafted by the ABA's Utah Stars. The Stars offered a reported five-year, $3 million contract, and, with Driesell's blessing, Malone got himself a lawyer. This was historic: Moses Malone became the first player ever to go directly from high school ball to pro ball.

Malone's Pro Start

Malone was barely 19 when he went to Salt Lake City to play for the Stars. If Mohammed won't come to the mountain, at least Moses did. He made the adjustments very well: he averaged almost 19 points and 15 rebounds per game in his 83 games. In Malone's second year, he only played half a season after fracturing his foot. By the time he recovered, the Stars had gone bankrupt, and then the ABA itself folded.

At the start of the 1977 season, Malone spent a total of three weeks with NBA teams in Portland and Buffalo before being shipped down to Houston (there was some sort of prearranged deal involving draft choices). Buffalo didn't want him and did him a favor by shipping him to the Rockets, which needed his scoring and rebounding. The second season in Houston—1978—was the first of 13 consecutive seasons that Malone would average 19 points or more per game. He averaged at least 10 rebounds per game for 14 seasons in a row.

Malone was all work ethic. He couldn't jump a lick compared with some of the other players in the league. He wasn't bigger than any centers, either. He just wanted the ball more.

Doug Collins: "In 1977, Houston was in the East and my Philadelphia team met the Rockets in the Eastern Conference finals. Moses looked like Caldwell Jones then. He was thin as a twig. He was so skinny you wouldn't have believed it. He could always play, though."

His first three years in the league Malone was a forward. After his second year in Houston, the Rockets traded away their center, Kevin Kunnert, and Coach Tom Nissalke decided Malone would be the center. Back then, Malone weighed 220 pounds, so he started working out and lifting weights. He bulked up to 255 pounds. He was still one of the shortest starting centers in the league, but he became the most dominant.

Joe Maloof: "Moses Malone: he could do anything. He was tenacious. Greatest rebounder I ever saw. He was so smart. A real workhorse. He had great agility. Not muscular like players of today, either."

Cedric Maxwell: "Moses Malone is one of the best rebounders on the court. Not only then, but now. He played in the three-on-three sponsored game at the All-Star Weekend with women and celebrities and was just throwing those elbows around."

Fortunate Timing

Good Timing No. 1 Malone was a high school star when there were two pro basketball leagues competing for players and attention. The ABA offered Malone a chance and $3 million—at a time when the NBA wouldn't entertain the thought of a teenager entering its league. Moses became such a good player that when his contract expired, the Rockets made him the first player in team sports history to earn (listen up, Austin Powers fans) *one mil-lion dollars per year.* In 1981, Magic Johnson would sign a 25-year, $25 million contract that was very shortsighted (within a couple of years, that contract became a 10-year, $25 million deal for Magic). When Malone became a free agent following the 1982 season, the 76ers were willing to make Malone a six-year, $13.2 million contract. He was the first to make more than $2 million per year. It was good timing, but Malone earned every dime. Malone was the MVP in the 1982 season.

Good Timing No. 2 The NBA began keeping track of offensive rebounds in 1974. Three years later, Malone entered the NBA and dominated that category, setting almost every season and career mark. Previously, guys like Moses were supposed to work hard on every possession at rebounding their team's missed field goals. Now, Moses was being singularly praised for the job. It's as if they started keeping track of diaper changes almost immediately after a woman gives birth for the first time.

Good Timing No. 3 At a time when the NBA was suffering from too many players and stars doing drugs, Malone stayed out of harm's way. He had the respect of opponents such as Larry Bird and the friendship of teammates, including Julius Erving. He was not a threat to white fans, as Kareem Abdul-Jabbar was. Malone was a hardworking stiff like the fans—and could there be a more Judeo-Christian-friendly name than "Moses"?

He had two memorable quotes that really endeared him to fans. Before the 1981 NBA Finals, with his Rockets the decided underdogs, Malone said that he could beat the Celtics by himself with four guys from his Petersburg neighborhood. And after the Sixers went 12–1 in the 1983 postseason (winning three playoff series, 4–0, 4–1, and 4–0) Malone boasted that the Sixers went "Fo, Fi, Fo" to win it all.

Bob Ryan: "Moses Malone: really, really good. Fo, Fi, Fo. His 1983 [season] is still the gold standard for center play. Larry Bird was the president of the Moses Malone fan club. He liked him because he worked hard for everything."

Who's Better, Who's Best
Moses Malone or Kareem Abdul-Jabbar
Malone entered the NBA in 1977. Once Malone entered the league, it was hard to call Kareem the best center in the league.

MVPs

1978	Walton (Abdul-Jabbar was fourth)
1979	Malone
1980	Abdul-Jabbar
1981	Abdul-Jabbar third, Malone fourth
1982	Malone
1983	Malone

In 1984 neither center got an MVP vote. All votes went to Larry Bird, Bernard King, or Magic Johnson. In 1985, Malone was third with 218 points and Abdul-Jabbar was fourth with 206 points. The following year, 1986, Hakeem Olajuwon was fourth with 193 points and Abdul-Jabbar was fifth with 135 points.

The last year Malone would gather MVP votes was 1985 and 1986 was the last for Kareem. By then, Olajuwon was the best center in the game. Although Abdul-Jabbar would win his sixth (and last) MVP in 1980, you can see that other centers had passed Kareem following the 1977 season. If Bill Walton hadn't gotten hurt, it might have been the Walton-Malone era.

Offensive Rebounding Stats

How important is it to be the best offensive rebounder? Everyone calls Moses Malone the best offensive rebounder ever, and he may be. But how important is that?

The teams that get the most offensive rebounds are generally losing teams that don't shoot very accurately.

Most Offensive Rebounds Per Game By a Team in a Season

1. 18.5   Denver   1991
2. 18.4   Dallas   1995

That Denver team was only 20–62. The Dallas team was 13–69.

Most Offensive Rebounds, Career

1. 6,731   Moses Malone
2. 4,598   Robert Parish
3. 4,526   Buck Williams

Offensive rebounds have been charted only since 1974. Of players who began their careers after that and accumulated at least 10,000 rebounds, no one is close to Malone.

This table ranks only players with at least 9,000 career rebounds who began their careers after 1973.

Percentage of Offensive Rebounds (Out of Total Rebounds)

1. Moses Malone   41.5 percent of his 16,212 rebounds
2. Dennis Rodman   36.5 percent of his 11,954 rebounds
3. Charles Barkley   33.9 percent of his 12,546 rebounds
4. Shaquille O'Neal   32.7 percent of his 9,012 rebounds
5. Charles Oakley   32.1 percent of his 12,158 rebounds
6. Hakeem Olajuwon   32.1 percent of his 13,748 rebounds
7. David Robinson   29.3 percent of his 10,497 rebounds
8. Karl Malone   23.9 percent of his 14,601 rebounds
9. Patrick Ewing   23.7 percent of his 11,607 rebounds

Shaquille O'Neal has averaged four offensive rebounds per game in his first 11 years. That still means he had less than three thousand offensive rebounds after his 11th season. At that pace, he would need about 950 more games (about another 12 seasons for Shaq, following the 2003 season). As you can see, it's not even close. Moses was dedicated to the craft of offensive rebounds. Only Dennis Rodman had appreciably more than a third of his total rebounds on the offensive end.

There were great rebounders whose careers spanned the 1950s and 1960s before offensive rebounds were kept. Is it possible that any of those players had more offensive rebounds than Malone's 6,731?

There are only a few men in history who even had a chance at bettering Moses Malone's career number of offensive rebounds.

First off, even Malone's number is low. The NBA and ABA record books should be combined. It is deceiving to say Malone has the record of 6,731 offensive rebounds. He had quite a few in his first two years in the ABA—where they didn't keep track of offensive boards.

I'm just trying to convey a sense of whether anyone else has approached seven thousand offensive boards.

Career Rebounds

1. 23,924   Wilt Chamberlain
2. 21,620   Bill Russell
3. 17,834   Moses Malone (ABA included)
4. 17,440   Kareem Abdul-Jabbar
5. 16,330   Artis Gilmore (ABA included)
6. 16,279   Elvin Hayes
7. 14,715   Robert Parish
8. 14,601   Karl Malone

Starting at the bottom, let's knock off the candidates one by one. We know Karl Malone's total of offensive rebounds isn't close. Parish's total is known: he pulled down 4,598 offensive boards (31.2 percent of his career totals). Some applause for Chief is due; that is a very impressive total.

Now, we're getting into examining the big boys. Elvin Hayes is a player we can judge more precisely. His offensive boards are totaled for the last 11 of his 16 seasons. In his last 11 years, he pulled down 2,798 offensive boards (or 28.6 percent of his totals). Even if we assume that Hayes was more of a monster his first five years—we can only give him, what, 30 percent of his remaining 6,258 rebounds. That would give him an additional 1,877. That puts the Big E up at around 4,675. That's slightly more than Parish, who is second all-time in the record books that began tracking matters in 1974.

Artis Gilmore played his entire NBA career in the "offensive-rebounding-charting" era. Unfortunately for us, Artis played a good chunk of his career in the ABA. We do know that the A-Train pulled in 2,369 offensive rebounds of his 9,161 NBA rebounds (25.8 percent of his NBA rebounds). You want to give him 27 percent of his 7,169 ABA rebounds because you were a fan? I have no problem with that. That gives him 1,935 more. Add that to his 2,369 and we have a projection of 4,304. That's awfully generous of us, I might add.

Kareem Abdul-Jabbar spent 16 of his 20 years in the league in the era that charted offensive boards. We know that 2,975 of his last 12,369 rebounds were offensive. That's 24 percent of his total. I know, I know. In his later years, the Lakers had Bob McAdoo or Kurt Rambis to work hard on the boards. Let's be at least as generous with the Big Fella as we were with Gilmore. Let's give Kareem, oh, 30 percent of his first four seasons (5,071 rebounds). That's 1,521 more offensive boards. Add that to the 2,975 that we are sure of, and we have a total of 4,496.

Malone had 6,731 plus 40 percent of his ABA totals of 1,622 rebounds. That's around 7,379 offensive rebounds. In the history of the game, only two men can approach that— Wilt Chamberlain and Bill Russell. And even they probably didn't topple that.

Chamberlain had 23,924 rebounds in his career. I only saw him extensively in his last seasons, but I remember he thrived in Coach Sharman's running style, where he would get the defensive board and throw an outlet pass to get the break started. Chamberlain, even then, played 46 minutes per game and would get his rest by "basket hanging," or occasionally not making the full trip upcourt. When he did play offense (and this is true his entire career), he took turnaround bank shots and fadeaways—moving away from the basket. There will be little negative here about the game's most dominant player, but I seriously doubt that his offensive rebounds were anything close to 40 percent of his total. If 25 percent of Chamberlain's total was on the offensive end, that would put him around 5,981. But if the Big Dipper decided in some years he wanted offensive boards, then by golly, he was going to get them. Let's see what his total would have to be to break Malone's record.

Chamberlain would need 30.8 percent of his boards to be offensive to get to 7,379. If we knocked Moses Malone down to his 19 years of NBA action, Chamberlain would need only 28.1 percent of his boards to be offensive. Hmmm. Very close call. My gut feeling is that Chamberlain didn't have that many offensive rebounds, but (a) there's no way of knowing, and (b) if he wanted that many, or needed that many, he would have gotten them.

Bill Russell had 2,304 fewer rebounds than Chamberlain. He would have needed a boatload of offensive boards. Russell would have needed 34 percent to get to Malone's projected ABA and NBA total. He would have needed 31.2 percent to part Moses from the NBA-only offensive rebound record.

I didn't see Russell play except for classic Finals games on ESPN Classic. I know he was a great rebounder. My guess is that similar to Chamberlain, he was a better defensive rebounder and outlet passer, getting the break started.

This much is certain. No great rebounder ever pulled down a higher percentage of offensive boards than Moses Malone. Chamberlain or Russell may have pulled down a few more (but probably didn't). No one else is even in the same area code.

Moses Malone was a great rebounder, period. In the 2003 season, the Pistons' Ben Wallace was the leading rebounder in the league, despite playing on the team that finished 25th in rebounds. In 2002, Wallace (despite missing two games) pulled down 32.7 percent of Detroit's rebounds.

Who's Better, Who's Best
Moses Malone or Ben Wallace

Cedric Maxwell: "Are you nuts? Moses would have chewed Wallace up and spit him out! Moses had those long arms. He had the quickness, the leaping ability. He was a tenacious rebounder—as I guess Wallace is. Just look at the name. Moses. When you're known by one name, you're better."

Wallace's rebound totals in the early 2000s rank right up there with the top totals.

1992 Detroit	Dennis Rodman had 42.1 percent of his team's rebounds.
1979 Houston	Moses Malone had 38.4 percent of his team's rebounds.

By way of comparison, here are Wilt Chamberlain's and Bill Russell's totals.

Chamberlain's Percentage of His Team's Rebounds

1960	32.8 percent (missed three games)
1961	36.1 percent
1962	34.5 percent
1963	36.3 percent
1964	32.4 percent (new teammate Nate Thurmond)
1965	played for two teams
1966	34.3 percent
1967	34.3 percent
1968	33.0 percent
1969	36.0 percent
1970	missed all but 12 games
1971	34.9 percent
1972	34.0 percent
1973	33.4 percent

Bill Russell had 33.6 percent of all Celtics rebounds in 1964, his best season.

Malone's Percentage of His Team's Rebounds

1979	38.4 percent
1980	32.9 percent
1981	33.1 percent
1982	32.2 percent

Del Harris: "Moses is the most underrated of all the truly great players. . . . A very deserving three-time MVP. Look at his rebound numbers. He was a better rebounder than Shaquille O'Neal or David Robinson. He never, ever took a night off."

Who's Better, Who's Best
Moses Malone or Charles Barkley
Barkley never won a title. Moses did. Moses delivered.

Who's Better, Who's Best
Moses Malone or Amaré Stoudemire
Bob Ryan: "Today, there's a player whose game reminds me of his: 6-foot-10, 245-pound Amaré Stoudemire with the Suns. Only time will tell."

Moses Malone had the peak value that few players in history ever had (three MVPs in a four-year period). He had the career longevity that no one else could better. Moses Malone played 21 years of professional basketball. He played the first two in the ABA and the last 19 in the NBA. Only one other player—Robert Parish—played as long. There is no one who played as long, as well, and as hard—as Moses Malone.

JULIUS ERVING
The Incredible Dr. J

NBA MVP: 1	
ABA MVP: 3	
MVP VOTING: 2nd in 1980, 1st in 1981, 3rd in 1982, 5th in 1983	
NBA TITLES: 1	
ABA TITLES: 2	
ALL-NBA FIRST TEAM: 5	
ALL-NBA SECOND TEAM: 2	
ALL-ABA FIRST TEAM: 4	
ALL-ABA SECOND TEAM: 1	

In this chapter, I'll defend the tough task of placing Julius Erving behind legendary forwards Bob Pettit and Elgin Baylor. The elite forwards are more tightly bunched than the guards or centers. Erving's 11 seasons in the NBA showed averages of *merely* 22 points, 6.7 rebounds, and 3.9 assists. He was brilliant. He was a fan-favorite, high-flying player who had the respect of everyone. Yet his NBA career didn't measure up in length or in dominance to Pettit or Baylor. That being said, I want people to remember the ABA days.

I have memorized a few of the NBA's 746 pages in its annual *Official Guide*, which serves as the league's history book. On pages 206, 207, and 208, you can find everything about the ABA—well, that's all they see fit to print, anyway. Erving, for example, won four MVPs—and scored more than 30,000 points. But you have to be Sherlock (Freakin') Holmes to find that out by reading the NBA's *Official Guide*. You can't even find out how his Virginia Squires did in that 1972 season. We're left with ABA Championship series results and the all-time (not single-season) records of teams. There is so much ABA history that is left out.

His ABA Career

Erving left the University of Massachusetts after his junior year to sign with the ABA. That was the modus operandi of the red, white, and blue league back then. The NBA still didn't allow underclassmen in its league, but the ABA welcomed them.

As a rookie with the Virginia Squires in 1972, Erving averaged more than 27 points and almost 16 rebounds—which compares quite favorably to the other elite forwards. In 1959, Baylor averaged 24.9 points and 15 rebounds per game. In 1980, Bird averaged 21.3 points, 10.4 rebounds, and 4.5 assists. Julius played four more seasons in the ABA, leading the league in scoring three times and winning (or sharing) the MVP three times.

After his first five seasons (all in the ABA), Erving averaged 28.7 points per game. Following the 1976 season, the ABA merged four teams—including Erving's Nets—into the league. At this same point in time, Bird—who would be forever compared and linked to Erving—was a transfer student at Indiana State, yet to play his first college basketball game.

Mark Cuban: "I can't give you the three best players of all time, but I can give you my two favorites. I grew up in Pittsburgh, and was one of the six hundred fans who would see Connie Hawkins play for the Pipers. I was a huge ABA fan, and my two guys were Connie and Julius Erving."

Since the NBA guide doesn't include the list of career scoring leaders for the ABA, I'll include it here.

ABA Scoring Leaders

1. 13,726 points   Louis Dampier
2. 12,823 points   Dan Issel
3. 12,153 points   Ron Boone
4. 11,705 points   Mel Daniels
5. 11,662 points   Julius Erving

There were a dozen players to score at least 10,000 points in the ABA, including my friend Steve "Snapper" Jones.

Who's Better, Who's Best
Julius Erving or Larry Bird

Kevin Loughery: "In the ABA, we played Denver in the finals that last year—and we asked Doc to do everything. His series versus Denver was simply incredible. I can't choose between Erving and Bird because they have different styles. I will say this: Put Dr. J with [Robert] Parish and [Kevin] McHale and those teams would have won a string of titles."

1976 ABA Finals

It was a matchup of the Denver Nuggets and the New York Nets. Larry Brown coached the Nuggets, and Loughery was in charge of the Nets. The first game of the series was a classic. A full house of more than 19,000 fans in Denver's McNichols Arena saw the best defensive player in the league—Bobby Jones—try everything to stop the Doctor. The score was tied at 118–118 when Julius hit a turnaround 21-foot jump shot over Jones that stunned the crowd. They were points 44 and 45 for Dr. J. He also grabbed 12 rebounds, had four assists, and hit 17 of 25 shots from the field.

In the second game of the series, Erving scored a whopping 48 points. Throughout the series, Erving and David Thompson waged a scoring battle. The sixth game would prove to be the last one in the nine-year history of the league. It was one of the best. The Nets were up in the series 3–2, and the Nuggets jumped out to a 22-point lead in the third quarter. The Nets came back and overcame a 42-point effort by Thompson. Erving was the MVP for the series, the season, and the entire history of the league.

That would be the last professional basketball championship the New York metropolitan area would win, to date. The WNBA Liberty team lost in the Finals a couple of times, as did the Knicks. The Nets lost in the Finals in 2002 and 2003.

That sixth game of the 1976 Finals would also be the last that Julius ever played for the Nets. The leagues merged, and a prolonged contract dispute occurred. Erving was dealt to the Philadelphia 76ers a day before the next season. Erving would remain with the Sixers for all 11 years of his NBA career.

Marv Albert: "The ABA was perfect for Erving, with its free-flowing game. Don't get me wrong, he was still an All-Star when he entered the NBA, but he wasn't the same player that ABA fans knew. The thing that I remember about Erving is that he—like Jordan in a later era—never took a night off. In his day, when a lot of games weren't televised, it would have been easy to hide a bad game. But Erving played hard every single night. He had to live up to his reputation. He always amazed me with how he dealt with people. There was so much pressure on him—but he was always the most courteous. The last player to leave and only after he answered everyone's questions."

Jerry Sloan: "I would probably compare Dr. J's game with Elgin Baylor's."

Who's Better, Who's Best
Julius Erving or Elgin Baylor

Erving was compared to Baylor because of his aerial, high-flying antics. He wasn't a great shooting forward like Rick Barry, a defensive specialist in the style of Dave DeBusschere, or a relentless rebounder à la Pettit. No, this was the next generation of Elgin Baylor.

- Baylor played 846 NBA games.
- Erving played 836 NBA games.

Give Baylor extra credit for playing the second half of his career with crippled knees (repaired with 1960s technology and know-how). Give Erving credit for starting his NBA career four chronological years later than Elg.

- Baylor averaged 27.4 points, 13.5 rebounds, and 4.3 assists.
- Erving averaged 22.0 points, 6.7 rebounds, and 3.9 assists.

Who's Better, Who's Best
Julius Erving or Bob Pettit

Pettit also played a comparable number of NBA games to the Doctor—792. Bob Pettit averaged 26.4 points, 16.2 rebounds, and three assists. Put it like this: Pettit had more rebounds in his 792 games (12,851) than Julius did in his 1,243 professional games (10,525).

- Erving was All-NBA First Team in five of his 11 NBA seasons.
- Pettit was All-NBA First Team in 10 of his 11 NBA seasons.

I'm not putting Erving down to place him behind the aforementioned superstars. His placement at fifteenth-best still seems low, I realize. He was a tremendous player.

Phil Jasner: "Julius: If you went to watch Julius Erving play every single night—you would learn something new that you hadn't seen before. You can't say that about too many players."

Erving's Place in the NBA

Erving became the role model and later the elder statesman of the league. His teammates and opponents looked up to him. He entered the NBA with a talented Philadelphia team that had won 46 games in 1976, despite losing forward Billy Cunningham to a career-ending injury. The team still had a pair of 20-point/game scorers in George McGinnis and Doug Collins.

Erving blended his talents so well that McGinnis and Collins averaged almost the same as they had the year before without the Doctor in the house.

The 1977 Philadelphia 76ers defeated the Celtics and Rockets to advance to the NBA Finals for the first time since 1967. They took the first two games, and Erving was close to winning back-to-back championships.

But the Portland Trail Blazers had other ideas. Forward Bobby Gross made Erving work hard for his points. An errant Darryl Dawkins elbow caught Collins by mistake, and the Blazers swept the final four games of the series.

That was the beginning of a frustrating playoff résumé for Erving. In the 1977 Finals, Philadelphia had the home court advantage and a 2–0 lead. They lost the series.

In 1978, Philadelphia won 55 games—best in the Eastern Conference—and they were the highest-scoring team in the league. But they were upset by the 44–38 Washington Bullets in the Eastern finals.

In 1979, the Sixers lost a Game 7 to San Antonio in the Eastern semis.

The following season, Philadelphia returned to the Finals in what remains the Golden Year in Philadelphia sports history (the Phillies went to the World Series, the Sixers to the NBA Finals, the Flyers advanced to the Stanley Cup Finals, and the Eagles made it to the Super Bowl).

Julius averaged 25.5 points per game against the Lakers in the six-game Finals, but it was not enough. Kareem Abdul-Jabbar averaged 33.4 points in the first five games. Then Magic Johnson played center for an injured Kareem and scored 42 in the sixth game.

In 1981, the Sixers blew a 3–1 lead in the Eastern Conference finals against Larry Bird's Celtics. The following year, the Sixers overcame the Celtics, but lost again in the Finals to the Lakers.

Erving had now played in the NBA six years and had lost in the NBA Finals three times. The common denominator in these defeats was the fact that Philadelphia was losing the battle in the middle. Bill Walton had dominated the 1977 series. Wes Unseld dominated the 1978 playoff series. Kareem Abdul-Jabbar (and Magic) won the center battle in 1980 and 1982. Robert Parish and Kevin McHale gave the Sixers fits.

The 76ers signed free agent Moses Malone when he was the best center in the game—and Philadelphia won its second (and last) NBA Championship.

After that season, Bird's career went into overdrive and Erving couldn't keep pace. Bird would win the league MVP in 1984, 1985, and 1986, leading the Celtics into the Finals each year. As Bob Ryan recalled earlier in the Larry Bird chapter, their rivalry culminated on November 9, 1984, at Boston when Bird and Erving got into their fight.

In the last three seasons, Erving would play a lot at guard, making way for young forward Charles Barkley. Dr. J was still a productive player, even with his average going down two points a season in his last four years (from 22 to 20 to 18 to 16).

In 1987, his last year—his 16th professional season—Erving still averaged 16.8 points per game at the age of 37.

Best Final Seasons for Elite Players Who Played at Least 16 Years

Julius Erving	16 years	37 years old	16.8 points/game	1987
John Havlicek	16 years	37 years old	16.1 points/game	1978
Charles Barkley	16 years	37 years old	14.5 points/game	2000
Dan Issel	15 years	36 years old	12.8 points/game	1985
Kareem Abdul-Jabbar	20 years	42 years old	10.1 points/game	1989

Julius was the second-leading scorer to Barkley on a 45-win Sixers team that went out in the first round.

Charles only played 20 games due to injury. If he had left after the 1999 season, he would have gone out in a season that saw him play 84 percent of the games (42 of 50) and average 16.1 points per game. He would have easily led the league in dribbles that season. He also had one last playoff game that year.

Issel scored more than 27,000 points in his ABA and NBA days—and was a 20-point scorer at the age of 35. In his final season, he averaged 12.8 points on a first-place Denver team that went all the way to the Western Conference finals.

Kareem was the fifth-leading scorer on a Lakers team that went to the Finals before being swept by the Pistons.

Hondo was the starting guard in a mess of a year for the Celtics—they were two years away from Bird. Midway through the season, the Celtics traded guard Charlie Scott for Kermit Washington. That meant Boston had a starting backcourt of 38-year-old John Havlicek and 35-year-old Dave Bing, also in his final season. Not all was lost for Boston. After the season, they dealt Washington (and others) to the Clippers for Nate Archibald (and others).

Most great players—including Jordan and Chamberlain—retired before playing a 16th professional season. The NBA had a different makeup when Erving retired. In today's NBA, the ages of the players range from their late teens to the early forties. It wasn't that way when the Doctor played.

At the end of the 1990 season (after Kareem finally called it quits), the league had only two players 37 years or older (Parish and John Lucas). There were only a handful of others (Alex English, Rickey Green, Walter Davis, and Dennis Johnson) who were 36.

Everyone in the league was pretty much between the ages of 22 and 32.

Now, they come early and leave late. There's more money to be made, and players aren't willing to leave any of it on the table.

And yet, they still can't approach what Erving did in his 16 seasons. When he retired, he was the third-leading scorer in professional basketball. Only Abdul-Jabbar and Wilt Chamberlain had scored more.

Erving saved the ABA and helped spur the merger. He was the game's unofficial ambassador and paved the way for Michael Jordan.

I don't take too many points away for the five years of ABA competition. He rates above all but a few forwards who ever played the game. Baylor retired in November 1971—just nine games into the season. That was Julius Erving's rookie season with the Virginia Squires. Erving bridged the gap between Baylor and Jordan. Baylor and Jordan were each the best at their positions for most of their NBA careers. You just can't say the same about Erving.

HAKEEM OLAJUWON
The NBA's Best in the Mid-1990s

MVP: 1	
MVP VOTING: 6 years in the top 5	
NBA TITLES: 2	
ALL-NBA FIRST TEAM: 6	
ALL-NBA SECOND TEAM: 3	

Hakeem Olajuwon grew up in Nigeria and didn't even pick up a basketball until he was nearly 17. It's an incredible story that just a few years later, he was playing for the National Championship at the University of Houston. No center in history has played more games for a franchise than Hakeem Olajuwon did for the Houston Rockets from 1985 to 2001. Only four players—John Stockton and Karl Malone of the Jazz; John Havlicek of the Celtics; and Reggie Miller of the Pacers—ever played more games for one team. Olajuwon grew to love the city of Houston, and the city of Houston loved him back.

He was the first player picked in the 1984 NBA draft. It's a testament to Olajuwon that no one ever criticized the selection, despite the Rockets bypassing Michael Jordan.

Most Games Played at Center for a Franchise

1.	1,177	Hakeem Olajuwon for Houston
2.	1,106	Robert Parish for Boston
3.	1,093	Kareem Abdul-Jabbar for Los Angeles
4.	1,039	Patrick Ewing for New York

Now, Olajuwon wasn't at the top of his game for each of those 1,177 contests. But he was at the top for a very long period of time. He was voted All-NBA Second Team in

1986 and All-NBA Third Team in 1999, making him one of the two or three best centers in the game 13 years apart. Olajuwon had so many skills. On March 29, 1990, he had a quadruple double against the Milwaukee Bucks—18 points, 16 rebounds, 10 assists, and 11 blocked shots.

The Rockets have really had a history of great centers. Following the 2003 regular season, three men who played at center for the Rockets (Moses Malone, Elvin Hayes, and Hakeem) were among the seven top point scorers of all time. And the 2003 season brought another all-star center to Houston—Yao Ming.

Postseason Performance

Hakeem is so highly thought of in large part because of his postseason play.

Most Points/Game, NBA Finals (min. 10 games)

1.	Rick Barry	10 games	36.3 points
2.	Shaquille O'Neal	19 games	34.2 points
3.	Michael Jordan	35 games	33.6 points
4.	Jerry West	55 games	30.5 points
5.	Bob Pettit	25 games	28.4 points
6.	Hakeem Olajuwon	17 games	27.5 points

Olajuwon blocked 54 shots in those 17 Finals games, more than three per game. Since they started keeping track of blocks in 1974, only one player (Kareem Abdul-Jabbar) has had more blocks in the Finals. And, of course, Abdul-Jabbar played many more games.

Olajuwon was unstoppable in the 1986 Finals, averaging more than 25 points, 12 rebounds, and three blocked shots against the greatest frontcourt in history. The 1986 Celtics were 40–1 at home and 10–0 in the postseason at home. Olajuwon's eight blocks in the fifth game cut the Celtics' lead to 3–2.

Olajuwon is one of the greatest big game players in history. Most of the other legendary players who were known as clutch or big game performers (Jerry West, Reggie Miller, and Michael Jordan) were perimeter players who handled the ball and were always able to get their shot off. Olajuwon was the finest big game center that ever played.

Olajuwon

1986 Rockets	23.5 points/game, regular season	26.9 points/game, playoffs
1994 Rockets	27.3 points/game, regular season	28.9 points/game, playoffs
1995 Rockets	27.8 points/game, regular season	33.0 points/game, playoffs

Scoring Averages

Regular season	21.8 points/game
First three rounds of playoffs	25.6 points/game
17 Finals games	27.5 points/game

Now, compare that to his two closest contemporaries.

David Robinson

Regular season	21.9 points/game
100 playoff games	20.4 points/game

Patrick Ewing

Regular season	20.9 points/game
139 playoff games	20.2 points/game

In mano-a-mano playoff action, Olajuwon clearly outplayed both Robinson and Ewing. In the 1995 Finals, he clearly outplayed O'Neal—although it was a little unfair since Hakeem was in the prime of his career and Shaq was only at the very beginning of his.

Olajuwon Meets Robinson: 1995 Western Conference Finals

First, let's set up the participants. Robinson was the MVP in 1995, the league's best player. The Spurs had the better team, and the home court advantage in the series.

Do you remember what happened?

The Rockets took the first two games in San Antonio. The Spurs came back and won the next two in Houston. The Rockets won the next two games and won the series 4–2. For the series, Robinson averaged 23.8 points, 11.3 rebounds, 2.7 assists, and 1.5 steals. Olajuwon's numbers were 35.3 points, 12.5 rebounds, five assists, 4.1 blocks. and 1.3 steals. Here's how it went game by game.

Game 1	Olajuwon	27 points	Robinson	21 points
Game 2	Olajuwon	41 points	Robinson	32 points
Game 3	Olajuwon	43 points	Robinson	29 points
Game 4	Olajuwon	20 points	Robinson	20 points
Game 5	Olajuwon	42 points	Robinson	22 points
Game 6	Olajuwon	39 points	Robinson	19 points

I can't find a more dominating performance against a league MVP on a superior team in the postseason. In the last two games, Hakeem outscored Robinson 81–41.

Sean Elliott: "It was the most dominating performance by a player that I was ever witness to. But I blame our (San Antonio's) marketing department. Hakeem had won the MVP award the previous year and felt he deserved it in 1995. David won it, and it was announced right before our [Western Conference finals] series started. The first game was in San Antonio, and they put together a tape with a collage of great Robinson plays. I found out later that the tape [and the naming of Robinson as MVP] spurred Olajuwon to new heights. Olajuwon was just unstoppable. But it wasn't just David's fault. Dennis [Rodman] was intent on getting every rebound, but he wouldn't come out and guard anyone. That's why Robert Horry killed us in that series. Dennis wouldn't guard him! That doesn't take anything away from Hakeem in the series. He was just awesome."

Olajuwon Meets Ewing: 1994 NBA Finals

Game 1	Olajuwon 28 points	Ewing 23 points
Game 2	Olajuwon 25 points	Ewing 16 points
Game 3	Olajuwon 21 points	Ewing 18 points
Game 4	Olajuwon 32 points	Ewing 15 points
Game 5	Olajuwon 27 points	Ewing 25 points
Game 6	Olajuwon 30 points	Ewing 19 points
Game 7	Olajuwon 25 points	Ewing 17 points
Ewing in series	18.9 points	.363 field goal average
Olajuwon in series	26.9 points	.500 field goal average

Olajuwon outscored Ewing in all seven games. In the two regular-season games played between Olajuwon and Ewing in 1994, Olajuwon averaged 33 points and 16.5 rebounds to Ewing's 12 points and 9.5 rebounds.

Olajuwon Meets Shaquille O'Neal: 1995 NBA Finals

Game 1	Olajuwon	31 points	O'Neal	26 points
Game 2	Olajuwon	34 points	O'Neal	33 points
Game 3	Olajuwon	31 points	O'Neal	28 points
Game 4	Olajuwon	35 points	O'Neal	25 points

Olajuwon outscored Shaq in all four games. By the end of those 1995 Finals, Olajuwon was clearly ahead of Robinson and Ewing.

O'Neal, in a 1995 interview, called Olajuwon the best center in the game. "He's got great moves, a great attitude. He's a class act. I have no problem with Hakeem being called the best player in the game." Of course, at the time, Olajuwon and O'Neal were represented by the same agent and agency. But O'Neal was giving respect to the right player.

Olajuwon and Moses Malone

Olajuwon	1,238 games	44,222 minutes	26,946 points	21.8 average points/game
Malone (NBA only)	1,329 games	45,071 minutes	27,409 points	20.6 average points/game

The numbers may have been close, but Moses and Hakeem scored their 27,000 points very differently. Malone did all his work under the basket or on the free throw line.

Olajuwon	7,621 free throw attempts (6.1 free throw attempts per game)
Malone	11,090 free throw attempts (8.3 free throw attempts per game)

Olajuwon used the shake-and-bake moves, ran the court better than most big men, and was able to time his jumps to block shots. He took a lot of outside shots and perhaps that added to his longevity.

Who's Better, Who's Best
Hakeem Olajuwon or Amaré Stoudemire

One of Hakeem's former teammates, Eddie Johnson, a radio analyst for the 2003 Phoenix Suns, observed the raw rookie Stoudemire and told me that Amaré mirrors Hakeem in so many ways. Hakeem had those cat-quick moves in the post. And so does Amaré. Hakeem had the spin moves, loved to harass guards, and was able to get a lot of steals. Johnson saw all of those traits in Stoudemire. Amaré has a long way to go, but to remind people of Olajuwon at such a young age speaks volumes about the rising Sun.

Other Ways to Measure Olajuwon's Greatness

I remember when Doug Collins would tell me how great Michael Jordan played for him in 1987 and 1988. He loved the fact that Jordan had at least 100 steals and 100 blocks in the season. (Jordan had 125 and 131 blocks those two seasons, the only two in which he had more than 100 blocks.)

Since they began keeping track of blocks and steals (1974), the feat of getting at least 100 of each has only been done about 110 times in almost 30 years.

Obviously, it favors a big man, because guards just don't average more than a block per game.

Malone never did it. McHale never did it. O'Neal never did it. Ewing did it twice. Robinson did it seven times.

Hakeem Olajuwon did it 12 times.

He would have done it 13 times, but in his rookie season, he had just 99 steals.

He would have also done it in 1999, but they only played 50 games that season. Olajuwon had 82 steals in those 50 games.

Olajuwon in 1989: 213 Steals, 282 Blocks

Olajuwon has the NBA record (again, since they began crediting blocks in 1974) for most blocks.

Most Career Blocks

1. 3,830   Hakeem Olajuwon
2. 3,189   Kareem Abdul-Jabbar
3. 3,064   Mark Eaton

Now, for a few drawbacks to Olajuwon's career record for blocks.

1. It is almost certain that Chamberlain and Bill Russell would have had more blocks.
2. Abdul-Jabbar had 3,189—and played his first four years without the stat being kept. In his 1974 season (Kareem's fifth in the league), he blocked 283 shots in 81 games. If we simply apply his per-game average to his first four seasons, we would have to credit him with another 1,122 blocks. That would bring him up to around 4,310. I'd feel a whole lot better calling Hakeem the all-time blocks leader (at least post Wilt/Russell) if his career total was up around 4,300. You can go to the bank on this one, folks. Abdul-Jabbar had more than 700 blocks in his first 321 games. In the first two years that they kept blocks, Abdul-Jabbar averaged 3.5 per game.
3. Dikembe Mutombo has averaged 3.38 blocks per game in his career and may approach Hakeem's total in the next few seasons.

Olajuwon in the 1990s

Olajuwon's 1995 Rockets eliminated four teams that won 50+ games, including the San Antonio Spurs (62–20), the Utah Jazz (60–22), the Phoenix Suns (59–23), and the Orlando Magic (57–25). The 1995 Rockets were also one of only three teams to defeat a pair of 60-win teams. In 1973, the Knicks defeated the 68-win Celtics and the 60-win Lakers. In 1993, the Bulls defeated the 60-win Knicks and the 62-win Suns.

On March 9, 1991, Olajuwon added an *H* to his first name for religious reasons. He also added a *C* for "controversy" to his newspaper clips; the first hint of controversy in his career to that point. Olajuwon never had anywhere near the largest salary in the league, and the Rockets offered a contract extension that didn't suit him. What happened next is a matter of which party to believe. Olajuwon claimed he was injured. The Rockets claimed otherwise. Olajuwon demanded a trade. The Rockets suspended Olajuwon. Eventually, the Rockets not only re-signed Olajuwon to a contract that was fair to both sides, they hired Rudy Tomjanovich as head coach. Olajuwon responded with his career-best seasons, despite being over age 30.

You had to drive a stake through this vampire to kill him. Olajuwon just wouldn't go down easily.

Once Tomjanovich came aboard in 1992, Olajuwon resolved his differences with the club and began a period as the best center in the game. And get this: beginning in 1992,

Olajuwon's teams were 14–6 when facing elimination. For a comparison, O'Neal's teams are 5–7 when facing elimination and 1–6 prior to the Lakers' three-peat.

In closing, I want to mention the vivid photo in this book of Hakeem Olajuwon, Yao Ming, and Moses Malone. It just fills my heart with joy knowing that one young man can grow up in Africa, another in China, and still another in the United States—and all three can spend the best part of their adult lives striving to win championships for the Houston Rockets.

KARL MALONE

The Compiler

MVP: 2	
MVP VOTING: 9 finishes in the top 5	
NBA TITLES: 0	
ALL-NBA FIRST TEAM: 11	
ALL-NBA SECOND TEAM: 2	

In this chapter, I'll state the case for Karl Malone, whose body of work on the hardwood most resembles Elgin Baylor and Charles Barkley. Other players had a career peak similar to Malone, but no one had the longevity. Many people call Malone the greatest power forward of all time. It's hard to argue with that. Malone started receiving MVP votes back in 1987. In 1988, he was in the top 10. In 1989, he finished third behind Magic Johnson and Michael Jordan. For a three-year period (MVPs in 1997 and 1999, sandwiched between a second-place finish in 1988 to Jordan), Malone was considered the best (or second-best, to Jordan). It is the sum total of the 18 years and the nightly 24 points and 10 rebounds that makes Malone unique. Entering the 2004 season, Malone needed just 2,013 points to overtake Abdul-Jabbar as the league's all-time scorer.

Malone's Consistency

Malone's career is filled with accomplishments that would highlight almost any other player's résumé. He was named First Team All-Defense three times. He was selected to 14 All-Star Games. It goes on and on. But Malone's career has been more workmanlike than flashy, more consistent than spectacular. So, where should this compiler of numbers and longevity records rank?

Malone's career is one reason I began work on this book. Prior to the 1998 NBA Finals, NBC was billing the matchup between the Chicago Bulls and Utah Jazz as a matchup that featured four of the 50 greatest players in NBA history.

Timeout. I remember telling Bob Costas that it was a disservice to Malone and Jordan to call them out as part of the 50 greatest. It was mind-boggling that the first honor and achievement under Karl Malone's name in the *Jazz Media Guide* (and the *NBA Official Register*) was being named to the 50 Greatest List (that list, of course, does not rank any players ahead of or behind anyone else).

When you talk about Malone, I told Costas, you are talking about one of the 20 greatest players in NBA history. He was a foundation player—one that every youngster learning about the NBA should know about. He was one of the three or four best forwards.

I also pointed out to Costas that Malone's career suffered from expansion.

Look, Major League Baseball has always had an American League and a National League. Despite interleague play and player movement that has long since dissolved any differences within the leagues, there are two distinct leagues that choose to each award an MVP—a batting champion, a home run champion, and so on.

The NBA has always had its Eastern Champion meet the Western Champion in the NBA Finals. Since expansion has bloated the league from 23 teams to 29 during Malone's career, it would have made perfect sense to award MVPs and scoring champions from both conferences.

NBA Expansion

1967	9 teams
1969	14 teams
1971	17 teams
1977	22 teams
1981	23 teams
1991	27 teams
2001	29 teams

It is harder to be a scoring champion or MVP when one is competing with 300 other players on 28 other teams. A player in 1969 (such as Elgin Baylor) competed for league honors with 150 other players on 13 other teams, for instance.

Not that it's the league's business to build up additional honors and awards for players, but I went back and imagined a world in which the NBA gave East and West MVPs and scoring champions.

Malone never won the NBA scoring title. But look at what the numbers would look like if a Western scoring champion had been awarded.

Malone Among Western Scoring Leaders

Year	Rank	Average
1988	1st	27.7 points/game
1989	1st	29.1 points/game
1990	1st	31.0 points/game
1991	1st	29.0 points/game
1992	1st	28.0 points/game
1993	1st	27.0 points/game
1994	3rd	25.2 points/game
1995	3rd	26.7 points/game
1996	2nd	25.7 points/game
1997	1st	27.4 points/game
1998	2nd	27.0 points/game
1999	2nd	23.8 points/game
2000	2nd	25.5 points/game

Malone would have won seven scoring titles, instead of zero. Malone finished second in the entire NBA to Michael Jordan in 1989, 1990, 1991, 1992, and 1997. It's as if Stan Musial (who won seven National League batting titles) had won zero, because he would have continually lost out to Boston's Ted Williams.

Malone, who won two MVPs when competing with the entire league, would have picked up an additional trophy in 1998 as the top vote-getter in the West.

His Amazing Longevity

In his first 18 NBA seasons, the Utah Jazz played 1,444 regular-season games, and Malone played in 1,434 of them (99.3 percent). Except for the first five games of his 1986 rookie season, he has started all that he has taken part in.

The first 263 games of Malone's career were coached by Frank Layden. Jerry Sloan replaced Layden 17 games into the 1989 season. With their blending of style and success, Sloan, Malone, and John Stockton formed one of the longest-lasting marriages in team sports history.

Karl almost didn't play his career in Salt Lake City . . . he almost spent 18 years in Sacramento (which, incidentally, can be done in almost any weekend). In 1985, the Jazz selected 13th in the first round of the NBA draft. That was the very first year of the draft lottery, and the bottom seven teams had a random chance to receive the top pick—in that year, all seven would have chosen Patrick Ewing. The Kings had won 31 games in their last season in Kansas City before moving to Sacramento. They drew the sixth overall pick. The first five teams chose big men: Ewing, Wayman Tisdale, Benoit Benjamin, Xavier McDaniel, and Jon Koncak went in quick order. The Kings thought about Malone, but instead picked Joe Kleine.

That, as much as anything, shows why Sacramento was destined for another 15 years of losing basketball. The players selected right after Kleine were Chris Mullin, Detlef Schrempf, and Charles Oakley. Malone was there for the Jazz with the 13th pick, the luckiest number 13 ever. It was lucky for the Jazz, at least, as Malone led them to a record number of consecutive winning seasons.

Who's Better, Who's Best
Karl Malone or Charles Barkley

In my opinion, Karl Malone (although close) was never the dominant—or best—player in the NBA. He never *took over the league*. For almost two decades his play set a consistent standard of excellence. He led his team by example. He led his team well.

Barkley, on the other hand, for roughly two to three years in the early 1990s—was the best player in the league. Better than Jordan. Better than Karl Malone. Sir Charles dominated the 1991 All-Star Game. Sir Charles dominated the first Dream Team (the one with Larry, Michael, and Magic on it). Charles dominated the 1993 season.

Pete Vecsey: "As great as Charles was—as much as he accomplished—he did himself, his team, his fans a tremendous disservice by never coming into camp in shape. Because he was so undisciplined, he fell way beneath his potential.

"Karl, on the other hand, doesn't have to apologize for anything in his career. No one got more out of his ability than Malone. You have to get the most out of what you have— and Karl exceeded it. Yeah, I'll take him over Barkley."

Who's Better, Who's Best
Karl Malone or Elgin Baylor

Baylor never won an NBA Championship and neither did Malone. One was denied by Bill Russell, the other by Michael Jordan. Taking championships out of the equation, Baylor suffered terrible injuries that curtailed the second half of his career. Malone never suffered injuries. Should Baylor be ranked ahead of the Mailman? In my opinion, Baylor (at

6-foot-5) was a much better rebounder than the taller Malone. Baylor and Malone each had a Hall of Fame backcourt partner (Jerry West and Stockton).

P. J. Carlesimo: "Karl was pure power, and Elgin had more finesse to his game. Karl put so much pressure on the transition defense because he ran the floor so well. Elgin operated on the blocks down low more than Karl. The interesting question in regard to Malone's career is how great he would have been without Stockton. In my opinion, both Stockton and Malone would not have been as good as they were without the other. They both would have been Hall of Famers, but neither would have achieved anything close to what they accomplished together.

"What really impressed me about Malone the most is how much he improved different aspects of his game. When he came into the league, he was not a good foul shooter. He wasn't a great passer. He had a decent perimeter shot. Over the years, he added different elements to his game, where he became a sensational perimeter shooter. Of course, he took tremendous pride in being the best-conditioned guy in the league. He has shown everyone coming up that when you work this hard—you can play as long and as hard as the Mailman."

The Case Against Karl Malone

That case revolves purely around his performance in the 12 most important games of his NBA career.

Malone in the NBA Finals

Some great players don't get a chance at the brass ring. Others get exactly one chance. Malone had three very good chances to win an NBA title. He didn't get the job done.

Karl Malone's Jazz teams had a 10-year run where they won 69 percent of their games. Beginning in 1990, the team won 55, 54, 55, 47, 53, 60, 55, 64, 62, and then 37 games. His Jazz teams reached the Western Conference finals five times in a seven-year period.

That's five trips to the NBA's Final Four.

In 1992, the Blazers were more experienced and a better team. In 1994, the Jazz ran into the Houston Rockets, who were riding Hakeem Olajuwon's heroics in his MVP season. Utah bowed in five games.

That left 1996, 1997, and 1998 as seasons the Jazz had great chances to win the NBA Championship.

1996 Season: Jazz Lose in Game 7 of Conference Finals

In the 1996 Western Conference finals, Seattle took the first two games at home. Back in Utah, the Jazz won Game 3 by 20 points. Seattle took the next game 88–86 to go up 3–1 for the series. Utah battled back in the fifth game, winning an overtime game in Seattle's Key Arena. Utah then took the sixth game by 35 points, setting up a deciding Game 7.

That Game 7 was the first game Karl Malone would ever play that could vault him into the NBA Finals. During the regular season, Karl Malone was a 72 percent foul shooter. But in the 1996 postseason, that number dipped to 57 percent. In the most important game of Malone's life, he missed 6 of 12 free throws in a very close contest. Seattle won 90–86 to advance to the Finals.

1997 NBA Finals: Jazz Fall 4–2 to Chicago Bulls

In the first Finals game of Malone's career, he went to the free throw line with eight seconds remaining, giving him a chance to steal the first game in Chicago's United Center. Malone—a 76 percent free throw shooter during the 1997 season—missed both. Michael Jordan calmly hit a game-winning shot as time expired.

In Game 2, Malone hit just 6 of 20 field goal shots, as the Bulls went up 2–0 in the series. After the Jazz tied the series up with victories in Games 3 and 4, the series headed back to Chicago.

In Game 5, Malone was terrible. He wasn't terrible for the average player, but he was below his usual production. He made 7 out of 17 shot attempts, scoring 19 points to go with seven rebounds. But in the second half, Malone made exactly one basket (in six shots) and shot an air ball at a crucial point. He also didn't foul with 10 seconds remaining and his team down a point. Chicago defeated Utah 90–88 to take a 3–2 series advantage.

In Game 6, the Jazz lost the series 90–86 back in Utah as Malone scored just 21 points on 7-of-15 field goal shooting.

1998 NBA Finals: Jazz fall 4–2 to Chicago Bulls

In the first two games (at home in Utah), Karl made only 3 of 22 field goals, from the perimeter.

In Game 3, the Jazz lost 96–54, as Sloan threw in the towel early. Malone took five shots after the first quarter and had only three rebounds (not one offensive board).

In Game 4, Malone played great as long as he went against Bulls center Luc Longley. When matched against Dennis Rodman, Malone didn't play as well. He scored only two points in the fourth quarter. In the three Jazz defeats in the first four games, Malone turned the ball over 15 times.

On June 12, 1998, in Game 5, the Jazz staved off elimination and Karl Malone finally played the kind of game one expects from a legend. It was the best game of his Finals career.

Heading into that game, no one thought Chicago would ever let this series go back to Utah for Game 6. In the first half, Chicago took a commanding 36–30 lead. Coach Sloan had a dilemma. He had to rest his then-36-year-old point guard, Stockton, but he knew the results would be dismal. Jordan and Scottie Pippen were unbelievable defensively, especially with the championship on the line.

Howard Eisley, Stockton's sub, played 11 minutes and scored zero points and had zero assists and zero steals. He did, however, turn the ball over five times under relentless pressure. Only one Jazz player would score as many as 10 points besides the Mailman (Antoine Carr scored a dozen off the bench), and, basically, Malone hitched the Jazz to his back. He hit 17 of 27 shots, along with nine rebounds and five assists, while staying on the court for 44 of the 48 minutes. The Jazz took the lead in the third quarter and survived a furious fourth quarter. Utah won Game 5 by a score of 83–81, setting up a sixth game.

In Game 6, Malone played his rear end off. He hit 11 of 19 shots and scored 31 points, along with 11 rebounds and seven assists. But he had five more turnovers—including the deciding final one—when Jordan stripped him, went downcourt, and completed a storybook final shot for the ages.

If the Jazz could have won that sixth game—and they came oh-so-close—then Game 7 would have been in Salt Lake City.

Malone in the NBA Finals

4 wins	30.0 points/game	50 of 100 field goals	.500
8 losses	21.6 points/game	64 of 141 field goals	.453
4 wins	20 of 26 free throws	77 percent	
8 losses	45 of 70 free throws	64 percent	

In 1997, Karl missed 19 free throws in the four losses. In 1998, he turned the ball over 20 times in the four losses.

In defense of Karl, he was swimming upstream against a current of sharks. Those Bulls teams were so tough in those situations. In 1997, Malone had to take on Rodman, who got into Malone's head and affected his play. In 1998, Rodman was imploding and had lost his starting spot in the previous playoff series to Toni Kukoc. Yet Rodman was still a force to be reckoned with, and the Bulls were an unbelievable defensive team.

Maybe it took a player of Karl Malone's magnitude to even make those series competitive. In the end, Malone was faced with the following postseason record:

- His teams played 172 playoff games.
- His teams were 85–87 in those games.
- His teams played 34 postseason series—and were 16–18 in those.

A great player? Yes, of course. An all-time great? Yes, of course. Does he rank above any of the players listed ahead of him? No. In the end, the biggest irony is that he played 18 seasons with the Jazz, when his own game had none of the jazz that one associates with that improvisational, free-spirited music.

18

KOBE BRYANT
The Air Apparent

MVP: 0	
MVP VOTING: 5th in 2002, 3rd in 2003	
NBA TITLES: 3	
ALL-NBA FIRST TEAM: 2	
ALL-NBA SECOND TEAM: 2	

When Michael Jordan retired for the first time, following the 1993 season, the NBA searched frantically to find the next Michael. It wasn't Grant Hill or Penny Hardaway, as many people thought. The heir apparent to Michael's throne was just 15 years old in 1993, the son of a former 76er named Joe "Jellybean" Bryant. Following the 1996 season, in which they won 53 games, the Los Angeles Lakers moved heaven and earth to sign the kid out of high school. In the off-season, they had found a way to sign free agent center Shaquille O'Neal by clearing out a lot of high-priced veterans. Gone was Anthony Peeler. Gone was Sedalle Threatt. Gone was George Lynch. The Lakers then traded their starting center—Vlade Divac—on draft day 1996 to Charlotte for a high school kid named Kobe Bryant.

The Payoff

When the dust cleared, the Lakers won 56 games in 1997 despite an injury that forced O'Neal to miss 32 games. Los Angeles had a pair of all-star-caliber guards in Nick Van Exel and Eddie Jones. Behind them were two raw rookies—Bryant and Derek Fisher. The roster moves made after the 1996 season were the seeds that sprouted into three consecutive NBA Championships.

The 1997 season was Bryant's internship. He was the age of a college freshman. He took his credits on a work-study program. He learned under Del Harris and by sitting behind Jones and Van Exel. Bryant only played 15.5 minutes per game that season.

In 1998, the Lakers improved to 61–21, one of only 39 teams in history to win that many games in a season. Kobe was up to 26 minutes per game. The 62-win Utah Jazz would sweep the Lakers in the Western Conference finals. But in those games, Bryant would gain the experience of playing big games against Karl Malone and John Stockton. In the series, he would play almost 22 minutes per game and average 10 points per game on 11-of-30 field goal shooting. His two-year internship was over.

After his first two seasons, Bryant's numbers were 21 minutes per game and 11.7 points per game.

Oh, he had his moments. In the 1997 All-Star weekend, Bryant won the Slam Dunk contest. In 1998, at the All-Star game in New York, 20-year-old Bryant went one-on-one with Michael Jordan in the fourth quarter, scoring 18 points in 22 minutes.

Who's Better, Who's Best
Kobe Bryant or Michael Jordan

Del Harris: "Kobe—almost immediately—reminded me of Jordan. Now, I'm not the first one to see that in him, or say it. But it's true. You couldn't help but notice the similarities."

Pete Vecsey: "Kobe: he is Jordan. It's like I told Julius when Michael was coming up: Julius, he's you—only he's got a jump shot. Kobe has that jumper that goes deeper than Jordan's. He plays great defense. He's Jordan upgraded. He wants to be the best. And has a chance to be the best."

Joe Maloof: "Jordan/Kobe: Kobe's a little better at the same age. But Jordan has stood the test of time. Right now, Jordan."

Derek Harper: "Michael Jordan is the greatest of all time. But Kobe isn't far behind him."

After their first two years in the league, the comparison looked like this:

After Two Years in the League

Bryant	150 games	21 minutes/game	11.7 points/game
Jordan	100 games	36 minutes/game	27.2 points/game

In his third season, Bryant finally played 38 minutes per game and averaged 19.9 points per game. He was hardly able to make headway on the player he was always compared with.

After Three Years in the League

Bryant	200 games	25 minutes/game	13.7 points/game
Jordan	182 games	38 minutes/game	31.7 points/game

Jordan was 24 years old after the 1987 season, his third in the league. Bryant, on the other hand, was 21 after the 1999 season, his third in the league. Bryant had scored zero points in college, but had 2,755 NBA points at an age where Michael had none.

Kobe wanted to be like Mike, but he was averaging 18 points per game less than Jordan after both had been in the league three years. Kobe was wondering if he was ever going to get his career scoring average above 20 points per game.

In the three following years, Bryant led his team to three consecutive NBA Championships. Jordan didn't win any NBA titles in his first six seasons. Bryant had three.

Should Bryant get the credit for the Lakers championships? There was a popular opinion that the Lakers could win without Kobe, but not without Shaquille O'Neal. Is there any validity for that?

Bryant's seventh season in the NBA looks a lot like Jordan's seventh season. In the 2003 season, Bryant scored 50 or more points in a game three times and scored more than 40 points in 18 different games.

Seventh Season Comparison

Jordan (1991)	31.5 points	6.0 rebounds	5.5 assists
Bryant (2003)	30.0 points	6.9 rebounds	5.9 assists

Who's Better, Who's Best
Kobe Bryant or Penny Hardaway

When playing alongside Shaquille O'Neal the game averages look like this:

Bryant

2000	22 years old	22.5 points	6.3 rebounds	4.9 assists
2001	23 years old	28.5 points	5.9 rebounds	5.0 assists
2002	24 years old	25.2 points	5.5 rebounds	5.5 assists
2003	25 years old	30.0 points	6.9 rebounds	5.9 assists
Totals		26.7 pts/game	6.1 rebounds	5.3 assists

Hardaway				
1994	23 years old	16.0 points	5.4 rebounds	6.6 assists
1995	24 years old	20.9 points	4.4 rebounds	7.2 assists
1996	25 years old	21.7 points	4.3 rebounds	7.1 assists
Totals		19.5 pts/game	4.7 rebounds	6.9 assists

In 1995 and 1996, Hardaway was on the All-NBA First Team. In 2000 and 2001, Bryant was on the All-NBA Second Team. He made the All-NBA First Team in 2002 and 2003.

Hardaway is listed at 6-foot-7, 215 pounds. Kobe Bryant is listed at 6-foot-7, 210 pounds.

You may ask why I compare Bryant to Hardaway. Merely this. Playing alongside O'Neal, talented perimeter players such as Hardaway or Bryant became superstars at early ages.

O'Neal signed with the Lakers as a free agent after three seasons with Hardaway. O'Neal didn't win a title with Bryant in their first three years together, either. It looked as if Shaq and Penny would form a dynasty together in Orlando. O'Neal left for Hollywood, and Hardaway proceeded to have one of the most disappointing careers in recent memory. Much of that was due to injury, but that is part of the problem in ranking players in mid-career.

It certainly looks as if Bryant is closer to a Jordan career than a Hardaway career. For one thing, Bryant has come through time and time again in the Lakers' championship runs.

In the 2000 postseason, the Lakers were in deep trouble in Game 7 against Portland in the Western Conference finals. Kobe rallied the Lakers to come back from a 15-point fourth-quarter deficit, as they outscored Portland 31–13 in that final quarter to get past the Blazers 89–84. Bryant had 25 points, 11 rebounds, and seven assists.

The Best 2:33 of Bryant's Career

In the 2000 NBA Finals, the Lakers won the first game and were leading early in the second game when Bryant sprained his left ankle rolling it on Jalen Rose's foot. Without the injured Bryant, the Lakers held on to win the second game and lost the third. Prior to Game 4, no one knew the status of the Lakers' all-star. Bryant had only six points at halftime, and the Lakers trailed 54–51. Kobe played brilliantly in the third quarter, scoring 10 points. But with 2:33 remaining in the fourth quarter of Game 4, O'Neal was called for his sixth personal, and fouled out. The Lakers were only leading 115–112 at this juncture. Shaq told everyone afterward that Kobe "looked at me and said, 'Don't worry about it. I got it.'" Bryant not only drilled a long jumper, but he rebounded Brian Shaw's miss and with perfect timing put the ball back in with 5.9 seconds remaining.

The Lakers went into overtime, and Bryant scored eight of the Lakers' 16 points in that extra session to lead the team to a 120–118 victory. On a bad ankle, Bryant had scored 28 points (22 after halftime) and had played 47 minutes. The Lakers had a 3–1 series advantage. On television, analyst Doug Collins was beaming. He was informing a nation that they were watching the first of many such performances by this young man. It was nothing short of Jordanesque.

More Postseason Stats

In the 2001 conference finals against the Spurs, Bryant put on a show for the entire series. The Lakers swept San Antonio, with Bryant averaging 33.3 points, seven rebounds, and seven assists per game.

In the 2001 Finals, with the Lakers down 1–0, Bryant scored 31 points in Game 2 and 32 points in Game 3 to lead the Lakers to consecutive victories.

In the 2002 postseason, the Lakers were in deep trouble in Game 7 against Sacramento. Bryant scored 30 points, pulled down 10 rebounds, and had seven assists on the road.

In the 2002 Finals, in Game 3, Bryant scored 36 points and had six assists to effectively end the Nets' chances.

In the 2003 postseason, Bryant averaged 32.1 points in the Lakers' 12 games. Despite an injured right shoulder, Kobe closed out the Timberwolves with an inspiring fourth-quarter performance in Game 6. It was Jordan-like. It wasn't the fact that he scored 14 points in the quarter. Bryant displayed the confidence, ability, and killer instinct of Jordan.

Bryant's Scoring Average

First three seasons	13.7 points/game
Next three seasons	25.4 points/game

Bryant's career scoring average after six seasons was 19.8 points per game. Early in the 2003 season, he finally pushed his career average safely above 20 points per game. After the 2003 season, his career average was at a robust 21.5 points per game.

Bryant had scored 8,197 career points after six seasons and was still only 24 years old. Remember, Jordan at that age had a career total of 5,762 points. But Jordan would have a commanding lead in points per game.

	Through 420 Games	
	Points/Game	40+-Point Games
Jordan	32.9	98
Bryant	19.9	9

But then, Kobe went crazy just when the Lakers' ship was springing a leak early in the 2003 season. Right before the All-Star game, Kobe began a streak of 40-point games that rivaled anything Jordan (or anyone else) had ever seen. Kobe tied for the fourth-longest streak of 40-point games ever, when he went nine straight games scoring 40 or more.

Think about that. He had only nine games in his first 420 where he scored 40 or more. Then he scored 40 or more in nine straight games.

But Bryant's Lakers began the 2003 season 3–9 without O'Neal. No matter how many points Kobe scores—no matter what percentage of the offense he takes over—Bryant cannot be O'Neal.

Kobe is the single toughest player to rank as I write this book. He has what it takes to be the very best in the game. But Tim Duncan has carried his team offensively and defensively for the same span of time that Bryant has been in the league. Bryant can make all the noise he wants with his spectacular play. If we picked sides in the schoolyard and I had a choice between Duncan and Bryant, I'm picking Duncan every time. This is not going to be a popular choice, I understand. But Bryant has been taken care of with this high ranking. He moved ahead of perennial all-stars such as Isiah Thomas and Walt Frazier, among fellow guards. He zipped past former MVP Allen Iverson. That still doesn't take away the fact that Bryant was the second-best player on his own team. Duncan was the second-best player in the NBA.

Kobe's accomplishments by his 25th birthday are extraordinary. But his place in NBA history is anything but decided. Injuries are not uncommon (see Grant Hill). And life offers a dizzying number of minefields to avoid.

He has the ability and confidence to one day join Michael Jordan as the game's greatest guard.

GEORGE MIKAN
The First Great Big Man

MVP: We'll talk about this one.	
MVP VOTING: Soon.	
NBA TITLES: 4	
ALL-NBA FIRST TEAM: 6	

The Hollywood Pitch: I had a dream about pitching a story to Hollywood executives with one of the big studios. The pitch went like this:

I have a movie that can't miss. It takes place in the early 1940s—so it can appeal to older ticket buyers as well. But it's about a kid. We have this average-sized kid—a little nerdy if you know what I mean—everyone could relate. We'll put him in the middle of the country, near Chicago, maybe. Yeah, Chicago. We'll call him George. We first see him at age 10 when he became marble champion of Will County, Illinois. Anyway, he suffers a broken leg in a parochial school basketball game—let's say doctors tell him it's a bad fracture and he'll never play again. He spends 18 months on crutches and during that time grows 12 inches. A whole foot.

All right, anyway, he doesn't even play high school basketball, so he enrolls in college to study law. One day, he goes down to the gym and decides to try out for the basketball team. He realizes he loves the game. The coach is too busy working with the varsity to have time for this gangly kid. George gets discouraged and decides to leave school. He goes to Notre Dame for a tryout, but their coach isn't impressed with George and tells him to forget about the game. By now, George is close to 6-foot-10. Maybe we get that guy from "Everybody Loves Raymond" to play him. How young can actor Brad Garrett play? Anyway, George gets depressed and is about to give up the game forever. He goes back to Chicago. All of a sudden, there's a new coach at his first school, let's say it's DePaul. Speaking of "Everybody Loves Raymond," this coach's name is Ray—Ray Meyer. I'm thinking we need a big star for this—Kevin Costner, perhaps. He's a hoops fan.

This Coach Meyer is so happy to have this big lug, he makes it his job in life to help him. Meyer teaches him to box, teaches him to skip rope, and even gets a girl from one of the sororities to teach George dancing! They work for months—you get a little Rocky-type music going and you can't miss.

What happens? What do you think? He raises the so-called respectability of the "big goon" in basketball. He helps build DePaul into a national basketball power. He makes the All-American Team three straight years and is voted the greatest college center of all time back in the middle of the last century. He becomes the biggest draw of the newly formed NBA, and is part of the league's first dynasty.

Quite a story, huh? It is the story of George Mikan's life.

Life Before the NBA

There was no National Basketball Association following George's graduation, so he played on the 1946 College All-Star squad. In the fall of 1947, Maurice White, owner of the Chicago American Gears (of the NBL—the National Basketball League) signed Mikan. And on the strength of one player, White seceded from the NBL and started a brand-new league. White's league failed after nine games, so he tried to rejoin forces with the NBL. The Chicago Gears were refused, so White's players were dispersed through a draft. The Lakers had first draft choice. They took Mikan. Mikan joined Minneapolis for the Lakers' fifth game of the 1948 season in Sheboygan, Wisconsin. The Lakers franchise transferred to the BAA (Basketball Association of America) for the 1949 season, and became part of the NBA upon merger of the BAA and NBL for the 1950 season.

Mikan's Career with the Lakers

Here are the highlights of Mikan's seven and a half years with the Lakers.

- He led the league in scoring six times (the first three years in the NBL or BAA and the last three leading the new NBA).
- He held most scoring records in the NBA at one time, including highest average points per game (28.4 in 1951), most points in a season (1,932 in 1951), and 47 points in a playoff game.
- The only time the Lakers missed winning a title in his seven-year career was in 1951, when he broke a bone in his ankle and Rochester eliminated Minneapolis from the playoff semifinals.
- The widening of the free throw circle to 12 feet was aimed primarily at Mikan.
- He only missed two games with the Lakers—in the 1952 season, with a virus.

- His best pro game of all time was on January 20, 1952, against Rochester at Minneapolis. He scored 61 points (22 field goals, 17 free throws).
- In 1952, Philadelphia owner Eddie Gottlieb offered to trade his entire 1951 club (with the exception of Paul Arizin) for Mikan. This was done for two reasons: economics and to give the fledging new business of sports-talk radio in Philadelphia something to talk about (only kidding!).

Joe Lapchick, one of the legendary coaches in the history of the game, was quoted as saying, "Mikan is the greatest all-around basketball player that ever lived and the highest paid and the greatest gate attraction. He's the Ruth, the Dempsey, the Hagen, the Tilden of basketball. And one helluva swell fellow along with it."

Back to Those MVPs and the MVP Voting

The first year the NBA awarded a Most Valuable Player award was 1956. Mikan had retired after the 1954 season, although he came back for 37 games in 1956. The voting for MVP in those days was done by the players.

Writers and broadcasters did select All-NBA teams. Mikan's first year in the NBA was 1950. Beginning in 1959, the All-NBA teams are listed like this: forward, forward, center, guard, guard. Prior to that, they listed five players that look an awfully lot like the five best players, ranked one to five. My assumption is that, prior to 1959, they were listed in the order of most to least votes. So, I can "award" Mikan some MVPs that weren't awarded then.

1950 MVP

1. George Mikan
2. Jim Pollard
3. Alex Groza
4. Bob Davies
5. Max Zaslofsky

1951 MVP

1. George Mikan
2. Alex Groza
3. Ed Macauley
4. Bob Davies
5. Ralph Beard

1952 MVP

1. George Mikan
2. Ed Macauley
3. Paul Arizin
4. Bob Cousy
5. Bob Davies, Dolph Schayes

1953 MVP

1. George Mikan
2. Bob Cousy
3. Neil Johnston
4. Ed Macauley
5. Dolph Schayes

In 1954, Cousy would have won the MVP, with Neil Johnston and George Mikan following him. In 1955, Johnston and Cousy would have placed first and second, as Mikan had retired.

So, Mikan would have won four MVP trophies. Four consecutive MVPs and four out of five NBA titles between 1950 and 1954 and six straight scoring championships—and you have a player who was as dominant as any who has ever played the game.

Who's Better, Who's Best
George Mikan or Shaquille O'Neal

Dr. Ernie Vandeweghe: "That's a great matchup. Both guys were just too physical for the opponents that they played—all they did was push guys out of the way. Hey, I played Mikan in three championship series—although I didn't actually guard him. I guarded Jim Pollard, who was as tough at the end of a game as anyone that has played. I think Shaq and Mikan were comparable in their physical domination over people. Hard to say which one was better. It's close."

How come Jack Dempsey, Bill Tilden, and Babe Ruth are still considered among the very greatest in the history of their sports—but Mikan is forgotten?

Because my movie wasn't made 40 years ago—that's why. People didn't go to movies to watch basketball flicks. (Imagine how successful a Jack Twyman–Maurice Stokes movie would have been—the story of teammates, the black one stricken, the white one spending a lifetime raising money and caring for him.)

Great writers wrote about boxing. Great actors such as Gary Cooper and Anthony Perkins played baseball players in the movies.

Even Minneapolis fans didn't know how great Mikan was in those days. The average attendance was probably less than three thousand per game. That's in the late 1950s, when the team essentially went bankrupt and was sold to Bob Short, who brought it west to Los Angeles.

The 24-Second Clock and Mikan's (and the Lakers') Decline

Following the 1954 season, the NBA adopted the 24-second rule, which prevented the "keep-away" strategy. On November 22, 1950, when the Fort Wayne Pistons came to Minneapolis battling for first place, they had figured the best way to defeat the Lakers was to keep the ball away from Mikan. The result was a 19–18 Fort Wayne victory in the lowest-scoring NBA game ever played.

When the NBA put in the shot clock, Mikan was only 30 years old but he retired. His ponderous nature in getting up the court was outmoded. Mikan accepted a new role as general manager. The next year, the Lakers were eliminated in the first round.

You didn't think Michael Jordan was the first, did you? After the Lakers opened the 1956 season by losing 15 of their first 20 games, General Manager Mikan made a bold move. He got back into playing condition and activated himself. He averaged 10.5 points per game in 37 appearances as the NBA's first—and last—player/general manager.

Is it fair to "punish" Mikan because the game wasn't as popular when he played? Did Mikan have the capabilities to go up physically against the likes of Wilt Chamberlain, Shaquille O'Neal, or Bill Russell? No, of course not. Did Mikan have the size and athletic ability of a David Robinson? No, of course not.

When Robinson and O'Neal entered the NBA, they traveled by team charters and stayed in five-star hotels with luxury beds. They had personal trainers and dietitians. It may not have been easy coming from certain backgrounds, but once in the NBA, life was easy street. Mikan, on the other hand, played in the 1950s.

Leonard Koppett: "When Mikan played, it was a bruising, body-contact sport. Players thought of playing the pivot as a test of manhood. How much guts did someone have? How much pain could he withstand? So, Mikan had to establish respect. But even once he did, it was very often strategic to hold and grab opponents. The refs couldn't call everything. Soon, they weren't calling enough. And it became a very rough game in the 1950s."

Mikan had tremendous competitive fire and determination.

Who's Better, Who's Best
George Mikan or Later Superstars

Leonard Koppett: "Who was a better all-around player than George Mikan? He stacks up against all the greats to the same degree but in a much earlier time, in a very different time. He didn't have to run up and down the court. Don't forget there was no shot clock and around the basket he was completely dominant . . . no one could deal with him. He didn't have the athleticism that Russell, Wilt, or Shaq have, but he didn't need it in the way the game was then."

Mikan was so dominating that beginning in 1952, the free throw lane, the area in which an offensive player is not allowed to be for more than three seconds, was widened from 6 to 12 feet. This meant that Mikan (or anyone else) had to take up his position farther from the basket. He obviously adjusted well. The Lakers won the NBA Championship that season.

In its own way, I feel that dominating the league in the 1950s was as much of an accomplishment as dominating it in the 1990s.

Mikan was named to the NBA's 25th Anniversary team, the 35th, and the 50th. He's not going to be knocked out of a new listing of any NBA all-time team. Not by me.

DAVID ROBINSON
The Admiral

MVP: 1	
MVP VOTING: 7 years in the top 6	
NBA TITLES: 2	
ALL-NBA FIRST TEAM: 4	
ALL-NBA SECOND TEAM: 2	

David Robinson fills up a stat sheet, and his résumé just can't be kept to a single page. There are references, of course. Heck, his most impressive scoring feat may have occurred in high school, when he scored 1,320—on his SATs. In this chapter, you'll see why ranking active players is such a gamble. Tim Duncan is ranked ahead of longtime teammate David Robinson. That is done, of course, in 2003, following all 14 seasons of Robinson's career and the first six of Duncan's. But if we had used Robinson's first six years—and only his first six years—Robinson would not only have placed higher than Duncan, he would have surged past several other players. Similar to Julius Erving, Robinson's NBA numbers are down because he entered the league at a later age. David was 25, after serving his military commitment following his college days at Annapolis.

Robinson played just one year of basketball at Osbourn Park in Manassas, Virginia. While at the Naval Academy, he grew seven inches. Following graduation, he was forced to sit out two seasons while serving in the Navy from June 1987 to May 1989 at Kings Bay, Georgia.

The Spurs took David Robinson with the first overall selection in the 1987 draft. Why did the Spurs take Robinson knowing that he wouldn't be able to help them for two years? The next three players taken were Armon Gilliam, Dennis Hopson, and Reggie Williams. Seattle did take Scottie Pippen with the fifth pick, but then immediately traded him to Chicago for Olden Polynice. There was no one within miles of the Admiral in terms of ability and talent. The Spurs not only stockpiled Robinson but were able to stay among the losing teams long enough to draft 10th overall in 1988 (Willie Anderson) and 3rd overall in 1989 (Sean Elliott).

David is the only male basketball player to represent the United States in three Olympics, having done so in 1988, 1992, and 1996. In his first seven seasons in the league, he won Rookie of the Year and Defensive Player of the Year honors, and he was named four times to the All-NBA First Team.

The Stats on Robinson

Robinson's career numbers won't look great compared to the horses that stuck around two decades, such as Kareem Abdul-Jabbar or Karl Malone. But Robinson needs to make no apologies for his career numbers. I'll give them anyway.

David Robinson spent four seasons at the Naval Academy and then spent two more years in military service. Back and foot injuries eliminated all but six games of another season. His first NBA season was the 1990 season—when he was 25 years old. Even giving him just the two seasons lost for his Navy commitment would bring him to around 25,000 points and 12,500 rebounds.

In his dominant seasons, he never got the Spurs to the NBA Finals. But when Tim Duncan came on board, the Spurs won the NBA title in the 1999 season. In those Finals, Robinson had 13, 16, 14, and 15 points in the four Spurs wins. In the lone Knicks win, the Admiral had 25. Clearly San Antonio was no longer David Robinson's team.

There were other great NBA players who willingly took a backseat to a younger superstar to win an NBA Championship, just as Robinson did. The closest comparison is one Oscar Robertson.

Robertson was traded from the Cincinnati Royals to the Milwaukee Bucks following the 1970 season and was teamed with second-year superstar Abdul-Jabbar. Oscar was 33 years old and had played 10 seasons without a title. But in 1971, the Bucks went 66–16 and easily won the NBA title by going 12–2 in the playoffs.

Oscar Robertson

1970	25.3 points/game with Cincinnati
1971	19.4 points/game with Milwaukee

In 1999, David Robinson was teamed with second-year superstar Duncan. Robinson was 33 years old and was in his 10th NBA season. In 1999, the Spurs went 37–13 in a lockout-shortened season and easily won the NBA title by going 15–2 in the playoffs.

There was also an MVP center that took a backseat to a younger, great teammate as well—Kareem stepped back for Magic Johnson.

Kareem Abdul-Jabbar

First 17 years	26.4 points/game	19.4 shots/game
Last 3 years	14.1 points/game	11.0 shots/game

Of course, Abdul-Jabbar won his last two rings in 1987 and 1988 without playing a major role offensively.

So, the question remains where to place Robinson among the all-time greats. The fact is, Robinson was on the All-NBA First Team more years than Bill Russell. Robinson was not as dominant a player as Russell. But make no mistake about it. If Dr. Frankenstein had attempted to construct the perfect body for a basketball player, he couldn't have done any better than coming up with Robinson's. Any mother in her right mind would be happy to have a son grow up and embody all of David's personality, work ethic, and compassion.

The fact is, though, something was missing in this perfect body and perfect personality. The very fact that Robinson knew there was more to life than basketball probably makes him a better person than Larry Bird or Michael Jordan or Kobe Bryant. (Do you think any of them give a hoot about playing the saxophone?) Robinson had the complete Wizard of Oz collection—brains, a heart, and courage. What he lacked as a player was the killer instinct. He lacked the self-centered attitude that might be needed to rank higher among the all-time greats. He'll be on the All-Heaven first team one day. Of course, most of the great players—and all of the referees—will be playing in the Southern Conference of the Great Beyond League.

All-NBA First Team Center

David Robinson	Four times
Bill Russell	Three times

1999 San Antonio Spurs

The 1999 Spurs are one of the most underrated great teams of all time. Part of it was that they accomplished their feat in a lockout-shortened season. Former Bulls head coach Phil Jackson spent that season on the sideline and belittled the Spurs' title because it came in the framework of a 50-game season. I remember the great NFL coach Joe Gibbs also having to apologize for winning Super Bowls in two different strike seasons. The fact is, the Spurs finished the Finals 46–7 to end the season. After the first two Finals games, they were 44–6 during a 50-game period. That's greatness. In any year. In any era. They were sandwiched between Jordan's theatrics on one end and the Shaq/Kobe run on the other end. The Bulls finished the 1991 season 31–7 and went 15–2 in the postseason (46–9 to end the season). At the other end, the Lakers finished the 2000 season 33–4 and went 15–8 in the postseason (48–12 to end the season). So, Robinson's window to win multiple titles came in the mid-1990s, when Jordan took himself out of the picture the first time. But Hakeem Olajuwon swooped in and grabbed those opportunities.

Robinson			
First nine years	25.1 points/game	11.6 rebounds	34.7 minutes
1999 title season	15.8 points/game	10.0 rebounds	31.7 minutes

Robinson was never the same player after Duncan arrived. Part of that was physical. The back injuries took their toll on the incredible chiseled body. Part of it was mental—Robinson allowed Duncan to take control of the game, on both ends of the court.

First 62 playoff games	45 games of 20+ points
Last 61 playoff games	8 games of 20+ points

First 62 playoff games	23.4 points
Last 61 playoff games	12.6 points

Robinson really had two careers in the NBA. In his first seven years, he was so close to Abdul-Jabbar. In his last seven years, he was a good center.

The Greatest Game Robinson Ever Played

The 1994 season was a year of transition for the Spurs, the Detroit Pistons, and the entire league. Jordan's retirement had left the league in a state of flux. Robinson was the best player still standing, and his Spurs made a bold move, sending Sean Elliott to Detroit for rebounding champ Dennis Rodman. There was not much left of the old Bad Boys in Detroit. Isiah Thomas was in the final days of his career. Bill Laimbeer had already left. When the Spurs played host to the Pistons on February 17, even Joe Dumars was out with an injury. Robinson was in the middle of his MVP season.

Sean Elliott: "I liked what Dennis Rodman did for David's game. He definitely pushed him. In San Antonio, it was like David walked on water."

In that February 17 game, Sean Elliott scored 20 points for the overmatched Pistons. Dennis Rodman would take a single shot and score on just a single free throw. He did pull down 23 rebounds and add five assists. David Robinson put on a show. He had 34 points on 12 of 20 field goals. He had 10 rebounds (five on the offensive end). He had 10 assists. He had 10 blocked shots. Although there is no way of knowing how many of these quadruple double games Chamberlain or Russell would have had, we know that since 1974—when they started keeping records of blocks and steals—it has been done only four times. Nate Thurmond did it in 1974; Alvin Robertson did it in 1986 with steals in place of blocks; and Hakeem did it in 1990.

The Last Game of David Robinson's Career

After 987 regular-season games and 122 postseason contests, David Robinson had one more game in him. His 1,110th game in a Spurs uniform was Game 6 of the 2003 NBA Finals. After everything Robinson had meant to the community, it was the perfect ending to his career. He not only played, but turned back the clock and performed like a much younger athlete. He hit six of eight field goals from the floor. He scored 13 points. He pulled down 17 rebounds and blocked two shots. In David's first regular-season game with the Spurs, on November 4, 1989, he hit six field goals and pulled down 17 rebounds—leading San Antonio to a victory over the Los Angeles Lakers. In his first game with the Spurs, he rejected one of Magic Johnson's shots. In his last, he blocked a Jason Kidd shot. His career had indeed come full circle.

Michael Jordan exited quietly as the 2003 regular season came to an end for the Wizards. John Stockton lasted one round in the playoffs, and then said his goodbyes. David Robinson ended with a victory. At home. In the NBA Finals. A champion.

Who's Better, Who's Best
David Robinson or Patrick Ewing

Leading Scorers of the 1990s

1. Karl Malone	21,370
2. Michael Jordan	18,014
3. Patrick Ewing	16,914
4. David Robinson	16,715

Pete Vecsey: "David Robinson over Ewing: He was an MVP, he won a scoring title . . . he's an officer and a gentleman . . . not like Patrick."

Bob Ryan: "Robinson didn't have the killer instinct that the other great players had."

Who's Better, Who's Best
David Robinson or Hakeem Olajuwon

Joe Maloof: "Olajuwon/Robinson: Hakeem. He's a little more mobile, and a better player. He won two championships. David only won one."

Sean Elliott: "David was a much better athlete than Hakeem. David had crazy athletic ability, freakish, for a player 7-foot-1."

Who's Better, Who's Best
David Robinson or Shaquille O'Neal

Sean Elliott: "Dave used to eat Shaq up by taking him outside. Shaq didn't have a chance against him. In San Antonio, the crowds used to chant 'M-V-P' to David in front of O'Neal. O'Neal had gone to high school in San Antonio and made statements that were just dumb. I mean, you have to understand San Antonio. David had turned the franchise around. Plus, he was a great guy. A religious man. Perfect for that city. Shaq comes in with this attitude—so he brought it on himself. You would think that by 1998, the rivalry would have turned around completely. But there were only a few times when Shaq would dominate against the Spurs."

A Better Analogy
David Robinson and Roger Staubach

P. J. Carlesimo: "David Robinson: If it's possible to have achieved as much as David has—and still not get the credit—then Robinson isn't nearly as appreciated as he should be. His greatness transcends the court. He has meant so much to the NBA. Why can't everyone be like David? It is similar to what Staubach meant to the Cowboys and the NFL."

This is partially what Carlesimo is talking about. Early in Robinson's NBA career, war broke out in the Persian Gulf and the United States was rushing a huge force into action.

Since David was in the reserves, there was a chance that he could be called to active duty. If it happened, he would probably have been assigned to the Naval Facilities Command in Washington.

Fortunately, David was never called. Because of his Naval Academy background, he was asked about the war wherever he went. He was like the NBA's unofficial spokesman for the Gulf War. David told the media that he would gladly go if called upon.

Now, that's a team player.

CHARLES BARKLEY

Sir Charles

MVP: 1	
MVP VOTING: 4th in 1988, 2nd in 1990, 4th in 1991, 6th in 1995	
NBA TITLES: 0	
ALL-NBA FIRST TEAM: 5	
ALL-NBA SECOND TEAM: 5	

He came into the NBA fresh from being cut from the 1984 U.S. Olympic team by Coach Bob Knight. He entered the league with a nickname—"The Round Mound of Rebound"—that spoke volumes about his physical fitness. But Charles Barkley left the league with a different moniker: Sir Charles. He was "knighted" somewhere along the way, as he did everything but win a championship. Barkley accomplished a great deal in his playing days. The above list should be sprinkled with even more platitudes. He had one MVP season, but was robbed of another. He came within a John Paxson three-pointer of forcing a beatable Bulls team to a Game 7 at America West Arena in Phoenix.

Barkley was All-NBA First or Second Team 10 consecutive seasons (1986–1995). The following year, he was All-NBA Third Team, so he didn't fall off the face of the earth.

In an age where the prototypical power forward was 6-foot-8 or 6-foot-9, Barkley was closer to 6-foot-4 (although listed at 6-foot-6). Sandwiched sometime in the period between Moses Malone's six rebounding titles and Dennis Rodman's seven—Sir Charles even managed to lead the league in rebounds one year.

Barkley deserves more respect on the all-time lists. I am a fan, and I wish I could place him even higher.

Matt Guokas: "When I coached him in Philly in 1985, he was very, very young and his game had not formed yet. He was not big for forwards, and defensively, he was bad. You had to hide him. But at the end of the game, he wanted to guard Bird."

Phil Jasner: "When he was drafted by Philadelphia, I'll never forget something Jack McMahon told me. Now, McMahon taught me more basketball than any other person ever. He told me that Charles would be the first of his body type to be a superstar in this league."

Kevin Loughery: "Pound for pound, Barkley and Wes Unseld are the greatest rebounders in the history of the game. Charles wasn't even 6-foot-5, you know."

Barkley and the 1990 MVP

Let's look at the 1990 season.

	1990 MVP Vote					
Player	**1st**	**2nd**	**3rd**	**4th**	**5th**	**Total**
1. Magic Johnson	27	38	15	7	4	636
2. Charles Barkley	38	15	16	14	7	614
3. Michael Jordan	21	25	30	8	5	571
4. Karl Malone	2	8	10	23	19	214

The total was weighted this way: 10 points for each first-place vote, 7 points for each second, 5 votes for each third, 3 points for each fourth, and 1 point for each fifth-place vote. So Barkley would have needed very little movement to win this election.

Let's look at Barkley's, Johnson's, and Jordan's numbers in that 1990 season.

Charles Barkley
Team record 53–29
25.2 points/game (sixth in NBA)
11.5 rebounds/game (third in NBA)
.600 field goal average (second in NBA)

Magic Johnson
Team record 63–19
22.3 points/game
11.5 assists/game (second in NBA)
.480 field goal average

Michael Jordan
Team record 55–27
33.6 points/game (first in NBA)
2.77 steals/game (first in NBA)
.526 field goal average

Tough choice, as the voters had to choose just on those regular-season numbers. The award is Most Valuable Player—not Best Player. The Bulls had a young nucleus featuring Scottie Pippen, Horace Grant, John Paxson, Bill Cartwright, and Stacey King. Their roster—minus Jordan—was better than the Sixers without the Round Mound of Rebound.

Johnson had the first season of his career without Kareem Abdul-Jabbar. But the Lakers still had James Worthy, Byron Scott, A. C. Green, and rookie Vlade Divac. Magic made himself a three-point threat that season. The fact that he added another dimension to his game—while keeping the Lakers at a high level without their ageless center—made him a popular choice.

But Barkley deserved the MVP that season. He made only 20 of 92 three-point attempts. If you take those out of the equation, Sir Charles was successful on 686 of 1,085 shots from two-point range (63 percent). If it seemed like he didn't miss a shot that season, that's because, well, he rarely did. In fact, Barkley's two-point field goal percentage for his *career* was more than 58 percent. Charles led a ragtag bunch to 53 wins. His 76ers defeated the champion Pistons 3–1 in the four regular-season games. They defeated the Celtics and their greatest frontcourt in history twice. They split their two meetings with the 63–19 Lakers. They split their two meetings with the 56–26 San Antonio.

The 76ers roster was made up of serviceable NBA players besides Barkley. Charles went to battle with Mike Gminski, Johnny Dawkins, Ron Anderson, and Derek Smith. Only Hersey Hawkins provided offensive support, though rarely on the order of Jordan or Joe Dumars.

Barkley suffered from many of the same attributes that Wilt Chamberlain was afflicted with. People perceived their "truths" as "ego." That didn't sit well with many.

In one year alone (1992, his last in Philadelphia), Barkley was misquoted in his own autobiography, was arrested in Milwaukee on charges of battery and disorderly conduct (acquitted of each, by the way), and accused the 76ers of racism for keeping a white player (Dave Hoppen) as the 12th man. He flagrantly elbowed a 176-pound Angolan player in an Olympic game and then defended his actions.

But, this guy could play.

Around the time Charles wore out his welcome in Philadelphia, I remember a long-form magazine article (I believe it was in the Sunday *New York Times Magazine*, but I could not locate it in their archives more than a decade later) that compared Barkley to Jordan. Barkley controlled the ground, while Jordan ruled the air. The article pointed out how both players were roughly the same height yet played so differently on the court.

Of course, even at his best, Charles was not in the same league defensively as Jordan. Barkley played defense sporadically—usually when his team needed him to, or against the bigger stars of the league.

Offensively, though, Charles held his own against anyone. He was a good dribbler and could rumble up the court. He was virtually impossible to stop one-on-one. In the half-court, he had all the spin moves with his back to the basket or he could take defenders off the dribble facing the hoop. He went to the hoop often and frequently drew contact—going to the free throw line 8,643 times in his career.

Barkley's Stats Broken Down
Field Goal Percentage
Charles Barkley finished his career in the top 15 of all-time shooters in field goal percentage. Most of the names ahead of him were centers whose shooting touch required little more than dunking or placing the ball in the hole. Even the forwards ahead of him were big, rugged power forwards who rarely took a mid-range shot, much less a three-pointer.

For example, Kevin McHale is one of the few shooters on the career field goal percentage list ahead of Barkley. But McHale took only 157 three-point attempts in his career. Barkley took more than two thousand.

Barkley's two-point field goal percentage is .581. Only one player in history—Artis Gilmore—tops that. Mark West and Shaquille O'Neal come close.

Free Throw Shooting
Barkley led the NBA in free throw attempts in 1988, when he went to the line 11.9 times per game. He averaged more than eight trips to the line per game for his career, and only a handful of players in history have made more free throws.

Rebounding
His 12,546 career rebound total says it all. Look at the following two lists. Notice that there are only five players who have more total rebounds, and only five with more rebounds per game than Barkley in the last 30 years. All are taller than Barkley.

Most Rebounds, Career, Rookie Season 1973 or Later

1. Moses Malone   16,212
2. Robert Parish   14,715
3. Karl Malone   14,257
4. Hakeem Olajuwon   13,748
5. Buck Williams   13,017
6. Charles Barkley   12,546

Most Rebounds/Game, Career, Rookie Season 1973 or Later

1. Dennis Rodman   13.1
2. Tim Duncan   12.2
3. Moses Malone   12.2
4. Shaquille O'Neal   12.2
5. Dikembe Mutombo   12.2
6. Charles Barkley   11.7

Barkley's 1993 MVP Season

Fifth in NBA in scoring (25.6 points/game)
Sixth in NBA in rebounding (12.2 per game)
Career-best 5.1 assists/game

In that 1993 season, he led the Suns in scoring 46 times, in rebounding 58 times, and in assists 22 times. Following that season (his ninth in the NBA) his career numbers stacked up like this: 686 games, 23.5 points per game, 11.7 rebounds, 3.9 assists, and a .569 field goal average.

Barkley was always concerned with his play declining and his place in history. Statistically, he never suffered the big decline that most of the other great players went through.

Barkley

First nine years	686 games	23.5 points/game	11.7 rebounds	3.9 assists
Last seven years	387 games	19.7 points/game	11.7 rebounds	3.9 assists

Barkley Had Plenty of Talent Around Him . . . at the Wrong Time

Charles was surrounded by great players at the wrong time in his career, and the wrong time in theirs. In his rookie season of 1985, his 76ers reached the Eastern Conference finals. He played on a 58-win team that featured Moses Malone, Julius Erving, Andrew Toney, and Bobby Jones. Of course, Erving was 35, Bobby Jones was 34, and Malone was 30. That team lasted one more season before time ran out on the Doctor, and the Sixers made one of the all-time worst trades in history (sending Malone and two first-round draft choices to Washington for Jeff Ruland and Cliff Robinson). Barkley went public, ripping the trade. Losing Moses was tough on Charles. Barkley would say that Malone was like his dad in ball, and it was Moses who taught Barkley that it wasn't enough to just be good. That playing hard, as Malone did, was its own reward.

By 1993, Barkley finally had talent around him in the Valley of the Sun who were in their prime (Kevin Johnson, Dan Majerle, and Cedric Ceballos)—but it still wasn't Hall of Fame talent, either.

Barkley's Suns could have won the 1993 Title. In 1994, the Suns won 56 games with the league's best offense despite Barkley missing 17 games for various reasons. They won the first two games of their second-round playoff series in Houston—and went back to Phoenix up 2–0. The Suns lost in seven games.

Finally, Charles was traded to the Rockets prior to the 1997 season. Barkley played with Clyde Drexler, Hakeem Olajuwon, and, in 1999, Scottie Pippen. All were past their prime. The 1999 team really didn't mesh, as Pippen (a cutter and slasher) was never content to watch Barkley dribble with his back to the basket, either to shoot or pass to one of three Rockets standing outside the three-point line.

The Last Great Game of Barkley's Career

On May 13, 1999, the Houston Rockets came home after losing the first two games of a best-of-five series in Los Angeles. During the season, the Rockets were 31–19, the same mark as the Lakers. Los Angeles had the home court, based on winning two of three regular-season matchups.

The Lakers had a genuine superstar in Shaquille O'Neal and another standout in first-year starter Kobe Bryant. The Rockets had three of the top 50 players of all time (in my estimation, they had three of the top 30). But, of course, Barkley and Olajuwon were 36 years old and near the end of their brilliant careers.

To watch that series was similar to being a Walter Matthau and Jack Lemmon fan for years and having to sit through some of those *Out to Sea* movies. The final movies they made together weren't good, but there were moments in each that reminded you how talented they were.

Olajuwon looked the most out of place. Shaquille had always given Olajuwon respect, but by 1999 the tables had turned and the student was now killing the teacher. In that game, attempting to stave off elimination, Olajuwon could only muster five points on 2 of 12 field goals. He picked up five fouls in a futile attempt at stopping O'Neal.

Pippen, however, still had enough to take on Bryant. Pippen had his best game away from a Bulls uniform, playing 48 minutes and scoring 37 points. He added 13 rebounds and held Bryant to a mere 13 points.

But I'll remember the game for another reason. Barkley turned back the clock to the early 1990s, when he dominated the league. Sir Charles played 43 minutes and scored 30 points. He pulled down an amazing 23 rebounds and had five assists for good measure. The Rockets won 102–88.

Two days later, Shaquille put up 37 points and the Lakers prevailed to take the fourth game—and the series. Barkley would play 20 games the next season before getting injured in Philadelphia (of all places) and not being able to have his farewell tour à la Julius Erving and others.

Charles's 1993 rebuttal about why he never was as valuable as Magic Johnson or Michael Jordan, i.e., the way great players raise their teammates' level of performance:

"Magic Johnson got to raise the level of James Worthy's game, Michael Jordan got to raise the level of Scottie Pippen's game. But I got to raise the level of Shelton Jones's game."

Who's Better, Who's Best
Charles Barkley or Elvin Hayes

Elvin Hayes dominated the paint. But Barkley did, too, and Charles was at least five inches taller.

Barkley's career stats	22.1 points/game	11.7 rebounds
Hayes's career stats	21.0 points/game	12.5 rebounds

Barkley gets the edge, though, in several categories. Charles averaged almost 4 assists per game, compared to 1.8 for Hayes. Charles was able to put the ball on the floor better than Elvin.

Who's Better, Who's Best
Charles Barkley or Dolph Schayes

Barkley	1,073 games played
Schayes	1,059 games played

These guys are very comparable. Schayes was the best forward, for a while, until Bob Pettit (and later, Elgin Baylor) came along. Barkley was the best forward until it became clear that Karl Malone (and later, Tim Duncan) would pass him. Schayes averaged more than 18 points per game (playing several years before the 24-second shot clock). That is very comparable to Barkley's averages. Barkley faced better competition.

A Better Analogy
Charles Barkley and Elvis Presley

- Presley was born in the deep South (Tupelo, Mississippi).
- Barkley was born in the deep South (Leeds, Alabama).

- Presley spent his early years in poverty.
- Barkley spent his early years in poverty. (Remember Barkley has said that he never eats vegetables because when he was growing up, his mom and granny were too poor to have vegetables so they ate meat instead.)

- Presley had his greatest success recording for Sun Records.
- Barkley had his greatest success setting records for the Suns.

- Presley had a celebrated career that made him "King" in the music business.
- Barkley had a celebrated career that made him "Sir Charles."

- Presley did a hitch in the Army in the late 1950s, an unlikely choice to represent his country.
- Barkley played in the Olympics in 1992 and 1996, an unlikely choice to represent his country.

Presley's final years of public performances were filled with personal disappointments and problems. Other artists (an entire British invasion) had come into style, and Presley was left to perform in showrooms in Las Vegas. Often bloated and heavy, Presley would squeeze into his uniform and belt out old material. But, his career marks are more impres-

Shaquille O'Neal displays his power and dominance over the Spurs' Tim Duncan.
Never in league history has the best player been more dominant over the second best.

(© Andrew D. Bernstein/NBA Entertainment/Getty Images)

Kevin Garnett was the All-Star Game MVP in 2003, joining many others from the Greatest 50 to receive that honor. (© Nathaniel S. Butler/NBA Entertainment/Getty Images)

Orlando's Tracy McGrady drives against the Spurs' David Robinson. (© Fernando Medina/NBA Entertainment/Getty Images)

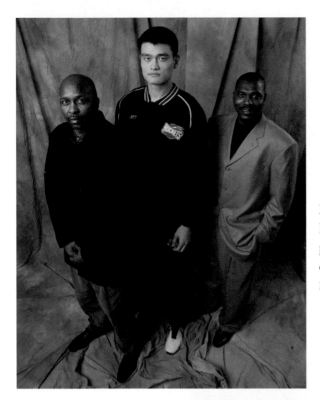

Moses Malone, Yao Ming, and Hakeem Olajuwon in a portrait of Houston Rockets centers. (© Bill Baptist/NBA Entertainment/Getty Images)

Reggie Miller—the consummate three-point shooter—being defended by Jason Kidd, the NBA's best pure point guard in the early 2000s. (© Noren Trotman/NBA Entertainment/Getty Images)

One of the best defensive players of all time on the perimeter, Scottie Pippen faces one of his toughest challenges in guarding Kobe Bryant. (© Robert Laberge/Getty Images)

For 18 years, John Stockton and Karl Malone ran the screen and roll to perfection. Here, Gary Payton fights to stay with Stockton. (© Jeff Reinking/NBA Entertainment/Getty Images)

Dennis Rodman left many images in a bizarre career that ended in March 2000 with the Dallas Mavericks. (© Ronald Martinez/Getty Images)

Isiah Thomas streaks past Magic Johnson, his friend off the court and rival on the court. (© Rick Stewart/Getty Images)

Michael Jordan became a jump shooter by the late 1990s, and his mid-range jumper helped the Bulls past the Utah Jazz in the 1997 and 1998 Finals. (© Jonathan Daniel/Getty Images)

An open apology to Rick Barry: this is the form we should all have used growing up. We didn't, because it wasn't cool enough. (© Ron Modra/NBA Entertainment/Getty Images)

Lakers big men Kareem Abdul-Jabbar, George Mikan, and Shaquille O'Neal. (© Peter Read Miller/NBA Entertainment/Getty Images)

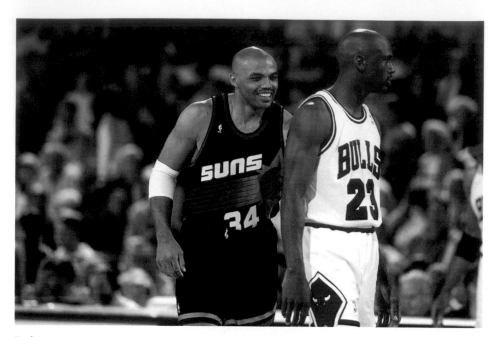

In his 1993 MVP season, Charles Barkley was the best player in the game—and that included Jordan, his opponent here in the Finals. (© Nathaniel S. Butler/NBA Entertainment/Getty Images)

There were moments between the 1977 Finals with the Blazers and the 1986 Finals with the Celtics that we saw Bill Walton on the basketball court. You missed it? You must not have seen many Clippers games from that era. (© Jonathan Daniel/Getty Images)

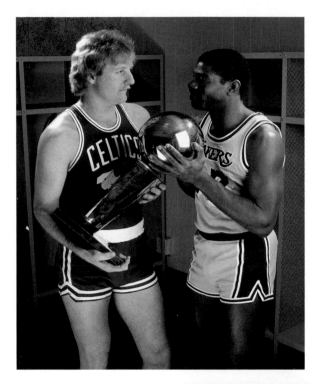

Larry Bird and Magic Johnson pose with the NBA Championship Trophy, which they battled for almost yearly in the 1980s. (© Andrew D. Bernstein/NBA Entertainment/Getty Images)

Dominique Wilkins poses with the trophy for winning the 1985 Slam Dunk contest. He was the standard for that event. (© Andrew D. Bernstein/ NBA Entertainment/Getty Images)

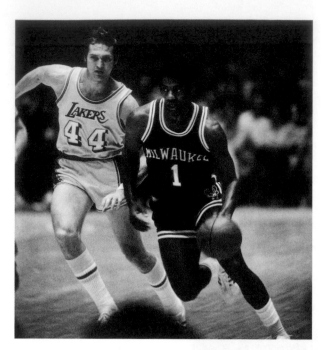

Who's Better, Who's Best? In the 1960s, it was between Jerry West and Oscar Robertson. (© Walter Iooss Jr./NBA Entertainment/Getty Images)

Is there a Doctor in the house? Julius Erving, with the cool ABA basketball and cooler Afro, at his absolute best. (© Walter Iooss Jr./NBA Entertainment/Getty Images)

Wes Unseld battled taller opponents (like Kareem Abdul-Jabbar) every single night. He remains one of the game's all-time best rebounders. (© Wen Roberts/NBA Entertainment/Getty Images)

Elgin Baylor, according to Bob Ryan, "took a mostly horizontal game, and made it diagonal. He brought in all the reverse layups, the double fakes. All the stuff you see today." (© Wen Roberts/NBA Entertainment/Getty Images)

Walt Frazier, according to Marv Albert, "was the type of player who could get three steals in the first quarter, but wouldn't. He would set up his opponent, and wait for the right time." Here he is against Celtics legend John Havlicek. (© Walter Iooss Jr./NBA Entertainment/Getty Images)

Who's Better? The veteran defender Jerry West, with the short hair and the textbook jump shot, or the creative young artist Pete Maravich with his long floppy hair, shooting off-balance and never the same way twice? (© Wen Roberts/NBA Entertainment/Getty Images)

Bob Pettit's game as described by Matt Guokas: "He was a tough, physical player. He had a mid-post game, not a deep low post. Kind of like how Yao Ming now plays. One hand over his head—a little push shot; similar to Oscar Robertson's shot." (© NBA Entertainment/Getty Images)

Dolph Schayes goes for a layup. Of the real big players of that era, according to Leonard Koppett, "Schayes was the best shooter and the best passer." (© NBA Entertainment/Getty Images)

While he was leading the league yearly in assists, Bob Cousy was also one of the leading scorers and always playing for the championship. (© NBA Entertainment/Getty Images)

Hakeem Olajuwon and Patrick Ewing battled for NCAA titles, NBA titles, and spots on the All-NBA teams for over 15 years. (© Bill Baptist/NBA Entertainment/Getty Images)

Dave Cowens, according to Bill Walton, was the only center who could play effectively against both Wilt Chamberlain and Kareem Abdul-Jabbar. (© Dick Raphael/ NBA Entertainment/Getty Images)

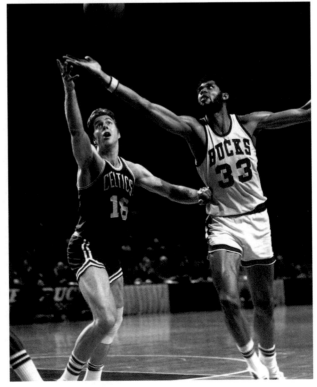

Bill Russell goes for a block. Russell was the greatest winner in team sports history. (© Walter Iooss Jr./NBA Entertainment/Getty Images)

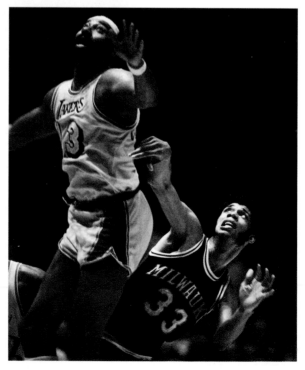

Kareem Abdul-Jabbar wrote in his 1983 autobiography that he played extra hard against Wilt Chamberlain. "Wilt demanded my best, and I gave it to him with a vengeance." (© Walter Iooss Jr./NBA Entertainment/Getty Images)

sive than Barkley's: 107 records on the *Billboard* charts and 18 records that were No. 1 hits.

Presley exhibited many compulsive and obsessive qualities throughout his life, which both helped and hindered his personal and public life. President Nixon once gave him a position as a special agent dealing with drugs. Elvis's lifestyle was hard for many to keep up with. He would sleep all day and party all night.

Charles, too, lived a nocturnal lifestyle and was a well-known Republican. (In his autobiography, Barkley recounts telling his mother that he was going to vote for George Bush. "But, Charles," his mother said, "Bush will only work for the rich people." To which, Charles replied, "But, Mom, I am rich.")

Elvis didn't like to be alone and would surround himself with friends. They were called The Memphis Mafia, and Elvis would frequent many nightspots in Memphis.

Elvis could have been taken as seriously as contemporary actor James Dean, but he wasn't. Charles was never taken as seriously as his athletic/entertainment contemporaries, either.

Hey, we can't all be like Mike or James Dean. Some of us have to provide comic relief and appear in movies like *Change of Habit*, where Presley woos nun Mary Tyler Moore. Some of us genuinely *like* peanut butter and banana sandwiches that are fried in butter.

Presley and Barkley share a lot in common. They were craftsmen, not innovators. They were not role models. For a time, they were the most popular and most successful in their fields—only to be passed by a new generation of performers who were far more youthful and athletic and who were taken a whole lot more seriously than Presley/Barkley.

Barkley: Love him tender.

RICK BARRY
Larry Bird Before Bird

MVP: 0	
MVP VOTING: 5th in 1967, 7th in 1974, 4th in 1975, 4th in 1976	
NBA TITLES: 1	
ABA TITLES: 1	
ALL-NBA FIRST TEAM: 5	
ALL-NBA SECOND TEAM: 1	
ALL-ABA FIRST TEAM: 4	

I asked Rick Barry's son, Jon, a guard with the Detroit Pistons, if there was any player's game that reminded him of his dad's. He quickly answered Larry Bird. No matter whom I asked, I got the same answer.

Rick Barry was Larry Bird before Larry Bird. He was a great shooter and a great passer. He was All-NBA or All-ABA First Team in nine different seasons. He was a Rookie of the Year. He was a Finals MVP. He was an All-Star Game MVP. He was a spectacular scorer from the corners, who became the first player ever to outscore Wilt Chamberlain for a season, when he averaged 35.6 points per game in 1967. He was not only Larry Bird before Larry Bird, he was Curt Flood before Curt Flood—challenging the reserve clause in his contract. He was the first and the most prominent NBA player to jump to the ABA.

Barry was born in Elizabeth, New Jersey, the son of a grammar school basketball coach who indoctrinated his son in the purity of the jump shot.

Number 24

You want to talk about the All-American kid? Barry grew up tagging after his older brother Dennis, an all-star player in high school. His first basketball coach was his father. His college basketball coach became his father-in-law. As a rookie in 1966 with the San Francisco Warriors, he chose #24. The fans were able to cheer San Francisco's #24 in baseball (Willie Mays) and basketball (Barry). Barry was a Mays fan back in the 1950s, when he used to see the Say Hey Kid play at the Polo Grounds. Wearing #24 in high school, Barry made all-state in basketball in high school. He also had honor grades and planned to attend the Naval Academy at Annapolis. But then he would meet Bruce Hale, coach at the University of Miami. By his senior year at the U. of M., Barry was such a celebrity that his church wedding (to his coach's daughter) was televised in Miami.

Barry had a terrific rookie season (25.7 points, 10.6 rebounds per game) and led the Warriors from their last-place 1965 season (17–63) to a much improved 35–45 mark. Barry was fourth in the league in scoring that first season. The Warriors' future was even brighter the next year, 1967, when San Francisco finished 44–37 and made the NBA Finals against the 68–13 Philadelphia 76ers.

Warriors' Record

1965	17–63	Year before Barry
1966	35–45	Barry was fourth in league in scoring in his rookie year
1967	44–37	Barry was first in league in scoring; team made NBA Finals
1968	43–39	Barry sat out season to challenge reserve clause; Warriors missed playoffs

Jumping to the ABA

This was an era where the players were using the two pro leagues against each other for leverage. Barry was the first star to jump from the NBA to the ABA. The Oakland club in the ABA was owned by singer Pat Boone. The coach was (now, what a coincidence) Bruce Hale, Barry's coach at the University of Miami.

Barry not only had family ties to the Oakland franchise, he was being offered entertainment deals by Boone and a cut of the gate. But it didn't turn out to be such a hot deal. For one, Rick had to sit out the 1968 season in a court dispute. The judge ruled that Barry had violated the option provision he had freely signed—the reserve clause. But the judge also ruled that Barry had the right to sit out one year and then play for Oakland. Barry spent that 1968 season as a broadcaster for the Oakland team. In those pre–Curt Flood days, there was no way Barry could play out his option year. All he could do was sit out.

Barry went to an inferior league where it was impossible to hit attendance marks. He received $75,000 a year plus a portion of the gate (5 percent of the home-team gate more than 600,000). He also received 15 percent ownership of the team. For a championship playoff game, the attendance reached seven thousand. The competition wasn't great and the crowd sizes weren't great, but at least Barry won a championship. Oakland defeated Indiana 4–1 to win the 1969 ABA Title.

The Oakland franchise folded after the 1969 season. When the Oakland Oaks owners announced that they were moving their team to Washington, Barry became involved in another contract dispute. Since the Oaks no longer existed, Barry felt that he was free to sign anywhere, with anyone. The court ordered Rick to honor his ABA contract, as the contract was one of the chief assets of the franchise.

Barry was swimming in very rocky waters. One year later, the Washington team moved to Virginia and became the Squires. Barry wanted to play either in New York (near his hometown) or in San Francisco. He didn't want to play in Virginia. There was a famous quote (Pete Vecsey remembers it being in *Sports Illustrated*, I thought I remembered it from a *Sport Magazine* article) that Barry had about not wanting to go to Virginia. "I don't want my son going to a nursery school and coming back with a southern accent, saying, 'Hi, y'all.'"

Barry got his way and played two years with the New York Nets. Finally content playing in New York—the courts intervened again and forced Rick back to the Warriors for the 1973 season.

Returning to the NBA

Rick reentered the NBA a more complete player. He was 198 pounds when he left and was 220 pounds when he returned. He was a much better passer. In his first stint with the Warriors, he averaged 2.9 assists per game. In his second stint, he averaged 5.7 assists per game. Barry's explanation was that by playing in the ABA, where he had to do it all to win, he'd been forced to develop latent talents.

In his 1,020 pro basketball games, he averaged 24.8 points, 6.7 rebounds, and 4.9 assists. If you take away his final two seasons, when he finished up with the Rockets, he had a 26.9 average after those first 12 pro seasons.

Through 12 Pro Seasons

Barry	868 games	26.9 points	7.3 rebounds	4.8 assists	.893 free throw average
Bird	897 games	24.3 points	10.0 rebounds	6.3 assists	.886 free throw average

Barry's career and Bird's career overlapped by only one season. 1980 was Larry's first year and Rick's last. It was also the first year of the three-point shot in the NBA.

1980 Three-Point Field Goal Percentage Leaders

1.	Fred Brown	39 of 88	.443
2.	Chris Ford	70 of 164	.427
3.	Larry Bird	58 of 143	.406
8.	Rick Barry	73 of 221	.330

Barry made 73 three-pointers in that 1980 season. That was more than 16 of the 21 other NBA teams in the league. Only one player (San Diego's Brian Taylor with 90) made more treys that first year. It is safe to say that Barry's scoring average would have been higher had the three-pointer been in effect earlier. If he made one per game, his average would be higher by a full point.

The Best Game of Barry's First Two Seasons

The 1967 NBA All-Star game was in San Francisco. The East had won the last four All-Star games and were probably heavily favored to win a fifth. For one of the few times in their careers, Bill Russell and Wilt Chamberlain were teammates—on the Eastern squad. Oscar Robertson, Jerry Lucas, Willis Reed, John Havlicek, and Hal Greer were also on the East. But Rick Barry poured in 38 points in 34 minutes, by hitting 16 of 27 field goals. He also contributed six rebounds. Barry wasn't exactly playing by himself. His Warriors teammate Nate Thurmond played 42 minutes at center against Chamberlain and Russell and had 16 points and 18 boards. The two fabulous Lakers combined for 36 points. The West won 135–120.

As with other great players, Barry saved his best games for the ones at the very end of the season. Barry's career average in the regular season was 23.2 points per game. His career average in postseason work was 24.8 points.

Barry in the NBA Finals

Rick Barry's career average peaked in the NBA Finals.

Highest Scoring Average in NBA Finals (min. 10 Games Played)

1.	36.3	Rick Barry (10 games)
2.	34.2	Shaquille O'Neal (19 games)
3.	33.6	Michael Jordan (35 games)

The Biggest Game of Barry's Career: 1975 Finals, Game 3

The 1975 Finals had a 1-2-1 format, with the series starting in Washington, D.C., and moving to the West Coast for the second two games. The Warriors broke serve in the opening game and took the second game at home. In the third game, Rick Barry scored 38 points to go along with four rebounds and six assists. He went to the line 16 times and hit 14 of them. He outscored Bullets superstar forward Elvin Hayes by 14 points. The Warriors took the game 109–101 to take a convincing 3–0 lead. The Bullets were swept out two nights later back in Washington.

Brent Musburger: "In 1975, Barry was a one-man show. Rick carried that team to the title. He would demand the basketball from his teammates. If you overplayed him and fouled him, he was automatic at the free throw line. If you doubled him, he would find journeymen like Clifford Ray and hit them with perfect passes. Rick was the best rhythm shooter I ever saw."

The 1975 MVP Vote

First, a word about Barry's MVP voting results. Until 1980—Barry's last season—the MVP was selected by a vote of players. Barry was by all accounts the most unpopular player and would never win an MVP award.

There is no other way to say this: he got robbed of the 1975 MVP. He finished fourth, behind Bob McAdoo, Dave Cowens, and Elvin Hayes.

In 1975, Barry:

- Led Golden State to the best record in the West
- Was second in the NBA in scoring (30.6 points/game, trailing McAdoo)
- Was first in free throw percentage (.904)
- Led the league in steals (2.85 per game)
- Tied for sixth in assists (6.2 per game)
- Was part of a Warriors team that led the NBA in scoring (108.5 points/game)

Why does former Oakland Raiders punter Ray Guy deserve mention in a chapter on Rick Barry? I was talking with my friend Peter King recently. Peter is the pro football writer for *Sports Illustrated* and one of the voters for the Pro Football Hall of Fame. We got into a heated debate when he told me that he hadn't voted for Ray Guy for the Hall.

I told him that he endorsed several candidates that were—at best—no more than the third- or fourth-best at their position during their careers. How could King not have the premier punter of his—and perhaps all—time? I argued that the NFL is a game of field position. And Ray Guy gave his team—the winningest team in his playing days—better field position.

King's response was that punters are interchangeable. He also said that punting has not changed over the course of the years. A punt is a punt is a punt. And Guy's punting numbers don't look as good in 2003 as they might have in 1976.

While I conceded some points to King, the thought came to me that if punting hasn't changed over the years, then the art of free throw shooting has really stood in a time capsule. The act of shooting a free throw remains unchanged throughout NBA history. The distance between the charity stripe and the basket has never been changed. The height of the basket has not moved up or down an inch. The free throw has never been defensed. It has always been worth exactly one point. There is a purity about comparing the free throw percentage of Rick Barry to Scottie Pippen or to George Mikan. A free throw is a free throw is a free throw.

Free Throw Leaders

It is interesting to see how league-wide free throw percentage has varied on a yearly basis. I remember Jim Bouton, in his 1970 book *Ball Four*, writing that if a major-league pitcher could take a pill that would guarantee him 20 wins in a season but that would also take off five years of his life, he and most all other pitchers would happily take it. There isn't a pill, but something better in the NBA. If he practices enough, any player could raise his scoring average one to two points per game, without any side effects or deals with the devil. All one has to do is practice free throw shooting.

Barry led the NBA in free throw percentage six times in his career. Larry Bird led the NBA in free throw percentage four times. Rick Barry retired as the all-time leader in free throw percentage, and since his retirement, only one player—the Cavs' Mark Price—has a better career percentage.

The NBA league average has been between 70 percent and 76 percent for every season since 1949. The league average was .748 in both 1972 and 2001. The league average was .751 in 1957. It was .752 in 2002.

All-Time Career Leaders in Free Throw Percentage

1.	Mark Price	2,135 made	2,362 attempted	.904
2.	Rick Barry	3,818 made	4,243 attempted	.900
5.	Larry Bird	3,960 made	4,471 attempted	.886

If Barry had made simply the league average (75 percent) of his career free throws, he would have made 3,126 free throws. He actually made 3,818. He was 692 free throws above the league average in his NBA career (1,020 games). His NBA career scoring average is 24.8. If he was an average 75 percent free throw shooter, his career average would be 24.1. If he was a 65 percent free throw shooter, his career average would be 23.7.

Now, while Rick scores points with me for making all his free throws, he played a forward position that didn't have the physical inside game that would get him to the line 9 or 10 times per game. If you look at the great forwards of all time, Barry's numbers really resemble Bird's the most.

Eight Great Forwards in NBA History

Rick Barry	4.1 free throw attempts/game	.900 percent
Larry Bird	4.9 free throw attempts/game	.886 percent
Julius Erving	6.4 free throw attempts/game	.777 percent
Tim Duncan	7.5 free throw attempts/game	.710 percent
Charles Barkley	8.1 free throw attempts/game	.735 percent
Elgin Baylor	8.7 free throw attempts/game	.780 percent
Karl Malone	9.1 free throw attempts/game	.741 percent
Bob Pettit	10.2 free throw attempts/game	.761 percent

Pettit scored 7.6 points per game from the foul line. Barry scored only four points per game from the line. The term "power forward" wasn't used in the earlier decades of the league, but it is clear that Pettit and Baylor played closer to the basket than Bird and Barry (who played, more often than not, on the traditional wings).

Score One More Point for Barry

Rick Barry only averaged four made free throws per game in his NBA career. But in the 10 biggest games of his life—the NBA Finals games—he made 87 free throws (8.7 per game).

Rod Thorn: "Rick Barry was a different kind of personality. He never got the credit he deserved because of it. He could score on the break like few others, and if he caught you on the break, forget it . . . great passer . . . didn't rebound . . . but tremendous shooter."

Bill Walton: "Rick Barry: He belongs in the all-time list. He didn't play on great teams, or in major media markets . . . like Barkley—loved to have the crowd on his case . . . the rarest of assets. Until Larry Bird came along, Barry was the best forward I ever saw play basketball. Rick and Larry were very similar players. They could do everything, particularly on the offensive end of the floor. Barry, like Bird, was a poor individual defensive player, but exceptional on team defense."

Kevin Loughery: "Rick Barry was not a good defender, he concentrated on offense. But one of the great offensive players of all time. He could pass. He could shoot. He was quick. One of the most underrated players of all time."

Marv Albert: "Rick was sensational. He was one of the smartest players of all time. He was a terrific passer. There have been a lot of great players, but you can't forget about Barry."

Pete Vecsey: "Rick Barry: Bird before Bird. He could rebound. He was so fundamentally pure. He led the league in pissing off opponents. I never saw a guy get beat up so much. In the ABA and the NBA. By everyone. White and black. Teammates and opponents."

Why Was Rick Barry So Unpopular?

I've been told he was very dogmatic in his beliefs and held little regard for other opinions. Brent Musburger, who worked with Barry as a broadcaster in the 1970s, thinks that's a bit unfair.

> Perhaps people didn't like his personality, or ego. Some were jealous of his talent. He went into broadcasting while he was an active player—we would use him when the Warriors were knocked out of the postseason—and he had a glibness, a good voice, and I thought he would be a star for years to come. But there were pockets of people who didn't like him, thought he was out for their jobs, and hung him out to dry.

Barry could put the ball in the hole almost better than anyone else his size in history. He averaged 35.6 points per game during one NBA season (1967). In the 35 years since then, only one player (a guard, Michael Jordan, in 1987) averaged more points per game for a season. No one other than Chamberlain and Jordan ever averaged as many points per game (minimum 70 games played; Baylor averaged 38.3 points in 48 games in 1962). He could score better than anyone at his position. He played on teams that won. He was labeled a selfish player but proved the label wrong by being a terrific passer. He was tabbed a poor defensive player but then led the league in steals.

Barry was living proof that one could be a terrific passer and perhaps selfish, too. He proved that one could get a lot of steals and still not be a terrific defensive player. A lot of players would welcome what Barry (and Dennis Rodman) brought to their teams in terms of talent. A lot of them would still have rather played with others.

Still, few players possessed the talents that Larry Bird did. Barry did, in abundance. One difference, though, was that Bird's teammates loved him and Barry's teammates mostly did not.

An Open Apology to Rick

An apology on behalf of all teenage basketball players who didn't shoot free throws the way Rick Barry did: You proved that you were right to shoot them underhanded. We all fooled around with it in practice. We all hit a better percentage of our shots like that. And we all chose to shoot them the conventional way. Perhaps if a cooler athlete such as Michael Jordan or Kobe Bryant had taken to shooting his free throws underhanded, then we all would be emulating that style. So, on behalf of all of us, we apologize, Rick. No one wanted to hit more free throws, if it meant looking like a sissy. Which is what it looked like to all of us.

But then again, people used to think that men who wore their hair long were sissies. Then, people thought if men wore earrings, they were sissies. Sometimes, you need more than results. You have to look cool.

Who's Better, Who's Best
Rick Barry or Elgin Baylor

That's reaching a little too high for Barry. Baylor and Karl Malone are in another league. Baylor had a complete game with an inside game to complement a terrific outside shot. Baylor wasn't any taller than Rick, but he sure was a more physical force who couldn't be stopped once he started driving to the basket.

Who's Better, Who's Best
Rick Barry or Allen Iverson

No one has ever made this comparison, but hear me out. There is no modern-day player who carries a team offensively as Barry did, other than A.I. Both were able to find the open man, hit their free throws, and lead a pack of journeyman teammates to the Finals. Both had MVP talent—and MVP ego. Barry replaced Chamberlain as the scoring champ in 1967, and Iverson replaced Jordan in 1999. Barry was a better player for a longer period than the Sixers star. But it's not so one-sided as one might think. Because of their personalities, both get overlooked when people discuss the all-time greats.

23

DOLPH SCHAYES
The NBA's Best in the Mid-1950s

MVP: 0	
MVP VOTING: 5th in 1956, 5th in 1957, 2nd in 1958,	
6th in 1959, 9th in 1960, 7th in 1961	
NBA TITLES: 1	
ALL-NBA FIRST TEAM: 6	
ALL-NBA SECOND TEAM: 6	

D olph Schayes had a 16-year career in the NBA and was one of the most durable players the world has seen, even now. In his first six years, he was among the five best players and ranked in the top 10 for 12 years. His first season was 1949, so he was one of the forefathers of the NBA. When he retired in 1963, he was the league's all-time leading scorer (19,249 points) even against such newcomers as Wilt Chamberlain, Bob Pettit, and Bob Cousy.

In the first six seasons that the MVP was awarded, he was in the top seven of the voting each time. If they had voted for a most valuable player in the years preceding 1956, he would have garnered a few more top five finishes. (I'm using the same logic as I applied in the George Mikan chapter.)

He was named to the NBA's 25th Anniversary All-Time Team in 1970 (one of the 12 greatest players whose careers had ended by then).

Dolph Schayes: "My game was one of perpetual motion. I was taught to keep moving. I set backside picks and worked to get open. If you're asking me about my game, I guess you could say somewhere between Keith Van Horn in today's game and Larry Bird's."

Schayes's NBA Career

In 1954, his Syracuse Nationals lost in Game 7 of the Finals to the Minneapolis Lakers 87–80. But the following season, 1955, the Nats defeated the Fort Wayne Pistons in the

NBA Finals in seven games with the home team winning all seven games. In the final game, Syracuse won 92–91.

Those were milestone series for the NBA. The 1954 season was the last one played without the 24-second clock. The NBA instituted the clock, and the game was officially in the modern era. It was Schayes's Syracuse owner, Danny Biasone, who implored the league to institute a shot clock. He fooled around with the numbers, settling for 24 seconds by coming to the realization that it took about 12 seconds to work the ball upcourt and attempt a field goal. He figured that would work out to 60 possessions per game. Anyway, it worked. He sold the league on a shot clock and was rewarded when his team won the NBA title the first year it was instituted.

The last year before the 24-second clock was instituted, 1954, the average team scored 79 points per game. In 1955, the average team scored 93 points per game.

Average Team Field Goal Attempts/Game

1954	75.3
1955	86.4
1956	91.3

A typical game from the 1954 season was the NBA Finals Game 6, ending with the score Syracuse 65, Minneapolis 63. Check out the box score of that game. Dolph Schayes started at a position known as left forward, or LF. Paul Seymour was the left guard. A Dugie Martin (now, there's a name!) free throw tied the game at 60–60 with 4:05 remaining. Without a shot clock, the game stalled to a crawl. There wouldn't be another field goal until a miracle dropped in for a player named Jim Neal with four seconds left.

With Syracuse shorthanded, they held on to the ball. In the third quarter, they held Minneapolis to just six points.

Now compare that with a typical 1955 game, the NBA Finals Game 6, which ended with the score Syracuse 109, Fort Wayne 104. The game was still marred by excessive fouling. Fort Wayne was charged with 31 personal fouls and Syracuse 33. But there was more scoring. Dolph Schayes scored 28 points. Of course, 14 of them came on foul shots.

How rough was the game then?

A fight between Wally Osterkorn of Syracuse and Don Meineke of Fort Wayne in the second quarter brought the fans on the court and police had to quell the disturbance.

You would probably guess that Osterkorn and Meineke were suspended for Game 7 of the Finals.

You would be wrong.

The next night, Syracuse defeated Fort Wayne in the seventh game for the NBA title. Osterkorn was back starting in his customary right forward spot. Meineke came off the bench at left forward. Schayes had given Syracuse a 91–90 lead with 80 seconds remaining by making good with two free throws. But George Yardley tied the game with a free throw. George King then made a free throw with 12 seconds left and stole the ball to ensure the Syracuse win.

By 1956, the average team was scoring 99 points per game—more than teams scored on average in the early 2000s.

In the last days of the 1956 season—George Mikan's last in the league—Dolph Schayes passed Mikan's career NBA point total and became the all-time leading scorer in the NBA's short history. Schayes remained the all-time leader until Bob Pettit passed him in 1964. Remember, Schayes spent the first half of his career in the "dead ball era," prior to the 24-second shot clock.

As late as 1970, when Jerry West zoomed past in point scoring, Schayes was the fifth-leading scorer in the history of the game (trailing, by then, Wilt Chamberlain, Elgin Baylor, Pettit, and Oscar Robertson).

NBA's All-Time Leading Scorers Following 1958 Season
1. Dolph Schayes   11,764
2. George Mikan   10,156

NBA's All-Time Leading Scorers Following 1963 Season
1. Dolph Schayes   18,304
2. Bob Pettit   17,566
3. Bob Cousy   16,955

A couple of native Philadelphians—Paul Arizin and Chamberlain—rounded out the top five. Yes, Chamberlain was the fifth all-time leading scorer after just three seasons in the game. Now, the game had changed totally since Schayes had entered the league. In the 1962 season, the average team had 107 shots per game and scored 118.8 points per game. Assuming that Schayes had spent the first six years in a league that scored a "normal" 100 points per game, we could hypothetically kick Schayes's scoring up 20 percent in those pre–shot clock years. That would add another 1,300 points to his career. Plus, his first year out of college was 1949, when there was no NBA. He played for Syracuse in the NBL. So, he scored 19,247 NBA points, but on a level playing field would have scored another two thousand or so. It doesn't move him past the eight forwards ahead of him, but it does make me comfortable placing Dolph ahead of the next three forwards (John Havlicek, Scottie Pippen, and Dennis Rodman).

What people remember about Schayes is that four decades after his retirement, his class and hustle remain vivid to those who saw him play. After each basket he scored, he would dash at full speed to the opposite end of the floor, fist clenched triumphantly over his head.

Matt Guokas: "He was the first guy who showed elation after a big play. Now, it wasn't like today's elaborate celebrations. He would put his fist up to ear level. I saw him play with my father—and after Schayes put his hand up, my father looked at me—he didn't say anything—but a look that said, 'Don't you ever do that.' "

Pete Vecsey: "Schayes: one of the all-time scorers. He was the Mark Jackson of his day. He would put his arm over his head every time he scored . . . he had a great shot, was a great rebounder. . . . He played one year with a broken right wrist."

What My Mother-in-Law, Barbara Levinson, Remembers About Schayes: "It must have been 1948, and Dolph was the boat boy for the Neville Hotel in the Catskills. The boat boys used to get the canoes or the rowboats ready for the guests. He would work all day and play at night. I remember Paul Arizin and a guy named Maury were on the same team. They used to play other hotel staffs. He was a very nice boy."

When I asked Schayes about his days at the Catskills, he was only too happy that I had said my mother-in-law and not my grandmother. But he and Arizin weren't the only top basketball players to play in upstate New York. Ernie Vandeweghe played against Schayes and Arizin with a neighboring resort.

In Wilt Chamberlain's autobiography from 1973, there is a photo of Wilt as a 7-foot busboy at Grossinger's hotel in the Catskill Mountains from the late 1950s. A half century later, high school kids from the inner-city projects can get loans to buy $70,000 automobiles. In the early days of the NBA, not only did prep stars attend and graduate college, but they had to work in the summers during their college years. So I gained a deeper appreciation for the stars of yesteryear. They did without charter airplane travel, personal trainers, and entourages. Even worse, they battled mosquitoes each summer and had to fight their way through endless buffet tables in the Catskills. It's no wonder they were ready for the aggressive play of the NBA.

Schayes was the last and the greatest of the deadly two-hand set shot shooters. For a tall player of his era (6-foot-8), he wasn't particularly aggressive and preferred to shoot outside. When he graduated from New York University, scouts said that he was a fine two-hand set shooter, an excellent foul shooter, and tall and heavy enough—but that he might not be tough enough for the rough NBA. The Knicks had first shot at Schayes but didn't pursue the Bronx native. The Syracuse team never regretted their offer to Schayes, who became the first player ever to reach 15,000 career points.

Schayes retired as the all-time leader in personal fouls, committing 3,667. Even today, that figure ranks high. The all-time leader is Kareem Abdul-Jabbar (4,657), with Robert Parish (4,453) and Hakeem Olajuwon (4,338) trailing him.

Schayes held so many career marks in the NBA when he retired, including games played, minutes played, playoff games played, foul shots made, and total points scored. He was the fourth all-time leading rebounder when he retired. In 1951, he was the very first player to lead the NBA in rebounds. His rebounding totals in 1949 (in the NBL) and in 1950 weren't even recorded.

He refused to let injuries force him out of games. He piled up what was then a record 705 consecutive games, not counting his 103 playoff games. From the beginning of the 1949 season until 1962, when a broken cheekbone forced him to miss 24 games, he missed just three games.

Leonard Koppett: "Schayes: of the real big guys (6-foot-8) . . . that would be comparable to a 6-foot-10 player now . . . Schayes was the best shooter, best passer, best all-around moving player. Titles don't mean anything when you judge an individual—I believe that is the result of interaction of a team of six to nine players, so I don't hold it against Dolph that he only won a single title. He was a tremendous outside shooter. If they were allowed to play with a three-point basket, no telling how many points he would have scored."

Rod Thorn: "Dolph Schayes: He was a great scorer. He had that two-hand set—he was the consummate scorer."

Dr. Ernie Vandeweghe: "Dolph shot a lot outside. He had pretty good range, too. I played against him in college and in the pros. He was strong under the boards. He was a very smart player. I would compare him to Dirk Nowitzki."

Matt Guokas: "Schayes: He was Larry Bird long before Larry Bird. He was a shooter, scorer. He was one of the few players who took faraway shots that would have been three-point shots. He took these two-hand set shots. He was very tough—he didn't mind getting hit. He wasn't much of a passer/defender."

Who's Better, Who's Best
Dolph Schayes or Rick Barry

Both players were outstanding forwards in NBA history. Barry was a better shooter and Schayes a better rebounder. But both had an influence on the league long after they retired. Schayes had a son, Dan, who played 18 years in the league. Between father and son, there was a Schayes in the NBA (and that meant at least one Jewish player in the league) for an astounding 34 years. Barry, not to be outdone, had three of four sons in the league. The Barry boy with the most experience, Jon, finished his 11th season in the league in 2003. Rick Barry was All-NBA First Team five times and All-ABA First Team another four years. Schayes was All-NBA First Team six years. Dolph and Rick each won an NBA title. It's close, which reflects the rankings in this book. But Rick Barry was a better player.

Who's Better, Who's Best
Dolph Schayes or Bob Pettit

Leonard Koppett: "I'd have to say Schayes. He was truly excellent. His style made Syracuse a great team to watch."

Pete Vecsey: "Wow. Leonard said that? He would know. I defer to Koppett."

That is one call that I just can't defer to the excellent scribe Koppett on: Schayes was not better than Pettit. Pettit was four years younger but only played one more year after Dolph. Schayes played 16 years and Pettit only 11. Except for longevity, Pettit had it all over the Syracuse and Philadelphia star. These men made their marks in cities that no longer have NBA basketball (Syracuse and St. Louis). One should not make the mistake of underrating or forgetting about either one.

Pettit won a pair of MVPs and Schayes did not. Pettit was All-NBA First Team in 10 of 11 seasons. Schayes and Pettit both retired as the league's all-time leading scorer. I'm going Pettit over Schayes for a few reasons.

1. Both won exactly one NBA title. In the seventh game of Schayes's 1955 championship, he scored only 13 points in that 92–91 victory. On the other hand, Bob Pettit scored 37 points in Game 1 of the 1957 Finals. In the seventh game of that series against the Celtics (and Bill Russell), he scored 39 points. In 1958, Pettit scored a then-Finals record 50 points in Game 6 to lead the Hawks to their only NBA Championship.

2. Pettit's Hawks went to four Finals in five years against the best of the Celtics dynasty. It is to their credit that they won one. Schayes and the Nats won their NBA title against Fort Wayne after changing the rules in the previous off-season to suit their style. Fort Wayne essentially played seven road games in the Finals, as a bowling tournament was booked in their home arena. So the three "home" games for Fort Wayne were switched to Indianapolis. The Pistons lost all three games there.

3. Pettit was a power player, a superior rebounder, and an offensive rebounder. Schayes was a better outside shot and (what you would expect from an iron man) lasted longer in the league.

Why, then, you might wonder, does Pettit rank so much higher than Schayes? Pettit's skills were more transferable to later generations—as Cousy's were. Pettit was four years younger than Dolph, but those were a big four years. It meant Schayes was dominating the NBA in 1950 and leading the league in rebounds in 1951. Pettit didn't enter the league until 1955. Pettit played against better competition in a slightly more modern era. In today's game, Pettit would have played the power forward, Schayes the shooting forward. I'm sure there will be people who feel that 23rd is too high for Schayes. But as it is, there are precious few players on my list from the early years of the NBA. The best deserve a place among the all-time greats.

JOHN HAVLICEK
The Best Mid-Sized Player of His Era

MVP: 0	
MVP VOTING: 4th in 1972, 5th in 1973	
NBA TITLES: 8	
ALL-NBA FIRST TEAM: 4	
ALL-NBA SECOND TEAM: 7	

If Jerry West is the greatest player in NBA history to never win a league MVP (he finished second in four different seasons), then John Havlicek is the greatest never to finish in the top three. Universally respected by fans, teammates, opponents, and coaches, Hondo played in the shadows of some great players in college (Jerry Lucas), the early years with the Celtics (Bill Russell), and his later days with the Celtics (Dave Cowens).

John Havlicek won eight NBA Championships, and although he did it all with one franchise, he did it performing several different functions. Havlicek won the first three rings by being the best sixth man in history. Red Auerbach didn't start Havlicek, preferring to bring his energy into the game to lead a second unit. Then, in the late 1960s, Coach Bill Russell started Havlicek. In the 1974 and 1976 championship seasons, the team was led by Dave Cowens.

Mr. Versatility

Hondo was terrific in every role asked of him. He was superb coming off the bench. He was a terrific starter. He could play 48 minutes without slowing down or losing productivity. He was good offensively and defensively.

Havlicek was named to the NBA All-Defensive First Team five times and the Second Team three other times. It is entirely possible he would have had more selections, but they didn't start voting for the All-Defensive teams until after Hondo's first six seasons.

It is also entirely possible that he—not John Stockton—had the most career steals. But they didn't record steals until 1974. Havlicek played 1,270 games—so if he averaged three steals per game in his first 11 seasons before they kept that particular statistic, he would have had a career total around 3,100 steals (adding the totals to his known 1974–1978 seasons). Only Stockton has more than 2,500 career steals officially since they began charting steals. I doubt Havlicek stole more than Stockton—but he damn sure stole the ball more than Michael Jordan, Scottie Pippen, Maurice Cheeks, Clyde Drexler, and anyone else you want to name. Havlicek also had the most famous steal in NBA history to nail down the 1965 Eastern Conference finals.

Mostly because the Celtics kept his minutes down, Havlicek didn't make All-NBA First Team until his ninth season. There is no other player that made All-NBA at least four times that didn't make his first until his ninth season. Kobe Bryant didn't make All-NBA First Team until his sixth season.

Havlicek the Legend

Although John Havlicek never played football at Ohio State, he was a seventh-round draft choice of the Cleveland Browns as a wide receiver and went to their training camp. From Ohio, Havlicek was a huge football fan. In his career, he was drafted by teams that featured Jim Brown in one sport and Bill Russell in another. He lasted with the Browns until the final cuts in football camp but never lost his football mentality.

In keeping with that football mentality, he played hurt. He not only played hurt, but he played courageously.

The best regular-season team that Havlicek ever played on was the 1973 Celtics team. That season, Hondo averaged 24 points, six rebounds, and six assists per game. In the Eastern Conference finals against the Knicks, Havlicek had 26 points, nine rebounds, and 11 assists in the first game, a Boston victory. He got caught in a pick in Game 3 and hurt his shoulder. He missed the fourth game in New York. In the fifth game, he scored 18 points while shooting only with his left hand. The Knicks finally realized he was a one-handed player for the rest of that series, and New York took the seventh game 94–78.

By the 1976 Finals, Havlicek had already turned 36 years old and was no longer the focus of the team. In those playoffs, he was battling a torn fascia in his right foot that required him to carry a plastic wash basin wherever he went so that he could constantly ice his foot. Despite the nagging injury—which forced him to miss three games of the Eastern semifinals against Buffalo—Havlicek played a key role in the 1976 Finals.

Bob Ryan: "By 1976, Havlicek was a shell of his old self . . . but picture Michael Jordan with the Wizards in 2003 and add 15 percent—that's what Hondo was to the 1976 Title team."

He averaged 17.8 points per game in the four Boston victories and averaged 4.5 assists per game in the series. What everyone remembers, however, is the classic Game 5 that went into triple overtime.

Brent Musburger: "Havlicek was virtually playing on one foot and yet managed to play 58 minutes that night. He scored 22 points, to go along with nine rebounds and eight assists. In the second overtime, Havlicek hit an off-balance shot that gave the Celtics a 111–110 lead with two seconds remaining. This is when the Suns' Paul Westhead called a timeout, without his team having one left. That brought a technical foul, allowing the Celts' JoJo White to sink a foul shot, putting Boston up a deuce. Garfield Heard hit a shot to tie the score and send it into a third overtime. The Celtics finally pulled away, and won the game—and two days later, the series."

Havlicek played in 13 All-Star games in a row, missing the first 3 in his career, mainly because he came off the bench and he averaged less than 30 minutes per game.

Bob Ryan calls Hondo the best mid-sized guard/forward combo ever in the league. It makes Havlicek sound like a mid-sized auto (maybe he's the Camry of NBA players?), but the point is valid. Havlicek was able to guard big guards such as Oscar Robertson and small forwards, including Bill Bradley, Jim McMillian, and Bobby Dandridge.

Big Game Player

Havlicek was one of the best big game players ever. In Game 7 of the 1969 Finals, he poured in 26 points. It was the last game of Bill Russell's career and the last game of Sam Jones's. The game ended with Wilt on the bench and Jerry West getting the Finals MVP in a losing effort. Havlicek's heroics were easy to overlook.

In 1974, Hondo was the Finals MVP. But again, he was overshadowed by an even greater performance. In the first three Boston victories in the 1974 Finals, Hondo scored 26, 28, and 28 points. Boston needed more from him in Game 6 if they were going to overcome Kareem Abdul-Jabbar. So, Hondo scored 36 points and added nine rebounds and four assists in the sixth game. He even had a record nine points in the second overtime session (nine of Boston's 11 final points). Kareem hit his game-winner at the buzzer to give the Bucks a 3–3 tie, sending the series to a seventh game.

Havlicek won eight NBA Championships and was the leading scorer on four of those clubs during the regular season.

Hondo's Eight NBA Championship Seasons

1963	Team's fourth-leading scorer
1964	Team's leading scorer
1965	Team's second-leading scorer
1966	Team's second-leading scorer
1968	Team's leading scorer
1969	Team's leading scorer
1974	Team's leading scorer
1976	Team's fourth-leading scorer

Leading Scorer on Most Championship Teams

Michael Jordan	6
John Havlicek	4
Kareem Abdul-Jabbar	4
George Mikan	4

Bob Ryan: "He played 48 minutes a night. . . . How many times did I see him outplay West and Robertson—the gold standards for guard play? Many."

Kevin Loughery: "Havlicek had a pull-up jumper from around 12 feet that was deadly. He had that in-between shot mastered."

Who's Better, Who's Best
John Havlicek or Billy Cunningham

Pete Vecsey: "Havlicek. It's not even close."

Kevin Loughery: "John Havlicek versus Billy C: They had different styles to get similar results. Hondo was a great scorer and a better defender than Cunningham. Hondo could be 0 for 15 field goals and he would keep shooting. I remember one game we were playing Boston, and Hondo was 0 for 17 at the half and hit for 30 points in the second half. He was a good passer and never stopped running."

Who's Better, Who's Best
John Havlicek or Rick Barry

Mike Dunleavy: "Hondo provided much more energy than Barry and much better defense. I played with Barry, and I don't mean to put him down. But I would take Havlicek."

Most Assists by Nonguards

1.	John Havlicek	6,114
2.	Scottie Pippen	6,085
3.	Larry Bird	5,695
4.	Kareem Abdul-Jabbar	5,660
5.	Julius Erving	5,176

In the end, Havlicek has to go down as one of the greatest forwards of all time. No nonguard in the history of the league has more career assists. He was an integral part of eight championship teams. That should say it all.

25

ISIAH THOMAS
Leader of the "Bad Boys"

MVP: 0	
MVP VOTING: 5th in 1984	
NBA TITLES: 2	
ALL-NBA FIRST TEAM: 3	
ALL-NBA SECOND TEAM: 2	

When Isiah Thomas entered the NBA, he joined a terrible Detroit Pistons team that had won only 16 and 21 games in the previous two seasons. Immediately, Detroit improved by leaps and bounds in Thomas's rookie season, winning 39 games. In that 1982 season, Detroit made two in-season trades. One brought a bruising center named Bill Laimbeer (from Cleveland) and the other brought the microwave—Vinny Johnson (who got hot early; acquired for Greg Kelser).

There were more changes in the following years. By 1984, head coach Chuck Daly was aboard. The 1985 draft was memorable for the drafting of Joe Dumars. The Pistons selected John Salley and Dennis Rodman in the 1986 draft. A team was being built to topple the mighty Celtics and Lakers. There would be enough time to squeeze in a pair of NBA Championships and three Eastern Conference championships in a row before the sleeping giant in Chicago awoke.

The Leader of the "Bad Boys"

Thomas was a big part of the Bad Boys, of course. They weren't confused with the popular Celtics. They were hated in every NBA arena outside Detroit. They practiced in black jerseys—complete with skull and crossbones—given to them personally by Oakland Raiders owner Al Davis. From that point, the moniker was official. Thomas was the captain, the unquestioned leader.

He was also the Most Valuable Player of the 1990 Finals, when he averaged 27.6 points, seven assists, and 5.2 rebounds against Portland. In Game 1, Isiah scored 16 points in the fourth quarter (finishing with 33 for the game), rallying the Pistons from 10 points down with seven minutes remaining. Later in those Finals, he would score 22 points in a quarter.

But that was only a small chapter in Thomas's big game heroics.

He had 24 points in the third quarter of a 1987 playoff game against the Atlanta Hawks. A player earns millions of dollars if he scores 24 points in a playoff game—much less a quarter. It is a feat not even Michael Jordan, Shaquille O'Neal, or Wilt Chamberlain has ever matched.

Thomas set an NBA Finals record in 1988 when he scored 25 points in the third quarter of Game 6. He did that with a severely sprained ankle. The Pistons lost that game and the series, after going back to Los Angeles up 3–2. Despite Thomas's big game, the Lakers prevailed 103–102.

The 1984 Playoffs

Maybe Thomas's most memorable playoff performance was in the 1984 playoffs versus the Knicks, when he scored 16 points in the final 94 seconds in the fourth quarter of the deciding fifth game.

During the regular season, the Pistons won 49 games and the Knicks won 47. Detroit had won four of six against New York during the season.

Both franchises were awakening from some doldrums. The Knicks hadn't won anything more than a best-of-three playoff series since 1974. The Pistons hadn't been in the playoffs since 1977 and hadn't advanced in the postseason since 1976. The Knicks were led by Bernard King, who was a scoring machine, averaging more than 26 points per game during the season.

New York struck first in Detroit's Silverdome, winning by a score of 94–93. King scored 36 points.

In the second game, Detroit jumped out to a 38–33 first-quarter lead. Then King had 23 consecutive points for New York in the quarter. He would score 46 points in the game. Isiah dished out 13 assists and scored 11 points. But it was Bill Laimbeer (31) and Kelly Tripucka (27) who did most of the offensive damage for the Pistons.

New York pushed Detroit to the brink of elimination in the third game, winning 120–113 as King scored 46 more points.

Isiah Thomas was always a great playoff performer. In the fourth game, he scored 22 points, pulled down seven rebounds, and dished 16 assists. The Pistons sent the series back to Detroit—this time at Joe Louis Arena. King scored 44 points in the deciding game, but Isiah led a furious rally (16 points in 94 seconds!) to send the game into overtime. The Knicks won the game 127–123, but Isiah played valiantly, scoring 35 points and getting 12 assists.

Matt Dobek: "I remember Bernard King averaged about 40 points per game in that series, and in the fifth game we were down late in the game. Isiah willed the game into overtime. I've never seen anything like those 16 points in 94 seconds."

A Closer Look at Thomas's Stats
He always scored more in the postseason than in the regular season.

Career regular season		19.2 points/game		
Career postseason		20.4 points/game		
1986	Regular season	20.9 points/game	Postseason	26.5 points/game
1987	Regular season	20.6 points/game	Postseason	24.1 points/game
1988	Regular season	19.5 points/game	Postseason	21.9 points/game
1989	Regular season	18.2 points/game	Postseason	18.2 points/game
1990	Regular season	18.4 points/game	Postseason	20.5 points/game

Despite those numbers, Thomas was always in the shadow of Magic Johnson.

Isiah and Magic
- Magic Johnson won a National Championship in college in 1979.
- Isiah Thomas won a National Championship in college in 1981.

- When Magic's Michigan State team won, it was against Larry Bird's Indiana State team in a contest that was so hyped it became the highest-rated basketball game of all time.
- When Isiah Thomas won a National Championship, it was on the same day that the President of the United States got shot. The game was an afterthought to most Americans.

- Magic Johnson was All-NBA First Team for nine straight seasons, beginning in 1983.
- Isiah Thomas was All-NBA First Team for three straight seasons, beginning in 1984.

- Magic Johnson was MVP of the All-Star game on two separate occasions.
- Isiah Thomas was MVP of the All-Star game on two separate occasions.

- When Magic was MVP of the 1992 All-Star game, it represented one of the all-time "feel good" stories in the NBA. Johnson, forced to retire prior to the 1992 season due to contracting the HIV virus, was still on the ballot and was voted in as a starter. Despite not playing all season, Johnson scored 25 points with 9 of 12 field goals and nine rebounds in the 1992 game.
- The most memorable All-Star memory of Isiah Thomas is probably the 1985 game, where big-fish Isiah "froze out" Jordan in his first All-Star game. Jordan would hit only two of nine field goals in 22 minutes in that game. No one mentioned anything about a freeze during the game. It was the hot rumor after the All-Star game had ended.

"Anything you can do, I can do better" is the theme of these comparisons: Isiah would lead the league in assists—Magic did it four times. Isiah would lead the Pistons to back-to-back NBA Championships in 1989 and 1990. So what? Magic had led the Lakers to back-to-back titles first, in 1987 and 1988.

Isiah couldn't win for losing. Even when Thomas led the Pistons past the Lakers in the 1989 Finals, everyone remembers that the Lakers were shorthanded as both starting guards (Magic Johnson and Byron Scott) had hamstring injuries. Magic really only played one game of that series.

Isiah was not only competing (and losing) to Magic Johnson all those years, but then Michael Jordan came along.

Jordan's arrival in the mid-1980s posed a unique threat to Thomas. Johnson was at least out on the West Coast, performing his Magic. But Jordan—damn it, did he have to land in Chicago, of all places!

Chicago was where Thomas was king of the courts growing up. Isiah was a schoolboy hero in the Windy City. By 1984, Thomas was one of the truly elite players in the NBA. Jordan was drafted by the Bulls—and suddenly, the Bulls were competitive. The Detroit Pistons (and anyone wearing the uniform) would be the bad guys.

Is it any wonder that Thomas would adopt the persona of his favorite football team—the Oakland Raiders? "Just Win, Baby."

Magic and Larry and Michael were credited with reviving the league. Isiah and the Pistons were credited with bringing down the beauty of the game with their "Bad Boy" antics.

The Olympics Story

Magic and Larry and Michael were able to join forces in the summer of 1992 (the "Good" Power Rangers) against the forces of evil. They were teammates on the Dream Team—the first professional team selected to represent the United States in Olympic play. The innuendo and world's worst-kept secret those days was that Jordan wouldn't give up his summer and play if Thomas was a part of the team. Many people were saying and writing that Thomas's walking off the court with Laimbeer as the Pistons were being dethroned by the Bulls hurt him in his bid to be on the Olympic team.

It's a joke that Thomas wasn't a part of that 1992 Olympic team. Thomas was a part of a more meaningful Olympic team—the 1980 squad—that never got to compete because the President of the United States said so (more meaningful because it was comprised of amateurs). Thomas should have had the very first invitation to the ball. In a "make-good" of sorts, Thomas was asked to compete as a member of the 1994 U.S. Team in the World Championships. Why Thomas even accepted is a mystery. (None of the original Dream Teamers would be on this team; it would be made up of secondary stars past their prime such as Dominique Wilkins, wanna-bes like Derrick Coleman and Larry Johnson, and rookies such as Shaquille O'Neal.) Of course, Isiah tore his Achilles tendon on April 19, 1994, and was unable to compete even in this. He then announced his retirement on May 11, 1994.

Thomas's Legacy

Isiah wasn't even accepted as a true hero by the Pistons fans or its management. Isiah retired in a season the Pistons won 20 games and lost 62. Instead of handing the keys of the kingdom to Isiah, they kept Don Chaney as head coach for another season. It was teammate Joe Dumars who eventually became president of basketball operations and stepped into the Detroit front office as soon as his playing days ended. A rift with Pistons owner Bill Davidson meant that Isiah ultimately was forced to go elsewhere—leave the country, in fact—as a part owner (figurehead) of the Toronto Raptors.

For various and complicated reasons, it was a no-win situation and Thomas parted ways with the franchise a few years later. Thomas was the majority owner of the Continental Basketball Association (1999–2000), but the NBA (with their own designs on a minor league) helped kill the CBA. The league now has its own NBDL (National Basketball Development League).

Is it any wonder that Thomas sometimes put his foot in the mouth and said the wrong things? Sometimes, this great leader said and did things that upset people. The two most memorable:

1. In 1987, the Pistons were on their way up—and the Celtics on their way down. Boston was the defending champion and unbeatable on their home court. In the crucial Game 5, Dennis Rodman blocked a shot by Larry Bird and the Pistons had the ball out of bounds with seconds to go. As Chuck Daly was trying to call a time-out, Isiah inbounded the ball to an unsuspecting Bill Laimbeer—and the Celtics made a miraculous steal and won the game. After the series, a distraught Rodman made the claim that if Larry Bird were black, he'd be just another guy. Isiah then made a mistake far worse than his pass in Game 5. He went on record as agreeing with Dennis. Bird accepted the apology at a hastily called press conference before the NBA Finals.

2. In 1991, the Pistons were on their way down—and the Bulls were on their way up. Detroit had held off Chicago in playoff series in 1988 (five games), 1989 (six games), and 1990 (seven games). By Memorial Day weekend, it was clear that the Bulls would not be denied any longer. Chicago took the first two games in Chicago, and Detroit needed a pair of victories on that holiday weekend to defend their championship. In Game 3, Isiah played his ass off. He played 47 minutes and scored 29 points with seven rebounds and six assists. Teammate Dumars made just three field goals in 10 tries, and the Bulls took the game 113–107 to go up 3–0 in the series. In the fourth game, Isiah didn't go quietly (16 points, seven rebounds, five assists), but Dumars got into foul trouble and again hit just three of 10 field goals for six points. The Bulls were going to their first NBA Finals. In the final minute of Game 4, Thomas, Dumars, and Laimbeer joined forces and walked off the court early before the game concluded. To me, it was a show of unity—of guys who had won together and who had now lost together. But it was not taken well by their opponents or the league. To them, it was a show of disrespect.

The good news is that Thomas found a team to coach. Eventually, he had to face the fact that the Pistons—and the league—would never treat him or hold him in the same regard as Magic Johnson or Michael Jordan.

In his playing days, Thomas made the All-Star game in his first 12 seasons. He retired fourth on the all-time list for career assists. He took a franchise that began in the league playing in 1949 in Fort Wayne and delivered the only two NBA Championships the team has ever won.

You have to hand it to Thomas. He had few allies among the NBA's big boys. He battled Karl Malone and Michael Jordan and Larry Bird. Despite his size, he more than held his own.

Who's Better, Who's Best
Isiah (Zeke) Thomas or Walt (Clyde) Frazier

Isiah Thomas: "We were different. Clyde depended on size and savvy to score. I had quickness and savvy."

Walt Frazier: "Isiah was the quintessential point guard. He rarely turned the ball over. I saw some aspects of his game that were similar to mine. First off, composure. He never got rattled and took good percentage shots."

Pete Vecsey: "A tie. I can't choose. I love them both."

Kevin Loughery: "Frazier versus Isiah Thomas: I have to go with Clyde. He was a better rebounder and better defender. Isiah had the toughness, though. Zeke was an incredible streak shooter."

Nate Archibald: "Clyde could do more than handle the basketball. He was an all-around guard. He could guard big guards or small forwards. Remember, he had guys on his team who could handle the ball and were distributors. Those Knicks had four or five of the most knowledgeable players ever."

Matt Guokas: "Clyde was so . . . elegant . . . graceful . . . he moved so smooth. Isiah— more bulldog—feisty—he played with a vengeance. Frazier accomplished the same as Thomas, but did it with a much different gait. Isiah did whatever it took. I played against Frazier for 10 years, and I never saw him change facial expression. Isiah would take on the big guys—he would shoot his team back in the game—he did whatever it took."

I always told Zeke that he was my fifth guard of all time, trailing only the big four of Oscar Robertson, Jerry West, Magic, and Michael. Of course, that was long before Kobe Bryant came on board. And before I seriously studied Bob Cousy. It's harder to keep this favorite of mine as the seventh-best guard. I've had to re-examine all my preexisting rankings. I'm not sure that the New York legend (Frazier) can take a backseat to Thomas. But then, Frazier played on a bigger stage with a better cast. Thomas will rank ahead of Frazier for now. But here comes Tracy McGrady, speeding along the expressway to stardom, as well. Isiah was everything right about the NBA. He played the game with a passion. He played the game with emotion. He played like he had a chip on his shoulder. So what if he didn't become Michael Jordan on the basketball court or Magic Johnson in the boardroom?

26

GEORGE GERVIN
Remember the "Iceman"

MVP: 0	
MVP VOTING: 2nd in 1978, 2nd in 1979, 3rd in 1980,	
5th in 1981, 6th in 1982	
NBA TITLES: 0	
ALL-NBA FIRST TEAM: 5	
ALL-NBA SECOND TEAM: 2	
ALL-ABA SECOND TEAM: 2	

There was one year that George Gervin was very close to winning the MVP. He was second in the league in 1978 and almost won it. Bill Walton had 96 votes and Gervin had 80.5. David Thompson was a distant third with 28.5 votes.

The Iceman was an outstanding scorer, one of the most prolific in league history. He was known as a player with such fluidity in his game that it appeared he floated smoothly down the court.

From ABA to NBA

Gervin started his career in the ABA, winning the ABA All-Rookie honors with the Virginia Squires as a teammate of Julius Erving. His contract was sold to the San Antonio Spurs because Squires owner Earl Foreman was looking to unload assets before selling the franchise. ABA Commissioner Mike Storen (Hannah Storm's dad, by the way) tried to block the deal. Foreman tried to back out of the deal, but Spurs owner Angelo Drossos filed a lawsuit against Foreman and the Spurs, forcing them to finish their transaction. It took a few weeks—with Gervin in limbo—but a judge eventually ruled that Storen had no right to block a legal deal and the Squires had to live up to their agreement. The league never filed an appeal. Gervin went on to average 23 points per game for the season, fourth in the ABA, and the Spurs lost to Indiana in the first round of the playoffs. Virginia went

28–56—even with Erving—then won only 15 games in each of the next two seasons and folded before the merger with the NBA in 1976.

Gervin is one of the few players in these pages who never won a championship. He is in an even smaller minority as one who never reached the NBA Finals. He is probably the greatest player never to appear in an NBA Finals game.

Just look how close he came.

1979	Eastern Conference finals Game 7	San Antonio 105 at Washington 107
1981	Western Conference semis Game 7	Houston 105 at San Antonio 100
1982	Western Conference finals	Lakers sweep Spurs 4–0
1983	Western Conference finals	Lakers win series 4–2

Three times in four seasons, the Spurs were among the final four teams, but they lost all three conference finals they played in. In 1984, the Spurs' defense fell to last in the NBA, allowing 124.8 points per game.

Gervin's Career (ABA and NBA)

1,060 games	25.1 points/game	5.3 rebounds	2.6 assists	26,595 total points

Quinn Buckner: "Gervin may be the best scorer I ever played against. . . . You could do whatever you want, and it wouldn't matter."

Rod Thorn: "Gervin: smooth as silk . . . quick . . . great shot maker . . . difficult to defend . . . it was a sight to see his spin shots."

Bill Walton: "George Gervin: near the top of any list . . . not a complete player . . . just a scorer . . . he had the pull-up 15-foot shot . . . he had the finger roll . . . teams had no idea how to defense him . . . impossible to guard him . . . graceful to watch."

Steve Jones: "Nobody in history scored points easier than Gervin. He would light you up and you didn't even know the match was lit. He had the efficiency and ability to be unstoppable."

Who's Better, Who's Best
George Gervin or Dominique Wilkins

Kevin Loughery: "It was so easy for Iceman. He was unique. He had his own, individual style. He was incredible to watch. He scored so easily. You would think you held him to 15 and look up—and he had 45. What a great shooter. But he didn't play defense—he was strictly a one-way player. Nique was a better rebounder and a better defender."

Who's Better, Who's Best
George Gervin or Allen Iverson

Steve Jones: "Allen Iverson takes a lot of bad shots and, like a lot of modern-day players, makes some questionable decisions. But Iverson has a competitive fire and willingness to do whatever it takes to win. Gervin was unstoppable. He could make 10 or 11 shots in a row. Now, Iverson could do that, too—but Gervin could do that on a consistent basis. Gervin had what modern players don't have—that mid-range shot. Iceman could score so many ways, from so many places on the court."

The Most Memorable Quarter of Gervin's Career

On April 9, 1978, the Spurs played the New Orleans Jazz in the season finale. The only thing at stake in this game was the NBA scoring title. George Gervin knew he needed 59 points to move past David Thompson and capture his first NBA scoring title. Earlier in the day, Thompson poured in 73 points. He finished his round first and signed his score card at 27.15.

Now, it was the Iceman's turn.

Gervin would score an NBA-record 33 points in a quarter. He broke a record that was held by Thompson for just a couple of hours. (Thompson had scored 32 points in the first quarter earlier that day against the Pistons in Detroit.) That broke the mark set by Wilt Chamberlain, who had scored 31 points in the fourth quarter of the contest in which he scored 100.

The Iceman would melt Thompson's record for points in a quarter—and capture the scoring championship. Gervin would need only 33 minutes to accumulate 59 points. It was the first of four scoring titles for him.

Gervin's NBA Scoring Titles

1978	Gervin 27.2 points/game	Second place David Thompson 27.15 points/game
1979	Gervin 29.6 points/game	Second place World B. Free 28.8 points/game
1980	Gervin 33.1 points/game	Second place World B. Free 30.2 points/game
1982	Gervin 32.3 points/game	Second place Moses Malone 31.1 points/game

Most Scoring Titles

1. Michael Jordan   10
2. Wilt Chamberlain   7
3. George Gervin   4

The 1978 MVP Vote

In 1978, Bill Walton was dominating the league and was on his way to his first MVP season. The Blazers got off to a blazing start and had already stashed their first Championship rings in their safe deposit boxes the previous June. Walton was averaging 19 points, 13 rebounds, and five assists. He was shooting more than 52 percent and blocking shots. He was one of the best passing centers of all time. But then he went down to injury and missed the last third of the season.

Gervin played all 82 games that season, leading the league in scoring. The Spurs won 52 games. Portland had the best record in the NBA that season, winning 58.

Walton received 96 votes. Gervin received 80.5.

It was a curious decision to vote a player MVP who missed so much time, when the leading scorer in the league was a deserving candidate.

Gervin's 26.2-per-game average in the NBA is eighth best of all time. If you include his ABA numbers, his 25.1 points per game is 10th best. He played with Erving at the beginning of Dr. J's career. He played with Michael Jordan at the beginning of Jordan's career. He made the All-Star team all nine seasons he was with the Spurs in the NBA. Even in 1986 with the Bulls (Jordan played only 18 games that season due to injury), Gervin averaged 16.2 points per game. He turned 36 that April and was finished in the league.

Gervin played briefly for the Bulls in that 1986 playoff series against the great Celtics. That was the series Jordan set a postseason record with 63 points in Game 2. Gervin played in two of those three games in that series, but didn't score a point in the 11 minutes he was on the floor. Everyone was probably too busy saying hello to Michael to say goodbye to George.

Why Gervin Can't Be Ranked Higher

The answer is *defense*.

Spurs Defensive Rankings with Gervin

1977	allowed 114.4 points/game	Last in NBA at 22nd (NBA average: 106.5 pts/game)
1978	allowed 111.1 points/game	18th in NBA (NBA average: 108.5 points/game)
1979	allowed 114.1 points/game	20th in NBA (NBA average: 110.3 points/game)
1980	allowed 119.7 points/game	Last in NBA at 22nd (NBA average: 109.3 pts/game)
1981	allowed 109.4 points/game	17th in NBA (NBA average: 108.1 points/game)
1982	allowed 110.8 points/game	18th in NBA (NBA average: 108.6 points/game)
1983	allowed 110.7 points/game	13th in NBA (NBA average: 108.5 points/game)
1984	allowed 120.5 points/game	22nd in NBA (NBA average: 110.1 points/game)

Follow me here. The average points an NBA team scored in a game between 1977 and 1984 was 108.7 points per contest. The Spurs allowed 113.8 points per game in that same eight-year period. San Antonio in those 656 regular-season games gave up more than 3,345 more points than the league average.

George Gervin played 640 of those 656 games in that eight-year period. And in those 640 games, he played 22,380 minutes for the Spurs (35 minutes per game).

Let's not be too hard on George. He was only on the court 75 percent of the time for San Antonio in that eight-year period. And he was only one of five players at any given time. So let's knock off 25 percent of those 3,345 points that the Spurs were over the NBA average (2,508 points—and only "charge" Gervin for 20 percent of them, since he was only one of five responsible at any given time). That means we have to hold Iceman accountable for 501 points during that period. And that's if we just wanted an average NBA defense.

Obviously, Gervin was the NBA's leading scorer in that same eight-year period, and head coaches Doug Moe and Stan Albeck were able to live with the lack of defensive intensity. Indeed, they probably encouraged it. They viewed the Spurs as an up-tempo team, rather than a poor defensive one. Gervin and the Spurs *did* score a lot more than the NBA average over that time, remember. But in the postseason, the Spurs couldn't turn a switch and begin playing defense.

In 1980, the Spurs' season ended when Houston knocked them out of the playoffs, scoring 141 points (a 141–120 victory).

In 1982, the Spurs came back to San Antonio down 0–2 against the Lakers in the Western Conference finals. They "held" the Lakers to 246 points in losing the last two games in Texas.

Did the Spurs score enough to justify the strategy? Well, the Spurs did average 116 points per game over that eight-year period.

1977–1984
The Spurs averaged 116 points per game.
The Spurs allowed 114 points per game.
The NBA average was 109 points per game.

One way of determining if a team's defense is good is by opponents' field goal percentages.

Opponents' Field Goal Percentages

Year	Opponent	NBA Avg.
1977	.490	.465
1978	.472	.469
1979	.477	.485
1980	.500	.482
1981	.472	.486
1982	.483	.491
1983	.485	.485
1984	.505	.492

It's a mixed bag. It looks like the Spurs were terrible defensively in 1977, 1980, and 1984. It also looks like they were actually about the league average in 1978 and 1983. The Spurs were a little better than the league average in 1979, 1981, and 1982.

Would the Spurs have won more games by slowing down the tempo? I believe so. Gervin led the NBA in shot attempts in 1979, 1980, and 1982. The plan was obviously to get the ball up the court for the Iceman to shoot as much as possible. You would think at some point, someone would have figured it out. "Hey, maybe we would win more if we took fewer shots, concentrated a little more on defense, and took better care of the basketball."

My guess is that a team with so much offensive firepower often ran teams out of the gym. Which means that although they won games by an average of 2.2 points during that period, there were lots of losses offset by big wins. They won an average of between 46 and 47 games per season. They never won more than 53 with Gervin.

In summary, Gervin was one of the great offensive talents the game has ever seen. There have only been two guards in history that scored more points than Gervin—and their names are Michael Jordan and Oscar Robertson.

Gervin	1,060 games	25.1 points/game
Jordan	1,072 games	30.2 points/game
Robertson	1,040 games	25.7 points/game

In downtown San Antonio, next to the Convention Center and on the delightful River-walk, is a street marked George Gervin Drive. It is the location of the old Hemisfair Arena, where the Spurs used to play. In a city that treasures history ("Remember the Alamo"), I say, "Remember the Iceman." George Gervin was a poor defensive player. But no worse than Shaquille O'Neal is as a free throw shooter . . . or Kevin McHale was as a passer . . . or Dennis Rodman was as an offensive player. A George Gervin drive to the hoop with that nasty finger roll was as good as it got in the late 1970s/early 1980s. And the fact that he never went to the NBA Finals? Heck, do you think Davy Crockett won his battle in San Antonio in the mid-1800s? Sometimes, it's about making a stand, defending your turf, and getting your shot off.

JOHN STOCKTON
The Tortoise

MVP: 0	
MVP VOTING: 10th in 1988, 7th in 1989, 9th in 1990,	
12th in 1991, 12th in 1992, 10th in 1993,	
8th in 1995, 11th in 1996, 15th in 1997	
NBA TITLES: 0	
ALL-NBA FIRST TEAM: 2	
ALL-NBA SECOND TEAM: 6	

John Stockton is the unlikeliest of players to rank in the top 30. He's never been the best player on his team, much less in the league. He's never won a championship or a scoring title, nor has he scored as many as 40 points in a game. He wasn't even one of the 15 highest-ranked players coming out of college!

1984 NBA Draft

1. Akeem Olajuwon, Houston
2. Sam Bowie, Portland
3. Michael Jordan, Chicago
4. Sam Perkins, Dallas
5. Charles Barkley, Philadelphia
9. Otis Thorpe, Kansas City
11. Kevin Willis, Atlanta
16. John Stockton, Utah

This is one of the toughest players for me to rank, because he owns some important records. What I had to decide was if Stockton was ever one of the best players in the league during any given season.

Stockton's Numbers

Look at the MVP voting. He was never in the top six in the league in MVP voting. He was never close to being a better player than teammate Karl Malone.

On the other hand, I have to respect the numbers.

Career Assists

1. 15,806   John Stockton
2. 10,215   Mark Jackson
3. 10,141   Magic Johnson
4. 9,887   Oscar Robertson
5. 9,061   Isiah Thomas
6. 7,704   Rod Strickland

That assists number is mind-boggling. If you cut it in half—to 7,903—it is more than all but a handful of players. If someone split John Stockton's 19-year career in half—and counted his statistics as John Young Stockton and John Old Stockton—then both players would have Hall of Fame credentials.

Young John Stockton	Elder John Stockton
1985–1993	1994–2003
734 games	770 games
13.1 points/game	13.2 points/game
11.4 assists/game	9.7 assists/game
31.6 minutes/game	32.1 minutes/game

Young John Stockton's assist total of 8,352 would place him behind only Magic Johnson, Mark Jackson, Oscar Robertson, and Isiah Thomas. The elder John would also trail Rod Strickland, Gary Payton, and Maurice Cheeks.

Stockton began his NBA career in 1985 but didn't break into the starting lineup until the 1987 season. He became a permanent starter in 1988 when he broke the single-season record for assists. Following his seventh season (1991) he was already 12th on the all-time list. By the 1993 season, he was fourth on that list. He broke Magic's all-time assist mark on February 1, 1995. On February 20, 1996, he broke the record for career steals.

This guy has made his name as vital in the NBA record books as Wilt Chamberlain. Of the nine times in history that a player has accounted for 1,000 assists in a season,

Stockton has seven of them. Only Isiah Thomas and Kevin Porter have also reached 1,000. It is not Stockton's career-best seasons that stand out. It is the consistent nature of his game.

First seven years	570 games	6,239 assists	10.9 per game
Since then	934 games	9,567 assists	10.2 per game

Who's Better, Who's Best
John Stockton or Any Other Modern-Day Point Guard

Mike Dunleavy: "Stockton over Payton: Stockton had the playmaking ability. He was the essence of a playmaker. Stockton and Cousy are the two best playmakers ever. Magic Johnson was the best all-around combo."

Rod Thorn: "Stockton was incomparable at delivering the ball."

Del Harris: "Excluding Magic, I'd put Isiah first, with Stockton second and Payton behind them."

The most amazing statistic when it comes to Stockton is his durability. Playing one of the toughest defensive positions to play, Stockton had perfect attendance in a remarkable 17 seasons. After being on the roster for 1,500 Jazz games, Stockton had managed to play in all but 22 of them. Here is a list of the excused absences.

Stockton Absences

Jazz Game	Reason	Result
Nov. 22, 1989	sprained left ankle	Jazz lost
Nov. 25, 1989	sprained left ankle	Jazz lost
Jan. 7, 1990	viral infection	Jazz won
Jan. 8, 1990	viral infection	Jazz won
Oct. 31–Dec. 5, 1997	left knee surgery	Jazz 11–7

That means he played in almost 99 percent of the Jazz games during a 19-year period. That he did most of it with a buddy—Malone—is even more remarkable. No pair of teammates had ever been together 14 years, much less 18.

Most Years Played Together as NBA Teammates
1. 18   John Stockton and Karl Malone
2. 13   Bill Laimbeer and Isiah Thomas
   13   Kevin McHale and Robert Parish

Stockton's 182 Playoff Games

He has played in a remarkable number of postseason games—more than two full regular seasons. The highlight of those 182 postseason games happened in 1997. It was the Western Conference finals against the Houston Rockets. Utah took the first two games, and then the Rockets stormed back to tie the series. The Jazz would win their first-ever trip to the NBA Finals, but it would not come easy. The Rockets were down 3–2, but the sixth game was tied in the final seconds. Stockton took an inbounds pass from Byron Russell with 2.8 seconds remaining, worked off a screen set by Malone, and sunk a 26-foot three-pointer that propelled the Jazz to victory.

In the 1997 and 1998 NBA Finals against the Chicago Bulls, Stockton's 12 games had a few memorable moments. In Game 1 of the 1998 Finals, Stockton scored 24 points (including 7 in overtime) and had eight assists to lead the Jazz to an early series lead. In Game 4 of the 1997 Finals, Stockton had six points and seven assists in the fourth quarter and lofted a perfect 50-foot pass to a streaking Karl Malone to lead the Jazz to a come-from-behind victory that tied the series at 2–2.

A Better Analogy

John Stockton and Cal Ripken Jr. Cal Ripken Jr. and John Stockton both played demanding defensive positions for close to two decades for the same team. They became heroes and legends, despite a lack of championships. They were both what my mother and grandmother before her would call *schwer-arbiters* (meaning "hard workers" in Yiddish and German).

Ripken played 3,001 total games in a sport that played 162 per season. Stockton played more than 1,500 in a sport that played 82 per season. No one in their generation matched their attendance records.

Cal is credited with saving baseball because his 2,632 consecutive games shattered the record of legendary hero Lou Gehrig. Stockton's work habits, ability to play through pain, and commitment to never taking a night off, rival Ripken's.

Ripken was the best player in the American League early in his career. Later in his career, he moved to a less demanding defensive position (from shortstop to third base). Just as Ripken would miss a few innings in his final seasons, Stockton's minutes were monitored and went down. Remarkably, though, Stockton's game remained at a high level despite playing point guard.

In Stockton's 19th season, he was among the top five players in the league in assists per game. He was still in the top 12 in steals per game. He was still one of the highest-percentage shooters in history.

And Stockton was doing this at the advanced age of 41. He didn't stop the clock for several seasons—as Jordan did. This car turned over the odometer a couple of times and was rarely in the shop for service. He played hurt, and he played hard. He set an example for the younger generation to follow. He didn't turn down All-Star invitations or Olympic roster spots. The worst one could say about him was that he didn't enjoy opening up to the media, giving tight, short responses. He never opened up in a way that others have.

No one ever called him a great scorer, but this tortoise has scored close to 20,000 points—a feat reached by less than 30 others. He did it in short bursts, for in his 1,500 career contests, he never scored as many as 35 points in a game. In 19 years, he scored more than 7,000 field goals himself and assisted on close to 16,000 more for the Utah Jazz. Remarkable.

JASON KIDD

The Closest Thing to Magic

MVP: 0	
MVP VOTING: 2nd in 2002, 5th in 1999, 9th in 2003	
NBA TITLES: 0	
ALL-NBA FIRST TEAM: 4	
ALL-NBA SECOND TEAM: 1	

Jason Kidd was the second overall pick of the 1994 NBA draft, behind Glenn Robinson. He was co-Rookie of the Year in his first season (with Grant Hill), and he has been one of the premier point guards in the game since then. He has been voted to the All-NBA First Team for four consecutive years. There are not many players who have accomplished that—especially the players who are guards.

Guards Who Have Been All-NBA First Team at Least Four Times

1. Bob Cousy   10
2. Jerry West   10
3. Michael Jordan   10
4. Oscar Robertson   9
5. Magic Johnson   9
6. George Gervin   5
7. Jason Kidd   4
8. Bill Sharman   4

The primary responsibility of the point guards is to distribute the ball to teammates for baskets. There aren't many guards who have more assists per game in their careers than Jason Kidd.

Highest NBA Average Assists per Game, Career

1. 11.2   Magic Johnson
2. 10.5   John Stockton
3. 9.5   Oscar Robertson
4. 9.4   Jason Kidd
5. 9.3   Isiah Thomas

The Stats—From Assists to Rebounds

In a six-year period from 1998 through 2003, Kidd had more assists than anyone.

Most Assists 1998–2003

1. 4,234   Jason Kidd
2. 3,889   Gary Payton
3. 3,636   John Stockton
4. 3,589   Stephon Marbury

Kidd's Assists per Game

1995	Tied for ninth
1996	Second to Stockton
1997	Fourth
1998	Second to Strickland
1999	First
2000	First
2001	First
2002	Second to Andre Miller
2003	First

Kidd has finished first four times and second three times.

Kidd has never put up the assists that Stockton compiled in the late 1980s. Nor has he scored as many points as Gary Payton. But—of the best guards in NBA history—Kidd has few peers when it comes to rebounding.

Elite Guards in NBA History

Oscar Robertson	7.5 rebounds/game	7,804 rebounds
Magic Johnson	7.2 rebounds/game	6,559 rebounds
Michael Jordan	6.2 rebounds/game	6,175 rebounds

| Walt Frazier | 5.9 rebounds/game | 4,830 rebounds |
| Jason Kidd | 6.4 rebounds/game | 4,157 rebounds |

But there's more to his game than rebounds. Kidd plays great defense. He is a supreme playmaker. He has improved his field goal shooting. He has improved his free throw shooting.

Rod Thorn: "Kidd—top-flight defender, rebounder . . . scores when he has to."

But Jason Kidd couldn't shoot . . . like everyone else.

Worst Field Goal Percentage Since 1955 and the Shot Clock (min. 7,000 Attempts)

1.	.378	Guy Rodgers
2.	.379	Bob Cousy
3.	.384	Dolph Schayes
4.	.386	Howard Komives
5.	.396	Gene Shue
6.	.398	Vernon Maxwell
7.	.399	Frank Ramsey
8.	.405	Tom Heinsohn
	.405	Ray Scott
	.405	Jason Kidd

That means this is also true.

Worst Field Goal Percentage Since 1970 (min. 7,000 Attempts)

1.	.398	Vernon Maxwell
2.	.405	Jason Kidd

In his postseason career with the Nets, Jason became his own "go-to guy," preferring to take more shots than to pass to reluctant or poor-shooting teammates. This has had mixed results.

2002 Season

Regular season:	13.8 field goal attempts/game
Playoffs:	17.7 field goal attempts/game
Finals:	20.0 field goal attempts/game

2003 Season

Regular season:	15.6 field goal attempts/game
Playoffs:	17.1 field goal attempts/game
Finals:	20.1 field goal attempts/game

Or, put it like this. In the 2003 Finals, Jason Kidd (the premier distributor of the basketball) took 12 more shots than Tim Duncan. In the 2002 Finals, Kidd took 10 more shots than Kobe Bryant (and only four less than Shaquille O'Neal). Is it any wonder that the Nets won only two of 10 Finals games?

In the 2003 Finals, Kidd shot 36 percent. He had games where he made four of 17 field goals (Game 1 defeat), six of 19 field goals (Game 3 defeat), and five of 18 field goals (Game 4 victory).

Kidd has always been described as a "Magic Johnson type," a player who can impact a game without scoring a point. But Magic (who also lost five NBA Finals series) won titles because his teammates were able to hit a shot. A quarterback can put the ball in the perfect spot, but if the receiver drops the ball there is no touchdown.

Who's Better, Who's Best
Jason Kidd or Magic Johnson

Isiah Thomas: "There is definitely a comparison. Kidd is the closest thing to Magic in this league. They both weren't great shooters. But they both had size, energy, brains, and that made them great."

Walt Frazier: "At his size, 6-foot-4, 212, Jason is probably the quickest ever off the dribble. He's even faster than Magic."

George Karl: "Some people are going to say Magic was the best passer ever . . . Stockton was the best passer ever . . . some old-timers might say Cousy. But Jason Kidd is among the top five playmaking guards in basketball ever in my opinion."

Magic Johnson: "Myself, Michael, Larry—we made guys better. That's what Jason does. He makes guys better."

Pat Riley: "Size was probably the only thing Magic would have over him. He had the size, but they both could really think. They were winners, they were leaders, and they had the talent to back it up."

Byron Scott: "His competitive nature stands out. Earvin had it, but he was much more vocal. Jason is the quiet type. People see him and they think he is a mild-mannered, quiet guy. But he's like the quiet assassin. The only thing that separates him from Earvin is five inches. He has the heart and desire. No one else can win games without scoring like Kidd can."

What Jason has become known for is his ability to turn around a team. He has done it more than once. Of course, turning the downtrodden Nets into a Finalist was the attention-getter.

Turnarounds

Team	Year Before Kidd	Year Kidd Arrived	Improvement
U. of Calif.	1992 (10–18 record)	1993 (21–9 record)	11 wins
Mavericks	1993 (13–69 record)	1994 (36–46 record)	23 wins
Suns	1997 (8–19 to start season)	(32–23 with Kidd)	23 wins
Nets	2001 (26–56 record)	2002 (52–30 record)	26 wins

Sean Elliott: "I used to watch Jason play in college. Remember, I was an Arizona guy and Jason is from California—so I watched the Pac 10 a lot, and I knew he would be great. We played them in his rookie year with Dallas. He really did make Jimmy Jackson and Jamal Mashburn better."

Jimmy Jackson: "I played with Jason in Dallas, and he wasn't the same player he became in New Jersey. The biggest things: Jason's confidence just grew and grew. He became a leader. And he became a much better threat to score. Back then, teams would just back off him, because they didn't respect his shot. Even from the beginning of his NBA career, though, he would get you the ball in perfect position."

Before the first game of the 2002 NBA Finals, I asked Jason who was the greatest player he ever played with. He responded with guys from the 2000 U.S. Olympic team. (I can't be certain, but if asked a year later, he might say Kenyon Martin, a player of whom he has been very complimentary and protective.) You get my point, however. Jason—unlike the other great point guards—has never played with anyone approaching what the others had.

Kidd's Greatest Teammates
Jimmy Jackson
Jamal Mashburn
George McCloud
Cedric Ceballos
Danny Manning
Antonio McDyess
Tom Gugliotta
Shawn Marion (before he became a star)
Kenyon Martin
Richard Jefferson

Not Hall of Fame material. Kidd made them all better.

Bob Cousy had his pick of Hall of Famers to pass to. John Stockton had his very own Karl Malone to treasure. Magic Johnson had Kareem Abdul-Jabbar—and James Worthy.

That brings to mind the question: Which player in NBA history has had the greatest collection of teammates?

I've narrowed it down to three candidates.

Greatest Collection of Teammates

1. **Horace Grant** This guy was always surrounded by great talent. He played six years with Michael Jordan—in Jordan's prime. He played seven years with Scottie Pippen—in Pippen's prime. He played two years with a young Shaquille O'Neal in Orlando. He played one year with a mature O'Neal in Los Angeles. He played with both Penny Hardaway and Kobe Bryant. He played with Gary Payton in his prime. He played with Tracy McGrady and Grant Hill. He even played with an old Patrick Ewing. And Grant was a major contributor everywhere he went. He wasn't just along for the ride.

2. **John Havlicek** He played one year with Bob Cousy. He played seven years with Bill Russell. He played with Sam Jones and Dave Cowens and Paul Silas and Tom Heinsohn. He wasn't the same as Don Chaney (a trivia answer because he played one year with Russell at the end and Bird at the beginning). Hondo was a major star who caught the first wave of the Celtics dynasty.

3. **Dennis Rodman** He played with Isiah Thomas, Joe Dumars, and Bill Laimbeer in Detroit. He played with David Robinson in San Antonio. He played with Jordan and Pippen in Chicago. He played with Kobe and Shaq in Los Angeles.

Ultimately, I would choose Grant and his teammates for a simple reason. Grant played with the better Michael Jordan. Also, it would be hard to beat a team with Tracy McGrady and Kobe Bryant on it.

Those are the kind of teammates Jason Kidd gets to play with—once a year at the All-Star game—and once every four years at the Olympics.

Who's Better, Who's Best
Jason Kidd or John Stockton

This is one of those classic confrontations that could produce endless arguments. Kidd is a better rebounder. Stockton is a better shooter. Kidd has recorded 49 triple doubles—fifth on the all-time list, trailing only Oscar Robertson, Magic Johnson, Wilt Chamberlain, and Larry Bird.

Stockton is a good shooter. Kidd is not. Stockton is an incomparable passer. Kidd is right there. Stockton's assist numbers are through the roof. But Jason has been a near-MVP and picked four times for All-NBA First Team in his nine seasons. Stockton made it twice in his 19 years.

Steve Jones: "Stockton has played hurt and has never had a bad year. Jason will be remembered for his play with the Nets, but he had some iffy years in Dallas."

Here, courtesy of the New Jersey Nets, is a look at Stockton and Kidd through a like number of games. This was for their first 629 games each in the NBA.

	Points/Game	Assists/Game	Rebounds/Game	Field Goal Percentage	All-NBA First Team
John Stockton	12.7	11.1	2.4	.517	2
Jason Kidd	14.6	9.3	6.4	.406	4

I made a case to many of my friends, intending to push Jason ahead of John Stockton. Ultimately, I couldn't do it. Stockton's numbers (like Chamberlain's and Rodman's) are too compelling. Even forgetting the edge Kidd has in rebounding, Stockton was a much more accomplished shooter. The Utah guard was the best in the business for years and years.

Jason Kidd can move ahead of Stockton, however. He needs to win an MVP or win a championship. Until then, Kidd has matched Stockton with consecutive losses in the NBA Finals and finds himself about nine thousand assists shy of the incredible Stockton. Kidd will be a Hall of Famer, but Magic Johnson or Isiah Thomas he's not. Although it would be very interesting to see him with Worthy/Malone/Duncan-type teammates.

SCOTTIE PIPPEN
The Second Banana

MVP: 0	
MVP VOTING: 9th in 1992, 3rd in 1994, 7th in 1995, 5th in 1996, 11th in 1997, 10th in 1998	
NBA TITLES: 6	
ALL-NBA FIRST TEAM: 3	
ALL-NBA SECOND TEAM: 2	

Despite the fact that he has so many credentials to bring to the table to prove his status as one of the all-time greats, Scottie Pippen has more than his share of critics. Until I started writing this book, you could have counted me among them. One of the experts that I interviewed for this book thought that Pippen was the most overrated of all the great players. The question is essentially this: Could any number of players have played next to Michael Jordan and won just as much?

Scottie Pippen has had the standard textbook career arc of a great player. His lowest scoring and rebounding averages came in his rookie year. He improved each year for the next four or five seasons. He won his first ring in his fourth year. He made All-NBA Second Team in his fifth year. He had a three-year run as—if not the best perimeter player in the game—certainly one of the top three. His play has remained consistent on offense and defense deep into his 16th season.

After 208 playoff games—many on national television—Pippen's hits and misses have become etched in our memories. In 2003, the outspoken Pippen made the playoffs for the 16th consecutive season. Only the two Jazz musicians (Karl Malone and John Stockton) have had playoff streaks as long as Pippen's.

Bill Walton has long maintained that the toughest thing for a truly great player to do is be the best player on a bad team. I'm not debating that, but a close second would be to have an even greater teammate in the prime of one's career. Pippen has had to fight for his turf his entire career.

Pippen's Tour with the Bulls

Pippen didn't join the Bulls as Michael Jordan did, with three years of exploits at the University of North Carolina, playing for a storied franchise and a legendary coach. Pippen played his college ball at Central Arkansas. It was Chicago general manager Jerry Krause who loved Pippen and made a draft-day trade with Seattle to secure the rights to Pip. Ironically, it was Krause who later coveted European forward Toni Kukoc. Pippen would view this as a sign of disrespect toward him. In fact, it was a shrewd and brilliant move. Scottie's defensive play on Kukoc in the 1992 Olympics was memorable. Krause would eventually add another Pippen nemesis to the Bulls roster—Dennis Rodman.

In Pippen's 1988 rookie season, he played fewer minutes than fellow rookie Horace Grant. They were young pups and thrown to the wolves 35 times together against the Detroit Pistons in their first three years.

Chicago Against Detroit

1988	Detroit 4–2 in regular season	Detroit 4–1 in Eastern Conference semis
1989	Detroit 6–0 in regular season	Detroit 4–2 in Eastern Conference finals
1990	Detroit 4–1 in regular season	Detroit 4–3 in Eastern Conference finals

That rivalry is hard to forget. Detroit had spent several seasons getting beaten by the Boston Celtics. It was those defeats at the hands of the Celtics and Lakers that educated the Pistons on how to win. By the late 1980s, Detroit was clearly the best team in the NBA, and their physical style had helped defeat the Bulls 26 of 35 times between 1988 and 1990.

During that period, Scottie Pippen had to guard players like John "Spider" Salley and Dennis Rodman. Pippen did not always distinguish himself. In 1988, he could be excused from doing more; he was merely an eight-point-per-game scorer playing 21 minutes per game in that rookie season. But by 1989, Pippen had earned starter's minutes (28 per night) and was the team's second-leading scorer behind Jordan.

So, in the 1989 Eastern Conference finals, when the Bulls stole the first game in Detroit and came back to sweet home Chicago for Game 3, it was inexcusable for Pippen to put up a clinker (two of 10 field goals on the way to just seven points plus five fouls) in a two-point game. No one was going to point fingers at Michael. Someone was going to have to take the blame. In Game 5 of that series, Pippen had only seven points. He didn't play at all in the sixth game, coming down with the most famous migraine since Kareem Abdul-Jabbar's in the sixth game of the 1980 Finals.

The next year, the teams met again in the Eastern Conference finals. This time, the Bulls pushed the Pistons to a seventh game. Pippen shot 10 times. He made one basket, scoring two points in 42 minutes. The Pistons went on to the Finals for the third consecutive season, beating the Bulls each year along the way.

Even after an NBA title, whispers about Pippen's play in the postseason continued. Pat Riley's Knicks continued the physical assault on the Bulls. In the 1992 playoffs, the Knicks (with forwards Xavier McDaniel and Charles Oakley) tried to intimidate Pippen. Scottie was seen as a complainer, especially after a two-of-12 field goal performance in Game 2 of that series.

In fairness, Pippen had a triple double in Game 7 of that 1992 series with the Knicks (17 points, 11 rebounds, 11 assists).

That's the maddening thing about getting a handle on Pippen. He's had so many great moments in postseason play. He's also had his share of boo-boos.

Consider 1994, when free from Jordan's shadow, Pippen was finally "The Man" in Chicago. The Knicks and Bulls were tied at a game apiece, and the third game came down to the final shot. Chicago coach Phil Jackson designed a play for Toni Kukoc to take with Pippen as a decoy. Pippen refused to go into the game with 1.8 seconds remaining. Everyone remembers Pippen refusing to go in. Kukoc hit the game-winner.

In 1996, Pippen was All-NBA First Team, and played on a 72–10 team, the best of all time. But in the Finals, the Sonics frustrated him. Pippen—a 47 percent shooter—hit just 34 of 99 field goals against Seattle, including just 9 of 37 (24 percent) in the two Chicago losses.

By now, though, Pippen had learned to contribute mightily even when his shotmaking ability was off. His disruptive defense helped the Bulls win back-to-back titles against the Utah Jazz, despite Pippen shooting two of 16 field goals in Game 5 of the 1998 Finals.

The Playoff Highlight Reel

Pippen had some of the most unbelievable playoff lines in history, certainly in the last 30 years. In the sixth game of the 1992 Eastern Conference finals against the Cleveland Cavs, Pippen closed the door on the Cavs by amassing 29 points, 12 rebounds, five assists, and four steals. In the third game of the 1996 first round against the Miami Heat, he had his usual triple double (22 points, 18 rebounds, 10 assists) to close the door on Alonzo Mourning and company. In Game 3 of the 1999 series against the Lakers, Pippen (by now a Rockets player) helped stave off elimination with a 37-point, 13-rebound game. In Game 5 of the 2000 series against the Lakers, Pippen (now with the Blazers) put off elimination by putting up 22 points, six rebounds, and six assists to cut the Lakers' lead to 3–2.

Scottie Pippen has played 208 postseason games. Only one player in NBA history, Kareem Abdul-Jabbar, has ever played in more. But the first 57 of Kareem's postseason game were played in the early 1970s with the Bucks. Kareem's 89th to 93rd postseason games were in the 1980 Finals, when the weekday games were not even shown live. So even though Kareem played more playoff games, many more people saw Pippen's. Pippen, on the other hand, had as much exposure on prime-time network television in the 1990s as Kelsey Grammer had playing Frasier Crane. Similar to Grammer on "Cheers," Pippen was a supporting star on the top show in television. When that team was broken up, Pippen continued in the same role for many more years than anyone thought possible.

There are only a handful of NBA players in history who have won more championships than Pippen's six. Of course, those players played for the Celtics in the 1960s, when they won 11 of 13 titles. But Bill Russell never had to win four playoff series to win a single title. So, it is possible that no one has approached Pippen's postseason victory count.

In the first round of playoff series, Pippen's teams were 12–4. By my count, his teams were 39–18 in first-round games. At one point, his teams were 11–0 in the first round.

In the Finals, Pippen's teams were 6–0 in series and 24–11 overall.

In the Conference finals, Pippen's teams were 6–3 in the series (losses twice to the Pistons, and the 2000 Blazers lost a Game 7 to the Lakers). His teams were 32–16 in the Conference finals.

That leaves the Conference semifinals. In second-round series, Pippen's teams were 9–3 (losses to the Pistons in 1988, the Knicks in 1994, and the Magic in 1995). That's another 42 wins in second-round games, compared to 26 defeats.

That puts Scottie Pippen's career playoff record at 137–71, for a .661 winning percentage. Now, his detractors (me no longer being one of them) would point out that Michael Jordan was his teammate for 124 of those victories.

Oh, by the way: In three playoff seasons without Pippen, Jordan's teams were 1–9. In five playoff seasons with Jordan, Pippen's teams were 13–17. If Pippen, Steve Smith, or Rasheed Wallace could have hit some shots in the fourth quarter and held on to a double-digit lead in Game 7, Pippen would have made the Finals without Michael.

Again, the question remains: Is there another player in NBA history who could have taken part in 137 winning postseason games?

Let's first look at Bill Russell, the only player to play on all 11 title teams with the Celtics. The Celtics won 108 playoff games between 1957 and 1969. Russell didn't even suit up for a couple of the 1958 Finals games, but you get the point.

Magic Johnson was considered one of the great winners in NBA history. His teams did play in an era where it took four series to win a championship. He led his team to the Finals nine times. Johnson's teams were 127–63 in the postseason (.668).

Of course, Abdul-Jabbar has been in more winning playoff games. Kareem's teams were 154–83 (.649).

Kareem played second banana himself in many of those 237 playoff games, remember. Pippen's teams had a better winning percentage than Abdul-Jabbar's or Jordan's teams. Scottie won more postseason games than anyone except for Kareem. He was one of the main winners in the history of American team professional sports.

What Type of Player Was Pippen?

One of the best defensive players in the game, with the ability to guard—lock up and shut down—virtually anyone under seven feet tall. In the 2003 season—his 16th—Pippen would guard anyone from Atlanta power forward Shareef Abdul-Rahim to San Antonio point guard Tony Parker to Boston small forward Paul Pierce. This gave his teams incredible versatility. He was a great leaper in his youth, and had the ability to dunk off the dribble on his drive and tip-dunk the offensive rebound. He would often take defensive rebounds and go the distance. He actually played point guard for the Chicago championship teams in the Bulls' triple-post offense. He had excellent ball-handling skills and was a skilled passer.

Doug Collins: "Scottie and Michael were the two best perimeter defensive players ever. Scottie could shut down anyone and take away half the court."

Who's Better, Who's Best
Scottie Pippen or John Havlicek

Mike Dunleavy: "Hondo versus Pippen: very similar players. Pippen is more athletic. Hondo was stronger. Pippen a better playmaker. Hondo a better offensive player. Pippen a better defensive player."

Matt Guokas: "Pippen versus Havlicek: First off, Havlicek was a good defender—for that era. Pippen was a better passer than Hondo, and more of a playmaker. John was relentless. He never stopped running. He was always looking to score. He was a better shooter than Pippen ever was."

P. J. Carlesimo: "Pippen or Hondo. I'll take Hondo."

Rod Thorn: "Hondo versus Pippen: When Scottie was at his peak, he was the perfect complement to Jordan. Scottie gave his team big shots and energy, and was probably a little more talented than Havlicek. But Hondo would run as hard in the 40th minute as he would in the first."

Bob Ryan: "Scottie Pippen: best mid-sized forward/guard since Hondo, but not in his league. At Scottie's peak, he was the second-best player in the league. But without Jordan, Pippen plunged to about the 20th best in the game. Havlicek was better—look at his 1970 season."

Actually, Bob, I was intending to do so. Pippen's best season came in 1994, one year after Michael Jordan retired. Havlicek's best season came in 1970, one year after Bill Russell retired.

In 1970 Havlicek (30 years old, eighth year) led his team in:

Points	1,960
Rebounds	635
Assists	550
Minutes	3,369

Havlicek's averages in 1970	24.2 points	7.8 rebounds	6.8 assists

Funny, that looks similar to Pippen's line from 1994, the year after Michael Jordan retired.

Pippen's averages in 1994	22.0 points	8.7 rebounds	5.6 assists

After the 1994 season, Horace Grant departed the Bulls as a free agent. In the 1995 season, Pippen (at 30 years old in his eighth season) duplicated Hondo's feat.

Pippen in 1995: He led his team in scoring (21.4 points per game), rebounding (8.1), assists (5.2), steals (2.94), blocks (1.13), and minutes (3,014). That year, Pippen led the NBA in steals. Of course, they didn't keep steals or blocks for Havlicek in the early 1970s.

In short, I have to go back to the set of numbers I trust:

Pippen	All-NBA First Team three years (1994, 1995, 1996)
Havlicek	All-NBA First Team four years (1971, 1972, 1973, 1974)
Edge:	Hondo

Pippen	All-Defensive First Team eight times
Havlicek	All-Defensive First Team five times (not awarded until his seventh year)
	Tie

| Pippen | 18,804 points | 7,426 rebounds | 6,085 assists |
| Havlicek | 26,395 points | 8,007 rebounds | 6,114 assists |

They have the two leading assist totals in history for nonguards (although both played guard at times in their careers).

Pippen	Six championships (6–0 in Finals)
Havlicek	Eight championships (8–0 in Finals)

Havlicek was one of the most multiskilled players in NBA history. Pippen was not really in his class as a scorer and shooter. Pippen didn't have the durability of Havlicek, nor was he able to provide 48 minutes on a nightly basis. Havlicek won without Russell and Sam Jones. He was his team's leading scorer on four different NBA Championship teams.

A Better Analogy

Scottie Pippen and Clarence Clemons Pippen was closer to being the NBA's answer to Clarence Clemons. Bruce Springsteen didn't make it big until the big man joined the band, just as Jordan didn't win until Pippen got up to speed with the Bulls. Clemons released some solo albums, but only hit it big—real big—when he recorded and toured with "The Boss." In fairness, Springsteen needed Clemons and Stevie Van Zandt and Max Weinberg—the longtime members of the E Street Band. Springsteen needed a backup band, and Jordan needed Pippen. Springsteen and Jordan both needed their supporting cast. Together, they complemented each other.

DENNIS RODMAN
The Greatest Defensive Forward Ever

MVP: 0	
MVP VOTING: None to speak of	
NBA TITLES: 5	
ALL-NBA FIRST TEAM: 0	
ALL-NBA SECOND TEAM: 0	

Dennis Rodman is one of those controversial players whose selection has caused some head-scratching by some and vehement arguments from others. But quite simply, this guy was passed by in 1996 when the league chose its 50 greatest. In fact, Rodman was the greatest defensive player in the history of the game.

Stay with me. Dennis Rodman was on the NBA All-Defensive First Team seven times in eight years. He was on the Second Team the other year. He was the league's rebounding champion a record seven years in a row. He was the Defensive Player of the Year in two consecutive seasons (1990 and 1991).

All those head coaches who preach defense and rebounding and unselfishness can't ignore the player they called "The Worm."

A Winner

Rodman was—above all—instrumental in making his teammates better. He was a winner.

Rodman's Teams

1987	52 wins
1988	54 wins—Pistons 20–4 with Rodman in starting lineup; Pistons lose Finals Game 7
1989	63 wins—best record in NBA; Pistons win NBA title
1990	59 wins—Pistons 34–9 with Rodman in starting lineup; Pistons win NBA title

1991	50 wins
1992	48 wins
1993	40 wins—Pistons 36–26 with Rodman; 4–20 without him
1994	55 wins
1995	62 wins—best record in NBA (Spurs 42–7 with Rodman; 20–13 without him)
1996	72 wins—best record in NBA history; Chicago wins NBA title
1997	69 wins—best record in NBA
1998	62 wins—tied for best record in NBA

It sounds incredible, but the magic continued. In 1999, the Lakers signed Dennis on February 23. On February 24, they relieved Del Harris as head coach. The Lakers were 6–6 when they signed Rodman (and replaced Harris). They won their next nine games immediately after signing Rodman. Dennis would last only another 14 games with the Lakers and 12 games with the Mavs the next season.

Rodman led the NBA in rebounds with three different franchises. He won two rebounding titles with the Pistons. He won twice with the Spurs. He was the league's leading rebounder with the Bulls three consecutive seasons.

For a three-year period that encompassed the 1993, 1994, and 1995 NBA seasons, Dennis Rodman averaged 18.1 rebounds per game. Of those 223 games, he grabbed 20+ rebounds in 94 of them.

And why is that so impressive?

No other player has averaged as many as 18 rebounds per game in a single season (never mind three consecutive seasons) besides Rodman since 1974. In 1974, Hayes averaged 18.1.

The Chicago Bulls lost Horace Grant to free agency following the 1994 season. In 1995, without Grant, they were a very average rebounding team. Trading for Dennis, the Bulls became a terrific rebounding team.

Chicago Bulls Rebounding

1993	+269 rebounds than opponents
1994	+309 rebounds than opponents
Grant leaves	
1995	+80 rebounds than opponents
Rodman joins team	
1996	+541 rebounds than opponents
1997	+403 rebounds than opponents
1998	+426 rebounds than opponents

Bulls Rebounding Averages

| 1995 | (before Rodman) | 41.4 per game |
| 1996 | (with Rodman) | 44.6 per game |

In Rodman's three seasons in Chicago, the Bulls outrebounded their opponents by more than 5.5 rebounds per game. In the year before he came, their rebounding edge was less than one board per game.

It was a familiar story for Rodman. The arrival of Dennis in San Antonio in 1994 shored up a big weakness on the Spurs—offensive rebounds. The Spurs finished first in offensive rebound percentage (pulling down more than 35 percent of their missed shots) after finishing dead last in that category a year prior.

Rodman's Erratic Attendance

It's impossible to evaluate Rodman without considering his attendance on the court.

Rodman's Attendance Record

1987	missed five games
1988	perfect attendance
1989	perfect attendance
1990	perfect attendance
1991	perfect attendance
1992	perfect attendance
1993	missed 20 games (team 4–16); missed 14 with torn right calf muscle, also suspended twice by Pistons due to team violations
1994	missed 3 games; suspended by Spurs twice, one DNP (coach's decision)
1995	missed 33 games; Spurs suspended him for 17 games (Spurs 8–9), injured for 16 others
1996	missed 18 games
1997	missed 27 games; 13 due to sprained ligaments in knee, 12 due to league suspension, and 2 due to team suspension
1998	missed 2 games
1999	missed 4 games (Lakers called it "personal issues")

The Bulls figured out that one way to keep Dennis in step with the program was an incentive-filled contract. It worked out great for both parties in the 1998 NBA Championship season. Rodman played 80 of 82 games and all 21 postseason games.

Rodman's 1998 Contract
$4.5 million base salary
$5.8 million in incentives ($3.8 million for playing 80 games, another $1 million for
                    playing every playoff game, $500,000 for leading the league in
                    rebounds, and $500,000 for a 1.5–1.0 assist-to-turnover ratio)

Rodman at His Best

1996 Eastern Conference Finals Against Orlando

Game 1	13 points	21 rebounds
Game 2	15 points	12 rebounds

During that 1996 series (in which the Bulls swept Shaquille O'Neal's Magic team) Dennis averaged 11.5 points and 15.8 rebounds in 37 minutes per game.

1996 Finals

Later, in the 1996 NBA Finals, Rodman deserved consideration for the Finals MVP, which went to Michael Jordan. It was Jordan's worst Finals performance, although he still averaged 27 points per game.

During those Finals, Rodman averaged 7.5 points and 14.7 rebounds in 37.5 minutes per game. He tied an NBA Finals record for most offensive rebounds in a game with 11. And he did that in Game 2 *and* in the deciding Game 6.

Doug Collins: "Dennis—an all-time great? You know, in Detroit, for those seven years, he was great. Before all the other stuff—before the distractions. . . . Yeah, I'll buy Dennis as one of the all-time greats."

Would this be distracting, Doug? In the 1997 playoffs, Dennis Rodman was called for technical fouls in 13 consecutive playoff games.

Del Harris: "Dennis was an all-time rebounder. He could have been an all-time great if he didn't go crazy. I can't say he was a great player, because he was only great on one end of the court."

"But, Del," I countered. "Do you consider George Gervin or Dominique Wilkins great players? Most people consider their games great only on one end of the court—the offensive end."

Del—a studious and gracious man—thought for a minute and countered back with this: "It's harder to be great on the offensive end. But that's a good comeback."

Sorry to have the last word, Del, but this is my book. No, it is not easier to be a great defensive player. Certainly, one doesn't need the skill that a great shooter possesses, but being a great defender is not any "easier." My point is that Rodman made his teams better. He made his teammates better.

I thought "illegal use of hands" was a football penalty.

Prior to a Bulls shootaround in November 1996, Dennis was served with court papers for a sexual harassment lawsuit filed by a Delta Center usher. In the lawsuit, usher Lavon Ankers claimed Rodman touched her in an inappropriate manner after diving into the stands for a loose ball during a playoff game in 1994, when Rodman was a member of the Spurs. I have my own thoughts about that incident. Rodman would frequently hurl his body in any direction, with great body control. One weekend, he was displeased with previous comments made by play-by-play announcer Bob Costas. Dennis let Bob know as only he could. In the second quarter just before halftime, Dennis dove for a ball at midcourt and landed on Costas's lap. I had to help pick Dennis off the floor, and I'll never forget his smile. He wanted to shake Costas up and instill some fear. But it wasn't really malicious. It was just Dennis.

Pistons teammate Isiah Thomas told me that Rodman was "a genius when it came to the game of basketball. He saw the game in ways that I never imagined."

When the Pistons were eliminating Michael Jordan's Bulls teams three years in a row, Rodman was a big reason why. Joe Dumars would start on Michael—and do as well as anyone in the league. But Chuck Daly would use Dennis on Michael a lot—especially late in the games.

Spurs teammate Sean Elliott told me, "I liked what Dennis did for David Robinson's game. He pushed him. He pushed him on the court. You have to remember, before Dennis came to San Antonio, Robinson was the savior—he was making holy water, if you know what I mean. When Dennis came to the team—and was a fan favorite—it pushed David."

The amazing thing was this: Dennis—by not taking shots offensively—gave his teammates more chances to score. And, he didn't take rebounds from them.

Robinson's rebound totals in two years with Rodman were 10.7 per game and 10.8 per game. Do you know what Robinson's career average is? It was 10.8 rebounds per game.

Scottie Pippen's rebound totals in three years with Rodman were 6.4, 6.5, and 5.2 per game. Scottie's career average for rebounds was 6.6 per game.

Michael Jordan's rebound totals in three years with Rodman were 6.6, 5.9, and 5.8 per game. Michael's career average for rebounds was 6.2 per game.

Robinson won the scoring title in 1994 with Rodman as a teammate. Jordan won the scoring title in 1996, 1997, and 1998 with Rodman as a teammate. They both won MVP playing alongside Rodman.

The Bulls never knew which Dennis Rodman would show up. In 1998, look at the difference a week made.

Rodman

Against Charlotte in 1998 Eastern semis	7.0 points	17.6 rebounds	41.6 min./game
Against Indiana in 1998 Eastern finals	4.7 points	9.8 rebounds	29.4 min./game

He was a self-promoter who is remembered for the tattoos and earrings and makeup and dressing in drag. He should be remembered for being the player who hustled non-stop—and did all the dirty work. He would dive on the floor. He would deny the entry pass. He would pass up shots so his teammates would be happy. He gave his team more extra possessions than anyone.

Chuck Daly used Rodman to play four different defensive positions. Phil Jackson had the 6-foot-7 Rodman take on Shaq one-on-one in the 1996 Eastern Conference finals. Rodman shut down O'Neal by denying him his spot. Dennis was 220 pounds, yet he regularly was assigned to defend players such as Karl Malone, Charles Oakley, and Chris Webber.

In 1996, the Chicago Bulls were 34–2 in games that Rodman grabbed 15+ rebounds.

Rodman was probably the most versatile defender to ever play in the league. Who identified with Rodman? Kids who played the game with reckless abandon. Gay people, liberals, and hippies. People who looked different than others. Social misfits.

I'm not sure Rodman didn't get picked on for things other superstars have always gotten away with. It was Magic Johnson who contracted the HIV virus. It was Michael Jordan who skipped town during a New York playoff series to go to Atlantic City and gamble. It was Charles Barkley who spit on fans (Rodman did kick a photographer). Wilt Chamberlain and Allen Iverson missed practices. We excuse Shaquille O'Neal for his jokes in poor taste on Asians. No one excused Dennis Rodman. No one gave him his due—at least on the court.

The Aura of Having Dennis Rodman on Your Team

Dennis Rodman was drafted by the Pistons—and they became NBA Champions for the first time ever within three years.

He was traded to San Antonio, and they became NBA Champions—for the first time ever—within five years.

He was traded to Chicago, and they became NBA Champions for three consecutive years.

He was signed as a free agent by the Lakers in 1999, and, only a year later, they became NBA Champions for three consecutive years.

He was signed as a free agent by the Mavericks for a month in the 2000 season. Since then, the Mavs have had a great record and might win an NBA title or two or three before long. Yes, he played with the game's best players, but Rodman was an integral part of every team he was on.

Who's Better, Who's Best

Dennis Rodman or Dave DeBusschere

Who is the greatest *defensive* forward of all time? My choices:

1. Dennis Rodman
2. Dave DeBusschere
3. Scottie Pippen
4. Bobby Jones
5. Kevin Garnett

All-Defensive First Team Selections Among Forwards

Dave DeBusschere	1969, 1970, 1971, 1972, 1973, 1974
Bobby Jones	1977, 1978, 1979, 1980, 1981, 1982, 1983
Dennis Rodman	1989, 1990, 1991, 1992, 1993, 1995, 1996
Tim Duncan	1999, 2000, 2001, 2002, 2003

Rodman came into the league a Piston, and a piston—a vital piece or cog. He left the league a Maverick, and a maverick (an independent individual who does not go along with a group or party).

Rodman was the greatest defensive forward of all time. If he had been six inches taller, he would have been the greatest defensive player of all time. He maximized his abilities and played to an old age in the NBA, especially considering his entire game was based on hustle and battling under the boards. He was unique as a teammate and required so much attention that it detracted from his play on the court. Yes, he was high maintenance, but his play merited all the extra work. What team wouldn't be excited to have a player who did all the dirty work, shut down the opposing team's leading scorer, and dove for every loose ball? So what if he threatened to strip naked on his exit from the NBA? Of course, that didn't happen. His last game came and went without incident. It was game number 911 of his career.

WALT FRAZIER
The Coolest Guy in the Room

MVP: 0	
MVP VOTING: 4th in 1970, 6th in 1974	
NBA TITLES: 2	
ALL-NBA FIRST TEAM: 4	
ALL-NBA SECOND TEAM: 2	

He dressed cool. He had a cool nickname, "Clyde." He owned New York in a way few athletes have during the last 40 years. But his play on the court is what elevated Walt Frazier to his elite status among the all-time greats. His outstanding play in the championship games puts him in a grouping with the other clutch guards of all time: Jerry West, Kobe Bryant, Isiah Thomas, Sam Jones, and Reggie Miller. In this chapter, I'll defend why I think Frazier belongs well behind the two Lakers, well ahead of Jones and Miller, and just short of Isiah Thomas.

If Walt Frazier had grown up in a different, less prejudiced time, he might never have made the NBA. He might have been a great NFL quarterback. When he graduated from high school in Atlanta, there were more offers for his football talents. Frazier was a pretty good quarterback in high school. The problem was that there were no major schools that had a black quarterback. At 6-foot-4, Frazier would have been big enough to play the position—especially in the 1970s. In late March 2003, I asked Frazier about football, and he confirmed that his idol growing up was Johnny Unitas. He might have chosen football if he grew up today. Instead, he quarterbacked the Knicks for a decade. For six straight seasons Frazier was All-NBA, either First or Second Team. For those six years, plus an additional one, he was All-Defense First Team.

A Better Analogy

The late Pete Axthelm wrote in 1970 in his book *The City Game* that "Frazier is akin to Joe Namath when he quarterbacked the Jets to a world title: both were capable of dreadful moments—but only in games that scarcely mattered. In the big games, they exuded confidence and took charge. Both were apt to lose statistical battles. But when the game-saving plays were required, they made them. And then they talked about them, freely and candidly, playing the starring role to the hilt."

Bill Walton: "Walt Frazier: Fifth-best guard of all time . . . maybe one of the 10 or 12 best players of all time."

His Defense Ruled

Frazier's calling card, of course, was his defense. NBA coaches started to vote for All-Defense teams beginning in 1969, which means that there is no tangible evidence to suggest Frazier was among the top defensive guards in his rookie season of 1968. Even without the rookie year accounted for—or steals being kept—we can assume Frazier was among the top defensive guards of all time. Of course, Frazier was an understudy in his first year on Broadway. He played only 21 minutes per night during his rookie season, coming off the bench.

First Team All-Defense Among Guards (Voting by Coaches; Since 1969)
1. 9 years   Michael Jordan
2. 9 years   Gary Payton
3. 7 years   Walt Frazier
4. 5 years   Dennis Johnson

Marv Albert: "He was the type of player who could get three steals in the first quarter, but wouldn't. He would set up his opponent, and wait for the right time. He would try to sucker guys. When the Knicks played the Lakers, he often didn't play Jerry West. I recall Frazier would play Dick Garrett. Dick Barnett would take West. But the Knicks played a help defense and would often switch."

The Two Greatest Games in Frazier's Career

Frazier's two best games came during postseason play.

1970 Finals: Game 7, Series Tied 3–3

Walt Frazier was the spectacular player on a team of destiny. Even though the seventh game was decided early—with Willis Reed's appearance being the showstopper—it was Frazier who scored 36 points and added 19 assists. It was one of the great Game 7 performances of all time. He played 44 minutes, hit 12 of 17 field goals, and pulled down seven rebounds. The Knicks had 113 points. Frazier scored 36, and his 19 assists led to 38 more. That's 74 of 113 points.

1973 Eastern Conference Finals: Game 4, New York Up 2–1

The Celtics had won 68 games, 11 more than the Knicks in the regular season. During the season, the Knicks and Celtics had split eight games. The Knicks took two of the first three games of the playoff series, and John Havlicek was going to sit out the fourth game with an injury. Boston would have had a great chance to win the series if they could have evened the series at 2–2 by winning Game 4 at Madison Square Garden.

In the fourth game, it wasn't as if the Knicks weren't shorthanded themselves. Earl Monroe did not play. An aging Dick Barnett had only four minutes in him in a 58-minute double-overtime game. Rookie Henry Bibby had only 14 minutes of action. And Dean Meminger played 38 minutes before fouling out. Walt Frazier was forced to play 57 of 58 minutes. He scored 37 points and had nine rebounds and four assists. More important, when the Knicks trailed by 16 points in the fourth quarter, Frazier put on a one-man show, not allowing the Knicks to lose. The Knicks sent the game into overtime, outscoring Boston 33–17 in the fourth quarter.

The Knicks needed that fourth game, as the Celtics came back and won the next two games to tie the series 3–3.

Game 7 In the seventh game, everyone remembers Dean Meminger making some big shots. But it was Clyde Frazier who made history—sending the Celtics to defeat in a Game 7 in Boston. Frazier had 25 points and 10 rebounds in that game.

For that historic 1973 series, Frazier led the Knicks in scoring all seven games, averaging 26.1 points per game.

Frazier had other huge games. In Game 2 of the 1970 Finals, Frazier had a triple double (11 points, 12 rebounds, 11 assists). Check out his numbers in the last two games of the 1973 Finals: Frazier had 19 points, eight rebounds, and eight assists in Game 4, and in Game 5, had 18 points, nine rebounds, and five assists.

The Greatest Regular-Season Game in Frazier's Career

On January 3, 1972, at Madison Square Garden, Frazier scored the Knicks' final 13 points, including the winning basket with three seconds left, in a 101–99 victory over the Bucks. Frazier scored 31 points in that game, to overcome Kareem Abdul-Jabbar's 38 points. That was against a 32–7 Milwaukee team that would end the Los Angeles Lakers' 33-game win streak less than a week later.

Who's Better, Who's Best
Walt Frazier or Lenny Wilkens

Although Wilkens was named in 1996 to the NBA's list of the 50 greatest players, he fails to make the cut just seven years later. Still, he wasn't that far apart from some of the great guards of all time, including Clyde.

Lenny Lewin's 1971 book *The Knicks*, with Red Holzman, details how the Hawks offered Wilkens to the Knicks early in the 1969 season for the young, unproven Frazier. The Knicks must have thought about acquiring Wilkens but were sure they were right in drafting Frazier. The Hawks found a buyer for Wilkens, and on October 12, 1968, the Hawks traded Wilkens to Seattle for guard Walt Hazzard.

Frazier's career	18.9 points	5.9 rebounds	6.1 assists
Wilkens's career	16.5 points	4.7 rebounds	6.7 assists

If these two started their careers at the same time, you would have to pick Frazier. Frazier led the Knicks in scoring five consecutive seasons, in addition to his playmaking abilities and defense. In 1968, though, it wasn't as clear. Wilkens had just turned 31 in October. He was coming off his best season, finishing second in the MVP voting in 1968. Frazier had shown promise as a rookie, averaging nine points and four assists per game. It is a fascinating trade that never happened. The Hawks were moving to Atlanta, which was Frazier's hometown. He would have been the conquering hero in Atlanta. A year later, the Hawks drafted Pete Maravich. Imagine a backcourt of Frazier and Maravich. New York would have Brooklyn native Lenny Wilkens to quarterback the Knicks. He would have fit in with Holzman's heady bunch. Frazier had four productive seasons after Wilkens's last good year (1974)—but both were pretty much like rock music: neither had much to offer after 1975.

Who's Better, Who's Best
Walt Frazier or Reggie Miller
Now that I've shown Frazier was better than Wilkens, let's climb the ladder and compare Frazier to Reggie Miller. Miller has hit a truckload of huge playoff shots. But Miller was never one of the top guards in the league. He never made either the All-NBA First or Second Team. Frazier was on the All-NBA First Team four times and the Second Team twice. Plus, Frazier's defense was his calling card.

Who's Better, Who's Best
Walt Frazier or Sam Jones
Sam Jones was a classic clutch performer in the postseason. But during the regular season, he didn't measure up to the best. He was never on the All-NBA First Team and was on the Second Team only three times. I don't want to hear about Jones missing out because of West and Robertson. Frazier made First Team in 1970 with West *ahead of* Robertson. Frazier was a better defensive player and a better playmaker than Jones.

Who's Better, Who's Best
Walt Frazier or Isiah Thomas
I don't argue too vehemently with fans of Frazier on this one. It's close. Both won two championships. Frazier made one more year on the All-NBA First Team. Thomas won one additional All-Star game MVP. Both players picked up their scoring averages in the postseason. Neither lasted a long time. Thomas was forced to retire in 1994 at the age of 33. Frazier only played 15 games past his 33rd birthday.

Who's Better, Who's Best
Walt Frazier or Patrick Ewing
Who's the greatest Knicks player of all time? It's between Frazier and Ewing. Besides the fact that Frazier led the Knicks to their only two championships and Ewing came up empty, there has to be some style points involved. Frazier moved gracefully on the court, and his play had an elegance to it. Ewing sweated like a pig—it is the visual picture most people are left with. Ewing played more games and scored more points. Frazier was the better player.

Frazier's career ended way too soon. According to Clyde, the Knicks made a decision that they didn't want him around in a lesser role. He would have agreed to groom Ray Williams and Michael Ray Richardson in the late 1970s, but the Knicks chose otherwise and traded Frazier to Cleveland. There wasn't much left in Frazier's game, as a recurring sprained ankle never really healed right. So Frazier is like rock music. Even if there was nothing of note to offer after 1975—boy, those tunes from the late 1960s and early 1970s still sound so good.

DAVE COWENS

The Fifth-Greatest Celtic

MVP: 1	
MVP VOTING: 1st in 1973, 4th in 1974, 2nd in 1975, 3rd in 1976	
NBA TITLES: 2	
ALL-NBA FIRST TEAM: 0	
ALL-NBA SECOND TEAM: 3	

O n any other franchise (except the Lakers) it would mean nothing to be the fifth-best player. But when the four players in front are Bill Russell, Larry Bird, Bob Cousy, and John Havlicek, it's quite an honor.

Dave Cowens was the fourth overall pick in the 1970 NBA draft—but was still unknown to most basketball fans. One reason was that Florida State had been on two separate NCAA violations in three seasons. Cowens was a natural forward and probably would have been a bigger superstar if he was left to play his natural position. Red Auerbach said in 1988, "Bill Russell told me he knew just by looking into Cowens's eyes that he would be a great center."

I'm sure that placing Cowens as high as he is here will rattle some modern-day fans. Cowens would have been a power forward in the modern game, banging every night against the Karl Malones and Chris Webbers. He could have also played center in today's game, with an outside touch that would consistently place him in the All-Star game.

Cowens had to face high expectations when drafted by the Celtics. Essentially, he had to replace Bill Russell as the man in the middle of the most storied franchise in league history. The Celtics won a pair of championships under his watch and would have won a third if John Havlicek hadn't gotten injured late in the glorious 68-win season of 1973.

During the 1970s, Cowens was instrumental. He placed in the top four of the MVP voting in each of four consecutive seasons. That's the kind of greatness that only 14 players have ever achieved. And this during an era of one of the great individuals (Kareem Abdul-Jabbar) and one of the most celebrated teams (New York Knicks) of all time.

Cowens places behind Tim Duncan (who has done everything Cowens has done, including earning Rookie of the Year and MVP honors and an NBA Championship ring) and ahead of the other modern-day power forwards (Nowitzki, Garnett, Webber) except for Karl Malone.

Why Cowens Was So Valuable to the Celtics

1970	Celtics 34–48	out of playoffs; draft Cowens after the season
1971	Celtics 44–38	+10
1972	Celtics 56–26	+12
1973	Celtics 68–14	+12
1974	NBA Championship	
1976	NBA Championship	

Cowens wasn't solely responsible for the Celtics' resurgence, of course. John Havlicek played more minutes and took more shots than any player in the game. Boston became a very good fast-break team. They acquired Paul Silas, who was good at starting the break, and Havlicek could run 48 minutes. Since plays weren't run for the center, Cowens had to crash the boards.

In 1972, the Celtics averaged 115.6 points per game—third most in the NBA. In 1973, the Celtics averaged 112.7 points per game—second in the league, a shade behind Houston's 112.8 points per game. Since Boston got up the court quickly, they took 250 more shots than any other team in the league. That 1972 season, Boston won 68 of 82 games.

Tommy Heinsohn, the Celtics coach at the time, was often quoted as saying, "For our running style of play, I'd rather have Dave Cowens than any center in the league except Jabbar and Reed, when he's healthy. Dave runs and shoots better than Unseld and he's much faster than Chamberlain."

Heinsohn created a system of spreading the players over the court, with Cowens at the high post and the guards on the wings. This style was perfect for Dave's speed, quickness, hustle, and full-court play.

Cowens from 1973 to 1976
19.7 points/game
15.7 rebounds/game
 4.5 assists/game

Dave Cowens Against Wilt Chamberlain

In 1973, the Los Angeles Lakers were the reigning NBA Champions, defending their 1972 record of 69–13. In that 1973 season, the Lakers were still an elite team, finishing 60–22. Only the Celtics (68–14) won more games in the 1973 regular season, and they were 4–0 against Los Angeles. The big reason was their MVP center, Dave Cowens. In the four games, the Celtics outscored the Lakers by 21 points, and Cowens outscored Chamberlain 125–57.

Cowens Versus Chamberlain in Head-to-Head Matchups, 1973

Cowens	31.3 points	20.0 rebounds/game
Chamberlain	14.3 points	14.5 rebounds/game

If you're wondering if that was just a case of Cowens—in a career-best year—going against Chamberlain in his final season, here's how Cowens fared against Chamberlain in earlier years.

Cowens-Chamberlain Matchups

1970	Chamberlain injured
1971	Cowens 16.2 points, 14.2 rebounds/game in five games (Boston 3–2 vs. L.A.)
1972	Cowens 20.6 points, 14.4 rebounds/game in five games (L.A. 4–1 vs. Boston)
1973	Cowens 31.3 points, 20.0 rebounds/game in four games (Boston 4–0 vs. L.A.)

In total, Cowens won eight games to Chamberlain's six. Dave Cowens averaged more than 22 points and 15.9 rebounds per game against Chamberlain.

Bill Walton: "Dave Cowens: only player successful versus Wilt Chamberlain and Kareem Abdul-Jabbar. He was only 6-foot-8, but he outworked and outran everyone. He was a complete player."

It is rebounding that made Cowens special. Despite being an undersized center, he was a great rebounder.

Cowens's Rank Among the Rebound Leaders

1971	seventh in NBA	15.0 per game
1972	fifth in NBA	15.2 per game
1973	third in NBA	16.2 per game

1974	second in NBA	15.7 per game
1975	second in NBA	14.7 per game
1976	second in NBA	16.0 per game
1977	left team for three months, played only 50 games	
1978	third in NBA	14.0 per game

The only men who ever averaged more rebounds per game during the course of a season than Dave Cowens in his first eight seasons were Wilt Chamberlain, Wes Unseld, Elvin Hayes, Kareem Abdul-Jabbar, Jerry Lucas, Bill Bridges, Nate Thurmond, Truck Robinson, and Moses Malone. For his career, Cowens averaged 13.6 rebounds per game.

Cowens in NBA Finals

The other aspect of his game that moves Cowens up among the all-time greats is his play on the biggest stage: the NBA Finals.

Entering the 1974 Finals, the Celtics hadn't won a championship in five seasons and the Celtics faced the Milwaukee Bucks, led by Kareem Abdul-Jabbar. Abdul-Jabbar was only 26 years old and had just won his third MVP.

Despite numerous injuries, the Bucks won 59 games and finished first in the Midwest Division in the regular season. Milwaukee won eight of its first nine playoff games and swept the Chicago Bulls 4–0 in the Western Conference finals.

In those days, very few coaches believed in double-teaming. That meant that 6-foot-9 Cowens would be responsible for stopping the unstoppable: Kareem's sky hook.

In Game 1 in Milwaukee, the Celtics upset the Bucks 98–83 as Cowens had 19 points, 17 rebounds, and seven assists in 45 minutes. Cowens would outscore the Big Fella 30–26 in Game 3 in Boston to give the Celts their second win of the series. In a crucial Game 5 in Milwaukee, the Celts went up 3 games to 2 as Cowens scored 28 points, to go along with his six rebounds and six assists.

Game 6 was one of the greatest games in NBA history. Abdul-Jabbar's sky hook from the corner in the second overtime gave the Bucks a 102–101 victory to tie the series at 3–3.

In Game 6, the strategy of having Cowens play man-to-man with Kareem was wearing on the redhead. So Coach Heinsohn decided to double-team Kareem and allow Cowens to concentrate more on offense. The result: Cowens had 28 points, 14 rebounds, and four assists to outscore Abdul-Jabbar and the Celtics won NBA Championship No. 12.

Those 1974 Celtics remain one of three teams in history to win a Finals Game 7 on the road. The 26-year-old Cowens—with help—shut down Abdul-Jabbar, holding him to zero field goal attempts during one 18-minute period.

Tommy Heinsohn: "I remember that game well. We played man-up against Abdul-Jabbar the whole series. Our strategy was to cut down his angles. They won Game 6 on a Friday night, and the final game was on Sunday. I decided we would double the big fella. We used Silas—Cornell Warner was the player we doubled off of. And then, it worked. We got up by 17, and it was never a game. It really was against my belief to double, though."

In 1976, the Celtics returned to the Finals—this time against Phoenix—and Cowens was just as superb. In Game 1, Cowens had a triple double (25 points, 21 rebounds, 10 assists). Of course, this was before Magic Johnson had popularized the stat, and scant attention was paid to Cowens's remarkable game.

In Game 5, which went into triple overtime, Cowens played 55 minutes before fouling out, scoring 26 points to go with 19 rebounds and four assists. That was the game that Gar Heard hit a 22-foot shot to tie the game for the Suns and send it into a third overtime. In the next overtime, the Celts built a six-point lead and outlasted the Suns 128–126.

Finally, the Celtics clinched the series on Phoenix's home court in Game 6, sealing their 13th NBA Championship. Cowens had 21 points and 17 rebounds in the final game.

The Quick End to Cowens's Career

Following the 1976 championship, Paul Silas's contract ran out. He had made $175,000 in 1976 and was looking to cash in. But Red Auerbach wasn't about to pay anyone on the team more than Cowens, the star. Cowens asked the Celts to pay Silas whatever it would take to keep him in Boston. But at the last minute, Auerbach traded Silas's rights to Denver in a three-way maneuver that brought former UCLA stars Sidney Wicks and Curtis Rowe to Boston.

Without the physical support of power forward Silas, Cowens fatigued quickly. Ten games into the 1977 season he left the team, burned out, and said he wasn't returning. The 29-year-old Cowens ended up staying away three months. That year, the Celtics won only 44 games, but defeated San Antonio in the first round of the playoffs. In the second round, Boston pushed Philadelphia to a seventh game—and came within a game of advancing to the Eastern Conference finals.

In 1978, Tom Heinsohn was replaced by Tom Sanders when the record showed a dismal 11–23.

In 1979, Sanders was at the helm for only 14 games before being replaced by Cowens, as a player-coach. Cowens coached the team to a 27–41 record. Although it was standard practice in the early days of the league, by the late 1970s the days of the player-coach were long over. Cowens was the last of the breed, in fact.

Cowens stayed with the Celtics to see the mountaintop again. In 1980, after just two losing seasons, Boston made a series of moves and won 61 games, led by a remarkable rookie named Larry Bird.

After 10 seasons of wearing green, Cowens saw the handwriting on the wall. Auerbach had staged a trade, sending center Robert Parish to Boston. The Celtics also drafted Kevin McHale in the same deal. Once holdout rookie McHale signed and newcomer Parish proved he could handle new coach Bill Fitch's system, Cowens retired prior to the start of the season. The Celtics would go on to win the 1981 NBA title, just as the Lakers went on to win the 1972 NBA Championship right after Elgin Baylor retired.

Cowens was similar to Sandy Koufax and other baseball pitchers of the 1960s and 1970s. Koufax was forced to retire at 30 years old. The left arm simply threw too many pitches, too many complete games. Today, pitchers don't pitch in a four-man rotation and don't throw 350+ innings a year. They stay on pitch counts. Similarly, NBA players don't play 45+ minutes per night, banging the boards against taller, bigger players night after night.

Who's Better, Who's Best
Dave Cowens or Kevin McHale

Cedric Maxwell played with both men, often alongside them in the same frontcourt. Who better to settle this one?

Cedric Maxwell: "McHale."

Cedric Maxwell (two seconds later): "Wait a minute. Let me take that back. McHale never won an MVP, right? [Jeez, he's beginning to sound like me.] They both were great players, but Cowens had to play center—a lot of times, for teams that weren't as good. Now, that being said . . . I still think Kevin McHale is the second-greatest power forward to ever play this game—much as I hate to say it—behind Karl Malone."

Bob Ryan: "You're talking to the absolute scholar on Dave Cowens. He was my favorite Celtics player to watch. Seeing him take on the Goliaths of the NBA. Cowens had grit. He had advantages. Tommy Heinsohn knew his strengths and weaknesses and built an offense around them. Cowens did a better job on Abdul-Jabbar than anyone except perhaps Nate Thurmond. But—out of context—Kevin was a better player."

Heinsohn had the same dilemma choosing between Cowens and McHale. McHale has an aura around him. Fans just loved McHale. But so did the media. *Boston Globe* sportswriter Dan Shaughnessy swears that McHale was the most unstoppable inside force in NBA history behind only Abdul-Jabbar. And former teammates like Bill Walton, Quinn Buckner, and Danny Ainge all feel the same for McHale.

But in the end, Maxwell hit it correctly. You want to say McHale—and you might, immediately. But if you think about it, it is hard for a reserve such as McHale to be greater than a center like Cowens. Both were great. Cowens should get some credit for playing out of position. The great athlete demands the top assignment. He wants to guard the top opponent. In Dave Cowens's day, that meant playing center. A quality cornerback is more valuable than a quality safety. A good hitting shortstop is more valuable than a good hitting third baseman. In the NBA, quality centers don't grow on trees.

ALLEN IVERSON
The Fifth-Greatest Sixer

MVP: 1 (2001)	
MVP VOTING: 4 years in the top 6	
NBA TITLES: 0	
ALL-NBA FIRST TEAM: 2	
ALL-NBA SECOND TEAM: 3	

There is absolutely no shame in being the fifth-greatest 76ers star, trailing the legendary Wilt Chamberlain, Julius Erving, Moses Malone, and Charles Barkley. The aforementioned four all had either titles or MVP seasons outside of Philadelphia. Allen Iverson has somehow managed to stay the course for seven years in the City of Brotherly Love.

He came into the NBA as positively the fastest man with a basketball in his possession and hadn't lost a step seven years into the league. Allen Iverson has won Rookie of the Year, MVP, and three scoring championships, and has led the league in steals twice.

By the Numbers

He has had three different All-Star games where he scored at least 25 points.

He has picked up his scoring in the postseason from 27 to more than 30 per game, despite overall scores declining in the playoffs.

There is no one who has taken the physical punishment that A.I. has, driving into the lane against bigger, bruising opponents on a nightly basis. Yet, no one appreciates him. One prominent columnist called him "a flavor of the month."

Even in his hometown city of Philadelphia, reaction seems muted.

Stephen A. Smith: "He is not yet among the all-time greats. He is a prolific scorer. An unbelievable talent. Don't get me wrong. I'm a big Iverson fan. He is not scared of anything. He is an assassin. But he's limited because of his size. He will never be the basketball player that Kobe Bryant is because of that size. He is not great defensively because of it. He is essentially a playground ballplayer."

I can't believe it. Shaquille gets penalized because he's bigger than everyone else. Iverson gets penalized because he's smaller than everyone else. You can't win.

Iverson—no matter what anyone says—is among the greatest guards in NBA history. He is, in fact, one of only five guards to win the league's MVP trophy.

MVP Guards
Bob Cousy
Allen Iverson
Magic Johnson
Michael Jordan
Oscar Robertson

Who's Better, Who's Best
Allen Iverson or Gary Payton

Joe Maloof: "Iverson: He's great. I love that guy. What a fighter, so tough. He gives 110 percent in each game he plays. Maybe he shoots a little much, but so what? I compare him a little to Gary Payton, who also has that nasty streak in him."

Both Payton and Iverson have carried teams on their backs. Iverson has had a consistently tougher task, mostly playing without a second big scorer.

Who's Better, Who's Best
Allen Iverson or Nate Archibald

It is my belief that if Iverson could have played in Archibald's era and in Archibald's system—when NBA teams routinely ran the ball—Iverson would have gotten eight or nine layups a game easy. Instead, Iverson plays in the early 2000s—when the zone defense is legal. Instead of running, teams play all sorts of isolation, two-man games. But not everyone thinks like that.

Nate Archibald: "People compare us because of our scoring and our size. I handled the ball 90 feet, though. He could score better than me, though."

Pete Vecsey: "I would take Tiny over A.I. First off, he could score with Iverson. And Archibald was an all-time teammate. Guys loved him. They would pay to play with Tiny."

Harvey Pollack: "Allen Iverson would get killed if he played in the old days. Imagine him driving against Jungle Jim Loscutoff? I'm telling you, Iverson wouldn't have lasted. Remember, they didn't have such a thing as flagrant fouls."

Harvey has seen all of Philadelphia's home games—and seen the man get pummeled. Here is a list of the injuries he suffered and missed games for in his first seven seasons.

Iverson's Injuries

1997	left shoulder separation
1997	sore left shoulder
1997	sprained left ankle
1999	right quadriceps contusion
2000	broken right thumb
2000	synovitis, left knee
2000	broken left big toe
2001	right shoulder dislocation
2001	left knee contusion
2001	left hip pointer
2001	tailbone contusion
2001	right elbow bursitis
2001	left sacroiliac joint contusion
2002	right elbow rehab
2002	sprained left thumb
2002	sprained right big toe
2002	fractured left hand

In Iverson's first seven seasons, the Sixers were 22–34 without him in the lineup. He missed 53 of those 56 games due to the above injuries, and three due to suspension.

Forget that pain threshold . . . he's also put up with the pain of acquiring all those tattoos.

The Greatest Game in Iverson's Career

That greatest game would be the first game of the 2001 NBA Finals on June 6, 2001. The Los Angeles Lakers were hosting the Philadelphia 76ers. The Lakers had swept three consecutive playoff series that year, winning 11 consecutive postseason games. They had won their final eight regular-season games, as well. Not only had the Lakers won 19 straight games—but they were well rested, with 10 days between the Conference finals and the NBA Finals.

On the other hand, the Sixers had struggled in each of the first three rounds.

In the first round, Philadelphia lost the first game at home in a best-of-five series to the Indiana Pacers.

In the second round, the Sixers struggled to defeat the Toronto Raptors, finally bringing the dinosaurs into extinction in seven games, with Philly escaping with a one-point win.

In the Conference finals, Philadelphia again went seven games, this time with the Milwaukee Bucks.

No one thought the 76ers could defeat the Lakers. Not at the Staples Center, anyway. But Allen Iverson scored 48 points—the sixth-most points ever in a Finals game. It went into overtime—and it was A.I. who hit the go-ahead three-pointer in overtime. The game was one day shy of Iverson's 26th birthday, and he was able to celebrate his birthday with a lead in the NBA Finals. It was also 19 years to the day since the Philadelphia 76ers had last won an NBA Finals game.

Iverson's Tattoos

Thanks to the diligent research of Harvey Pollack and his staff, I am able to report the locations and identifications of Allen Iverson's tattoos. He has a tattoo on the right side of his neck (Chinese for loyalty), right shoulder ("Hold my Own"), right chest (his kids' names Tiaura and Deuce), right upper arm (soldier's head), right upper arm ("Cru Thik," the name of guys with whom he grew up—it's also in three other locations), right forearm ("Virginia's Finest"), right wrist (Chinese for respect), right side of stomach (Tawana, his wife's name), right thigh (a panther), left neck (Cru Thik again), left shoulder (cross of daggers with "Only the Strong Survive"), left elbow ("The Answer"), left chest (a set of praying hands between his mother's and grandmother's initials), left forearm (a bulldog), left upper arm (strength, in Tibetan), left forearm (a screaming skull with "Fear No One"), and left thigh ("Newport Bad News").

The Great 2001 Postseason Run by Iverson

All season long, Allen Iverson was there to bail out the Philadelphia 76ers. He had averaged 31.1 points per game to lead the league in scoring—and it marked the first time since 1996 that anyone averaged 30 or more for the season. He took 25.5 shots per game for a team that averaged only 79 per game. The team was set up for him to take a lot of shots—and often turned Iverson misses into second-chance points. The Sixers were fifth in offensive rebounds that year—no doubt because Iverson had shot just 42 percent. He missed 11 games due to an assortment of injuries—and the Sixers were 6–5. They were 50–21 when Iverson suited up.

They had worked so hard for the home court advantage in the Eastern Conference, but blew it in Game 1 of their first round series against Indiana. In a must-win Game 2, Iverson scored 45 points to lead Philly to victory.

In the next round, the Toronto Raptors were the opponent. Once again, Philadelphia lost the first game at home, and, once again, Iverson was there to bail them out in the second game. In Game 2, he scored 54 points to tie the series. With the series tied 2–2, Iverson dropped in another 52 to give the Sixers a 3–2 lead. (For you trivia buffs, only one other player ever had a pair of 50-point playoff games in the same series. Michael Jordan did it in 1988 against the Cleveland Cavs—which means Lenny Wilkens was the only coach who allowed an opponent to score 50 or more twice in the same postseason series. Wilkens was the coach against Jordan and Iverson.)

In that 2001 fifth game, the Sixers' first without starter George Lynch (who had broken his foot in Game 4), Iverson hit eight three-pointers. Toronto took Game 6 and had a chance to win Game 7 at the buzzer, but Vince Carter was just long on a jumper in front of the Sixers bench. Iverson played one of the greatest seventh games in history, passing for 16 assists.

During Game 7 against Toronto, Iverson suffered a left sacroiliac joint contusion that forced him to miss one of the Conference finals games (a Sixers loss). Those Conference finals were memorable because of Iverson's heroics in Games 6 and 7. In Game 6, the Bucks—down 3–2—took a huge lead. At that point, most players—especially injured warriors like Iverson—pack it in early and rest in preparation for Game 7. Allen Iverson, however, scored 26 of his 46 points in the fourth quarter to get Philly back in the game—but the Bucks hung on to force a seventh game. In the final game, Iverson scored 44 points—the fourth most ever in a seventh game. (And Iverson's 44 came in a 108–91 victory. Sam Jones's 47 points in Game 7 in 1963 came in a 142–131 victory over Cincinnati. Iverson had a much greater degree of difficulty.)

Then came the 48-point effort in Game 1 of the Finals. Overall, Iverson scored 32.9 points, 4.7 rebounds, and 6.1 assists per game in the playoffs. In the 22 games that he played in, he scored 36 percent of the Sixers' points.

I saw Jordan up close in 1993. I saw Olajuwon up close in 1995. No one was ever more valuable to a team than Allen Iverson. If Jerry West or Rick Barry or Bob Pettit was any better in one year's playoffs—I just wouldn't believe it.

With each passing year, Iverson's accomplishments in that playoff season fade away. No one remembers players who come in second. When I asked various experts about Iverson and the all-time greats, they point to one thing: Frazier and Thomas and Bryant and Archibald all won titles. "What has Iverson ever won?" they ask.

People didn't embrace Allen Iverson for a variety of reasons. He was "too black" for some. The NBA's official magazine once airbrushed his tattoos off him in a cover photograph. His rap lyrics weren't politically correct. He didn't show up at media sessions and give witty remarks at press conferences.

I don't know. I've always thought that Iverson was the most exciting player to watch once Jordan became a jump shooter. He's tough and dangerous and unpredictable. Even if he never wins an NBA Championship.

He represents Philadelphia—and has for years. He's tough enough to flourish in a city famous for booing Santa Claus. He provided more electricity than Ben Franklin's kite. He's had more heart-stopping moments than the Cheez Whiz–laced cheese steaks. He is one of the all-time greats.

KEVIN McHALE

The Unstoppable Low-Post Moves

MVP: 0	
MVP VOTING: 4th in 1987	
NBA TITLES: 3	
ALL-NBA FIRST TEAM: 1	
ALL-NBA SECOND TEAM: 0	

K evin McHale played 13 seasons in the NBA—all with one team, the Boston Celtics. The record for most years playing with just one organization belongs to John Stockton, with 19 seasons with the Jazz.

McHale's Career Numbers

In those 13 seasons, McHale averaged 10 points per game in his first and last seasons. He averaged a little more than 13 points per game in his second and 12th seasons. His scoring average was a perfect graph—he increased his scoring average from 10.0 to 13.6 to 14.1 to 18.4 to 19.8 to 21.3 to 26.1 points per game—then went slowly down, from 26.1 to 22.6 to 22.5 to 20.9 to 18.4 to 13.9 to 10.7.

His two highest-scoring NBA games came consecutively. He scored 56 points against Detroit on March 3, 1985. Then, two nights later, he scored 42 at New York against the Knicks. Those were the only two (out of 971) games that Kevin would score more than 40.

When McHale scored his 56 points in one game, it was an all-time Celtics record. That was more than John Havlicek, Sam Jones, or Dave Cowens had ever scored in a game. McHale also pulled down 16 rebounds in that game—including 10 on the offensive boards. McHale said later he was "in a zone." After the game, Larry Bird said that McHale should have scored 60 points. So, nine days later, Bird went out and scored 60 against Atlanta at the New Orleans Lakefront Arena.

McHale started only 399 games in his NBA career. For the majority of his career, he was the sixth man. Of course, that also meant that McHale played most of the important minutes. If he averaged 30 minutes a night, he would play 30 of the game's final 38 minutes.

Beyond the Scoring Numbers

McHale made the All-Defensive First or Second Teams no less than six times, including in 1983 when he wasn't even a starter.

Kevin would have scored more—a lot more—on a different team. He would have had to provide more numbers, higher-scoring games. He probably wouldn't have won as much, or been as good a player, however.

He is the perfect example of a player whose place in history can't be judged according to numbers. In more than 1,140 games (regular and postseason), McHale averaged just 18 points, 1.7 blocks, and 7.3 rebounds per game.

When you refer to McHale, you have to listen to his peers: his teammates and opponents, as well as the men and women who covered his 13-year career in Boston.

Bill Walton: "He was the second-best low-post player of all time, after Jabbar. In his strategy against bigger guys, he was brilliant—subtle finesse, deft fakes, and all. He was so complete as an offensive threat that a defensive player had no defense against him."

Quinn Buckner: "Kevin was the best low-post forward I've ever seen. A couple of things about McHale. Not only could he score at will in the post, he could defend it, as well. Now he wasn't a great passer—we called him "The Black Hole"—but he could shoot. Eventually, he became a good three-point shooter, but his shot was really a step inside the three-point area. But Larry was always around, so Kevin could stay on the block, where he was most effective."

Danny Ainge: "Kevin was fantastic. He was virtually unstoppable. He just struck fear in the hearts of defenders."

The Most Memorable Play of McHale's Career

That play was the takedown of Kurt Rambis. In 1984, the Celtics and Lakers met in the Finals. Los Angeles was up 2–1 and had taken control of the series by winning the third game by a score of 137–104. In Game 4, McHale stopped a fast-break basket by clotheslining Kurt Rambis in the second quarter. The momentum of the game—and the series—changed. Boston went on to win Game 4 in overtime, and they won the series 4–3.

You have to remember the players in this little drama. Lakers coach Pat Riley loved the open-court game he had going with Magic Johnson. He talked of Lakers basketball as being poetry in motion and the Celtics being Neanderthals. People, he thought, wanted to see "Showtime," not some scrum match under the basket. McHale took down Rambis after Boston teammate M. L. Carr had urged McHale and his teammates to be tougher.

What was the significance of this play? One era was ending and another was beginning. Earlier in those same 1984 playoffs, Knicks head coach Hubie Brown had started preaching that his team was not allowed to permit an opponent a layup. Now, it was official. Soon, the Detroit Pistons would come along and win a pair of NBA Championships based on defense and being the "Bad Boys." Shooting percentages would go down and rules would have to be changed. A new era of physical intimidation and hard defense had begun.

Even Pat Riley came around to this new era of NBA basketball. His Knicks in the early 1990s were effective, but as far apart from the "Showtime" and "poetry in motion" as one would ever find.

NBA League-Average Field Goal Percentage

1984	.492	111 points/game
1988	.480	108 points/game
1991	.474	106 points/game
1994	.466	101 points/game
1997	.455	97 points/game
1999	.437	92 points/game

The Most Memorable Game of McHale's Career

By the 1993 season, the Celtics had turned their club over to Reggie Lewis. Bird had retired, and Parish and McHale had little left physically. McHale was really banged up. His ankles hurt all the time, and his feet were constantly bothering him. In the first round of the playoffs, Boston played up-and-coming Charlotte. Celtics star Lewis slumped to the floor and the seriousness of the condition was not immediately known. He would not play again. In Game 2, McHale played what proved to be his final home game of his 13-year career. That game went into double overtime, and the Hornets won 99–98. But

McHale scored a season-high 30 points on 13-of-18 field goal shooting. He pulled down 10 rebounds. At one point in the game, McHale and Robert Parish scored 28 consecutive Boston points, starting with 4:12 remaining in the third quarter and continuing until a Kevin Gamble hoop interrupted their streak with 1:47 left in regulation.

The Most Heralded Frontcourt in History

McHale, Bird, and Robert Parish each received a Jeff Hamilton leather jacket for being named three of the 50 greatest players back in 1996. What's remarkable is that this frontcourt stayed together for 12 seasons. During Kevin's first eight seasons (which ended in 1989, when Larry Bird went down with a double heel surgery), the Big Three averaged 61 wins a year and won 86 playoff games. They won three out of five NBA Finals.

Celtics radio announcer Glenn Ordway remarked, "It was amazing how much of that nucleus stayed together for their whole careers. Marriages don't stay together that long."

While it has almost been accepted lexicon—calling the trio the greatest frontcourt in history—there are others equally worthy. While the Celtics stars were at their peak in the early 1980s, they were slow and a liability on defense by the last four seasons together. Bird's back and McHale's feet gave out first.

Who's Better, Who's Best
Kevin McHale or James Worthy

Although both Kevin McHale and James Worthy were named in 1996 to the NBA's list of the 50 greatest players, there's only room for one at the 2003 ranking.

| McHale | Three NBA Titles | 17.9 points | 7.3 rebounds |
| Worthy | Three NBA Titles | 17.6 points | 5.1 rebounds |

Quinn Buckner: "I would take McHale, definitely. Worthy wasn't a post-up player, but in many ways was at the forefront for what the power forward would look like in the modern game—especially in the Western Conference. But Kevin was unstoppable."

Matt Guokas: "Worthy was not nearly as good a defender as Kevin. James was an excellent finisher. And to give him credit, Worthy got better in time at catching the ball at the 17-foot line and either shooting or doing a quick, hard move to the basket. McHale was a good, solid rebounder—although he didn't get volume rebounds because of Bird and Parish. I would take McHale."

So, where do you place a player who started only a couple of seasons? Very high. Let Chris Webber and Dirk Nowitzki win a few titles before they come looking for McHale's spot on the all-time list. Worthy was a Top 50 choice in 1996, and he gets squeezed out by 2003. McHale's spot is secure. He was a dominant player on a dominant team in a dominant era.

ELVIN HAYES
The Big E

MVP: 0	
MVP VOTING: 5th in 1974, 3rd in 1975, 3rd in 1977	
NBA TITLES: 1	
ALL-NBA FIRST TEAM: 3	
ALL-NBA SECOND TEAM: 3	

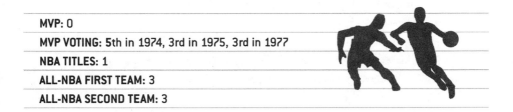

There is simply no criterion that could justify taking Elvin Hayes off a list of the 50 greatest players in NBA history. In the history of the game of basketball, only Kareem Abdul-Jabbar and Karl Malone have played more minutes. Only Wilt Chamberlain, Bill Russell, and Oscar Robertson have played more minutes per game. Only Chamberlain, Russell, and Abdul-Jabbar have more rebounds. Only Abdul-Jabbar, Karl Malone, Michael Jordan, Chamberlain, and Moses Malone have scored more points in the NBA. Hayes shows up on more leader boards than Tiger Woods.

The Stats

The Big E had 12 seasons with a per-game average of 20 points and 10 rebounds and averaged 20 and 10 for his career. He had four great statistical seasons to start his career, and he led his teams to four NBA Finals late in his career. He won an NBA title. Is it any wonder that he is ranked ahead of some great big men (including Bill Walton, Patrick Ewing, and Wes Unseld)?

Elgin's teams failed to make the playoffs in three of his first four seasons, and Hayes developed a reputation as a troublesome player to coach. But that was to change. He was traded to the Bullets, where he led his team to the NBA Finals in 1975, 1978, and 1979. In the 1978 season, they won the NBA title.

Hayes's NBA career lasted 16 seasons and 1,303 games played. So he has the longevity and career marks to be among the greatest. He also has a brilliant seven-year period in which he was one of the top players in the game (1973–1979).

He came quite a long way from his small town of Rayville, Louisiana. As a 6-foot-2 high school freshman, he went out for the basketball team and was cut. The next year, as a sophomore, he was cut. To top it off, Hayes's best friend—his father, Chris (a boiler supervisor in town)—died when Elvin was in ninth grade. By Hayes's junior year in high school, he was 6-foot-5. This time, the coach kept him on the squad. After high school, he chose the University of Houston, where he and Don Chaney became the first blacks to play for the basketball team.

Although Elvin played 16 years in the NBA, the most important game of his life was played at the University of Houston. In January 1968, Hayes's Houston team (with 17 wins in a row) took on UCLA (with 47 consecutive victories). With 28 seconds remaining in the game, Hayes sank two foul shots to unlock a 69–69 tie. Overall, Hayes scored 39 points to Lew Alcindor's 15. Hayes also outrebounded Alcindor—although, it must be pointed out that Alcindor (now Abdul-Jabbar) played the entire game with an eye injury that blurred his vision.

That, of course, was the night at the Astrodome that literally put the University of Houston on the map. There were 55,000 fans watching a college basketball game chanting "E-E-E." Of course, the teams would meet again in the NCAA semifinal game. The teams were ranked first and second in the nation, and UCLA got the better of Houston in the rematch, 101–69. That time Alcindor outscored Hayes 19–10.

Hayes's Graduation to the NBA

Hayes, though, would be named the 1968 collegiate player of the year, and was the first player selected in the draft. The San Diego Rockets won the coin toss with the Baltimore Bullets, who picked Wes Unseld with the second pick.

Baltimore would go from last place to first place, and Unseld was selected Rookie of the Year and MVP. Hayes won the scoring title in his rookie season, yet Unseld won the awards.

In the next three years, the Rockets and Hayes would go through several coaches. Jack McMahon and Alex Hannum were the first two, neither of whom had good things to say about the Big E. Recognizing that Hayes was still a major hero and draw in Houston, new ownership moved the franchise to Texas and hired a longtime college coach, Tex Winter, to be the head coach. So Hayes played an important role in bringing the NBA to the city of Houston.

Tex Winter, a former Kansas State and University of Washington head coach, became a head coach with the Houston Rockets in 1972. He brought along a rather complex and elaborate system—a triple-post offense, which had been his trademark and calling card in college. It would have worked, too, in Houston, except for one problem. Elvin Hayes. Hayes was virtually a shrine in Houston, back to his college days, and didn't want to play Winter's new triple-post offense. The Big E insisted it would hurt his offensive stats. Interestingly, the triple-post offense would give Winter nine NBA Championship rings as an assistant to Phil Jackson, first with the Bulls and then with the Lakers many years later. The offense didn't hurt Michael Jordan's offensive stats, that's for sure.

In the 1972 off-season, the owners backed Winter—and traded Hayes to Baltimore for Jack Marin, a fundamentally sound player from Duke.

Hayes, 1971–1973

1971 (before Tex Winter)	28.7 points/game	2,215 shot attempts (led NBA)
1972 (with Tex Winter)	25.2 points/game	1,918 shot attempts
1973 (with Baltimore)	21.2 points/game	1,607 shot attempts

Career Numbers

First 4 years	27.4 points/game	16.3 rebounds	44 minutes/game
Next 12 years	18.8 points/game	11.2 rebounds	35 minutes/game

Hayes, in his first four years, outscored everyone else in the league—and only Wes Unseld had more rebounds in those four seasons. But Elvin became a better, more complete player once he joined the Bullets.

Doug Collins: "Once he got to the Bullets, and he and Wes were together . . . he was pretty damn good. He had an unbelievable turnaround jump shot."

Leading Scorers of the 1970s

1. Kareem Abdul-Jabbar   22,141
2. Elvin Hayes   18,922
3. John Havlicek   15,747
4. Pete Maravich   15,359
5. Gail Goodrich   14,692

Hayes played on teams that went to the Finals in 1975, 1978, and 1979. None of those were great teams.

Interesting Fact About the 1975 Finals

Bullets coach K. C. Jones and Warriors coach Al Attles were the first African-Americans to oppose each other for a championship in a major team sport. It went mostly unnoticed. The NFL made news in January 2003 when the Jets' Herman Edwards opposed the Colts' Tony Dungy in a wild card playoff game.

Of course, nothing made news about the 1975 Finals. Rick Barry of the victorious Warriors noted that *Sports Illustrated* didn't even give the Finals a cover story.

Amazing Hayes Stats
- He played exactly 50,000 minutes in his NBA career.
- Since he entered the NBA in 1969, only one player has more career rebounds (Kareem Abdul-Jabbar).

Who's Better, Who's Best
Elvin Hayes or Chris Webber

Pete Vecsey: "They're kind of the same. Each one disappeared in crunch time. Hey, I vote for Hayes to be Top 50. He was a great scorer, an excellent shot blocker, a very good rebounder. But I used to call him 'The Silent E.'

"But you're asking me Hayes versus Webber. Hey, now we know where Webber goes in the fourth quarter of tight games. He's probably hanging out with Elvin somewhere! Webber is probably a little better. He could pass and dribble. Elvin couldn't put it on the floor. Webber can create for teammates."

Hayes moved cities a lot, but not franchises.

Hayes played for the San Diego Rockets when they moved to Houston. He played for the Bullets as they changed cities twice in his first three years (they were Baltimore then Capital then Washington).

Stu Lantz: "I played with Elvin with the Rockets in those early years. We were rookies together. You know, that year Wes Unseld won Rookie of the Year and MVP. Now, no offense to Wes—he's one of my best friends—but Wes should have received the MVP, and Hayes should have been awarded Rookie of the Year. Elvin had the numbers. Hayes used to post up and hit that 15-foot shot better than anyone. I'll place him over Webber—for now."

Walt Frazier: "He was a prolific scorer and rebounder. Guys who get 20 points and 10 rebounds like he did have always been a rare commodity. He was an excellent shot blocker, too."

Elvin Hayes had the durability that Webber has lacked. Webber has played 10 years in the NBA. In his first season, he missed six games. He's missed more than that in every season since. In 10 seasons, Chris has not even accumulated 600 total games. And Webber isn't as good a rebounder or shot blocker. That being said, Webber is a much more accomplished passer and puts the ball on the floor better. With Webber's career in midstream, it is easy to see how he might one day surpass the Big E. He hasn't done it, yet. Hayes was closer to Abdul-Jabbar than Webber is to Shaq. Hayes was as dominant in the 1970s as any player except for Kareem.

36

GARY PAYTON
"The Glove"

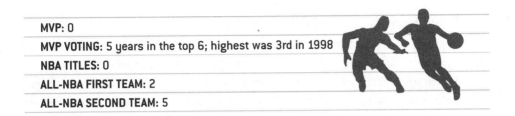

MVP: 0	
MVP VOTING: 5 years in the top 6; highest was 3rd in 1998	
NBA TITLES: 0	
ALL-NBA FIRST TEAM: 2	
ALL-NBA SECOND TEAM: 5	

Gary Payton has put a face on a franchise in a way that only a handful of players have ever done. He was Seattle's first-round pick (second overall) in the 1990 draft and has been one of the best offensive and defensive guards in the league since. He was Seattle's best player for 12 consecutive seasons—something that is quite rare in this league. Only a handful of players have even played for a franchise for as many as 12 years.

Most Games Played for a Franchise

1.	1,422	John Stockton, Utah
2.	1,353	Karl Malone, Utah
3.	1,270	John Havlicek, Boston
4.	1,177	Hakeem Olajuwon, Houston
5.	1,173	Reggie Miller, Indiana
6.	1,122	Hal Greer, Philadelphia
7.	1,106	Robert Parish, Boston
8.	1,093	Kareem Abdul-Jabbar, Los Angeles
9.	1,039	Patrick Ewing, New York
10.	1,018	Joe Dumars, Detroit
11.	1,002	Calvin Murphy, Houston
12.	999	Gary Payton, Seattle

Of these dozen players, not all are as readily identified with their franchise as Payton has been. For instance, Hal Greer played for the same franchise, but in his first seasons they played in Syracuse. Dumars is identified with Detroit, but he was never the best player on his team. Abdul-Jabbar spent the first six years of his career with the Milwaukee Bucks. It was Magic Johnson who was the "face" of the Lakers organization during the 1980s. Stockton and Malone are inseparable; forever they will be remembered as one with the Utah Jazz. Ewing is the same way with the Knicks.

The Glove Man

Payton is known as "The Glove," a reference to his defense, which has always been outstanding. People have whispered that as Payton's offensive game has grown, his defensive game has dropped. Still, look at the All-Defense First Teams. Payton made the First Team for nine straight seasons beginning in 1994. Do you want more defensive recognition? How's this? The NBA has awarded a Defensive Player of the Year award since 1983. It has been awarded mostly to centers. Payton is the only guard to win the award (in 1996) since 1988, when Michael Jordan captured it.

Who's Better, Who's Best
Gary Payton or Jason Kidd

Both players are from Oakland. Both entered the NBA as the second overall pick in the draft. Both have made the Finals.

They call this The Kidd against The Glove . . . and it is a matchup that has taken place 28 times in the regular season since Jason Kidd entered the NBA in 1994. Payton is 12–16 in games against Kidd (so, of course, Kidd is 16–12 in games against Payton).

Payton	Kidd
20.6 points	14.7 points
5.6 rebounds	6.3 rebounds
7.2 assists	11.1 assists
2.5 steals	2.3 steals

They met again for six postseason games in the first round of the 2003 playoffs. Jason again got the upper hand. But Payton's defense on Kidd at the end of games gave Milwaukee victories in Games 2 and 4.

Payton	Kidd	
18.5 points	18.8 points	
3.0 rebounds	6.8 rebounds	
8.7 assists	9.2 assists	
1.3 steals	1.6 steals	

Payton is a better shooter, and they're both great defensive players.

Stephen Smith: "To me, Kidd is the quintessential point guard. He is limited in his ability to shoot the basketball. The fact that he can't shoot makes him an even greater point guard in my mind. If he shot well, that would draw out the defense. For years, teams didn't respect his shot—and Jason still was able to find teammates and set them up to perfection. He really could control a game, scoring only five points."

Isiah Thomas: "Payton is very underrated. Make no mistake about it, he's one of the best. You can look at his body of work, and it compares to Jason and most of the other great point guards."

Who's Better, Who's Best
Gary Payton or John Stockton

The day before the 2003 All-Star break, former Seattle coach George Karl said he would hate to see Payton wearing anything other than Sonics colors.

"I hope Gary retires a Seattle SuperSonic," Karl said. "I don't know what the compromise is or the figure is, but I look at Gary as John Stockton. Having him in another uniform would be very sad to me. It would be very sad." (Not that sad, as it turned out, since Karl traded for his ex-player two weeks after making that statement.)

Gary Payton and John Stockton have played each other more than any other two NBA opponents in the last 20 years. To find opponents who have played against each other more frequently, the following four guidelines would have to be met:

1. The opponents would have to play for 13 years each.
2. The opponents would have to play against each other (center against center, et cetera).
3. The opponents would have to play in the same conference since there are more games against conference foes.
4. The opponents would have to face each other in four different playoff series.

Stockton has missed 22 games in 19 years. Payton has missed five games in 13 years. They have played each other around 52 times in the regular season, with another 21 meetings in four playoff series. That means they have played against each other more than 70 times in their careers.

This is not like Chamberlain against Russell, in a nine-team league. This is in an era of 29 teams.

Playoff Meetings

1992 Second Round: Utah 4–1 Payton was hurt and did very little in this series. He didn't play the fifth and final game at all. In the fourth game, he played little, made his only shot, and had two assists.

1993 First Round: Seattle 3–2 With the series tied 1–1, Payton shot one of 10 field goals, and Utah went up 2–1 with the fourth game in Salt Lake City. But Payton came back strong and the Sonics won the last two games of the series. In the fifth and deciding game, The Glove hit 8 of 14 shots, scoring 17 points with seven assists and only one turnover.

1996 Western Conference Finals: Seattle 4–3 Seattle had a 3–1 lead in this series, but the Jazz came back to tie up the series and send it back to Seattle for Game 7. Seattle advanced 90–86, as Payton scored 21 points and added six rebounds and five assists.

2000 First Round: Utah 3-2 Utah led 2–1, and Payton staved off elimination with a brilliant performance. In a 104–93 victory, Payton had 35 points, 10 rebounds, and 11 assists. He came back with 27 in the deciding fifth game, but Utah advanced 96–93.

Derek Harper: "Stockton is better because Payton hasn't done it as long." When I pointed out that Payton was in his 13th season, Harper laughed and continued, "I have a ton of respect for Gary Payton. He has that overall ability to control both ends of the court. His defense is far above his offense, however. He could defend any guard of any size. His defense is tenacious."

Sam Cassell: "Gary Payton: He was on a great team in Seattle. Check the winning percentage that year. He's one of the all-time greats, in my eyes. Payton is a great team defender. He knew how to make team defense work."

Payton the Winner

In Gary Payton's first 13 seasons in the NBA, he played 947 of Seattle's 952 games. Seattle won 606 of those 952 games. That's a .636 winning percentage—an average of 52 wins per year for 12 consecutive seasons. That's more wins than the Los Angeles Lakers had in those same 12 seasons (603). That's more than the Portland Trail Blazers had (594). That's more than the Chicago Bulls had (494). Only two teams had more wins in that 12-year period—the Utah Jazz (639) and the San Antonio Spurs (609).

Gary's 1996 Seattle team won 64 games and lost in the Finals to Chicago.

Most Regular-Season Wins, Without Winning NBA Title

1. 68   Boston, 1973
2. 64   Seattle, 1996
         Utah, 1997

As great as Payton has been, he was considered a disappointment in his first two seasons in Seattle. His defense was up to speed immediately, but his offense and decision making were often questioned. The organization brought in George Karl as head coach, and Payton made the most of his opportunity.

Playing in the left-hand corner of the country, Payton has gotten lost among the other elite players—even at his position. He became known for his trash-talking and not his play. That is unfortunate, because between 1995 and 2001, he had seasons where he was among the very best players in the league. I'm not sure you can say that about John Stockton. This is one case where I listened to the three dozen experts I talked to. They were mostly unanimous. I had to include John Stockton. He had to be above Kidd and Payton. It wasn't one person. It was a landslide. But, hey, G.P., at #36, you're still in the top 1 percent of all NBA players that ever played!

BILL WALTON

The Textbook Center

MVP: 1	
MVP VOTING: 2nd in 1977, 1st in 1978	
NBA TITLES: 2	
ALL-NBA FIRST TEAM: 1	
ALL-NBA SECOND TEAM: 1	

There is no one who loves the game of basketball more than Bill Walton. There is no greater student of the sport. When legendary UCLA basketball coach John Wooden prepared for practices, he needed extra hours to handle the avalanche of questions that he knew Bill Walton would throw at him. Anyone who ever saw Walton play knew that it all paid off.

Walton is not on this list because he was the greatest college basketball player of all time (although he was). He's not on this list because he has been a hero of mine since I was ten years old as well as a friend of mine for more than a decade (although he is). He's on this list because no one gave up more to play this game at the highest level. He gave up nine years of his prime to injuries.

Walton's Brief Career

Not that I have to justify or smudge the record when it comes to Walton, but critics point out that he only played 468 career games in the NBA. When he was healthy—and that was rare—he was as good a center as there has ever been. He was a tremendous shot blocker. He was also a terrific defensive rebounder, with a wicked outlet pass. But despite a career shortened by injuries, Walton won an MVP, a Finals MVP, a Sixth Man award, and two championships.

Remember that last sentence. The man was a Most Valuable Player for a season.

That's hard to do. In the first 47 years that they awarded the MVP, it went to only 23 players. In the first 44 years they awarded an MVP, it went to only 20 different players. All 20 should go directly to the Hall of Fame, without passing go. If that honor doesn't automatically qualify them for the Hall, it will qualify them for a permanent spot in this book.

The way the Masters Golf Tournament draws its yearly field gave me this idea. This list shows how the Masters draws its field. In addition, the Masters Committee, at its discretion, invites international players not otherwise qualified.

1. Masters Tournament Champions
2. U.S. Open Champions (Honorary, noncompeting after five years)
3. British Open Champions (Honorary, noncompeting after five years)
4. PGA Champions (Honorary, noncompeting after five years)
5. Winners of the Players Championship (three years)

They fill out the field with the deserving players of the year. But the key is, they respect their past and hold a place.

How regal! How perfect! Notice the Masters Champion qualifies each year, merely because he won the prestigious event in the past.

NBA MVPs
Kareem Abdul-Jabbar
Charles Barkley
Larry Bird
Wilt Chamberlain
Bob Cousy
Dave Cowens
Tim Duncan
Julius Erving
Allen Iverson
Magic Johnson
Michael Jordan
Karl Malone
Moses Malone
Bob McAdoo
Hakeem Olajuwon
Shaquille O'Neal

Bob Pettit
Willis Reed
Oscar Robertson
David Robinson
Bill Russell
Wes Unseld
Bill Walton

All of these players are among the greatest players in the history of the game. But, if we had to divide the gymnasium and put the above list on one side, who would be left on the other side?

"All of you with an MVP trophy, go to the other side of the gym. Not so fast, Jerry."

Bob Ryan: "Bill Walton is one of the greatest centers to ever play the game. Arvydas Sabonis is the greatest player America never got to see. They say when he was young, he reminded people of Bill Walton with a three-point shot. To that, I have only one thing to say: 'Omigod.'"

Brent Musburger: "Walton was the best passing center I ever saw. The other two who were close were Arvydas Sabonis and Alvan Adams."

Dr. Ernie Vandeweghe: "Bill had the best outlet pass in the history of the game. Russell had a great one, too, but Bill was so quick and so athletic—wow!"

In his first four years with Portland, Walton averaged almost four and a half assists per game. Shaquille, not a bad passer himself, has never averaged as many as four assists per game in a season. Vlade Divac, considered one of the best passing centers, has a career average under three assists per game. Olajuwon finished his career with 2.5 assists per game. Robinson was about the same. Ewing was under two assists per game. Moses Malone and Elvin Hayes were pathetic. Wes Unseld averaged 3.9 for his career. Chamberlain had a career 4.2 assists per game—and was much higher for most of his career (although in his first two seasons, he averaged under two assists per game).

Most Career Assists by a Center

1. 5,660   Kareem Abdul-Jabbar (3.6 per game)
2. 4,643   Wilt Chamberlain
3. 4,100   Bill Russell
4. 4,012   Alvan Adams

Walton's Blocked Shots

| 1977 | 65 games | 211 blocks | 3.3 blocks/game (led league) |
| 1978 | 58 games | 146 blocks | 2.5 blocks/game (fourth in league) |

Those numbers make you think that if Walton had been able to play upwards of 1,000 career games, he might have been among the best ever in blocked shots.

Walton's Rebounds

| 1977 | 65 games | 934 rebounds | 14.4 per game (led league) |
| 1978 | 58 games | 766 rebounds | 13.2 per game (didn't qualify) |

Walton shot more than 52 percent for his career. He could not have played the center position better if Dr. Frankenstein had personally created him in his laboratory.

Bill Walton was like a student who had a lot of absences, but aced the final exams anyway. Walton's most important tests, of course, were against Kareem Abdul-Jabbar.

Who's Better, Who's Best
Bill Walton or Kareem Abdul-Jabbar

Here's what the man himself had to say.

Bill Walton: "Kareem was the best player *by far* that I ever played against. My battles with Jabbar, next to winning championships, were the most exciting moments of my professional career. Everything I did as a basketball player I did to beat him. I would be riding my bike up a hill, pumping iron, running, saying to myself, 'Jabbar. Jabbar. Jabbar . . . I'm going to get him.' He was my ideal opponent, my competition, my archrival, my motivation."

Walton's Average Game Stats Against Kareem

1976	18.5 points	15 rebounds	6.7 assists
1977	24.3 points	21 rebounds	5 assists
1978	15.5 points	15.5 rebounds	5 assists

In the 1977 season, Walton's Blazers met Kareem's Lakers 11 times (seven times regular season, four playoff games). Walton missed one game with an injury. The Blazers won eight out of 10 games that Walton dueled with Abdul-Jabbar.

Steve Jones: "What battles? Bill lost them all. Bill Walton got his fanny kicked by Abdul-Jabbar. Kareem had no team around him. Portland killed the Lakers in the backcourt. But Abdul-Jabbar was still Abdul-Jabbar. He was great."

In 1978, Walton played the two early games against the Lakers before suffering his season-ending injury. The Blazers were 0–2 in those games.

Dr. Ernie Vandeweghe: "Their games were different. Kareem's game depended on having a teammate who was a great passer. Bill was a better rebounder, a better all-around player. With a healthy Walton, you have a great center, coach, cheerleader—everything rolled into one."

Steve Jones: "If Bill had remained healthy, he would have been Hell on Wheels. But in truth, he was a one-year wonder. Everything else was hypothetical."

Bill Walton has a lot of musical heroes—men such as Bob Dylan and Jerry Garcia and Neil Young. It was Neil Young who capsulized Walton's career as a basketball player. "It's better to burn out—than it is to rust," wrote Young. Walton—maybe the most fundamentally skilled center to ever play the game—burned out long before he could have a Dylan/Abdul-Jabbar career.

38

PATRICK EWING
The Best Jump-Shooting Center

MVP: 0	
MVP VOTING: 6 years in the top 5; highest finishes:	
4th in 1989, 4th in 1993, 4th in 1995	
NBA TITLES: 0	
ALL-NBA FIRST TEAM: 1	
ALL-NBA SECOND TEAM: 6	

Patrick Ewing had the "almost" career. He was one of the all-time great college basketball players at Georgetown, where he was known as the "Hoya Destroya." He still is one of the last great college players to stay all four years. He played 137 college games, and game number 37 was indicative of Ewing's entire basketball career. In that 1982 game, his Hoyas were in position to win the NCAA National Championship, but a freshman Tar Heel named Michael Jordan hit a shot to win the game. Ewing won a national title at Georgetown in 1984 but lost in the finals of his senior year to a heavy underdog Villanova team.

Patrick Ewing was only a 15-point-per-game scorer in four seasons at Georgetown and was thought to be "the next Bill Russell." While at Georgetown, he played under head coach John Thompson, a former Russell understudy with the Celtics.

Ewing Takes the NBA by Storm

Ewing was the prize of the 1985 NBA draft—a draft that featured lottery picks for the first time. In 1986, Ewing justified his No. 1 selection by winning Rookie of the Year, averaging 20 points and nine rebounds. The Knicks had a center—Bill Cartwright—who was injured and missed all but two games of that 1986 season. The two centers would play together two seasons before Knicks management traded Cartwright to the Bulls for power forward Charles Oakley. (In those pre-9/11 days, two 7-foot centers playing alongside each other in New York were called the "Twin Towers.")

Oakley and Ewing were teammates for 10 seasons. Guard John Starks played with them for eight of those 10 seasons. Forward Anthony Mason was there for five of those years, as well. Ah, what a warm, fuzzy team for New Yorkers to embrace!

With that bunch, Ewing came close to several NBA Championships. He also came close to winning several MVPs. Always, it seemed, a man named Michael Jordan was there ahead of him.

Ewing played Wile E. Coyote to Jordan's Roadrunner. In other words, the Coyote spent his lifetime in pursuit of the uncatchable Roadrunner. He had the best game plan (sometimes, with elaborate charts and maps). He used only the finest products from Acme. It didn't matter. The Coyote would invariably fall off some cliff and have to peel himself together to hatch another plan. That was Ewing in pursuit of Michael Jordan. There wasn't one instance when Ewing's team caught Jordan's. If Ewing had caught the NBA's version of the Roadrunner, then a case could be made that Ewing would have been among the top dozen players of all time.

1989	Jordan's Bulls eliminate Ewing's Knicks 4–2
1991	Jordan's Bulls eliminate Ewing's Knicks 3–0
1992	Jordan's Bulls eliminate Ewing's Knicks 4–3
1993	Jordan's Bulls eliminate Ewing's Knicks 4–2
1996	Jordan's Bulls eliminate Ewing's Knicks 4–1

It would have benefited Ewing if his teammates had helped at key points along the way. John Starks missed all 10 of his three-point attempts in Game 7 of the 1994 Finals. Charles Smith missed four attempts at the end of Game 5 of the 1993 series—the one in which the Knicks had the home court advantage on Jordan's Bulls. But Ewing made his own bed a lot of times.

Bulls-Knicks Postseason Matchups

I want to examine those Bulls-Knicks playoff games a little more closely.

Michael Jordan played against the Knicks in five different postseason series. The Knicks and Bulls met in 1994, when Jordan was playing minor-league baseball, and Ewing's Knicks advanced.

In the five playoff series against Jordan, the Knicks were by far the inferior team in 1989, 1991, 1992, and 1996. The 1991 Knicks team snuck into the playoffs with a 39–43 record, in fact.

Pat Riley took over the Knicks in 1992 and improved the Knicks team from 39 wins to 51. The Knicks eliminated the Pistons in a deciding fifth game in the first round and advanced to play the 67–15 Chicago Bulls. By winning the fifth game of the Detroit series, the Knicks put an end to the Chuck Daly era in Detroit and prevented a Bulls-Pistons matchup for a fifth consecutive season. Ewing scored 31 points and had 19 rebounds against the Pistons, and New York withstood a 21-point fourth quarter by Isiah Thomas. The physical Knicks, with Xavier McDaniel, Charles Oakley, and Ewing, then took on the Bulls.

If You Can't Beat Him, Join Him

Ewing never won an NBA Championship, in large measure due to Michael Jordan. So Patrick did the next best thing: he joined Michael Jordan as a teammate on the Olympic Team and won gold medals in 1984 and in 1992. Michael Jordan also hired Ewing for a role in his movie, *Space Jam*. And in a move that reminded me of an aging Rocky Balboa hiring Apollo Creed to help him prepare for one last fight, Jordan's Wizards hired Patrick as an assistant coach. On Patrick Ewing Night at Madison Square Garden in February 2003, Jordan told reporters that he had tried to get Patrick to come to North Carolina with him way back in the early 1980s—but Ewing chose Georgetown instead.

1992

In the first game of the series, the Knicks snapped a 14-game losing streak against the Bulls and a 17-game losing span at Chicago Stadium by stunning the defending champions 94–89. This was the game that Patrick Ewing needs a copy of to show his grandkids one day. This was the one for the time capsule.

Ewing had 34 points, including 28 in the second half. He also had 16 rebounds and six blocked shots. The Bulls had a one-point lead with 2:26 remaining, but the Knicks outscored the Bulls 9–3 the rest of the way—with Ewing scoring eight of the points.

The Bulls pulled even in the second game and then defeated the Knicks in New York to win back their home court advantage. Ewing sprained his ankle in the third quarter of the sixth game. Yet, somehow, Patrick scored 11 points in the fourth quarter to send the series back to Chicago for a deciding seventh game. A hobbling Ewing wasn't going to interrupt a dynasty. The Bulls won 110–81 in that Game 7. Still, Ewing pushed Jordan like no one else. In Jordan's six championship seasons, this would be one of only two Game 7s they would need (Indiana in 1998 pushed the Bulls to a seventh game as well).

1993

In 1993, the Knicks peaked at 60 wins. They had a better regular-season record than the two-time defending Bulls. The Knicks went 7–2 in the first two rounds of the postseason, easily disposing of Indiana and Charlotte. They then had a rematch with the Bulls.

This was going to be Patrick Ewing's year. In the final minute of Game 2 at Madison Square Garden, John Starks had what many consider the most famous play in New York Knicks history. Starks split the Bulls defense for "The Dunk"—a driving left-handed tomahawk slam that sent the Garden into a frenzy. The play, coming with 47 seconds remaining, gave the Knicks an insurmountable five-point lead in their eventual 96–91 win. The Knicks were up 2–0 in the best-of-seven series.

Chicago was the site for two games on Memorial Day weekend. If the Knicks could take just one of those games, they would have a 3–1 lead with two possible games remaining at New York.

In the third game, Michael Jordan had one of his worst shooting days in his illustrious playoff career. He made just 3 of 18 shots. But Jordan still was able to get to the line, and Scottie Pippen picked up his game and scored 29 points. The Bulls got back into the series with a 103–83 win.

Two days later, in the Monday afternoon game, Jordan was back on his game. He scored 54 points, and the Bulls tied the series 2–2.

In the fifth game, the Knicks missed 15 free throws. The Knicks' Charles Smith had four chances to win the game in the final seconds, but the Bulls' interior defense, led by Horace Grant and Scottie Pippen, turned him back each time. The Bulls took the home court advantage, and the series never got back to New York for a seventh game.

1994 Postseason

In 1994, Michael Jordan had retired for the first time. The Knicks got past the Bulls and everyone else. In Ewing's first Finals appearance, he shot just 36 percent (58 of 160 field goals) and averaged just 18.9 points per game in the seven games. Remember, Ewing had averaged 24.5 points per game during the season on 50 percent shooting. In the Finals, against Hakeem Olajuwon, Ewing's numbers dropped with a thud. In the seventh and final game, he shot just 7 of 17 field goals on the way to 17 points. Olajuwon had 25 points and 10 rebounds in the same game. He averaged 26.8 points in those Finals.

Ewing's best game in those 1994 Finals was Game 5. On a Friday night, when the nation was keeping one eye (OK, both eyes) on a white Ford Bronco in southern California, Patrick Ewing put the Knicks up 3–2 for the series with a brilliant 25-point, 12-rebound, eight-block performance.

But, needing just one win in the final two games, the Knicks couldn't finish off the Rockets.

Ewing's Playoff Frustration

1992	lost a seventh game to Chicago
1993	lost a 2–0 lead to Chicago in a best-of-seven
1994	lost a 3–2 lead to Houston in the NBA Finals
1995	lost a seventh game to Indiana (at the Garden, with Ewing missing a finger roll at the buzzer)
1997	lost a 3–1 lead to Miami (Ewing suspended for Game 6, Knicks undermanned in Game 7)
1998	injured for first-round series, returned for second-round loss to Pacers
1999	missed final nine playoff games including the Finals (torn left Achilles tendon)

Ewing's playoff career was filled with frustration. It was so typical that Ewing was suspended for the sixth game of the 1997 series with Miami, following a fight at the end of Game 5 in which Ewing left the bench. The sixth game was played in New York, where the Knicks would have had a good chance of winning with Ewing and four NYC policemen. Instead, the Heat fought back and extended the series with a 95–90 win. Back in Miami for the seventh game, Ewing played great: 37 points and 17 rebounds. It didn't matter. The Heat won by 11 and advanced.

In the 1999 playoffs, Ewing was positively heroic in playing with Achilles tendon and rib-cage injuries. In the Eastern Conference finals against Indiana, he experienced a tearing sensation in his left Achilles tendon during warm-ups. Nevertheless, Ewing's two free throws with 45 seconds remaining in the game gave the Knicks an 86–84 lead. After Indiana moved ahead, the Knicks got the ball to Ewing for a potential game-tying 16-foot jumper. He missed at the buzzer. He showed increased swelling following the game, and he was done for the remainder of the playoff run. It was all so typical in Patrick Ewing's postseason career.

Who's Better, Who's Best
Patrick Ewing or Hakeem Olajuwon

Ewing had the championship at Georgetown over Olajuwon's crew at the University of Houston. Ewing and Olajuwon had parallel careers up until the 1994 Finals. Olajuwon outplayed and was clearly superior to Ewing in the Finals.

From then on, Olajuwon has been considered the better player. But it wasn't always that way.

Let's look at Ewing and Olajuwon at the halfway point in their careers.

Following the 1991 Season

	Years	Games	Field Goals	Percentage	Rebounds	Assists	Points
Ewing	6	438	4,066 of 7,650	.532	9.6	2.1	23.6
Olajuwon	7	524	4,774 of 9,287	.514	12.6	2.2	23.0

Ewing had 1,361 blocks (3.1 per game), while Olajuwon had 1,758 (3.4). Hakeem was slightly ahead in blocks, steals, and rebounds. Ewing was slightly ahead in shooting percentage and scoring.

Ewing was seen as a player who had to endure different head coaches—with wildly different philosophies.

Ewing's NBA Coaches, First Seven Years
Hubie Brown
Bob Hill
Rick Pitino
Stu Jackson
John MacLeod
Pat Riley

Despite this coaching turnover, Ewing performed like a true all-star. He flourished when John Thompson wanted him to be Bill Russell. He flourished when Hubie Brown was calling out plays as the Knicks walked the ball upcourt. He positively starred when Rick Pitino wanted to run.

All-NBA First Team Centers
1987 Hakeem Olajuwon
1988 Hakeem Olajuwon
1989 Hakeem Olajuwon
1990 Patrick Ewing

Olajuwon's career had a different arc than Ewing's. Hakeem started his NBA career with a better team and led his team to the Finals in just his second season. His career had a dip in the middle, and he clearly fell behind both Ewing and David Robinson in the early 1990s. Ewing started showing up in the MVP voting in 1989 and stayed. Olajuwon received a ton of votes early in his career, but then didn't get any votes in 1991 or 1992. Of course, unlike Ewing, Olajuwon would win an MVP and an NBA Championship (two of them). But halfway through their careers, you could say choosing between Ewing and Olajuwon was a real toss-up.

Ewing and Olajuwon: MVP Votes

1986	Olajuwon	4th		
1987	Olajuwon	7th		
1988	Olajuwon	7th		
1989	Ewing	4th	Olajuwon	5th
1990	Ewing	5th	Olajuwon	7th
1991	Ewing	11th		
1992	Ewing	5th		
1993	Olajuwon	2nd	Ewing	4th

Ewing's 1990 Season

This was his dominant season. This was the year—the only year—that Ewing was the best center in the NBA. Olajuwon was better earlier in their careers. Hakeem, David Robinson, and Shaquille O'Neal were better in later years. But for one year, Ewing was THE man. He was in the top six in the league in scoring (almost 29 points per game), rebounds (almost 11 per contest), blocks (a shade under four per game), and shooting (55 percent).

In the postseason, he was even better. He averaged 31.6 points per game, with 11.4 rebounds, against Boston in the first round. In the climactic Game 5, Ewing scored 31 points, with eight rebounds and 10 assists. In the Knicks' only victory in the second round against Detroit, Ewing poured in 45 points.

The Greatest Jump-Shooting Center . . . Ever?

Ewing's touch from the outside was beautiful. I think he was the greatest jump-shooting center of all time. I have seen his shot thousands of times. It is as ingrained in my head as Jimmy Connors's serve or as Joe Morgan's batting stance.

I remember the 1993 NBA All-Star game at Utah. Ewing sent the game into overtime with a clutch 15-foot baseline jumper with eight seconds left to knot the score. Ewing then scored six more points in overtime. He wasn't your classic, back-to-the-basket center. He was a below-average passer. What he was, was a good rebounder, a good defensive player, and a terrific jump shooter. He developed into a decent low-post player who could play in the lane. He was always most effective when his teammates drove and kicked the ball out to him for his jumper.

How did Patrick Ewing compare to the other great centers of his time (David Robinson and Hakeem Olajuwon)?

Del Harris: "I would rank them this way. Hakeem, David, Patrick. If David had Patrick's drive, he would be first."

Bill Walton: "David Robinson was more skilled than Ewing, very gifted. . . . Robinson was better. Ewing benefited greatly by playing in New York . . . Everything Patrick did was magnified—good and bad."

Pat Riley: "I think he is right up there; he is right there with both of them. You can't separate them at all. He had an incredible career for a long period of time and competed against the very, very best, night in and night out. There wasn't anybody that ever dominated Patrick and he got his numbers against all of them."

Mike Fratello: "Ewing is right there with Robinson and Olajuwon. Only a championship separates them. But I believe that if you took Patrick Ewing and plugged him into those Rockets teams or the Spurs championship team, then Ewing would have won."

The Greatest Play in Ewing's Career

Ewing had some wonderful playoff moments. I've already written about his play in the winner-take-all game of 1990, his play in Chicago in the first game of the 1992 series, and his unbelievable play against Olajuwon in the fifth game of the 1994 Finals.

I was courtside for so many of these games. So many times in the mid-1990s, my work, my vacation—my life—was tied up in the performance of Patrick Ewing.

In 1994, the Knicks advanced past the Jordanless Bulls in seven games and played the Indiana Pacers in the Eastern Conference finals. The Knicks took the first two games in New York but gave them back in Indiana. In Game 3, Ewing had the worst playoff game any player could ever have. The Pacers won 88–68, as Patrick Ewing scored one point. He missed all 10 of his shots from the field and made just one of four free throws. This was the first series that Reggie Miller went nuts against the Knicks (25 points in the fourth quarter of Game 5), and the Knicks were fortunate to win in Market Square Arena in the sixth game.

In Game 7, the Pacers took a four-point lead into halftime and built the lead to 12 points with four minutes remaining in the third quarter. With :34 left, Dale Davis's layup gave the Pacers a one-point lead. Following a timeout, Starks drove the baseline for a missed layup attempt, but Ewing was there to time the rebound perfectly and slam in the miss. Those two points sent the Knicks to the Finals for the first time in 21 years. Ewing had 24 points, 22 rebounds, seven assists, and five blocks.

Why Didn't Fans Appreciate Ewing?

Well, it started at Georgetown, where Ewing and his team were aloof and distant. Knicks fans were paying top dollar and wanted a title. That didn't happen. Patrick was also elected president of the NBA Players Association for a four-year term starting in 1997. He was the front man for the players during the lockout in 1998. He took criticism for the role that he played, being accused of dragging out the proceedings, but he had the players' best interests in mind. Then, his contract—and then, his trade—represented the end of the Knicks' run of success. As Walton said, Ewing's contributions were magnified because he played in New York.

During Ewing's tenure in New York, he saw the Mets win a World Series in 1986. He saw the Giants win a pair of Super Bowls. He saw the Rangers win the Stanley Cup. He saw the Yankees win four World Series in five years. Even the Devils won a Stanley Cup. Ewing's 15 years also saw the rise of sports-talk radio. Fans—who now had the capability to watch every single game—had a place to vent and be heard. Ewing was going to hear about his late-game misses. His perennial "guarantee" of a title. Even Ewing's personal affairs were discussed on the Howard Stern radio show.

Patrick Ewing became a symbol for New York. They didn't always come out on top, but they were always gritty, always tough. Ewing may not have been the game's greatest player—but his greatness brought out the very best in a host of players (Isiah Thomas,

Michael Jordan, Reggie Miller, Hakeem Olajuwon). He raised the bar for the rest of the stars.

By the end of Patrick's career, all was forgiven. The Knicks retired Ewing's number on February 28, 2003, and the Garden fans honored their warrior. Ewing was gracious (even saying that he wasn't the greatest Knick of all time). The fans, in turn, gave Ewing a lot of love. The Knicks teams had to stink before their fans would realize how much Ewing meant to their franchise.

39

WILLIS REED
Heavyweight Champ

MVP: 1	
MVP VOTING: 2nd in 1969, 4th in 1971	
NBA TITLES: 2	
ALL-NBA FIRST TEAM: 1	
ALL-NBA SECOND TEAM: 4	

Captain Willis Reed was a dominant player in the NBA—the dominant player on one of the most celebrated and popular teams in league history. He was the heavyweight champion of the world for a short time. But as you'll see, it was a very short time.

Heavyweight Champion of the World

In boxing terms, the center position is the heavyweight division, the most glamorous position. Willis Reed entered the NBA in 1965 with the Knicks, a time when the heavyweight bouts between Wilt Chamberlain and Bill Russell were holy wars. Reed was a forward with the Knicks, until a trade with Detroit in December 1968 brought forward Dave DeBusschere to the Big Apple in exchange for center Walt Bellamy. Suddenly, Reed moved up to the heavyweight division and started having spectacular results.

In 1969, Bill Russell retired, but not before taking out Willis Reed and the Knicks in the Eastern Conference finals and then Chamberlain and the Lakers in the NBA Finals. Of course, that would be the year Wilt's corner man (Coach Butch van Breda Kolff) didn't let Chamberlain come out for the final round in the seventh game.

Following the champion's retirement, the heavyweight division in 1970 was wide open. A season-ending injury to Chamberlain limited him to 12 games, leaving four contenders to battle for the belt. A pair of second-year centers were too raw and one-dimensional (Elvin Hayes was a sensational scorer, Wes Unseld a tremendous rebounder) to truly be in contention. That left the young, brash, recently converted Muslim against the proud black man that white America rallied behind and loved. Does that sound familiar?

Kareem Abdul-Jabbar versus Willis Reed was the NBA's answer to Muhammad Ali versus Joe Frazier. Same arena. Same fans. Same era.

Reed was Smokin' Joe Frazier—the safe choice for white fans.

Abdul-Jabbar had everything Ali had, in terms of physical talent. He had great hands, great agility, great spring, great moves, great savvy. He was quicker than other centers (you might say, he could "float like a butterfly"). Abdul-Jabbar sparked Power Memorial High School to three straight city titles, a 71-game winning streak, and only one loss in three years. You would think he would have been a New York hero from that alone.

But he wasn't. Kareem left New York for UCLA, where he led the Bruins to three NCAA National Championships. Shortly afterward, he became the first athlete to sign a million-dollar contract.

After playing against Kareem in the preseason, Willis Reed had this to say: "I lost one headache when Bill Russell retired. Now, I've got another. At this point, I'd rather have my Russell headache. Bill was quick as a cat, but at least he wasn't someone I had to look up to."

Reed and Abdul-Jabbar

Abdul-Jabbar first met Willis Reed for real on November 1, 1969, in New York. The Big Fella had a cold hand at the start, but Alcindor (as he was still being called then) got hot and almost led the second-year franchise to an upset over the eventual champs, who won112–108. Against Reed, the rookie scored 36 points and had 27 rebounds. Two nights later, the teams met again in Milwaukee. The Knicks pasted the Bucks 109–93, with Reed scoring 35 points while holding Abdul-Jabbar to 17.

In January 1970, the teams met for the third time. The Knicks had never lost to the Bucks, but Kareem scored 41 points and took down 16 rebounds. He completely out-played Reed, who had 16 points and three rebounds.

Reed started the All-Star game for the East, and Kareem backed him up. Willis scored 21 points in that game and was voted the Most Valuable Player. When the MVP voting for the regular season was announced a few months later, Reed was again the winner, beating out Jerry West and Abdul-Jabbar.

Reed and Abdul-Jabbar would meet in the Eastern Conference finals in April 1970 for the right to take on a now-healthy Chamberlain for the NBA Championship.

Reed was not only giving away five years—and five inches—he was playing on a bad left knee. In Game 1 at the Garden, the Bucks committed 19 turnovers—in the first quarter alone! The Knicks won 110–102, despite Abdul-Jabbar outscoring Reed 35–24 and out-rebounding the Knicks center 15–12.

In the second game, Abdul-Jabbar had a triple double. He scored 36 points, 23 rebounds, and 11 assists. The Knicks won 112–111, to go up 2–0 for the series. In that second game, Kareem missed a pair of free throws in the final minute with his team down by one.

The Bucks won the third game back in Milwaukee, as Abdul-Jabbar scored 33 points and had 31 rebounds—almost as many as the entire Knicks team.

In a crucial fourth game, the Knicks took a 20-point halftime lead. The Bucks then outscored New York 22–4 in a seven-minute burst. The Knicks regained composure and the game. They led the series 3–1. Kareem had 38 points and nine boards.

Back in New York, the Knicks showed their championship ways. They defeated Milwaukee 132–96. When the Big Fella left the game, the crowd in New York began chanting, "Goodbye Lewie!" Asked about it after the game, Abdul-Jabbar was quoted as saying, "Whenever I play in New York, the fans have rooted against me. It's their problem. Maybe they do it because they're scared."

Reed would go in the ring against a now-healthy Chamberlain in the Finals and win that battle, too. Reed was inspirational in the 1970 Finals and was the new NBA heavyweight champion. But Reed's window didn't last long. The Bucks would win 66 games and the NBA Championship the next season. Chamberlain would take back the crown for a year in 1972. After that, it was Kareem's league.

Who's Better, Who's Best
Willis Reed or Kareem Abdul-Jabbar

The two really only met in the 1970 season, the 1970 playoff series, and the 1971 season. After that, Reed was hurt in 1972 and was not the same in his final season. In the two seasons that Reed was healthy, his Knicks beat the Bucks 12 out of 16 games. In 1971, when the Bucks were 66–16, the Knicks defeated Milwaukee four out of five times.

Reed frustrated Kareem on several occasions, including three times when he outscored him.

Nov. 3, 1970	Knicks 112–108	Reed 35 points	Abdul-Jabbar 17 points
Nov. 27, 1971	Knicks 103–94	Reed 34 points	Abdul-Jabbar 33 points
Jan. 26, 1971	Knicks 107–98	Reed 35 points	Abdul-Jabbar 29 points

The Knicks won the 1970 title. The Bucks won the 1971 title. In 1973, the Knicks regained the belt. It would have been a wonderful battle throughout the 1970s if Reed had remained healthy. Kareem Abdul-Jabbar would wait a few years to face a formidable challenge. This time, it came not from a native New Yorker, but from another UCLA center. Bill Walton would win his share of battles with Kareem—as Willis did—but similar to Reed, Walton's body gave out far too soon.

Marv Albert: "It seems to me, trying to remember all these years later, that Willis used to kill Kareem. Reed would outplay him. I used to think Kareem was afraid of him. He watched him in New York, growing up. There was always that possibility that Reed would deck him."

Pete Vecsey: "Willis Reed was one of the fiercest competitors you'll ever find. He wiped the deck with opponents. He once beat up four Lakers—he broke John Block's jaw . . . another time, he was in the middle of a huge brawl in Atlanta. He was a great team player. . . . One of the all-time enforcers. His teammates loved him."

Marv Albert: "I remember what Vecsey was talking about. It was opening night at Madison Square Garden against the Lakers. John Block just happened to be in the way. Willis just lost it. He was being restrained, and I think he once got beat up as a child when restrained. So, a fight broke out, and Reed broke free from whomever was holding him back, and he just went up and down the Lakers bench. He got Rudy LaRusso as well."

Here's what happened that night. It was opening night of the 1967 season. Forward Rudy LaRusso was jostling with Willis. As Baylor attempted a free throw, Reed threw an elbow at LaRusso. LaRusso took a swing at Reed, touching off what is regarded as one of the most vicious fistfights ever seen during an NBA game. Reed lost his temper. Rookie John Block grabbed Reed and pulled him off LaRusso. Willis then hit him with his fist. From there reserve guard Emmett Bryant hit Darrall Imhoff a couple of times. Afterward Reed said, "I know that Walt Hazzard was trying to hold me. I resent someone trying to hold me. You don't know if they mean good or they mean bad."

Willis Reed wasn't Kareem Abdul-Jabbar. He had neither the size nor the skills. But then again, who does? Reed was Rookie of the Year in 1965. He was second in the MVP voting in 1969 and first in 1970. He was also All-NBA First Team in the 1970 season. In 1971, he was fourth in the MVP voting. Following that 1971 season (his seventh in the league), tendinitis in his knee limited him to just 11 games in 1972 (and only 99 games total after that).

In 1973, Reed had one last memorable season that culminated in the fifth game of the Finals, when he scored 18 points and grabbed 12 rebounds while completely taking

Wilt Chamberlain out of the game. That game would represent the Knicks' second title and the last. That would also turn out to be Chamberlain's final game in the NBA. Reed, himself, would only play 19 more regular-season games and 11 playoff games in his career, which ended in 1974.

1970 NBA Finals

This would be the seventh time in nine seasons that the Lakers would be in the NBA Finals. They had never won. They had also never faced any team except the Boston Celtics.

The Knicks began the 1970 season with 15 consecutive victories. They were also riding a wave of New York success in the sporting world. In October 1969, the Miracle Mets defeated the Baltimore Orioles in the World Series. It was only the Mets' eighth year of existence. In January 1970, the brash Joe Namath made good on his prediction and led the upstart AFL Jets to Super Bowl III. Now, three months later, the Knicks took on Baylor, West, and Chamberlain for the NBA Championship.

The Lakers got a split in the first two games, winning 105–103 in New York. In Game 3, West hit that incredible shot estimated to be 60 feet to send the contest into overtime. He also suffered a jammed thumb in that game, which the Knicks won because of Reed's overtime heroics. Reed had 29 points, 15 rebounds, and five assists.

The Lakers tied the series 2–2 as West, listed as a doubtful starter, played 52 of 53 minutes and scored 37 points, to go with 18 assists. His 20-footer put the Lakers up to stay in the overtime period. Chamberlain had 18 points and 25 rebounds. It was also a Lakers sub named John Tresvant who contributed three points, two rebounds, and two brilliant defensive plays—despite not playing the first 47 minutes of regulation.

In the fifth game, the Lakers raced to a 25–15 lead with 3:56 left in the first quarter. Then, Reed, who was driving toward the hoop, fell to the floor with a strained hip muscle. With 2:11 left in the second quarter, the Knicks trailed 51–35. The Knicks played without their captain the rest of the way and forced 30 turnovers, including 10 in the final quarter. Somehow, even without Reed, Chamberlain scored only four points of his 22 after halftime. West was held without a field goal in the second half as the Knicks double-teamed the Lakers guard. The Lakers had a 53–40 halftime lead and led by seven points going into the fourth quarter, but still relinquished the game and series lead.

Chamberlain scored 45 points and had 27 rebounds in the sixth game, sending the series back to New York.

It's considered one of the great moments in NBA history, the moments just prior to Game 7, when a hobbling Reed came onto the court to warm up. He hit two early shots and New York got off to a 19–10 lead, which grew eventually to 38–24 after the first quarter. The scripts were written long before the game had started: New York had to win a championship. The Lakers had to lose. Those were their roles in life.

Marv Albert: "No one knew if Reed was going to play the seventh game or not. I not only did the radio broadcast, I did the pregame show. I taped an interview with Willis at, I don't know, five o'clock, and he had just received an injection. He told me he was going to play. You can't believe all the anticipation among the fans as they filed into the Garden. Anyway, the teams come out for warm-ups, and Reed hasn't come out. I start figuring that perhaps Reed couldn't make it after all. I was on the air doing the pregame show, and that's when the 'Here comes Willis' came in. I was broadcasting the warm-ups live. The whole arena stopped and watched Reed. I remember Jerry West stopping his warm-up from the other side of the court. Wilt, too. The crowd went nuts—it was the loudest I can ever remember the Garden being. I was broadcasting each warm-up shot of Reed's. The crowd reacted to every shot he took. It is so unusual for a pair of first-quarter baskets to mean anything, and in truth, the Knicks wouldn't have won that night without a great night from Clyde. But Reed's playing definitely had an effect on the Knicks that night."

Who's Better, Who's Best
Willis Reed or Wes Unseld

Matt Guokas: "Willis was a better player because his team's offense revolved around him. The Knicks depended on him to score. Wes would play the high post—and have good games that consisted of eight points and 17 rebounds. Willis was a pretty good rebounder, too. I'd go Reed."

Rod Thorn: "Willis versus Wes: really, really good players . . . Willis had a more complete game."

Kevin Loughery: "I'd have to go with Willis because he had more offensive skills than Wes. And I'm biased because Wes meant so much to me, and so much to my game."

Who's Better, Who's Best
Willis Reed or Patrick Ewing

Pete Vecsey: "Willis Reed: No question. Willis over Patrick Ewing. When was the last time Ewing came through in the clutch?"

Marv Albert: "Patrick Ewing over Reed—slightly. Because Willis didn't play enough. Injuries stopped Reed."

Mike Dunleavy: "Reed or Ewing? Reed had the mental toughness. He had the ability to will himself to win."

Reed was a heavyweight champion who held the title for a short time. He boxed less effectively at the lower weight classes. But he really didn't have the size to compete with Chamberlain or Abdul-Jabbar. He didn't last very long, but he provided the Garden with an electrifying moment that many consider the greatest moment in the history of the league.

KEVIN GARNETT
Through the Looking Glass

MVP: 0	
MVP VOTING: 10th in 1999, 2nd in 2000, 5th in 2001,	
12th in 2002, 2nd in 2003	
NBA TITLES: 0	
ALL-NBA FIRST TEAM: 2	
ALL-NBA SECOND TEAM: 2	

When we consider Kevin Garnett, do we want to look at the glass as being half-full or half-empty? In his first seven years, he has accomplished so much and yet, at the same time, has endured so much criticism for not being able to lead his team past the first round of the playoffs.

The fact is, Garnett entered the NBA in the fall of 1995 as a 19-year-old kid. He entered a league with no other teenagers. And Garnett was the first player to come into the league without attending college since Moses Malone and Bill Willoughby did it two decades earlier. Partially because of Garnett's success—and mostly so players could cash in sooner on the NBA millions—the floodgates opened after Garnett, with players entering the league straight out of high school, often with mixed results.

Players Entering NBA Directly from High School

1975	Moses Malone (ABA)
1975	Bill Willoughby
1995	Kevin Garnett
1996	Kobe Bryant
1996	Jermaine O'Neal
1997	Tracy McGrady
1998	Al Harrington
1998	Korleone Young

1998	Rashard Lewis
1999	Leon Smith
1999	Jonathan Bender
2000	Darius Miles
2000	DeShawn Stephenson
2001	Kwami Brown
2001	Tyson Chandler
2001	Eddie Curry
2001	DeSagna Diop
2001	Ousmane Cisse
2002	Amaré Stoudemire

Garnett had a spectacular rookie season, when viewed against the 16 players who made the jump from high school in the seven years after Garnett's initial 1996 season. He played 28.7 minutes per game and scored 10.4 points per game. Only one player—the Suns' Amaré Stoudemire in 2003—has bettered that.

Rookie (freshman)	Year and Team	Minutes/Game	Points/Game
Moses Malone	1975 Utah Stars	38.6	18.8
Amaré Stoudemire	2003 Phoenix	31.7	13.4
Kevin Garnett	1996 Minnesota	28.7	10.4
Darius Miles	2000 Clippers	26.3	9.4

Evaluating the Numbers

Kevin Garnett has shown the ability to be an offensive force, a defensive presence, and a true superstar. He has a real history of the league and has never embarrassed himself or his organization.

After his rookie season, he began a run of All-Star game appearances. If you look at his statistics, you are struck by the constant improvement in his game.

Garnett's Average Rebounds/Game

1996	6.3
1997	8.0
1998	9.6
1999	10.4
2000	11.8

2001	11.4
2002	12.1
2003	13.4

Garnett's Average Assists/Game

1996	1.8
1997	3.1
1998	4.2
1999	4.3
2000	5.0
2001	5.0
2002	5.2
2003	6.0

The 2003 season would represent his fifth consecutive season of averaging 21–23 points per game. He has completed the first eight years of his career (611 games) about halfway through a Hall of Fame career. In those first eight seasons—completed before his 27th birthday—he has close to 12,000 points, more than 6,300 rebounds, and more than 2,600 assists.

Let me put this combination into focus. Garnett started so young—and put up big numbers so early—that a low projection would find him with 24,000 points, 12,500 rebounds, and 5,200 assists. His 16th NBA season, which will be the 2011 campaign, will end with Garnett being just age 35. He could do better than double his first eight years of NBA statistics.

There are only a handful of players to amass more than 20,000 points and 10,000 rebounds in their careers. And none were as skillful with their passing as Garnett.

We shouldn't merely double the assists for Garnett's first 600 games when projecting his career totals. His steady improvement has shown everyone that he is capable of much more in the second half of his career. If one takes away his first two seasons, he has averaged more than five assists per game in his career. If he keeps that pace up—and plays until he's 35 years old—he will amass somewhere between 5,200 and 6,000 career assists. There are only two nonguards (John Havlicek and Scottie Pippen) who have more than 5,700 career assists. And both Havlicek and Pippen played a lot at the guard position—especially late in their careers.

Look at players who had long and productive seasons in the NBA. James Worthy was one of the 50 greatest players in the league in 1996.

Garnett	611 games	19.4 points	10.4 rebounds	4.3 assists
Worthy	926 games	17.6 points	5.1 rebounds	3.0 assists

Let me get this straight. Kevin Garnett has scored 10 percent more points per game, has close to 50 percent more assists, and has more than doubled the rebounds per game of a 2003 Hall of Fame inductee (Worthy).

Willis Reed played 650 NBA games. He averaged 18.7 points and 12.9 rebounds in his career—comparable to Garnett. But Garnett has also averaged 4.3 assists per game in his career (closer to six assists per game over a four-year period), while Reed averaged just 1.8 assists per game in his career. Kevin McHale (Garnett's mentor) averaged 1.7 assists per game in his career. Moses Malone averaged 1.4 assists per game. Elvin Hayes averaged 1.8.

You can't find a big man who has passed the ball as well as Garnett (disregarding the superman Chamberlain, who averaged 4.4 assists per game in his career).

So let's look small and find players who were comparable scorers and playmakers—Magic Johnson and Julius Erving.

Garnett	19.4 points	10.4 rebounds	4.3 assists
Johnson	19.5 points	7.2 rebounds	11.2 assists
Erving (ABA totals included)	24.2 points	8.5 rebounds	4.2 assists

Julius not only had three years at the University of Massachusetts, his first five pro seasons were against somewhat inferior competition (in the ABA). Erving's NBA totals look like this: 22.0 points, 6.7 rebounds, and 3.9 assists per game.

The most comparable stats of all the great players belong to the Kangaroo Kid, Billy Cunningham. Again, let's combine Billy C's ABA and NBA numbers.

Garnett	19.4 points	10.4 rebounds	4.3 assists
Cunningham	21.2 points	10.4 rebounds	4.3 assists

Take away Garnett's rookie season (when he was 19 years old), and the numbers look very close.

| Garnett | 20.8 points | 10.9 rebounds | 4.7 assists |
| Cunningham | 21.2 points | 10.4 rebounds | 4.3 assists |

Cunningham compiled these numbers after training and maturing at the University of North Carolina. Cunningham compiled these numbers with great teammates, playing a sixth-man role on one of the greatest teams in NBA history. He also put up numbers for a declining team, without help from other teammates. He put up numbers in the somewhat inferior ABA.

The other player with similar numbers is Chris Webber.

| Webber | 22.2 points | 10.3 rebounds | 4.4 assists |

Any way you slice it, those numbers are comparable.

Garnett's steals and blocks are only a small measure of his defensive abilities. He has the size and speed to cover just about anyone on the court. Garnett has been selected by the league's coaches to the All-Defensive First Team three (probably four) seasons in a row. Along with Tim Duncan and Gary Payton, Garnett has to be figured among the best defensive players in the game in the early 2000s.

Mike Fratello: "If he wanted to be known as a defensive specialist—à la Bill Russell or Dennis Rodman—he would have to concentrate on that part of his game. He cannot do that. He has to play center sometimes. Sometimes he plays power forward. He's in a tough situation. Rodman always had the teammates to have the luxury to concentrate on defense. Russell, too, although he was mainly a shot blocker. He could be the best defensive player in the game, but it would hurt his team. He's quite a talent."

The Knock on Garnett

Garnett led his team into postseason play in seven of his first eight seasons. But his teams are 0–7 in playoff series. He has never made the second round. His teams have never been one of the final eight.

The Timberwolves have won only seven of 29 postseason games in their history. Garnett has played in all 29 games.

Charles Barkley first expressed the criticism during the 2002 playoffs. Garnett, he said, was too unselfish and didn't look for the ball in the game's waning moments.

I'll examine the evidence.

Garnett's Minnesota Teams

Year	Record/Seed	Opponent	Result
1997	40–42 sixth seed, drew 57–25 Rockets		Lost 0–3
1998	45–37 seventh seed, drew 61–21 Sonics		Lost 2–3
1999	25–25 eighth seed, drew 37–13 Spurs		Lost 1–3
2000	50–32 sixth seed, drew 59–23 Blazers		Lost 1–3
2001	47–35 eighth seed, drew 58–24 Spurs		Lost 1–3
2002	50–32 fifth seed, drew 57–25 Mavericks		Lost 0–3
2003	51–31 fourth seed, drew 50–32 Lakers		Lost 2–4

Only the top four seeds in each conference had home court advantage in those series. Which of these seven series were the Wolves expected to win, anyway? The problem for the Wolves came in the 82 regular-season games, not the postseason. Garnett doesn't earn points just getting the team into postseason, either. Not when more than half the teams qualify for the playoffs, and a handful don't even seriously try to make the playoffs. In 2003, the Timberwolves finally had home court advantage, but lost to the three-time defending champion Lakers.

The Wolves were spanked by Barkley's Rockets in 1997. They were swept by Houston by an average of more than 11 points per game. That's going to happen when one team has Dean Garrett at center and the other has a still-productive Hakeem Olajuwon.

In 1998, they had the Seattle Sonics on the ropes. Seattle had been upset in the first round in both 1994 and 1995 (in 1994, by the eighth-seeded Denver team!). Minnesota took a 2–1 lead in the best-of-five series.

Garnett had a chance to advance in the postseason in the fourth game of that 1998 series with Seattle. But the Sonics jumped out on top 28–21 after the first quarter, and it was uphill for Minnesota after that. Kevin Garnett took just 14 shots in the game. He scored a team-high 20 points along with 10 rebounds and five assists. Seattle tied the series as Gary Payton scored 24 points and did his usual great defensive work on Stephon Marbury (four of 16 field goals). In the fifth and deciding game in Seattle, Payton scored 29 points and Marbury scored seven points (on two of 10 field goals). Garnett took just

11 shots in the game, making just three. He scored just seven points total, and the Sonics avoided a third first-round upset.

In 1999, Garnett could have gone to battle with the greatest teammates of all time on his side and it wouldn't have mattered. The Spurs were on a serious roll to the NBA title, and Minnesota wasn't going to defeat them. Kevin did average 22 points and 12 rebounds per game in that four-game series.

In the next three years (2000–2002), Garnett's teams went 2–9 in the postseason, despite 50, 47, and 50 wins. In none of those seasons did Minnesota have to play the eventual NBA Champion Lakers. In 2003, Garnett's team had the Lakers on the ropes. But Garnett missed a pair of free throws at the end of Game 4. The Lakers tied the series and won the next two games to advance.

Throughout history, the great players in this league have made plays to win big play-off series. Garnett hasn't done that, yet. In his defense, he marks the turning point in NBA history. He signed the contract for the most money and then saw his team suffer because of it (salary cap restrictions left little money for additional stars). After the 2000 season, teammate Malik Sealy died in an automobile accident (leaving Garnett's house, actually). Then Joe Smith left after the 2000 season, when Minnesota management was caught trying to circumvent the rules.

Jerry West may not have won an NBA title until his 12th season, but he was in the Finals quite a bit. Oscar Robertson may not have won a title until his 11th season, but his Royals were in the semifinals back in 1963. Michael Jordan didn't win a title until his eighth season and Chamberlain his seventh—but they were knocking on the door. It is time for Kevin Garnett to knock some doors down in the postseason. If he does, then he'll leapfrog over many of the all-time greats.

41

TRACY McGRADY
The Sky's the Limit

MVP: 0	
MVP VOTING: 4th in 2001, 4th in 2003	
NBA TITLES: 0	
ALL-NBA FIRST TEAM: 2	
ALL-NBA SECOND TEAM: 1	

Tracy McGrady didn't go to college. He was so outstanding in the youth ranks at summer basketball camps that the sneaker company Adidas funded McGrady's expenses to attend Mount Zion Christian Academy in Durham, North Carolina. His first four years in the NBA—at the ages of 18, 19, 20, and 21—show a steady and shocking improvement.

McGrady's First Four Years in the NBA

	Points	Rebounds	Assists
1998	7.0	4.2	1.5
1999	9.3.	5.7	2.3
2000	15.4	6.3	3.3
2001	26.8	7.5	4.6

The first three years were in Toronto. After that third season, McGrady was sent to Orlando in exchange for a future conditional draft pick in a sign-and-trade deal on August 3, 2000. He exploded in the 2001 season, a year in which he was only 21 years old when the campaign started. In the 2002 season, McGrady and Kobe Bryant were the only two players to average at least 25 points, five rebounds, and five assists per game. The following season, both players actually picked up their numbers.

The sky is the limit for this player. If his team surrounds him with quality players, he could run off a string of championships. If his team doesn't, his individual numbers will compare nicely with almost any of the other players in this book.

McGrady's Stats So Far
He started young and produced early.

Highest Scoring Average for Players 21 Years or Younger at Season's End

1.	26.8	Tracy McGrady, 2001
2.	24.2	Bernard King, 1978
3.	23.5	Allen Iverson, 1997
4.	23.4	Shaquille O'Neal, 1993
5.	22.9	Isiah Thomas, 1983

McGrady also holds the fourth-highest scoring average in NBA history for players who *began* the season 21 years or younger.

Highest Scoring Average for Players 21 Years or Younger at Start of Season

1.	30.5	Oscar Robertson, 1961
2.	29.3	Shaquille O'Neal, 1994
3.	28.2	Michael Jordan, 1985
4.	26.8	Tracy McGrady, 2001
5.	25.7	Rick Barry, 1966

Sam Cassell: "People talk about Kobe, Iverson, and the other guys, but to me, Tracy is the best player in the league behind Shaq. More than anyone else, he does it all."

McGrady started only twice in 1998 and only twice in the lockout-shortened season of 1999. In his third year, he started 34 games. So, in his first three seasons he came off the bench 139 times.

John Saunders: "I really give a lot of credit to Isiah Thomas. He selected Tracy with the ninth pick in the first round. He was so high on this high school kid that he went on record saying that he would have selected McGrady with the first overall pick. But Tracy really struggled in that first year. His coaches—first Darrell Walker, then Butch Carter—were real tough on him. Think of what Tracy had to go through. He had to leave home. He had to leave his country. He slept all the time. He couldn't go out anywhere. He didn't have close friends on the team. I remember, though, by his third year, you could see how he could become a real star."

Proving People Wrong

On New Year's Eve during McGrady's rookie season, Coach Darrell Walker told a writer before the game that the teenager buried on his bench could well be out of the league when his first three-year contract expired. "By him telling me I'd be out of the league in three years, that just motivated me, and he's nowhere to be seen," McGrady said four years later.

Tracy has been adamant about his first coach. "If I would have had the opportunity early in my career to play and be thrown to the wolves my rookie year and my second year—I'd be a better basketball player right now. I'd have a better feel for the game, I'd be much smarter. That wasn't the case because I had a coach who basically didn't want me out there on the basketball court. Why? I don't know."

The Flip Side of McGrady's Argument

I'm not defending the Toronto coaching staff at the time, or Darrell Walker. But if McGrady wanted to play and have a better feel for the game and be smarter—he could have picked any college coach in the country. He would have played a lot. He could have selected some great teachers—Lute Olson or Bob Knight or anyone. The problem isn't that McGrady was buried on the bench his first year—he played behind solid pro Doug Christie—it's that by his third year, they still didn't see the jewel they had.

The First Glimpse of McGrady's Greatness

The 2000 playoff series between the New York Knicks and the Toronto Raptors was an important one for Tracy. The Knicks were the defending Eastern champs and had won 50 games in the 2000 season. They had Allan Houston, Latrell Sprewell, Patrick Ewing, Larry Johnson, and Marcus Camby. Toronto had a single star going into that playoff series: Vince Carter. The Knicks would win the first-round series 3–0. All three games were decided late in the games. Vince Carter made only 15 of 50 field goals (30 percent) and averaged six points below his season average. Tracy McGrady averaged 16.7 points and seven rebounds per game. People started saying that if Toronto ran their offense through McGrady rather than Carter, they might have won the series.

John Saunders: "Tracy was always a quiet, unassuming kid—and he always looked unhappy. But on the few occasions that he did smile, he had a smile that would light up the room."

Who's Better, Who's Best
Tracy McGrady or Penny Hardaway

Jack Givins: "In all aspects, T-Mac is better because of the way he does things. McGrady handles the ball better. He's probably a half-step quicker than Hardaway was."

John Saunders: "Tracy's a better shooter, a better jumper. He has a lanky body that reminds me of Scottie Pippen. For a guy his size that's able to handle the ball, there's no one better. McGrady could play point guard if he had to."

Who's Better, Who's Best
Tracy McGrady or Kobe Bryant

Bill Walton: "They're both as close to perfect as anybody playing today, maybe as close to perfect as anybody who's ever played the game. I can't choose between the two."

John Saunders: "Tracy has two or three inches on Kobe, so by virtue of that, there are things that McGrady can do that Bryant just cannot."

Jack Givins: "Kobe's won titles. You walk with a different swagger when you've won. Kobe is on a slightly higher pedestal."

Givins and I spent some time talking about McGrady and who is a comparable player. We decided that McGrady is a combination of several of the all-time greats. He's a great scorer—similar to George Gervin. He goes to the hoop with either hand just as the Iceman did. T-Mac is also like Magic Johnson, because he understands the game so well. Similar to Michael Jordan, McGrady has the ability to play defense and shut down opponents. Tracy hasn't made defense his calling card to this point in his career, however.

McGrady has a sense of history. After being the leading vote-getter to start the 2003 All-Star game, Tracy offered to give up his spot so that Michael Jordan could start in one final All-Star game. While Jordan rejected the offer, McGrady (an Adidas endorser) crossed party lines to assist Nike's All-Time All-Star. It was a goodwill gesture (also made by Allen Iverson, by the way) that went a long way. Former teammate (and McGrady's cousin) Vince Carter—also selected a starter—made the same offer at the last minute, and Jordan replaced Carter (who had played far less during the season due to injury).

The 2003 Season in Review

Tracy McGrady has to do it all for the Orlando Magic. In the first half of the season, T-Mac led the team in points, assists, and blocked shots. The last player to do that during an entire season was Scottie Pippen in 1995. McGrady went from being a superstar to one of the all-time greats. He started transcending the court. On December 23, he sat out his third consecutive game with a lower back contusion. Two days later, he started on Christmas Day and scored 46 points to lead the Magic to a five-point victory over the Detroit Pistons. What made the game extra special was Tracy's guest: Washington sniper victim Iran Brown, the young teen who told the nation that McGrady was his favorite player. Then, there was the positive publicity that McGrady made with his goodwill gesture toward Jordan concerning the All-Star game.

McGrady is the youngest player to average 30+ points for a season since 1977.

Age	Player	Average Points
1. 23 years, 328 days	Tracy McGrady, 2003	32.1
2. 24 years, 57 days	Michael Jordan, 1987	37.1
3. 25 years, 47 days	Adrian Dantley, 1981	30.6
4. 25 years, 58 days	Michael Jordan, 1988	35.0
5. 25 years, 313 days	Allen Iverson, 2001	31.1

Prior to the 1977 season, Bob McAdoo averaged more than 30 points per game in 1974, when he was only 23 years old.

A Typical Game for McGrady

On January 31, 2003, I sat courtside for the San Antonio–at–Orlando contest. The game featured three of the greatest players in the history of the game—including McGrady and Tim Duncan, who were in the prime of their careers. The game was memorable. It featured the mano-a-mano theatrics that only true superstars can provide (Dominique-Bird; Miller-Jordan; et cetera).

This game was a seesaw affair. The Magic jumped out to a 12-point lead in the first quarter. The Spurs took a 14-point lead in the second quarter. The fourth quarter was so close, there were 12 lead changes and two ties. The final 2:45 of the fourth quarter was priceless.

The Final 2:45

2:44 remaining	McGrady assist on Armstrong hoop	Magic up 99–98
2:23 remaining	Duncan dunk	Spurs up 100–99
2:11 remaining	McGrady driving layup and foul shot	Magic up 102–100
1:32 remaining	McGrady assist on Garrity jumper	Magic up 104–100
1:19 remaining	Duncan assist—an alley-oop to Robinson	Magic up 104–102
0:39 remaining	McGrady assist on DeClercq layup	Magic up 106–105
0:13 remaining	McGrady turnaround jumper from 17	Magic up 108–107
0:04 remaining	Duncan layup on his own miss and rebound	Spurs up 109–108
0:01 remaining	McGrady misses 16-foot jumper	Spurs win 109–108

In the fourth quarter, McGrady scored 12 points. He had three assists in the final 2:44 of the game. He had 35 points for the game, driving to the hoop against Tim Duncan and David Robinson. Without Grant Hill, the Magic lacked a second star to take some pressure off McGrady. He was required to do it all. Earlier in the game, McGrady had an impossible reverse slam that would be replayed hundreds of times and go down as one of his signature moves. Just another night at the office for McGrady, one of the best perimeter players ever.

McGrady carried the Orlando Magic on his back in the last weeks of the 2003 season, earning co–Player of the Month honors in March with Shaquille O'Neal. In McGrady's 15 games in the month, he averaged 36.5 points (in 39 minutes per night—almost a point a minute!), 5.7 rebounds, and 6.3 assists. Most important, he led the Magic to a 10–5 record that month, which vaulted them into the postseason.

Once in the postseason, McGrady was poised to take the national stage. Michael Jordan was safely back in retirement, and McGrady's Orlando team faced a matchup with the top seed in the Eastern Conference, the Detroit Pistons. McGrady scored 43 points in a 99–94 win in the first game, and Tracy was poised to advance to the second round for the first time in his six-year career.

The Magic would take a 3–1 lead in the best-of-seven series, and McGrady spoke prematurely about reaching the second round.

Bad move.

The Pistons won the final three games of the series, and made life miserable for McGrady. In Game 7—the biggest game of Tracy's career—rookie Tayshaun Prince hounded McGrady and the Pistons won, 108–93. McGrady shot only seven of 24 field goals and had only 13 points in the first three quarters.

McGrady knows that to be a great player in the NBA, you have to come back strong from losses like that one.

Tracy McGrady (and Kevin Garnett) are both young entering the 2004 season. Tracy might pass Kobe (and Garnett could pass Duncan), but as Yogi Berra once said, "It gets late early out there." It's time to start advancing deep into the postseason.

SAM JONES
The Bank Is Open

MVP: 0	
MVP VOTING: 4th in 1965, 5th in 1966	
NBA TITLES: 10	
ALL-NBA FIRST TEAM: 0	
ALL-NBA SECOND TEAM: 3	

Whenever the name Sam Jones is brought up among old-time NBA fans, the first two words that immediately come to mind are these: *bank shot*.

Sam Jones played fewer games, scored fewer points, and had fewer assists than his longtime rival Hal Greer. Greer was All-NBA in seven different seasons, while Jones made the list only three times. They were obviously the third- and fourth-best guards of the 1960s. Only three guards from that era even make this book. Jones beats out Greer and Lenny Wilkens and any guard from the 1960s that wants to make a case (including Guy Rodgers and K. C. Jones). The reason is not only the 10 NBA Championships or the 9–0 record in Game 7s, it is Jones's contribution in those title runs.

Big Game Player

Jones had a run of big shots in big games that modern-day fans have seen in another player: the Lakers' Robert Horry.

After Horry made his huge three-pointer to win Game 4 of the Lakers-Sacramento Western Conference finals in 2002, people started to say how Horry was one of the 15 greatest playoff performers of all time.

But no one—no one—had bigger shots at bigger moments than Sam Jones.

Sam Jones in Game 7s: 9–0

1.	1959 Game 7 vs. Syracuse	19 points
2.	1960 Game 7 vs. St. Louis	18 points (NBA Finals)
3.	1962 Game 7 vs. Philadelphia	28 points
4.	1962 Game 7 vs. Lakers	27 points (NBA Finals)
5.	1963 Game 7 vs. Cincinnati	47 points
6.	1965 Game 7 vs. Philadelphia	37 points
7.	1966 Game 7 vs. Lakers	22 points (NBA Finals)
8.	1968 Game 7 vs. Philadelphia	22 points
9.	1969 Game 7 vs. Lakers	24 points (NBA Finals)

In games facing elimination, Sam Jones's teams were 13–2. By my count, he faced elimination in those nine Game 7s. He lost a sixth game in the 1958 Finals when Bill Russell was injured, and the Hawks won the title. His teams lost a Game 5 in 1967, when the Sixers eliminated the Celtics 4–1. There were four other games (including winning Games 5 and 6 of the 1968 Eastern finals against Philadelphia) where Sam's Celtics held off the threat of elimination. It's not as if Sam was just along for the ride, either.

Bill Russell, in his 1979 book, *Second Wind: The Memoirs of an Opinionated Man*, said, "Whenever the pressure was greatest, Sam was eager for the ball. Sam Jones had a champion's heart. Under pressure, we had hidden on our team a class superstar of the highest caliber. In Los Angeles, Jerry West was called 'Mr. Clutch' and he was, but in the seventh game of a championship series, I'll take Sam over any player who's ever walked on a court."

I asked Don Nelson, a former Celtics teammate of Jones, if Sam indeed looked for the ball in those pressure-packed situations.

Don Nelson: "He'd go into hiding in the corner, if he could. [laughing] We had to force him to take the shot—then, he would hit it every single time. He was chosen a few years ago as one of the 50 greatest. I think that says all you need to know about Sam."

You Had to Be a Big Shot, Didn't You?

In the 1962 Eastern finals, Wilt Chamberlain tied the game with a three-point play in the final seconds. Although Chamberlain was only a 50 percent foul shooter, he made the pressure free throw for the tie. With just two seconds remaining, Sam Jones hit a jumper that sent the Celtics to the Finals—and denied Chamberlain a chance at his first trip to the NBA Finals.

In 1963, the Cincinnati Royals were the surprise team to play the Celtics in the Eastern finals. Boston probably took them too lightly. It came down to a seventh game. Sam Jones had a tough task, trying to defend the magnificent Oscar Robertson. Robertson scored 43 points, mainly on the strength of making 21 of 22 free throws. But Sam Jones had a career day of 47 points, with Oscar unable to stop him. Sam's big day was overshadowed by Bob Cousy's 16 assists in Cooz's last season.

In Game 7 of the 1965 Eastern finals, Jones had 37 points—a huge game. But all anyone remembers is Russell throwing the ball away, giving Philly a last chance at winning—and Havlicek then stealing the ball.

In 1966, Jones had 22 points in the Finals against the Lakers. His final deuce was a 35-foot shot with 25 seconds remaining. When the ball went in, Coach Red Auerbach lit up his last victory cigar before retiring from the bench.

Several other big Sam Jones moments I should bring up. In the 1962 Finals, the Celtics were down 3–2 and in danger of losing the series in Los Angeles. Jones kept the Celts alive with 17 points in the second quarter, on his way to a game-high 35.

In Sam's final season, the Celtics were down in the Finals 3–2 to the Lakers, with Game 6 at Boston Garden. Although Russell hardly played Sam (saving him for Game 7), he inserted him into the game with a minute left. The Boston fans gave the 34-year-old Jones one final ovation. Jones immediately hit a shot.

Who's Better, Who's Best
Sam Jones or Robert Horry

Walt Frazier: "Oh, come on. Sam was a starter. He had an unusual game, but his bank shot was uncanny. He was better than Horry. Sam was an adequate defensive player—[laughing] but then, we all would have been adequate defensively with Russell behind us."

Robert Horry's Big Moments It started in 1995, when Horry was with the Rockets, and in the Western Conference finals, he hit a 17-footer with 6.4 seconds left to win a game.

Later, in the 1995 Finals, Horry hit a huge three-pointer with 14.1 seconds left to seal another game. In the 2001 NBA Finals with the Lakers, Horry scored the Lakers' last seven points—all in the final 47 seconds of overtime—to defeat Philadelphia and go up 2–1 in the Finals.

In the Lakers' 2002 first-round series against Portland, Horry hit a game-winning three-pointer with 2.1 seconds remaining. Later in those 2002 playoffs, Horry turned the Western Conference finals around by hitting a game-winning three-pointer as time expired.

Horry, similar to Jones, was surrounded by Hall of Fame players. Horry and Jones never excelled much in the regular season, doing most of their damage when it mattered most. Jones did it in Game 7s for the most part. Jones had three-point range, but they didn't award three-pointers back in his day.

Tommy Heinsohn: "Sam Jones—great, great shooter . . . total game . . . he would bank it off the boards. . . . Two-hand set shot from 40 feet. He was one of the greats."

Walt Frazier: "I asked Sam once why he used the bank shot so much and he told me that his high school coach always told him to shoot the bank."

Marv Albert: "Sam Jones was a great player, a scorer who used to come off screens, use all the angles. He was like a modern-day Tim Duncan, the way he used glass."

Who's Better, Who's Best
Sam Jones or Hal Greer
Rod Thorn: "Sam Jones—as talented as anyone you could ever find. . . . Yes, I would take Sam over Hal Greer."

Pete Vecsey: "I'd take Sam Jones over Greer. I'd take him over a lot of people. I'd take him over Drexler."

Matt Guokas: "Now, I played with Greer, but that aside, he was a better defensive player than Sam. Hal also drove to the basket better and had a better middle-distance jumper. Sam was deeper—boy, he had range. But he was basically just a shooter. I'd take Greer."

Sam Jones deserves a place in the top 50 players of all time. Only one player ever won more rings. For all the people that go gaga over Bill Russell because of all his titles, I hope those same people remember Sam Jones. I'm not saying I would take him over T-Mac, but he was the third-best guard of his decade. It was tough, real tough, leaving another Celtics guard—Bill Sharman—off this list. Hopefully, putting Cousy as high as I did—and including Sam Jones—helps take the sting out for die-hard Boston fans.

43

NATE ARCHIBALD
The Best Player Nicknamed "Tiny"

MVP: 1	
MVP VOTING: 3rd in 1973, 5th in 1980	
NBA TITLES: 1	
ALL-NBA FIRST TEAM: 3	
ALL-NBA SECOND TEAM: 2	

The nickname "Tiny" refers to his height and weight, not his achievements in the sport. Nate Archibald is known to modern-day fans for one statistical accomplishment. He remains the only player to lead the league in scoring and assists in the same season—even though he has the slightest build of all the players featured in this book.

One thing about Archibald: he sure moved around a lot. He played with Cincinnati at the beginning of his career during the time the franchise moved to Kansas City/Omaha. He was traded to the New York Nets during the time the franchise moved to New Jersey. He was traded to the Buffalo Braves during the time the franchise moved to San Diego and was renamed the Clippers. He played more games for his college team—Texas-El Paso—than he did for the Nets, Braves, or Bucks.

A Quiet Start to His Career

Nate Archibald grew up on the streets of New York, playing against Julius Erving, Dean Meminger, and Charlie Scott. He then went to Texas-El Paso, where he starred. But in those days (the late 1960s), games weren't on television as they are today.

Let's just say Tiny didn't suffer from overexposure early in his NBA career. In 1972, when he averaged more than 28 points a game for the last NBA team ever in Cincinnati, he didn't even make the All-Star team. His team didn't play a single game on national television, and cable television was something distant in the future.

His first coach, Bob Cousy, once said, "I never saw him play in college. On the recommendations of our scouts, we took him in the second round as a sleeper."

Nate Archibald: "The best thing that ever happened to me was having Bob Cousy as my first coach. I consider him my stepdad. He gave me a chance to blossom in the league. He gave me a chance. He saw things in me. And he came from an organization that loved to run. He let me run his team at a very early age."

Having Cousy as your first coach was akin to having Albert Einstein as your physics professor. Cousy instituted a running game and let Tiny have the ball. The comparison people made with Archibald was not Cousy, however, but Lenny Wilkens. Wilkens was left-handed, quick, from New York, and black.

Who's Better, Who's Best
Nate Archibald or Lenny Wilkens

I've had this conversation often with friends, most recently my very informed friend Ethan Cooperson. When I ask him about a player's greatness, he values the longevity. I suppose I value the peak, which is the reason Archibald is in this book and Wilkens is out. It is also the reason Jason Kidd is almost neck-and-neck with John Stockton, and it is the reason Bob McAdoo is in and Robert Parish is out.

Lenny Wilkens played 15 seasons and 1,077 games in his NBA career. His career averages were 16.5 points, 6.7 assists, and 4.7 rebounds per game. He played in nine All-Star games. He had significant MVP votes only in 1968—when he was second.

1968 MVP Vote

Player	1st	2nd	3rd	Total Points
1. Wilt Chamberlain	88	21	1	504
2. Lenny Wilkens	26	22	20	216

In that 1968 season, Lenny averaged 20 points and was second in assists to Chamberlain. He was never All-NBA First Team. He was never All-NBA Second Team. His teams never won an NBA Championship. He never led the league in points, or assists, or in anything. Even in that career-best 1968 season, the Hawks won 56 games but were upset in the first round by the San Francisco Warriors (who were playing without Rick Barry).

Archibald did a little of everything. He won late in his career, with the right team. He led the league in scoring, and he led the league in assists. He was third in the MVP voting in 1973—and fifth in 1980.

1973 MVP Vote

Player	1st	2nd	3rd	Total Points
1. Dave Cowens	67	31	16	444
2. Kareem Abdul-Jabbar	33	49	27	339
3. Nate Archibald	44	24	27	319

Cowens was playing with Havlicek and JoJo White. Abdul-Jabbar was playing with Oscar Robertson. Archibald squeezed out 36 wins with a team consisting of John Block, Sam Lacey, Nate Williams, and Matt Guokas.

Career Highlights

Archibald had one of those special seasons in 1973. He led the league in minutes played, field goals attempted, field goals made, free throws made, free throws attempted, and assists. Two years later, in 1975, he came right back and averaged 26.5 points (fourth in the NBA) and 6.8 assists (third in the NBA, trailing Kevin Porter and Dave Bing). More important, he led the Kings to a 44–38 record. In 1976, he had another dream season, averaging nearly 25 points and eight assists per game.

This was not a one-year wonder.

Peak of Archibald's Career

1972	2nd in scoring	3rd in assists
1973	1st in scoring	1st in assists
1974	injured for all but 35 games	
1975	4th in scoring	3rd in assists
1976	4th in scoring	2nd in assists

A month before the 1977 season, Archibald was traded to one of the four new NBA teams that had just merged from the ABA. Tiny was sent back home to New York to play for the New York Nets. The Nets were the last ABA champion and had fellow native New Yorker Julius Erving on the team. But the Nets paid a steep admission price to join the league—steeper than Denver, Indiana, and San Antonio had to pay. The Nets had to pay territorial rights to the Knicks for cutting into their turf. And management was forced to deal Julius to Philadelphia as Erving and the Nets found themselves in a contract dispute. Once again, Archibald found himself the star of a very bad team.

Some Trivia for Nate Archibald Fans

There are only two other players to ever lead the league in scoring and assists (in different seasons). Jerry West led the NBA in assists in 1972 (he defeated Wilkens 9.7 to 9.6 by having a big final game). West led the league in scoring in 1970 (when Chamberlain missed all but 12 games and Elgin Baylor's knees were shot). The other player to lead in both categories, of course, was Chamberlain. Wilt led the league in scoring in each of his first seven seasons. In 1968, Chamberlain had the most total assists, although Oscar Robertson averaged more per game. Two years later, the league moved to averages per game to determine statistical leaders. Most assist leaders, including Stockton, Kidd, and Mark Jackson, don't get within a mile of the league's leading scorers.

Nate Archibald scored 30 points for the Nets in their very first NBA game—a two-point win over the Golden State Warriors. Kevin Loughery gave him the ball, and Tiny did what he always did. The Nets were 11–15 after their first 26 games. But Archibald suffered a season-ending, career-threatening Achilles injury two weeks later. The Nets finished the year winning only 11 of their remaining 56 games.

Archibald is one of the three players prominently featured in this book who had great peak values at the beginning of their careers and then cemented their places in history with well-timed contributions to championship years at the end of their careers. The other two players are McAdoo and Bill Walton. Their last years were enough to kick several of these players up into the all-time greatest 50. If Lenny Wilkens had gone to a title contender and helped win a championship, he would have been on the list.

Nate never did get to play with Julius, but he sure got to feed Larry Bird. Archibald played four seasons in Boston and was a featured player in the 1981 championship run.

Down 3–1 to the 76ers in the 1981 Conference finals, Archibald scored 23 points in Game 5, then came back with 19 points in Game 6. In Game 7, he added 13 points.

In the clinching Game 6 of the 1981 Finals, Archibald played 43 minutes, scored 13 points, and had 12 assists.

Archibald was second in minutes played on that 1981 team. After that season, he was 34 years old, and although he played for a few more seasons, he was near the end. In 1984, he played his final season for the Milwaukee Bucks and Coach Don Nelson.

Archibald began his NBA career as a Royal—playing for NBA royalty. He would be turned into a King in just his third season. Cousy was from Queens and Archibald was from the Bronx. They are two NBA legends who grew up on the streets of New York.

BOB McADOO

Much Adoo About Something

MVP: 1	
MVP VOTING: 2nd in 1974, 1st in 1975, 3rd in 1976	
NBA TITLES: 2	
ALL-NBA FIRST TEAM: 1	
ALL-NBA SECOND TEAM: 1	

Bob McAdoo often gets overlooked on the lists of the all-time greats. He was even bypassed for the league's 50 greatest list in 1996. Although his last NBA game was played in 1986, he didn't get voted into the Hall of Fame until 2000. Yet there aren't many players in the history of the NBA with this guy's credentials. He's one of 23 players to ever be elected MVP for a season. Throughout the game's history, a benchmark for a big man's greatness has been an average of 20 points and 10 rebounds per game. McAdoo averaged more than 30 points and 15 rebounds in a three-year period.

McAdoo won a Rookie of the Year. He won three consecutive scoring titles in the mid-1970s. He played in five All-Star games. He won two NBA Championships. When he was finished, he wasn't finished. After he wore out his welcome with seven different franchises, Big Mac went overseas and played seven years in the Italian League, averaging 26.6 points per game.

McAdoo did a lot of things David Robinson did in his career, although I can't think of anyone else who has ever compared them. But think about it. Both were Rookies of the Year, among the two or three best centers in their eras, and big-time scorers. They both would win NBA Championships by changing their game and sacrificing their offense for a more talented, frontcourt teammate (Kareem Abdul-Jabbar and Tim Duncan). I'm not saying McAdoo was even close to Robinson defensively. But don't be so quick to knock McAdoo.

The Case for McAdoo

Of all of the thousands of NBA playoff games ever played, a player has hit for 50 or more points in only 29 of them. Michael Jordan did it 8 of those 29 times. Wilt Chamberlain did it four times. Jerry West did it twice. McAdoo is among the 15 other players to score 50 in a postseason game. He did it against Washington in Buffalo on the 18th of April in 1975. Hardly a man is now alive who remembers that famous time and year. Hey, forget Paul Revere's ride 200 years earlier. McAdoo's ride was more thrilling: one if by free throw, two if by field.

More Reasons for Supporting McAdoo

He finished his career at the age of 34 with a scoring average of 22.1 points per game.

But if you take away his last four years (or 212 games), his career numbers look like this:

McAdoo's Career
640 games
25.0 points/game
11.1 rebounds/game
1.8 blocks/game

Those numbers include most of the good (the Buffalo years), the bad (the Knicks years), and the ugly (almost single-handedly taking down the proud Celtics franchise in just 20 games) of McAdoo's career. It also includes replacing the injured Mitch Kupchak and helping the Lakers to their 1982 NBA Championship. Let me explain what I mean when I say he single-handedly almost brought down the Celtics franchise. Celtics ownership made the trade for him against Red Auerbach's judgment. That decision nearly led to Auerbach's departure from the franchise. McAdoo put up numbers with the Knicks, but something didn't click. He made mistakes at the wrong time.

Sweet Caroline . . . good times never seemed so good. . . . I'm taking the same argument my friend Bob Costas used in a discussion with Bruce Springsteen about where Neil Diamond should rank. Don't laugh, this gets interesting. It was Costas's contention that if Diamond had died young, as Buddy Holly did, Diamond would be revered today as a first-rate, heralded singer/songwriter. His early material would be held in much higher regard by critics. If Holly had lived, he might have turned into a Vegas-style crooner who got less and less relevant to the younger generation. It might have been Holly who would have been mocked, and Diamond who would have been acclaimed.

If McAdoo had been taken by aliens in a spaceship and left us after the 1982 season, his stats in the record books would look far different.

After the 1982 season, McAdoo finished the season as the fifth-leading active scorer in the NBA, trailing only Kareem Abdul-Jabbar, Elvin Hayes, Bob Lanier, and Calvin Murphy. McAdoo at the time was 24th all-time in league history in points scored. His 25.0 points per game was eighth all-time, trailing the legendary Chamberlain, George Gervin, Abdul-Jabbar, Elgin Baylor, West, Bob Pettit, and Robertson. He scored 30 points in the 1977 All-Star game, and scored 40+ in 56 regular-season games.

How impressive is that, you wonder?

Most 40+-Point Games, Career

1. 271   Wilt Chamberlain
2. 171   Michael Jordan
3. 87   Elgin Baylor

Playoff Action

McAdoo's 42-win Buffalo team faced the 56-win Celtic team in the first round of the 1974 playoffs. The Celtics had defeated Buffalo five times during the regular season and would go on to win the NBA Championship. McAdoo gave them all they could handle in the playoff series, which the Celts would eventually win in six games. McAdoo averaged almost 32 points and 14 rebounds per game in that series. The following year, 1975, McAdoo's Braves would extend the Washington Bullets to seven games. McAdoo averaged more than 37 points in that series against Hayes and Unseld. When Bob joined the Lakers, he said, "I want a championship. I want people to stop thinking of me as a guy who couldn't play for a winning team."

In the 1982 postseason run by the Lakers, McAdoo averaged more than 16 points per game. In the final game of the Western Conference finals against San Antonio, McAdoo hit 12 of 16 shots for 26 points, as the Lakers advanced to the NBA Finals. In Game 5 of the 1982 Finals, McAdoo hit 11 of 14 shots and scored 23 points, adding five blocked shots.

McAdoo's career-high 29 rebounds came on December 7, 1976—and two days later he was traded to New York. After only one full season with New York, he was traded on Washington's Birthday by the Knicks to the Boston Celtics for three first-round draft choices in the 1979 draft.

Who's Better, Who's Best
Bob McAdoo or Chris Webber

Chris Webber has a lot to compare to McAdoo. Webber was Rookie of the Year, as was McAdoo. Webber was traded after not getting along with his head coach. Webber's career numbers (22.1 points and 10.2 rebounds) are also similar to McAdoo's. Both players were listed between 6-foot-9 and 6-foot-10 and 225 pounds. For the moment, McAdoo gets the spot on the all-time greatest 50 list. Webber does not. If Webber leads the Sacramento Kings to a title or two and continues to have all-star seasons, there is no reason he wouldn't overtake McAdoo. But, for now, Webber has never led the league in scoring and is way behind McAdoo as a rebounder.

McAdoo through 583 games	26.6 points/game	11.8 rebounds/game
Webber, 596 games	22.2 points/game	10.3 rebounds/game

Cedric Maxwell: "Bob McAdoo had the height and speed and shooting ability that no big man had. You can't imagine the range he had—and he could put it on the floor. Webber doesn't have the shooting ability that McAdoo had—although Chris is a better passer. But it's no contest. McAdoo."

Dr. Jack Ramsay: "Yeah, Webber was a little bit like Mac. McAdoo was better. He was a shot blocker and a strong rebounder. McAdoo led the NBA in total rebounds one year, although Unseld had more per game. McAdoo was quick as a snake. He had so many baskets off back-cuts going to the hoop. He was too quick for other centers to play."

Who's Better, Who's Best
Bob McAdoo or Dirk Nowitzki

Del Harris: "Dirk has McAdoo's range and does more things. Nowitzki has a broader game than McAdoo. McAdoo may have been a better rebounder in his prime, though. For big men, they both could put the ball on the floor and handle it as well as anyone."

Who's Better, Who's Best
Bob McAdoo or Bill Walton

Bill Walton: "Bob McAdoo was as difficult an opponent for me as I had. He was so good at transition—he played for Dr. Jack (Ramsay) as I did, but Ramsay used me as a screener and someone who set picks on offense. McAdoo was used more as an offensive threat than I was."

Both Walton and McAdoo were MVPs of the league in the 1970s, and each won a pair of NBA titles. But Walton's contributions to his teams made his teammates better and he played a more important role in his team's NBA titles. Neither Walton nor McAdoo had a long career peak, but both were great NBA players. Walton was slightly better.

BILLY CUNNINGHAM
"The Kangaroo Kid"

MVP: 1	
MVP VOTING: 3rd in 1969, 5th in 1970	
NBA TITLES: 1	
ALL-NBA FIRST TEAM: 3 (also All-ABA First Team in 1973)	
ALL-NBA SECOND TEAM: 1	

Bill Cunningham was known as "The Kangaroo Kid"—a Brooklyn, New York, native who was listed at 6-foot-7 and yet was a great scorer and rebounder. There is only one other player among the all-time greats who was born in Brooklyn, went to the University of North Carolina, and became an NBA star. That would be a player named Michael Jordan.

His Career with the Philadelphia 76ers

In the preseason of his rookie season, 76ers coach Dolph Schayes figured Cunningham's best position would be guard. But that lasted only a few games. He was shifted to the frontcourt, where he pumped in 14.3 points per game.

Billy C had the moves to go around defenders or to lean back to take his 15-foot jumper. For the first few years in the pros, Cunningham was used for his instant offense. He was the Sixers' answer to the Celtics' sixth man (John Havlicek in the mid-1960s). At the time, Billy the Kid alternated at forward with Luke Jackson and Chet Walker, with Wilt Chamberlain in the middle. It was one of the best frontcourts in NBA history. It didn't stay together that long, however, as Walker and Chamberlain were traded.

Cunningham became the cornerstone of the Philadelphia franchise. But the team fell apart quite quickly. The year after their NBA Championship, the 76ers again had the best record in the league, eight games better than the Celtics in the East. The familiar foes met in Game 7 of the 1968 Eastern Conference finals—in Philadelphia. Boston defeated

Philadelphia 100–96 to advance to the NBA Finals. Wilt looked awful in that final seventh game against Bill Russell and the Celtics.

When Chamberlain insisted that he receive a percentage of the team as promised by late co-owner Ike Richman, general manager Jack Ramsey traded the superstar center to the Lakers in exchange for Darrall Imhoff, Archie Clark, and Jerry Chambers.

That was the start of the slide for the Sixers. They went from 68 wins in 1967 to 62 wins in 1968 to 55 wins in 1969 to just 30 wins by 1971. After Billy C left after the 1972 season of 30–52, Philadelphia fell to a record-worst 9–73.

Cunningham would prove to be so valuable to that franchise that when he returned from the ABA two years later, the Sixers improved their win total from 25 to 34 to 46.

Cunningham the Player

Cunningham loved to drive to the hoop and never stopped hustling. By the end of the 1971 season, he had been named All-NBA First Team three consecutive seasons.

He was also an emotional player, drawing 32 technical fouls in one year. In 1972, he fouled out of 12 games.

When was the last time a Philadelphia 76ers player had three triple doubles in a row? Billy Cunningham did it in December 1970. (It's also the only time in the history of the franchise that a player has had three consecutive triple doubles.)

Cunningham's Consecutive Triple Doubles

Game	Opponent	Points	Rebounds	Assists
Dec. 20, 1970	Portland	31	27	11
Dec. 22, 1970	Phoenix	25	11	10
Dec. 25, 1970	Detroit	21	18	13

Here's more proof that Cunningham was a dominant player in his era.

1969	All-NBA forwards	Elgin Baylor and Billy Cunningham
1970	All-NBA forwards	Connie Hawkins and Billy Cunningham
1971	All-NBA forwards	John Havlicek and Billy Cunningham

In 1972, Cunningham was on the second team, behind Havlicek and Spencer Haywood. In 1973, Billy C chose a $200,000-a-year contract to play for Carolina in the ABA (he was a major drawing card in the area, based on his college career). After two seasons, he returned to the league. In another era, he would have come back from his 1976 career-ending knee surgery, thanks to advances in surgery and physical therapy.

The best measure of Cunningham's great play can be seen in the following list of players.

Players Averaging at Least 20 Points, 10 Rebounds, Four Assists/Game for Career
Elgin Baylor
Larry Bird
Wilt Chamberlain
Billy Cunningham
Chris Webber

Doug Collins: "I had the good fortune of playing with Billy, and he would take risks with his passes—but I'll tell you what—I was on the receiving end of some of the most beautiful passes you'll ever see from Billy C. I'll never forget the play that ended his career—the sound of him going down has stayed with me. What a shame."

Collins is referring to the awful knee injury that Cunningham suffered 20 games into the 1976 season. He went down without being hit by another player, and his scream could be heard by everyone in attendance.

Kevin Loughery: "Billy was one of the great offensive rebounders of all time. His second jump—and that's what offensive rebounding is all about—was as quick as anyone's. He was one of the toughest competitors—and truly a great offensive rebounder."

Steve Jones: "You are talking about a freak of nature. He was a 6-foot-7 guy who could jump out of the gym. He was a great scorer. He wasn't a great passer, but he was with the game on the line. He would go inside and mix it up with anybody. He played hard; he played hurt. I played with Billy—and when the game was on the line, that's when he was at his best."

Fred Carter: "Billy was a great player that all the brothers respected. They had nothing on him. He was the first white leaper. He could handle the ball, pass. He could do everything Tracy McGrady can do, but he wasn't as quick."

Who's Better, Who's Best
Billy Cunningham or John Havlicek

Phil Jasner: "Hondo was perfect for what his Celtics team needed from him. They had everything else in place. Now, the one year the Sixers had everything around Cunningham, they won 68 games and Billy C was maybe the best sixth man ever.

"Cunningham didn't have the longest career, but his impact was felt long after he retired. He was forced into early retirement, and showed up as the head coach not long after that. He might not have been as great as Havlicek, but he sure was for that one year."

Who's Better, Who's Best
Billy Cunningham or Paul Arizin

Paul Arizin has a lot of credentials to argue that he has earned his own chapter in this book. In fact, Arizin and Cunningham were named in 1996 by the NBA as being among the 50 greatest. There's not room for both of them this time around, though, so I had to eliminate one.

Arizin—just as Cunningham did—played his entire NBA career in Philadelphia. Arizin didn't want to move with the Philadelphia franchise to San Francisco following the 1962 season and played his final three seasons in the Eastern Basketball League, playing with the Camden team. Cunningham spent two seasons in the prime of his career in the American Basketball Association, returning to Carolina (where he played his college ball).

Both Arizin and Cunningham played with Wilt Chamberlain, so their eras were not too far apart.

Cunningham	21.2 points	10.4 rebounds	4.3 assists/game
Arizin	22.8 points	8.6 rebounds	2.3 assists/game

Cunningham was a much better passer and rebounder. Their scoring averages were similar. Both won a title. They were comparable players, but Cunningham had a more complete game in an era with better competition.

Who's Better, Who's Best
Billy Cunningham or Vince Carter

Vince Carter and Billy Cunningham played their college ball at the University of North Carolina. Carter spent the first five seasons of his NBA career playing in Michael Jordan's shadow. Even if he tried to compare himself to Cunningham (another North Carolina alum) he would have had trouble. Cunningham was 6-foot-7, 210 pounds. Carter was 6-foot-6, 225 pounds.

| Cunningham | 21.2 points | 10.4 rebounds | 4.3 assists |
| Carter | 24.1 points | 5.4 rebounds | 3.7 assists |

Not bad for Carter's first 300 or so NBA games, but Vince can't measure up to Cunningham. Billy C was a much better rebounder, played many more minutes, and averaged more assists.

Cunningham's contributions to the game as a head coach help push him ahead of some others on the list of the 50 greatest. While there have been some NBA coaches who were terrific as players (Lenny Wilkens, Bill Sharman, and K. C. Jones, for instance), only 2 of my 50 greatest players have won NBA Championships as coaches. Bill Russell won a pair with the Celts, and Billy Cunningham won a title with the Sixers.

Billy Cunningham wasn't only a great player. He was a great coach. Look at that winning percentage.

NBA Head Coaches (by Win Percentage, min. 400 Games)
1. .738 Phil Jackson
2. .698 Billy Cunningham
3. .679 Pat Riley
4. .674 K. C. Jones
5. .662 Red Auerbach

Phil Jasner on Cunningham's Coaching: "As a coach, Billy taught me his philosophy. Don't substitute to merely rest your starters. Put subs in to either improve your team or to change the pace of a game. That is how he used Bobby Jones."

Maybe because Cunningham is remembered as a head coach, people forget how tremendous a player he was. He was behind contemporaries like Havlicek, for sure, but not by much. Only a select few had the combination of skills Cunningham possessed.

46

EARL MONROE
"The Pearl"

MVP: 0	
MVP VOTING: None to speak of	
NBA TITLES: 1	
ALL-NBA FIRST TEAM: 1	
ALL-NBA SECOND TEAM: 0	

If Earl "The Pearl" Monroe had been born 30 years later, he would have had an even longer and more distinguished NBA career. As it was, he entered the NBA a month before his 23rd birthday. Monroe graduated from high school but decided he was tired of going to school. Remember, the NBA wasn't an option for teens then. So Monroe took a job as a shipping clerk. He said later that he learned what possibilities faced him without a college education. So after a year as a clerk, he quit and left for Winston-Salem State.

There he played for Coach Clarence Gaines, and their relationship grew as close as father and son. Gaines was one of the great influences in Earl's life. The most memorable game in Earl's college career came during Winston-Salem's visit to Akron for a regional championship. Their star was a guy called Something Smith. So they had a big sign across the top of the field house, "Earl Monroe Just a Myth, Can't Compare to Something Smith." Earl scored 49 points, and when the game was over there were three of Earl's teammates standing on each other to get the sign down.

Monroe played four years for Winston-Salem State. Those years coupled with the year as a shipping clerk meant he lost a lot of NBA playing time compared to other modern-day players. His style took a toll on his knees, as well. But even with the late start and the injury problems, Monroe deserves a spot on the 50 greatest of all-time list.

Why? Let's go back to 1968 when Monroe burst on the scene as Rookie of the Year.

1968 Rookie of the Year

Monroe was the second pick overall in the NBA draft. The Detroit Pistons took Jimmy Walker from Providence. Providence was a major school, and Walker was more of a known factor than Monroe. The Bullets were also on record as coveting Walker. They were never happier to be wrong. Monroe was a playground legend in Philadelphia and averaged 41.5 points per game in his final year at Winston-Salem State. Playing on the playgrounds of Philadelphia and in an all-black conference helped him develop his famous "spin" move, which became unstoppable.

Nate Archibald: "I knew all about him years before anyone else. My best friend in the world, Ernie Brown, was from Philly and went to Winston-Salem. We played in summer leagues against Earl. He had an uncanny way of scoring. He was known for his spin moves. One of the best, I'm telling you."

In the NBA draft, the Pistons took Walker, who averaged 8.8 points per game. The Bullets took Monroe, who averaged 24.3. Baltimore went from 20–61 the year before Monroe's arrival to 36–46 in his rookie year of 1968 to an NBA-best 57–25 in 1969. His lightning-quick head fakes, his blind passes to teammates, and his style made him the most exciting player in basketball. He was compared favorably to Bob Cousy. His coach that year, Gene Shue, said, "With all the things he can do, Earl Monroe makes Bob Cousy look like a little boy." In one 1968 game against Los Angeles, Monroe had 56 points. That remains the second-most points scored in a game by a rookie. (Wilt Chamberlain once had 58 points in his rookie season.)

Kevin Loughery: "He was one of my favorites. He revolutionized guard play. When we played, we didn't designate point guards or shooting guards. There were just guards. And we were taught to never turn our back. No one turned their back. Earl was the first to play with his back to the basket. Oh, Oscar would do it—from the interior—play with his back to the basket. But never would the Big O play on the perimeter with his back to the basket. Earl was the first. He had those spinning moves. I think he led all guards in rebounds his rookie year."

Thanks, Kevin, for giving me extra work to look up. The 6-foot-3 Monroe grabbed 465 rebounds (5.7 per game) his rookie season. Oscar Robertson averaged more rebounds per game (slightly more than six) but played only 65 games, so Monroe's 465 rebounds were the highest total.

1968 Most Rebounds/Game, Guards

1. 6.0   Oscar Robertson
2. 5.67   Earl Monroe
3. 5.65   Jeff Mullins
4. 5.4   Hal Greer
5. 5.4   Dick Van Arsdale
6. 5.3   Lenny Wilkens

NBA Playoff Action

Following that Rookie of the Year season, the Bullets drafted Wes Unseld and vaulted to the top of the NBA. But each year, they would battle the Knicks in the playoffs.

Pete Vecsey: "Those were great matchups. At every position. Marin versus Bradley. Gus Johnson against Dave DeBusschere. Wes Unseld versus Willis Reed. Kevin Loughery versus Dick Barnett. And, of course, Monroe versus Frazier."

Bullets-Knicks Playoff Matchups

1969	New York 4	Bullets 0
1970	New York 4	Bullets 3
1971	Bullets 4	Knicks 3
1972	New York 4	Bullets 2
1973	New York 4	Bullets 1
1974	New York 4	Bullets 3

Kevin Loughery: "I'd have to say the 1971 Eastern Finals was one of the greatest playoff series of all time, when my Bullets defeated the Knicks 93–91 in the seventh game. You have to understand, Baltimore was always losing to New York—we couldn't beat the Knicks, the Colts couldn't defeat the Jets, the Orioles couldn't defeat the Mets. When we finally beat the defending champion Knicks, that was our championship." (They then lost four straight in the NBA Finals to the Bucks.)

Get this—between 1969 and 1974, the New York Knicks eliminated the Bullets five out of six seasons. Monroe looked at the series from both sides, having been traded to the Knicks early in the 1972 season. In the six Bullets-Knicks series he played in, Monroe played for the winning team four years.

1969 Knicks-Bullets Series

Earl averaged 28.3 points in the four-game Knicks sweep. Walt Frazier helped contain Monroe to just 39 percent shooting in the series. (Earl needed 114 shots in the four games to score his 113 points.)

1970 Knicks-Bullets Series

Earl averaged 28.0 points in this seven-game series. This time, he shot 48 percent for the series. He did everything he could but could not overcome the Knicks' destiny that season. In his 1971 book *The Knicks*, the late Red Holzman wrote, "We tried everything on Monroe in that first game. We tried to steer him into certain lanes. We double-teamed him. We had Frazier pressure him and tried to sneak Barnett in off the blind side. How did we make out? The Pearl got 39 points."

The Knicks won that first game in double overtime. In that game, the Bullets had a chance to win at the end of regulation and again at the end of the first overtime. Each time, they isolated Monroe on Frazier. Monroe's jumper at the top of the key hit the rim and bounced out as time expired. In Game 6 of that series, the Bullets tied the series up. They really won the game in the third quarter, when Gus Johnson and Monroe took over and scored 28 of Baltimore's 30 points in that quarter.

Baltimore had a problem after that sixth game. Monroe's knees were bothering him and he needed a cortisone shot in the dressing room. In the seventh game, Monroe had 32 points, but the Knicks prevailed 127–114. After that game, Frazier was quoted as saying of Monroe, "I'm tired of dreaming of that cat. He's like a horror movie. It's a lot of sweat chasing him. He's such a great shooter."

In the 1971 season, the Bullets finally advanced past the Knicks and played in the NBA Finals, but ultimately lost to the Bucks. Following that season, the Bullets began to break up their team for one reason or another. They drafted rookie guard Phil Chenier (one of the very first "hardship" players—players who could make a case that they needed to earn money for their families earlier than their college class graduations would allow). Baltimore also traded Kevin Loughery to Philadelphia for Archie Clark.

Earl refused to play for Baltimore. He had checked out ABA teams in hopes of jumping leagues but decided he didn't think he would be comfortable living in ABA cities, such as Indianapolis. He approved a trade to the rival Knicks in early November 1971—even accepting a backseat role on that club that he had once tortured as an opponent.

Monroe had averaged 36.8 minutes per game in his Baltimore career. After being traded to the Knicks, he averaged just 21 minutes per game in that 1972 NBA season. But he put to rest any rumors that he and Frazier wouldn't be able to play together. And, Monroe got to return to the NBA Finals twice—in 1972 and 1973.

Walt Frazier: "We never let our egos get in the way of each other. We had a mutual respect for each other. The first year we played together, he was injured so it was an even easier transition. But it really never was a problem playing with him. We both handled the ball . . . it all just worked out. It depended on who was having the hot hand at the time."

Kevin Loughery: "Earl Monroe should never have left Baltimore. I mean, he blended in to the Knicks. He would have blended in anywhere he went. Erving was like that, too. They were not as assertive as they should have been. Jordan, for instance, would have taken over any team he went to. Monroe and Erving deferred some to their teammates in New York and Philadelphia. This is not a knock on Earl or Doc."

To add to Loughery's statement about Earl the Pearl blending in—perhaps too much—consider this. Walt Frazier had his best three (and highest-scoring) seasons playing with Monroe. And following the 1974 season, with Dave DeBusschere and Willis Reed gone, Monroe returned to his 20-point-per-game average. Monroe lasted with the Knicks longer than Bradley and Frazier and was a consistent scorer well into his late thirties.

Monroe					
Baltimore career	328 games	23.7 points	3.7 rebounds	4.6 assists	.445 field goal %
New York career	598 games	16.2 points	2.6 rebounds	3.5 assists	.478 field goal %

Monroe was initially used as a reserve with New York, in part because he was severely hampered by bone spurs in his left foot. After the 1972 season—which saw him go from 21.4 points to 11.9 points per game—things improved in 1973. That season he was entrenched as a starter and averaged 15.5 points during the regular season and more than 16 in the postseason. In the clinching 1973 Finals game, he scored 23 points.

Monroe in Postseason

1970	eliminated by Knicks	played against Walt Frazier
1971	eliminated by Bucks	played against Oscar Robertson in Finals
1972	eliminated by Lakers	played against Jerry West in Finals
1973	starter on NBA Championship Knicks team	

Bill Walton: "Earl Monroe: fighting a degenerative problem . . . such a champion but had no body . . . won and dominated strictly on skill and heart . . . knee and hip problems . . . he would control games with his creativity . . . dynamic attack to basket . . . he could never out-jump a soul."

Who's Better, Who's Best
Earl Monroe or Walt Frazier

Kevin Loughery: "Monroe versus Frazier: unfair to me. I'm biased toward Earl."

Who's Better, Who's Best
Earl Monroe or Dave Bing

Pete Vecsey: "Bing or Earl Monroe: Earl. Revolutionized the game. What ballplayer doesn't play like Earl—with the spin moves and flashy play. Black Jesus—it was a popular underground nickname . . . I couldn't get it in print back then." (Apparently, neither could Bill Bradley, who, in his 1976 *Life on the Run*, wrote that Monroe's feats "inspired nicknames that soon became the trappings of his reputation.")

Who's Better, Who's Best
Earl Monroe or World B. Free

Wouldn't that be a great one-on-one matchup? Free (from Brooklyn, New York's Canarsie High School) and Monroe (from the streets of Philadelphia) playing against each other with all their moves? Free was a prolific scorer who averaged more than 30 points per game in one season and more than 20 per game in a 10-year career. Monroe was a better all-around player. In the name department, though, even Black Jesus comes up short to World B. Free. The one-time Lloyd Free belongs in the Marketing Hall of Fame.

Who's Better, Who's Best
Earl Monroe or Tracy McGrady

Monroe was a terrific all-around player who led all guards in rebounds before Wes Unseld joined him and grabbed every available rebound. But Monroe—in his best days—could not play the game the way T-Mac plays. McGrady entered the NBA right from high school, and if Monroe could have, the NBA would have had a string of at least three or four additional Pearl seasons. McGrady has the benefit of a quick start and (so far) has remained injury-free. McGrady zoomed past an all-timer such as Monroe before he was 25 years old. The simple truth is, Earl never had a season like Tracy's 2003 season. Not many players have.

Monroe came into the NBA like a Bullet. He was one of the most exciting players in basketball. He adjusted his overall style of play to fit into the most team-oriented club in history. When that group of heady ballplayers retired, Monroe scored at will for a team that needed it. Many consider Monroe the finest one-on-one player ever (better than George Gervin, Connie Hawkins, Julius Erving, and Nate Archibald). His twisting, turning moves and uncanny passes were his trademark. It is one trademark that doesn't need any updating for a while.

PETE MARAVICH

The Floppy-Socked Magician

MVP: 0	
MVP VOTING: Never in top 5	
NBA TITLES: 0	
ALL-NBA FIRST TEAM: 2	
ALL-NBA SECOND TEAM: 2	

"Pistol Pete" Maravich's name still rings in the ears of basketball fans across America. Who can forget the floppy socks, the behind-the-back passes, the between-the-legs dribbling, and the wondrous assortment of shots that made him a basketball magician?

Maravich was a great basketball player who starred for the wrong teams in the wrong era when they used the wrong rules for his game. He played most of his career in the two worst cities for pro basketball (Atlanta and New Orleans). Most of the time, he played before empty seats. In the mid-1970s, the league's reputation was at its all-time low—that's when Pistol Pete played. Not that Maravich ever sniffed the Finals, but more people would have been exposed to his talents if he had.

Maravich the Showman

Maravich was a master showman. In an earlier era, he might have been as celebrated as Bob Cousy. In a later one, he would have been a billionaire, with endorsements and movies and television shows for his choosing. He was the fourth-leading scorer in the entire league for the decade of the 1970s. In 1977, he averaged 31.1 points per game, in a season where no other player averaged as many as 27 points. He led the New Orleans Jazz to 35 wins despite one of the worst supporting casts in history.

The 1977 Jazz had lost the aging Gail Goodrich to injury for all but 27 games. That left a depleted roster around Pistol Pete of the immortal Nate Williams, Aaron James,

Jim McElroy, and Rich Kelley. They were coached by Mr. Stats's 13th-ranked player, Elgin Baylor, who had a terrific strategy: put the ball in Maravich's hands.

Most fans are familiar with Maravich's scoring achievements, but Pete was an all-around player with a good floor game. For his career, he averaged 4.2 rebounds and 5.4 assists per game. In that 1977 season, Maravich had as fine an individual offensive year as Michael Jordan ever had. (But Michael still had it all over Maravich—and everyone else—defensively.)

Maravich's 1977 season	31.1 points/game	5.1 rebounds	5.4 assists
Jordan's 1987 season	37.1 points/game	5.2 rebounds	4.6 assists

Maravich was the greatest long-range shooter in the history of the game. Unfortunately, there's no way to prove that, as he played in an era without a three-point shot. Here's my attempt at putting some perspective into Maravich's career.

How many three-pointers would he have scored?

Well, let's see. Reggie Miller is generally considered the greatest three-point shooter of all time. His range is very comparable to what Maravich had. Miller has what is considered the deepest range in the league, with an accurate shot well beyond the three-point line. Let's determine what percentage of field goals Miller takes represent three-pointers. Of his 7,386 field goals, 2,217 are three-pointers. That translates to 30 percent of his career field goals.

Although the NBA had the three-point rule in effect for Reggie's entire career, the shot was not exploited till the 1990s. In Miller's rookie season of 1988, there were teams such as Washington that scored just 29 treys all season long. The average team scored about two long-range shots per game.

Let's look at Miller's career beginning with the 1993 season and ending with the 2002 campaign, since that's when we find teams exploiting the three-point shot. That's a 10-year period.

Miller, 1993–2002
1,667 three-point field goals
4,863 field goals

Okay, that's more like it. More than 34 percent of Miller's successful field goals during a 10-year period have been from long range.

Now, let's assume Maravich would have taken at least as many shots as Miller did. In fact, he probably would have taken more. Why in the world would he continue to pass inside to less effective teammates when his own shot would be worth 33 percent more points?

Miller was a 40 percent shooter from three-point range, and one has to assume Maravich would have been at least the same.

Maravich averaged 24.2 points per game in his career without the three-point shot. He scored 6,187 field goals. If we give Maravich even 33 percent of those for extra credit, then he would have scored an additional 2,062 points. For his career, that's another 3.1 points per game.

That puts Maravich up to 27.3 points per game in the modern three-point era. It also puts Pistol Pete's 1977 season closer to 35 points per game—narrowing the gap to Jordan's magnificent season a decade later.

The Great "What-Ifs" in Maravich's Career

Early in Maravich's career, his Atlanta Hawks tried to get Julius Erving out of his ABA contract with the Virginia Squires. If Erving had wound up in Atlanta with Maravich, Pistol's career would have been much different. At the end of Maravich's career, he finished up with the 1980 Celtics, playing his final 43 games with rookie Larry Bird. In that 1980 season, the NBA finally adopted the three-point shot. Maravich was teased early and late.

Talk about being born 20 years before your time and dying 20 years before your time! If Maravich came along today, there is no way he would have stayed in college four years. His dad, Press (his college coach), would have come along with him to the NBA in some package deal.

Maravich averaged 43.6 points, 43.8 points, 44.2 points, and 44.5 points at LSU. There is no way he would have stayed the three last years. Of course, Pete didn't have the option. Spencer Haywood didn't challenge the draft at that point, and there was no hardship rule. If there was, it wouldn't have applied to Maravich anyway.

Maravich was 23 when he entered the NBA. He lost three to four years on the front end of his career and continuously battled to reach his potential.

In Pistol Pete's second NBA season, he developed mononucleosis and spent the first 14 games of the season flat on his back. Of course, he came back too soon and played at least 20 pounds underweight the entire season. At 6-foot-5, he played at only 178 pounds the rest of that 1971 season. No wonder his scoring dropped from 22.2 to 19.3. In that season, he scored 50 points in a game twice, had zero points once—and scored a total of 12 points in a five-game funk following his father's dismissal as coach of LSU.

Maravich also lost three to four years on the back end of his career as well, this time due to injury. And he passed away in early 1988 at the age of 41.

He was the flashiest of players, with his trademark floppy socks; behind-the-back dribbling; and no-look, behind-the-back passes. The son of a coach, he was very fundamentally sound. Maravich wore #23 in college (in honor of his brother, who wore that number in college), but when he got to Atlanta, that number was already being worn by Sweet Lou Hudson. So Pistol accepted #44.

The Career High

On February 25, 1977, the Knicks traveled to New Orleans for a game with the Jazz. The Knicks were just a .500 team that season, but they still boasted an aging Walt Frazier and Earl Monroe as guards. Maravich picked this game to score a career-high 68 points. At the time, only two other players (Wilt Chamberlain and Elgin Baylor) had scored more points in a single game. Interestingly, both Wilt (100) and Elgin (71) had also achieved their career highs against the Knicks. (Hey, if you want attention, do something against the Knicks!) It was the most points in a game ever scored by a guard and has since been bettered by only two other backcourt men: David Thompson and Michael Jordan. But Jordan's career high of 69 points actually came in an overtime game. So Thompson is the only other guard who has scored more points in a regulation 48-minute game. Robinson's feat came a year later in the season finale (in a futile attempt to win a scoring title).

Who's Better, Who's Best
Pete Maravich or Reggie Miller

This was a classic matchup of the longevity guy against the peak-value guy. Reggie Miller averaged at least 18 points per game for a dozen straight years. Maravich finished in the top five in scoring four times in a five-year period. Miller had the longer career and made one trip to the NBA Finals, but so what? When he got there, he proceeded to shoot one of 18 field goals in Game 1 in Los Angeles, and the Lakers won in six games in the 2000 Finals. Miller has averaged only three rebounds and three assists per game in his career—more than 40 percent less than Maravich. Pete was a true "combo" guard—one who had to handle the ball and run the offense, but still take a tremendous amount of shots. In fact, Maravich took 28 shots per game in 1977—more than even Michael Jordan or Allen Iverson has ever taken in a season.

Bob Ryan: "He was totally underrated. Pete was one of the saddest figures in the game's history. He would have been better off in college playing for anyone other than his father. His father made him a circus act. He could have been Magic before Magic. His passing was beyond belief. He was absolutely fearless. And if he had had the three-point line, there is no telling how many points he would have scored. Among modern-day players, Jason Williams has been compared to Maravich, but that is like comparing Appalachian League baseball to the Major Leagues."

Joe Maloof: "Maravich: my all-time favorite player. Remember, they didn't have the three-point play in his day. Some of the things he accomplished—my God, didn't he get like 65 points in some college games? We had a player—Jason Williams—who reminded me of Pete. But what separated Pete from Williams—and just about everyone else—was that Maravich was a student of the game. He put out four or five instructional videos—I still have them—on ball handling, passing, et cetera. He was a great, great player."

Maravich scored more in the 1970s than guys who went to Plato's Retreat or Studio 54. Take a look at his rankings.

1977	1st in scoring
1974	2nd in scoring
1976	3rd in scoring
1973	5th in scoring
1971	8th in scoring

There have been many players in history to score more points and accumulate more assists than Pete Maravich. But there absolutely was no better passer and shooter. The baseball pitcher turned author Jim Bouton once described his life like this: "You grip a baseball all your life, and one day find out it was the other way around all along." That quote applies as well to Maravich's mastery of handling a basketball. Basketball gripped him early. You can tell the kids today about Maravich—even show them the videos—but it pales in comparison to having seen the real deal. He could do anything to a basketball except make it sing. He was the only member of the 1996 Top 50 players who was deceased at the time. He's been gone since 1988, and we must make sure we never forget the style, the substance, and the superb play of Pistol Pete Maravich.

48

REGGIE MILLER

Master of the Game-Winning Three

MVP: 0
MVP VOTING: Never in top 5
NBA TITLES: 0
ALL-NBA FIRST TEAM: 0
ALL-NBA SECOND TEAM: 0

There are only a few spots left and a lot of worthy candidates remaining. In this chapter, I'll explain why Reggie Miller's name was chosen ahead of something old (Bill Sharman), something new (high school phenom LeBron James), something borrowed (European Dirk Nowitzki), or something Carolina blue (James Worthy).

The Stats on Miller

Reggie Miller has the career record for most three-pointers by a country mile. He has converted 89 percent of his career free throws. He's been remarkably consistent in the regular season—and consistently terrific in the postseason.

Miller averaged at least 18 points per game in 12 different seasons. There are only five other players who have accomplished that (using the standards for qualifiers of 70 games played or 1,400 points in a season, which eliminates Jerry West and Charles Barkley). Only Kareem Abdul-Jabbar, Karl Malone, John Havlicek, Elvin Hayes, and Moses Malone had a string of a dozen or more seasons averaging at least 18 points per game.

Miller was drafted in 1987 by the Indiana Pacers, which upset Pacers fans who wanted local hero Steve Alford.

In 1989, Chuck Person led the Indiana Pacers in scoring. Reggie Miller was second. After that season, the Pacers go-to guy was always Miller.

Miller was the Pacers' leading scorer in 1990, the first of 10 consecutive seasons he led the team in scoring. In 2000, Miller averaged 18.1 points per game, to finish second on the team to Jalen Rose (18.2).

Miller has played more than 1,200 games for the Pacers. That trick is hard enough to do when there is one coach and management in place for a decade (such as Utah's John Stockton and Karl Malone enjoyed). But unlike Stockton and Malone, who played virtually their entire careers under Jerry Sloan, Miller has played for seven different head coaches. Miller played for Jack Ramsay. He played for Larry Brown. Then Larry Bird was in charge for three seasons. Isiah Thomas also has been his head coach.

In his first seven years, Miller made the All-Star team exactly one time, in 1990. During his 16-year career, he made the All-Star game just five times.

Derek Harper: "Some guys just beg for the ball at crunch time. I played 11 years with Rolando Blackman—and he was right at the top of players with the game on the line. I've seen Miller do so much damage at the end of games—five points in less than eight seconds in New York."

Pete Vecsey: "Miller absolutely has to be part of the top 50 players of all time. You have to find a place for Reggie."

Isiah Thomas: "Reggie was one of the greatest scorers. Yet he couldn't jump as high as Michael Jordan. He couldn't run as fast as Jason Kidd or Mark Price. But he could beat anyone off the dribble. He got the maximum out of his abilities."

Free Throws, Three-Pointers, and Playoff Heroics
These are the three things Miller has done to merit inclusion in this book:

Free Throw Shooting
He led the league in free throw percentage four times. Only three other players have done that. Bill Sharman led the league seven times, Rick Barry six times, and Larry Bird four times.

Miller was only an 80 percent foul shooter in his first year. By his second season, he was up to 84 percent. Since then, he has been the best foul shooter of all time. His first 500 or so attempts were shot at an 82 percent clip. His career average is now 89 percent.

In 115 pressure-packed playoff games, he has hit 89 percent of his free throws.

Three-Point Shooting

The three-point field goal was not introduced into the NBA until the 1980 season, and in the first few years, no team really shot many. Miller entered the league in 1988. By 1998, he was the all-time leader. Now, he's putting serious distance between himself and all others. For his career, Miller has 2,330. Dale Ellis is second with 1,719.

During the 1997 season, Miller and Ellis went back and forth, each spending time atop the career three-point leader board. It was very similar to Steve Carlton's and Nolan Ryan's 1983 baseball seasons, when the two strikeout kings battled for the all-time lead. In the end, Carlton couldn't keep up with the Ryan Express, and Ryan would finish his career with 5,900 strikeouts compared to Carlton's 4,100. Miller had a later start than Ellis but quickly climbed the charts. In 1994, Reggie moved up to fourth on the all-time list. In 1995, he became the third player to reach 1,000. By 1996, he became the second (following Ellis) to record 1,200 successful three-pointers. It was during the 1998 season that Ellis and Miller went back and forth. At season's end, Miller had 1,596 compared to Ellis's 1,588. By 1999, it was still close. Miller had a 106–94 advantage, building his lead to 20.

Miller left Ellis in the rearview mirror in the 2000 season, hitting 165 three-pointers, to just 37 for the declining 39-year-old Ellis.

Playoff Heroics

Miller warmed up with some impressive performances in the early 1990s. But by the playoffs of 1994, he was ready for action.

1. **1994 Eastern Conference Finals, Game 5 at New York** He scored 25 points in the fourth quarter (39 for the game). He hit five three-pointers in that fourth quarter. The Pacers took the series back to Indiana up 3–2.
2. **1995 Eastern Conference Semis, Game 1 at New York** He scored eight straight points in 8.9 seconds, to give the Pacers a two-point win, 107–105. All it takes, kids, is to drill a three-point field goal, make a steal off the inbounds pass, step back and hit another three-pointer, and then finish it off with two free throws.
3. **1996 First Round Against Atlanta** He returned to action after missing eight straight games (the final four regular-season games, and the first four playoff contests). In Game 5, he scored 29 points, including 16 in the fourth quarter. It wasn't enough, as the Hawks won by two in the deciding game of the series.
4. **1998 Eastern Conference Semis, at New York** He had 38 points in the overtime Game 4. That was only his seventh 30-point game against the Knicks in the postseason.

5. **1998 Eastern Conference Finals Against Chicago** He hit the game-winning three-point field goal with seven-tenths of a second remaining to defeat the Bulls on Memorial Day and tie the series at 2–2.

6. **2000 Postseason** He averaged 31.3 points in the deciding game of each of the four playoff series. In the fifth and deciding game of the first round against Milwaukee, Miller had 41 points. In the fifth game of the Eastern Conference finals against the Knicks, Miller poured in 34 points.

7. **2000 NBA Finals** After a clinker in Game 1 (two of 16 field goals), Miller averaged 27.8 points per game in the last five games of the series. He hit on 45 of 46 free throws in those Finals.

8. **2001 First Round Against Philadelphia** Miller made his former coach Larry Brown work hard to advance to the second round on his way to the Finals. Miller averaged 36 points a game the last three games of the series, but the Sixers had a postseason weapon of their own in Allen Iverson.

9. **2002 First Round Against New Jersey** In the fifth and deciding game against the Nets, Miller had 31 points. He had a 40-foot three-pointer at the end of regulation that sent the game into overtime. He had a driving dunk at the end of the first overtime and sent the game into double overtime.

Appearing on Carson Daly's late-night show in February 2003, Miller ranked the fifth game against New Jersey as his greatest playoff moment.

Derek Harper: "Reggie might be at the very top of the most clutch performers ever. I saw him score those three-pointers in eight seconds. Wow. In front of Spike Lee and all. He belongs."

Miller has raised his scoring average in the playoffs each year. For his career, he averages about 19 points per game. In the postseason, it is a robust 23.5. Miller has had his share of off-nights in the postseason. In the 1998 Eastern Conference finals against Chicago, Miller shot just two of 13 field goals on the way to only eight points. In Game 1 of the 2000 Finals, Miller had seven points on two of 16 field goals. He's also been suspended for playoff games (following an altercation with 76er Matt Geiger).

My one criticism of him is that he is first and foremost a shooter. Shoot the ball. Miller is not on the court because he is Dennis Rodman on the boards. Or John Stockton at the point. He is on the court to shoot.

Do you realize how many times, in his 1,200+ regular-season games and his 115+ postseason games, he shot the ball 30 times?

None.

There's never been a playoff game in which Miller shot the ball as many as 28 times.

In that 1998 Eastern Conference finals against the Bulls, Michael Jordan shot the ball 167 times. Reggie Miller shot the ball 89. Jordan had 78 more shots in the seven games. In Game 7, with an opportunity to defeat Michael Jordan, Reggie Miller put up only 13 shots.

Miller reminds me of a young John Elway, the one that was coached by Dan Reeves. Remember, Elway's stats were nothing special until the final two minutes. That is when Reeves finally unleashed him. Elway could have had Marino-like numbers, and Miller could have had Jordan-like numbers. The question that begs asking all seven of Reggie's head coaches is: Why didn't Miller shoot as much when the game wasn't on the line as when it was?

Miller's postseason average is so much higher than his season averages. Jordan's career playoff numbers increased. So did Walt Frazier's, Isiah Thomas's, and Jerry West's. None, however, were spiked any higher by the playoffs than Reggie Miller's numbers.

DOMINIQUE WILKINS
"The Human Highlight Film"

MVP: 0	
MVP VOTING: 2nd in 1986, 5th in 1987, 6th in 1988, 8th in 1991	
NBA TITLES: 0	
ALL-NBA FIRST TEAM: 1	
ALL-NBA SECOND TEAM: 4	

He may not have a championship ring, but Dominique Wilkins has other memorable titles on his résumé. He won the Slam Dunk titles in 1985 and 1990 and finished second in 1987 and 1988. That's when the event meant something, and top players such as Michael Jordan competed yearly. Nique's first season was 1983, and by 1984 he was 17th in the league in scoring average. He was just an unbelievable scorer. He won one scoring title in his career—and that was in 1986, when Michael Jordan was injured and limited to just 18 games. If not for Jordan, Wilkins would have been the scoring champ many times.

Wilkins's Place Among the League's Top Scorers

1984	17th
1985	6th
1986	1st
1987	2nd (to Jordan)
1988	2nd (to Jordan)
1989	7th
1990	5th
1991	7th
1992	Didn't qualify; averaged 28.1 points in 42 games
1993	2nd (to Jordan)
1994	4th

He averaged 29.9 points per game in 1993. He needed nine more points in that 1993 season to become the oldest player to ever average 30 points per game in a season. Michael Jordan would turn 33 years old in 1996 and average just over 30 points per game.

Most Points/Game, Season In Which Player Was 33 Years or Older

1. Michael Jordan (33 years two months at end of season)	30.4 points/game in 1996
2. Dominique Wilkins (33 years three months)	29.9 points/game in 1993
3. Michael Jordan (34 years two months)	29.6 points/game in 1997
4. Michael Jordan (35 years two months)	28.7 points/game in 1998
5. Alex English (33 years three months)	28.6 points/game in 1987

Karl Malone had two years after turning 33 years old in which he averaged 27 points per game. Kareem Abdul-Jabbar checked in one year with a 26-point average in his mid-thirties. Rick Barry was still averaging 23 per game, as was Barkley in the 1996 season. Larry Bird's last big scoring season came at 33 years old: 24.3. Wilt Chamberlain decided to concentrate less on scoring, but he still had a 20-point average at 35 years old. Erving was a long way from his 30-point averages, but he managed 22 points per game. Moses Malone was at 20.3.

Kevin Loughery: "Dominique: What athleticism—as good as any athlete. He was a better shooter than people gave him credit for. He didn't make his teammates better, though. He was a scorer and rebounder."

Wilkins loved to play, and he was very easy to coach. He blocked shots—he was quite strong. Remember, in his day, no one lifted weights. He could defend but he was not a great ball handler. He never looked away when the pressure mounted and a last shot needed to be attempted. He was a genuine scoring machine.

Pete Vecsey: "I did not vote for Dominique last time on my all-time 50. I think I was wrong then. He was a great scorer. He could play defense—when he wanted to. He was a great athlete."

1986 MVP Voting

There were 78 voters for the 1986 MVP award. Larry Bird received votes from 73 of them. The other five votes went to Dominique Wilkins.

The Defining 5:57 of Dominique's Career

In 1988, Mike Fratello's Atlanta Hawks won 50 games and defeated the Milwaukee Bucks in the first round of the playoffs. The Hawks drew the Boston Celtics, a team that had been in the NBA Finals in each of the previous three seasons.

The Celtics were clinging to the remains of their dynasty. The year prior, the Detroit Pistons had their chance against the Celtics in a crucial fifth game that they let get away.

Boston won the first two games against the Hawks in Boston Garden. Atlanta went back to the Omni and won the next two games. Going into Game 5, the Hawks were facing a Celtics team that was 22–1 at home in the postseason over the last three years. History be damned, the Hawks broke through in Game 5—in Boston—and suddenly the Hawks were a game away from eliminating the Celtics.

Boston won narrowly in Atlanta in the sixth game, 102–100. That set up a Sunday afternoon showdown.

With 5:57 remaining in that series finale, Boston led 99–97. Then, the game turned into a mano-a-mano duel. Here are the play-by-play highlights:

5:57	Wilkins hit deep left-corner jumper: 99–99
5:42	Bird sank left-handed jumper in lane: Boston 101–99
5:25	Wilkins put stutter-step move on McHale and hit jumper from 18 feet: 101–101
5:06	Bird hit 17-footer from the left: Boston 103–101
4:38	Wilkins banked one in high from the right: 103–103
3:34	Bird hit in heavy traffic in the lane: Boston 105–103
1:43	Bird stuck three-pointer while in Dominique's face in front of Atlanta bench: Boston 112–105
1:31	Wilkins hit turnaround in lane: Boston 112–107
0:26	Bird drove to hoop for score: Boston 114–109
0:20	Wilkins missed dunk, got his own rebounds, and laid it in: Boston 114–111
0:01	Wilkins made the first of two free throws, purposely missed the second: Boston 118–116

In the final six minutes of a Game 7 on the road, Dominique Wilkins had scored 11 points and Larry Bird had scored 11 points. It was a memorable exhibition that few who were there would ever forget.

Mike Fratello: "I remember playing back the tape and I couldn't believe one of the announcers said after a Boston basket, 'This game is over.' It wasn't over. Dominique was on one of his incredible rolls. The only thing that stopped us from winning that game and series was we couldn't get that one stop on defense that we needed. I'll never forget Bird hitting a shot going from right to left, stumbling down. If we could have stopped them there, or stopped Bird on his three-pointer in front of our bench . . . we would have had a shot.

"We had the ball down three points in the final seconds, and the Celts paid Wilkins the biggest compliment. Danny Ainge just ran at Dominique and wrapped his arms around him, so he couldn't take a three-pointer to tie the game. We had Nique make the first and hoped we could get the rebound on the second."

Who's Better, Who's Best
Dominique Wilkins or Alex English

In 15 years, Alex English scored 25,613 points. In 15 years, Dominique Wilkins scored 26,668. But there was more to separate these two great scorers.

Pete Vecsey: "I would take Dominique because he could take over a game—and do it spectacularly. He had so much more flair than Alex English. Nique was bombastic. Alex was effortless and a master of the quiet game. Plus, Dominique could pass—although he wasn't known for it. Lastly, English had range from 18 feet and in—but Dominique could hit from three-point range."

Mike Fratello: "Dominique did it in a very different way than Alex English. Alex was like Gervin, you know, smooth. Dominique was powerful. He was a powerful dunker. He had great resiliency, loved to play. He was a real gamer."

Who's Better, Who's Best
Dominique Wilkins or George Gervin

Kevin Loughery: "Nique versus Gervin: So easy for Iceman. Unique. He had his own, individual style. He was incredible to watch. He scored so easily. You would think you held him to 15—and look up—and he had 45. What a great shooter. But he didn't play defense—he was strictly a one-way player. Nique was a better rebounder, better defender."

The best way to show Dominique Wilkins's sustained brilliance is with these season point totals.

Most 2,000-Point Seasons

1. 12   Karl Malone
2. 11   Michael Jordan
3. 9   Kareem Abdul-Jabbar
4. 8   Dominique Wilkins, Alex English

That's more than Wilt Chamberlain, Oscar Robertson, Gervin, Bob Pettit, Elgin Baylor, and anyone else. That alone should put Dominique ahead of other great scorers who competed for this spot in the top 50 (including Paul Arizin, Alex English, Dan Issel, and Paul Pierce). Some players earn style points—it's not only how much they score, but how they score. Dominique Wilkins earned enough style points to rate a spot among the top 50. In college, he was nicknamed "The Human Highlight Film." In the pros, he lived up to his nickname.

50

CLYDE DREXLER
Jordan-Lite

MVP: 0	
MVP VOTING: 5th in 1988, 2nd in 1992	
NBA TITLES: 1	
ALL-NBA FIRST TEAM: 1	
ALL-NBA SECOND TEAM: 2	

Clyde Drexler was one of many outstanding players who played in the shadow of Michael Jordan. Unlike some of the other great players of that era (Charles Barkley, Patrick Ewing, Karl Malone, and John Stockton, to name a few), Drexler played the same position and had the same strengths as Jordan. Drexler distanced himself enough from the rest of the mortals, however, to merit the final spot on this top 50 list. He was fourth in scoring during an eight-year period. Between 1985 and 1992, only three men—Jordan, Malone, and Dominique Wilkins—scored more points than Clyde. Clyde was also eighth in assists during those eight years with 3,961, and fourth in steals with 1,421.

Playing Behind Jordan

After Jordan, who was a better two-guard than Clyde in that era? He led his team into the NBA Finals in both 1990 and 1992. In 1991, his team was upset by Magic Johnson's Lakers. When Jordan retired for the first time, Drexler even earned an NBA Championship with the 1995 Rockets.

Drexler had Jordan-like talent. He should have won a little more, produced a little more. In the 1990 Finals, the Blazers split the first two games in Detroit. They proceeded to lose three straight home games. In 1991, the Blazers won 63 games—best in the league—but they couldn't make it back to the Finals. The following year, 1992, the Blazers were tied with the Bulls 2–2. But they were blown out of Game 5 at home and then blew a big lead in Chicago in Game 6.

Portland had a reputation for self-destructing in close games.

Eventually, in 1995, Drexler was traded in midseason to the Houston Rockets, where he helped the Rockets repeat as NBA Champions.

Drexler scored more than 22,000 points in his NBA career and finished with career averages of 20.4 points, 6.1 rebounds, and 5.6 assists per game. Following his rookie season, he averaged at least 17 points a game for 14 consecutive seasons.

Dr. Jack Ramsay: "Clyde was not very skilled coming out of college. He had so much raw talent and became a great player. He had tremendous athleticism."

That eight-year period (1985–1992) culminated with Drexler being the last NBA player selected to play on the Dream Team.

If you take a smaller subset—the 1992 season—Drexler was, without question, the second-best player in the game. In that year, Drexler averaged 25 points per game as well as 6.5 rebounds and 6.5 assists per game.

Those are big-time numbers.

In that 1992 season, only one team had a better record than Portland, and that was Chicago. Only one player finished ahead of Drexler in the MVP vote—Jordan. The Blazers lost 4–2 in the NBA Finals. If the Blazers had won, Drexler would have been Finals MVP. It just wasn't Clyde's year. Magic Johnson came out of retirement to play in the All-Star game, and he scored 25 points on nine of 12 field goals. Magic was the MVP of the All-Star game, while Drexler finished second, scoring 22 points with nine rebounds and six assists, in 28 minutes.

Although Clyde was All-NBA First Team only that 1992 season, it is not a sin to be ranked below Michael Jordan and Magic Johnson in the prime of their careers. Drexler won one championship, but probably should have won one with the Blazers.

Who's Better, Who's Best
Clyde Drexler or Reggie Miller

Drexler had the better eight-year run, and Miller had the more consistent 16-year numbers. Drexler won the title, but Miller had the more spectacular playoff moments.

Steve Jones: "Clyde was a better player, and I say that without hesitation and not just because I'm from Portland. Reggie was the greatest big-moment three-point shooter in the history of the NBA. He jackknifed them in. But Miller was not the all-around player that Drexler was. Clyde could carry his team for 10 to 12 games. He did it all the time for Portland. He did it for Houston and that carried them to the title. Clyde hated losing—and he had that 'get out of my way, I'm not losing' attitude."

Of course, the true test for both Drexler and Miller as shooting guards in that era was how they fared against Jordan. Jordan was the measuring stick that they would be judged by. Jones once thought Drexler should have approached the 1992 Finals as a personal challenge. According to Jones, there was "just an eyelash" between the two that year. Clyde was a better passer and rebounder. Jordan was a better on-the-ball defender. But Drexler was better at playing the passing lanes. Jones felt that Drexler should have approached the Finals as Phil Mikkelson approached the golfing majors—as if Tiger Woods were the one, singular opponent. Instead, Drexler felt it was a team game and didn't have the killer instinct that Jordan (and few others) possessed. In that regard, Clyde was very similar to Reggie. At least, Miller knew at the end of the close games that it was his team, his game to win, his ass on the line. That is why, in my opinion, Miller rates slightly ahead of Drexler.

Pete Vecsey: "Clyde falls into the Barkley category—he didn't always maximize his abilities."

P. J. Carlesimo: "He was very good. I had him for half a year. He could guard people. Do it all. He has to get some credit for that."

There's another player I found comparable to Drexler. Wes Unseld and Drexler are both 6-foot-7. Drexler lost his first couple of times in the NBA Finals. Unseld lost his first couple of times in the NBA Finals. Unseld was All-NBA First Team just once. Drexler was All-NBA First Team just once. Unseld won an MVP. Drexler was second to Jordan in the 1992 MVP vote.

Both won their titles after a former University of Houston center (Elvin Hayes or Hakeem Olajuwon) became their teammate.

Steve Jones: "Wes probably wasn't 6-foot-7 like he was listed. He was the best 6-foot-6-inch center in the history of the game. Another freak of nature. He did so much with so little. Imagine, every night this guy gave up three or four or five inches to an opposing center. He was able to defend and find a way to contribute offensively. The Bullets knew that this was a once-in-a-lifetime guy and knew how unique and special he was."

Kevin Loughery: "When Wes came to the Bullets, my scoring average jumped from 14 to 22—all because of him. The summer we drafted him, we met in some Jewish Community Center gym in Baltimore, and he was wearing this tight sweat suit. He started showing me how he could grab a rebound and throw it all the way downcourt before he hit the ground. All of a sudden, I became Paul Warfield—a wide receiver catching passes ahead of the field."

Unseld and Drexler both dominated seasons and had standout long careers. They both won championships. They helped Olajuwon and Hayes as much as those guys helped them. Unseld averaged 15 rebounds per game for his career and had a playoff game where he out-rebounded the entire Knicks squad. In football terms, Unseld was a fine quarterback, who threw the outlet pass better than anyone in history, except, perhaps, Bill Russell. Drexler was a fine cover corner similar to Deion Sanders. When he played the passing lanes and intercepted a pass, he was off to the end zone. The Blazers knocked their heads against better teams, and so did the Bullets. In my opinion, Drexler deserves this spot— but Unseld deserves mention. He's like Puerto Rico. He can be the 51st state, or first alternate. If any of the 50 contestants fails to be able to serve as one of the 50 greatest in history, then Unseld is there to step in and take the last spot, bumping everyone up a notch.

There you have it. The top 50 players ranked in order.

THE OTHER GUYS

Paul Arizin was seriously considered. How could I not? He was named to the NBA's 25th Anniversary All-Time Team. As recently as 1996, the NBA named him to their list of the 50 greatest players. He had some solid credentials. He won an NBA title and led the league in scoring. Arizin made All-NBA First Team three times and Second Team once. He played in eight All-Star games, winning MVP in the 1952 game. He made the final cut here, but he wasn't chosen because his contemporaries whom I spoke with didn't passionately make a case for him.

Dave Bing was another hard cut. Bill Walton, Doug Collins, and Stu Lantz all lobbied for Bing, one of the classiest men in league history. He was All-NBA First Team two times. In 1971, he was fourth in MVP voting. Collins remembers the Pistons coming out of the dressing room with Bing bouncing the ball to the beat of the blaring Elton John song "Benny and the Jets." Lantz, a former teammate of Bing, laughed at the recollection and confirmed they came out to warm up to that song every home game. Everyone told me what a tremendous person Bing was. I'm sure he's all that. But when the time came for choosing the guards from the early 1970s, I am confident that Walt Frazier, Earl Monroe, and Pete Maravich had it all over Bing.

Dave DeBusschere also was squeezed out. If Gil Hodges can't make the Baseball Hall of Fame, then DeBusschere fails to get into my book for essentially the same reasons. They were rock-solid players on memorable teams. They weren't Jackie Robinson or Roy Campanella or Willis Reed or Walt Frazier. I gave his spot on the list to Dennis Rodman. Rodman could never have done what DeBusschere did. Dave was the Pistons' player-coach in 1964, becoming the youngest coach in NBA history. But DeBusschere could never impact a game the way Rodman could.

Similarly, Hal Greer lost out to Sam Jones. Philadelphia always seemed to lose to Boston in the 1960s, and it is no different in this book. Greer was never All-NBA First Team but was on the Second Team seven times. That meant he merited a good look, but that was all. I'll get arguments from at least three of the men I spoke with who saw both play.

Jerry Lucas was a difficult decision. He wrote amazing memory books with Harry Lorayne in the early 1970s, and mastering those tricks improved my schoolwork and impressed my class to no end. I never tried to memorize the New York City phone book, but I remember phone numbers all right. That should be worth something to Lucas. He was a crazy rebounder. You get the feeling it was just numbers, however.

Robert Parish was selected as one of the NBA's 50 greatest players in 1996. I know Bill Walton and Chamberlain (in his 1991 and last book) have said some very nice things about the Chief. But Parish was the first player I eliminated when I started writing the manuscript. He goes against everything I've been talking about. He played 21 seasons—and was All-NBA First Team *zero* times. He was Second Team just once. At his peak, he would get regularly beat by a man who collected Social Security checks on his way up the court in the Finals.

Bill Sharman was also named to the 25th Anniversary All-Time Team. That team failed to name then-active players. Of course, if they had, then Oscar Robertson and Jerry West would have pushed Bill out of the way—and fast. Leonard Koppett and Dr. Ernie Vandeweghe told me how great Sharman was, however. He won four NBA titles. He made All-NBA First Team four different seasons and Second Team three additional seasons. He was more of a winner than Reggie Miller. He was even a better foul shooter than Reggie. He was a big part of NBA history. It is hard to leave this man off. In the final cut, however, Miller just barely squeezed ahead. Miller is one of those players that would be easy to bypass. He shouldn't be. It comes at the expense of Sharman. But remember, in almost every instance in this book, the ties have been broken like this: big over small, modern over past, prime over longevity, and winner over loser. Miller was bigger, played against better competition, and had enough huge postseason moments to squeeze past a Celtic with a truckload of NBA Championship rings.

Nate Thurmond averaged 15 points and 15 rebounds in his career. He had seasons where he averaged 20 points and 20 rebounds. If he did that twice in a month now, they would name a street after him. He has as much chance as Strom Thurmond of entering this book, however. In not a single year did he make the All-NBA First or Second Team. He also didn't win a championship. So, he's not even up to Parish's standards.

Lenny Wilkens has been in the NBA since 1961, as either a player, coach, or player-coach. He was a very, very, very good player. If this book had room for the top 65 players, he'd be a lock.

James Worthy had the television exposure, the flashy nickname ("Big Game James"), and the pedigree of Dean Smith and the University of North Carolina. But Magic Johnson and Kareem Abdul-Jabbar were the reasons the Lakers won those titles. Put Jerome Kersey in Worthy's spot and Kersey has the rings. In the early 2000s, the Dallas Mavericks featured a player with Worthy's talents. Michael Finley—similar to Worthy—is a tremendous player. They're not chiseling a statue of him to put in front of the arena, however.

Bernard King was on the All-NBA First Team just twice. His teams won a game past the first round just once in his career (losing 4–3 to the Celtics in 1984). He was some player, however. He lost the 1986 and 1987 seasons (when he was 30 and 31) to injury, as well as the last half of 1985. It came down to a choice between Dominique Wilkins and King, and King didn't score as much or last as long as the high-flying Hawk.

Chris Webber is more than halfway through a Hall of Fame career. He's got Elvin Hayes's spot as long as he doesn't take a left turn somewhere. Dirk Nowitzki has Bob McAdoo's slot. And time will tell whether Yao Ming or LeBron James will make the list one day.

APPENDIX
The Lists

The Centers

1. Shaquille O'Neal
2. Wilt Chamberlain
3. Bill Russell
4. Kareem Abdul-Jabbar
5. Moses Malone
6. Hakeem Olajuwon
7. George Mikan
8. David Robinson
9. Dave Cowens
10. Bill Walton
11. Patrick Ewing
12. Willis Reed
13. Bob McAdoo
14. Wes Unseld

The Forwards

1. Larry Bird
2. Tim Duncan
3. Bob Pettit
4. Elgin Baylor
5. Julius Erving
6. Karl Malone
7. Charles Barkley
8. Rick Barry
9. Dolph Schayes
10. John Havlicek
11. Scottie Pippen

12. Dennis Rodman
13. Kevin McHale
14. Elvin Hayes
15. Kevin Garnett
16. Billy Cunningham
17. Dominique Wilkins

The Guards

1. Michael Jordan
2. Magic Johnson
3. Oscar Robertson
4. Bob Cousy
5. Jerry West
6. Kobe Bryant
7. Isiah Thomas
8. George Gervin
9. John Stockton
10. Jason Kidd
11. Walt Frazier
12. Allen Iverson
13. Gary Payton
14. Tracy McGrady
15. Sam Jones
16. Nate Archibald
17. Earl Monroe
18. Pete Maravich
19. Reggie Miller
20. Clyde Drexler

Best Players by Era
1947–1962
1. Bob Cousy
2. George Mikan
3. Bob Pettit
4. Dolph Schayes
5. Bill Sharman
6. Paul Arizin
7. George Yardley
8. Jim Pollard
9. Vern Mikkelsen
10. Andy Phillip

1963–1983
1. Wilt Chamberlain
2. Bill Russell
3. Kareem Abdul-Jabbar
4. Oscar Robertson
5. Jerry West
6. Elgin Baylor
7. Julius Erving
8. Rick Barry
9. John Havlicek
10. George Gervin
11. Dave Cowens
12. Walt Frazier
13. Elvin Hayes
14. Bill Walton
15. Willis Reed
16. Sam Jones
17. Nate Archibald
18. Bob McAdoo
19. Billy Cunningham
20. Earl Monroe
21. Pete Maravich
22. Wes Unseld

1984–Present
1. Shaquille O'Neal
2. Michael Jordan
3. Larry Bird
4. Magic Johnson
5. Tim Duncan
6. Moses Malone
7. Hakeem Olajuwon
8. Karl Malone
9. Kobe Bryant
10. David Robinson
11. Charles Barkley
12. Isiah Thomas
13. John Stockton
14. Jason Kidd
15. Allen Iverson
16. Scottie Pippen
17. Dennis Rodman
18. Kevin McHale
19. Gary Payton
20. Kevin Garnett
21. Tracy McGrady
22. Reggie Miller
23. Dominique Wilkins
24. Chris Webber
25. Dirk Nowitzki

Best Single Seasons

1.	Chamberlain's 1968	1,992 points (3rd)	1,952 rebounds (1st)	702 assists (1st)
2.	Chamberlain's 1967	1,956 points (3rd)	1,957 rebounds (1st)	630 assists (3rd)
3.	Robertson's 1962	2,432 points (3rd)	985 rebounds (8th)	899 assists (1st)
4.	Abdul-Jabbar's 1972	2,822 points (1st)	1,346 rebounds (2nd)	370 assists
5.	O'Neal's 2000	2,344 points (1st)	1,078 rebounds (2nd)	299 assists
6.	Jordan's 1989	2,633 points (1st)	652 rebounds	650 assists (8th)

I chose the Chamberlain years from 1967 and 1968 because he was a much better defensive player in those years. He was a superior passer, and his teams won 68 and 62 games, including an NBA Championship in 1967. Robertson's season was the best ever by a guard, although Jordan came close in 1989 and 1987. I liked Jordan's 1989 season since his team won seven more games and it was Jordan's best rebounding season (eight per game). O'Neal's 2000 season also saw him finish first in field goal percentage and third in blocked shots. Jordan's great championship years, you ask? They're all great, but nothing that Rick Barry (30.6 points, 5.7 rebounds, 6.2 assists, and league leader in steals in 1975) didn't accomplish. Wilt led the league in scoring and rebounding in five different seasons, but his assist totals were lower. Archibald led the league in scoring and assists in 1973, but his rebounding (obviously) was under three a game.

Best Celtics Title Teams

In 1965, the Celtics won 62 games. It was the most they won during their run of 11 NBA Championships in 13 seasons. Counting the playoffs, this team was 70–22. Philadelphia defeated them eight times (five times during the regular season and three more times in playoffs). Take the Sixers games out, and the Celtics were 61–14. Red Auerbach expertly blended the old (Sam Jones and Bill Russell) with the new (Havlicek, who averaged 18.3 points). As a result, they had a point differential of 8.3 points per game.

In 1964, the Celtics were almost as good. They won 59 games and had a point differential of 7.9 points. Chamberlain was playing out west in San Francisco that season, so the Celtics defeated Philadelphia 10 out of 12 times during the season.

Best Bulls Title Teams

I don't want to hear about the 1996 Bulls team that won a record 72 games. The 1992 team was much better. I'll take that team—which won 67 games—in a heartbeat.

I'm big on point differential, and people will question my choice, even by my standards. The 1996 team was 72–10, with a point differential of 12.2 points per game. The 1992 team was 67–15, with a point differential of 10.4 points per game.

Start with Michael Jordan. In 1992, Jordan was 29 years old and at his peak. Even if you like the 33-year-old Jordan as much as the 29-year-old MJ, Scottie Pippen was a better player in 1992. Horace Grant had an amazing season as the third option. He was steady (he played 81 of 82 games) and averaged 14.2 points and 10 rebounds per game. He added 100 steals and 131 blocked shots. Luc Longley/Bill Cartwright is a wash. Steve Kerr/John Paxson is a wash. The teams were very close. But the NBA was much stronger in 1992. The Pistons had some bite to their bark left. The Cavs may have been one of the strongest teams ever not to make the NBA Finals. The Celtics had a young stud in Reggie Lewis to complement the great frontcourt. Pat Riley had molded the Knicks into a legitimate contender. Teams were not diluted by expansion the way they were just a few years later. Mostly, though, Jordan and Pippen were in their prime in 1992.

My All-Time Team

Forward	Larry Bird
Forward	Bill Russell (starting here as power forward)
Center	Shaquille O'Neal
Guard	Michael Jordan
Guard	Magic Johnson